Engaging American Novels

Engaging American Novels

Lessons from the Classroom

Edited by

Joseph O. Milner
Wake Forest University

Carol A. Pope
North Carolina State University

National Council of Teachers of English
1111 W. Kenyon Road, Urbana, Illinois 61801-1096

Figure 37.6: Material on feminist criticism and Marxist literary theory originally from LYNN, STEVEN J, LITERATURE: READING AND WRITING WITH CRITICAL STRATEGIES, 1st Edition, ©2004. Reprinted by permission of Pearson Education, Inc., Upper Saddle River, NJ. Reprinted by permission.

Manuscript Editor: Theresa L. Kay

Staff Editor: Bonny Graham

Interior Design: Doug Burnett

Cover Design: Frank P. Cucciarre, Blink Concept & Design, Inc.

NCTE Stock Number: 13585

It is the policy of NCTE in its journals and other publications to provide a forum for the open discussion of ideas concerning the content and the teaching of English and the language arts. Publicity accorded to any particular point of view does not imply endorsement by the Executive Committee, the Board of Directors, or the membership at large, except in announcements of policy, where such endorsement is clearly specified.

Every effort has been made to provide URLs that were accurate when the text was written, but because of the rapidly changing nature of the Web, some sites and addresses may no longer be accessible.

Library of Congress Cataloging-in-Publication Data

Engaging American novels : lessons from the classroom / edited by Joseph O. Milner, Carol A. Pope.
     p. cm.
   Includes bibliographical references and index.
    ISBN 978-0-8141-1358-5 ((pbk.))
  1. American fiction—Study and teaching (Secondary)—United States. 2. Lesson planning—United States. I. Milner, Joseph O'Beirne, 1937– II. Pope, Carol Ann.
    PS41.E47 2011
    813.0090071'2—dc23

                                  2011015634

Contents

Contents

Preface

Fire and ice—this book balances both. We urge readers to reach for the fire of classroom teachers' ideas to ignite their own ways of exploring Janie's growth in *Their Eyes Were Watching God*, or to take a fresh look at Twain's *Adventures of Huckleberry Finn* to see it as a runaway's journey into maturity. Some readers will start at the book's beginning to engage the cooler, more broadly applicable ideas of theorists who provide new and varied ways of exploring the ten novels discussed here or any other text. We know, too, that busy teachers will read for their own purposes—to see what a few classroom teachers have done to help *To Kill a Mockingbird*'s Maycomb, Alabama, come alive in their classroom, or to take a look at how John Noell Moore's critical stances might help their students consider new, fresh ways *Out of the Dust*, *The Giver*, or a classic novel might be understood. Some will see Robert Probst as almost challenging his earlier reader response stance while others will recognize Sheridan Blau's belief that ready-made, prefabricated critical postures are not as useful as more commonsense ones. Other readers (a host, we hope) may read our book from cover to cover, but most will dig in where the gold most readily lies. Some will plunge into the classroom teacher's ideas and leave the larger views of the opening five chapters to a less busy day. It's your book; use it selfishly.

We have intentionally constructed our book to pay homage to the worlds of both fire and ice. We champion the enduring wisdom of the statement, "There's nothing more practical than a good theory, and nothing so theoretical as sound practice." That's why the first five chapter authors refer repeatedly to the novels to be explored in the last ten sections, and many of the classroom teachers' lessons refer to the ideas in the first five chapters. That back-and-forth motion is a powerful feature of our book. We believe the lessons on the ten novels would be less enduring if they were not tied to the critical theory, and those ideas would be barren were they out of touch with the palpable world of teaching these novels.

We are inclusive about professional terminology as well. Some teachers like the broad idea of purpose and the larger sense of accomplishment it conveys. They sense its connection with essential questions and core learning. Others look for more specific determination and definition of their students' literary performance, so they refer to goals and objectives. Similarly, some of our contributors outline single lessons that help students explore small chunks of the novels they are teaching while others explain multiple days of instruction with lesson plans that completely envelop the novel. We have chosen to call these ideas and activities *lessons* and admire their useful, well-defined, instructional ideas, but we also like to think of them as lessons these classroom teachers offer all of us about teaching.

The novels we include represent a range of typical classroom use, too. Some are among the great classic American novels; some were early young adult blockbusters; some still seem new even though they have been around for a century or more. All provide a rich swatch of the American literary fabric and, whether dense and complex or simple and profound, have riches sufficient to engage you and all of your students.

Finally, this book is for teachers who hanker for new ways to open up a favorite text and who will use it as a part of a university course or as part of an informal reading group. We are particularly proud of the young teachers and first-time writers who have contributed so splendidly to *Engaging American Novels: Lessons from the Classroom.* It is, in part, the new light they bring to these texts that helps to make the collection so rich and brightens our sense of our profession's future. We started our construction of this book with the help of NCTE leaders who were willing to reach out to colleagues they knew to be fine teachers who would enrich the book with their fresh ideas. For all these voices we are grateful; they create the heat and cool strength of this book. We know you will appreciate and enjoy it, too, because you will use it.

Acknowledgments

*E*ngaging American Novels would have never seen the light of day were it not for two amazing graduate assistants: Mary Beth White and Greg Bartley. Both are outstanding teachers who will soon make their mark in English education. More specifically, each of them used their love and understanding of these American novels, as well as their technological savvy, to bring together in one coherent text the various editions and revisions of the five literary theorists and the forty or more lessons brought together by the ten editors of the novel chapters and their thoughtful colleagues and friends who created the exciting lessons on how they teach these remarkable novels. Mary Beth and Greg have been instrumental in making this complex and compelling book a reality. Robin Hawkins and Cindy O'Hagan were stalwart, too, in their support of this important undertaking.

I Some Helpful Theory

1 Fostering Authentic Learning in the Literature Classroom

Sheridan Blau
Teachers College, Columbia University

Louise Rosenblatt liked to say that taking somebody else's reading as your own is like having somebody else eat your dinner for you. That is a witty way to describe the intellectual and experiential poverty and fraudulence of what may be the typical pedagogical transaction of secondary school and college literature classes, where students may sometimes read the assigned literature (which is to say roughly decode and grasp a rough sense of a plot or situation) but rarely engage in the more serious intellectual enterprise of thoughtfully unpacking a difficult text or constructing a meaningful interpretation of what they have read.

Unfortunately, students (in middle schools and high schools and in college as well) typically come to class expecting their teachers to provide them with a sense of the meaning of what they have read. And that meaning or interpretation and the statements that elaborate it are what "good" students record in their notebooks and draw on later, as they write dutiful papers and exams for their courses or dutifully answer their teacher's questions in class. Some of the most dutiful students of all become English teachers who will then draw on the notes derived from their own teachers when it is their turn to provide the next generation of students with ideas about the meaning of the same texts taught in English classes from one generation to the next. And when they don't have their own notes, they will turn to those that are commercially available—CliffsNotes or SparkNotes, for example. Alan Purves (1993) observed that teachers even consult sources when preparing to teach from textbooks. But in that instance they get their notes from the ones dutifully prepackaged for them by publishers in the teacher's editions of whatever textbook their students will be using.

True and False Knowledge

The problem with such learning and such teaching is not merely that it frequently entails the communication from one generation to the next of reductive, misunderstood, or temporarily fashionable ideas about literary texts, but that it doesn't communicate or yield anything that can be called true or authentic knowledge at all. On the contrary, it represents a transaction that is likely to yield what John Milton dramatized and what we need to understand as false knowledge the only kind of knowledge that was forbidden to Adam and Eve in the Garden of Eden, because it is both false and an obstacle rather than a stepping stone to true and new learning.

But how can anything we can call "knowledge" be false and an obstacle to learning, especially in the context of literary study? The answer is, first, that knowledge is always false when it has not been learned by the person who claims or is presumed to possess it. Thus, literary knowledge said to represent the meaning of a text, when taken by a student from a teacher or when taken from SparkNotes or a similar crib, cannot be said to have been learned by its recipients who are now in possession not of anything they know for themselves, but only of what amounts to no more than hearsay knowledge—the kind of knowledge that is not admitted as evidence in a court of law because it is not the true knowledge of the person giving testimony; it is somebody else's knowledge. It is, at best, borrowed knowledge, representing only what has been understood of what was presumably said by somebody else who is presumed to have spoken authoritatively.

That is, when I tell you about the meaning of a text, you can't know the meaning of that text by virtue of my telling it to you; you can only know that I have a particular idea about the meaning of the text. What you have learned, in other words, is not the meaning of the text, but my idea about the meaning of the text. And you haven't actually learned that idea, either, but only that I have it. To learn my idea yourself, you must have it yourself, and that means coming to an understanding of the idea through your own reading and experience of it, as often happens when a student will suddenly say, "Oh, yes, now I get it," which usually means, "Now I understand what I have been told and have been saying, until now, only as words, but without true understanding."

What most students appear to know about literary texts as a result of being taught those texts in school is precisely this kind of false knowledge. It is not the product of their experience of the texts but hearsay knowledge derived from what their teachers have said about the texts, which itself is often merely what the teacher had been told by his or her teachers (or by the notes in a teacher's edition) and never experienced firsthand for himself herself. So when a teacher "teaches" that borrowed knowledge as if it were true knowledge and students take on such knowledge as if it were their own, both teachers and their students are engaged in a fraudulent transaction of teaching and learning, and what they are trading in is surely false rather than true knowledge.

Now, let us examine why such borrowed knowledge should be regarded not only as false but also as an obstacle to further learning. It is an obstacle in two ways. First, it is an obstacle to the learning of those who have borrowed it and now claim to possess it insofar as they value it and treat it as a treasure they are reluctant to relinquish. That is, insofar as a teacher or student trusts in borrowed knowledge as true, the teacher or student will resist challenges to that knowledge as challenges to his or her status as one who possesses knowledge. This is a particularly powerful temptation to teachers who borrow their knowledge from a publisher's notes or the authority of experts, since they feel obliged to borrow to establish their own authority as teachers. And if a teacher feels that authority depends on the teacher's borrowed knowledge of answers about meanings or about correct interpretations, then any questions that challenge the interpretation offered by the teacher will be experienced as challenges to the teacher's authority and expertise as a teacher, and therefore resisted. And that resistance will discourage questions and explorations of meaning that might refine or correct the interpretation offered by the teacher or lead to new insights about the text or the interpretation under interrogation. Hence, false knowledge is not only false in the sense that its possessors do not truly possess it; it is false to the degree that it obstructs rather then advances further learning.

True knowledge, on the other hand, is true to the extent that it advances learning and serves to lead those who hold it to larger and more capacious understandings. Interestingly, this suggests that even knowledge legitimately acquired through direct experience and not borrowed from any external authority can become false if it becomes overvalued by its possessor as a source of authority, status, and self-esteem. That is, whenever we hold on to our knowledge—even knowledge legitimately acquired through our own learning—and treat such knowledge as unalterable rather than provisional, that knowledge too becomes false. It is false because it insists on remaining ignorant of whatever information or ideas call it into question and require its modification, and it is false because it becomes itself an obstacle to further learning.

Unfortunately, direct observations of classroom practices (see Applebee, 1993; Marshall, Smagorinsky, & Smith, 1995; Nystrand, 1997) and collections of videotapes that I have personally reviewed from a wide range of secondary English classrooms provide abundant evidence that most English teachers—including those whose learning is most authentically acquired and most legitimately possessed—suffer from what I have elsewhere called "the anxiety of the right reading" (Blau, 2003, p. 147) and take great pains to give their students the reading they regard as standard or authoritative or, at best, the reading that accounts for why they regard a text to be worth reading in the first place. Moreover, such anxiety does not derive from an unworthy or dishonest impulse on the part of the teacher. It is natural that we English teachers would select literary texts for our students that we think most worthy of their study and that we would then want to ensure that our students derive from their study of the assigned texts the kinds of wisdom, insight, ideas that account for our selection of the text in the first place. So we tell them what they should be seeing or learning or feeling as a consequence of having read the assigned text. The problem, of course, is that in the generosity and caring of our instruction we short-circuit the process by which students themselves would otherwise have to construct their own understanding and interpretation of the text we are teaching them, and in that short-circuited process we tempt them to accept our true learning as their false knowledge, with the added unfortunate consequence of convincing them of their dependence on us as the source of any reliable knowledge about the meaning of the difficult texts we typically teach.

But the intellectual consequence of our honorable intention is that literary instruction in many if not most classrooms becomes part of a cycle for the reproduction and circulation of what amounts to false knowledge—knowledge not acquired through any legitimate experience but communicated from one participant to another as hearsay, something heard from others and taken as true without direct experience or examined evidence. Such knowledge, as I have already noted, is not counted as the basis for acceptable testimony in courtrooms, but it is even more worthless in a literary education because it serves as a substitute for genuine literary experience and deprives its recipients of the opportunity to discover what literature (rather than English teachers) can offer to them and why they might want to read literature for themselves without the coercion of teachers or fear of tests. No wonder so many studies suggest that students who graduate from high school (not to mention those who drop out) seem disinclined to ever read any serious literature again for the rest of their lives.

Literary Instruction and the Experience of Literature

The irony is that of all disciplines, the discipline of literary study should be most closely linked to an experiential model of learning or learning through direct experience rather than learning through instruction by intermediaries who are positioned between texts and their readers. That is, the defense of literature—from the time of Aristotle in the classic age, to Sidney in the Renaissance, to Johnson in the period of the enlightenment, to Wordsworth in the Romantic age, to Eliot and Frost and Rosenblatt and Stanley Fish among the modern and postmodern thinkers—has been that literary texts constitute uniquely powerful instruments for learning because they offer readers the opportunity to learn through something like direct experience, insofar as they allow readers who will submit themselves to the reading experience to imaginatively experience what it is like to endure a calm on a nineteenth-century sailing ship, or experience a gas attack in World War I, or endure the humiliation and degradation of life in a concentration camp in the 1940s. Literature, in other words, is a medium for learning through experience, not learning about experience. Yet, the history of teaching literature in schools and colleges, at least from the nineteenth century on, has been a history of submitting student readers to exercises and examinations that make knowledge about literary texts a substitute for direct knowledge and experience of those texts, and a screen that stands between a student reader and what might otherwise be a direct and informing experience of a text.

What, then, can a teacher do to enable students to understand and appreciate for themselves the difficult texts typically taught in high school English classes when students come to class already convinced that they can't interpret those texts by themselves? The problem becomes even more problematic when we consider that many students are also unwilling to do the work that would be required for a thoughtful interpretation and are inclined, if asked to produce their own interpretations, to create hastily constructed, inattentive, and irresponsible interpretations that cannot be respected or accepted as any kind of legitimate or intellectually valid knowledge.

I do not presume to have a simple or definitive solution to the problem, but I want to assert that any practice that will promote some small increment in genuine learning is better than all the practices that yield false knowledge and that discourage true learning. For a start, I would occasionally select a short (no more than half a page) but fairly difficult passage from a longer piece of literature that I was teaching and ask students to read it three times, each time rating their understanding of it on a scale from 0 to 10, 0 meaning they don't understand it at all and 10 meaning they understand it perfectly (if that is ever possible). Then I'd ask them to write out how their understanding may have changed over the course of their three readings and what questions they still have about the passage. I would then ask students to work in groups of three sharing their experience of reading the passage three times and dealing with the questions they still have, trying to answer those questions as fully as possible. Finally, I'd reconvene the entire class to talk about what happened to students as they read the passage three times and what questions the various groups still had that they didn't feel they had adequately resolved in their small groups. Those would be questions for the whole class to consider. It is likely that those questions are also questions that strong readers would have about the text, and I would want to emphasize at this point that being a strong reader usually means having to read difficult passages more than once and then having questions about those texts. I would argue that difficult texts by their nature are likely to present problems for even the best of readers. In other words, being a strong reader does not mean being a reader without questions. It means, instead, being a reader who pays attention to the difference between what he or she does and doesn't understand and is willing to identify and try to clarify questions about what the reader doesn't understand so that he or she can also begin to answer those questions, often with the help of other readers who may or may not have the same questions. I am inclined to say that the most important lesson to teach to our students about the reading of classic and often difficult texts is that strong readers of such texts are readers who pay attention to the questions they find themselves experiencing as readers, because they value and recognize the importance of their own questions as resources for advancing their understanding of any difficult text. Capturing and talking about the questions that students in groups identified and couldn't resolve within their groups is almost certainly a good way to help students see what productive and authentic questions look like and how they can be so productive for the readers who ask them.

Not surprisingly, then, my regular nightly homework assignment, when I am teaching a long literary work, is to ask students to identify the questions they have as they read assigned pages or chapters and bring their questions with them to class. To model productive questions I would recommend that teachers remind students of the questions that surfaced in groups and also bring to class their own (i.e., the teachers') questions and use all those questions as the focus for class discussions, demonstrating to students how the identification of real questions can advance a reader's understanding of a difficult text. I also recommend identifying difficult passages in a longer text and having students read the passage in pairs, aloud, stopping whenever either partner finds a line or portion of a sentence that he or she doesn't understand with perfect clarity. The questions that will arise from such an activity will be additional models of what constitutes a good question and demonstrate, once again, the efficacy of asking questions and seeking solutions to problems.

Teaching "The Story of an Hour"

In teaching Kate Chopin's widely anthologized story "The Story of an Hour," for example, it is crucial that teachers ensure that students read the story carefully enough to experience the irony of the final scene, a scene with a final sentence that constitutes what amounts to the narrator's interpretive commentary on the whole story. But for students to have such an experience they must have it for themselves, and this means they must ask the questions they have about the story and work through for themselves the kinds of confusion and problems that the story is likely to engender for readers who are engaged in understanding the story and construing its meaning for themselves.

In that final but sometimes problematic scene, Brently Mallard—the husband whose death in a train accident had been reported (mistakenly) at the opening of the story to his wife, Louise—enters his own home, shocking his friends and his wife who had for the past hour or so thought him dead ("The Story of an Hour" may be presumed to have taken place within an hour). His friend, Richards, tries "to screen him from the view of his wife." And then come two brief but telling paragraphs. First: "But Richards was too late." And then: "When the doctors came they said she had died of heart disease—of joy that kills."

Many students in my experience take that last sentence at face value, failing to see how it is both true and ironically mistaken. That is to say, readers who understand the story recognize the statement as a true report of the doctors' pronouncement as to the cause of Louise's death. After all, as we are told in the opening paragraph of the story, "Mrs. Mallard was afflicted with a heart trouble." That's why "great care was taken to break to her as gently as possible the news of her husband's death." So, the doctors who were summoned at the end of the story would presume that Mrs. Mallard's apparent heart attack upon seeing that her husband is alive and not dead was occasioned by the shock she experienced at now seeing him alive, after she had been told an hour before that he was dead. And from the perspective of these presumably male doctors, who do not know about Louise's emotional experience as described in the body of the story, the shock she experienced could be properly described as a shock of joy—a joy so shocking that they refer to it as a "joy that kills." But for a reader who remembers the narrated account of Louise's feelings and thoughts after learning of her husband's death, the doctors' analysis of Louise's fatal experience as caused by a shocking "joy that kills" is ironic and a telling commentary on conventional male assumptions or possibly a society's conventional assumptions about the need and dependence and love that wives feel for their husbands. Such irony is lost, however, on students who fail to understand exactly what happens in a final scene that is rendered so economically and with a surprise that so contradicts the facts of the opening of the story that readers can easily become confused in their own shock about what actually happened and why and with what narrative reliability on the part of the story's narrator or that of characters within the story.

To warn students to be prepared for irony in the final scene is to invite them to look for a special literary technique and to do something other than try to make the best sense they can for themselves of what they see happening in the story. And what must happen to a reader who experiences the irony of the ending of this story is that he or she must first take the doctors' report at face value and recognize that it is factually correct as a report of what the doctors said, and then, after a moment of accepting it in itself as also a factually correct report, realize that it can't be factually correct given the rest of the story as narrated by an omniscient third-person narrator, whose narration appears reliable throughout. Only then is the reader able to recognize the irony in the report, which is located in the difference between the conventional male perspective of what a wife would "naturally" feel upon seeing that her husband, who has been reported dead, is actually alive, and the unconventional set of feelings experienced by the recently liberated wife in this short story. Thus, to invite students to look for irony is likely to prevent them from experiencing it. They would also be denied the experience of the story if they were told by their teacher how to interpret the ending. Moreover, both tactics carry with them the additional lesson for the students who have trouble unpacking the meaning of the story that they cannot read such a story or any story that poses difficulties, unless they can call on some authoritative source or an expert teacher to provide an acceptable interpretation for them.

On the other hand, to invite students to reread the last scene of the story and to ask the questions it raises for them and to discuss those questions with other students in the class is to provide them with an opportunity to learn the power of their questions and the value of their own confusion as resources for interrogating a text in the manner of expert readers and accomplished literary critics. That is, what a student is likely to experience as a confusing section in a text and therefore as evidence of some insufficiency in the student's capacity as a reader, a literary critic or scholar is likely to see as a textual problem worthy of critical and interpretive attention and evidence of astuteness in discovering a place in the text where the text somehow resists easy interpretation. Thus the same problem that represents a frustrating moment of failure for a student becomes for an expert reader an exhilarating moment of discovery—wherein what is discovered is a problem worthy of critical and interpretive attention. Our responsibility as teachers is, therefore, to help students begin to recognize the productive value of the interpretive problems, confusions, and questions they encounter in their reading so that they will begin to embrace their questions and problems as occasions for advancing their understanding, rather than retreat from those same problems as obstacles to their success as readers. And the first step we must take as teachers toward helping our students adopt such a stance with respect to textual difficulties is to resist the temptation we experience to provide students with solutions to problems before they encounter them and have to experience the frustration and sense of failure that such problems occasion. We need to strengthen and refine our pedagogical dispositions as a first condition for strengthening those of our students as learners. Surely one of the saddest ironies of conventional practice in the teaching of literature is that English teachers are endlessly worried about teaching their students the skills and processes of critical thinking and seem constantly to be lamenting the failure of their students to think critically about the literary and nonliterary texts assigned to them in English classes. Yet, in trying to protect their students from the sense of failure that accompanies the confusions and problems that students inevitably experience in their encounters with difficult texts, teachers deprive students of the richest and most authentic opportunities that are likely to be found in an English class to engage deeply and productively in the kind of critical thinking that would allow them to recognize how and when they can exercise their own capacity for such thinking.

What is critical thinking, after all, except what Dewey (1910/1991) identifies as reflective thought and, most particularly, intensive thinking directed to resolving problems or clarifying confusion, precisely of the kind arising from the recognition of contradictions or inconsistencies in the logic or coherence of an argument or narrative. Hence, most of the problems that students encounter in their reading of literary texts (at least when those texts fall within the students' zone of proximal development [Vygotsky, 1962], which is to say within the students' ability to comprehend with some instructional assistance) are problems that call for the kind of reflective or critical thinking that Dewey identifies with the confusion occasioned by logical contradictions or narrative inconsistencies. And the best assistance that a teacher can provide at such points is the assistance of assuring the student that his or her own questions about the text are resources for making advances in understanding the text, particularly if the student will employ such strategies as rereading, writing out or explaining the questions and confusions that define the problem, and discussing the problem with classmates who may share it. In such discussions students are able to assist each other at a level where their collaboration allows everyone to contribute without leaving anyone far behind and with all participants experiencing their capacity to use their problems and questions as scaffolds for learning.

A Classic Interpretive Problem in *Adventures of Huckleberry Finn*

That the discovery of problems is a characteristic experience for leading literary scholars and theorists and not a mark of literary ineptitude is dramatically represented for the profession of English in a famous story told by Professor Gerald Graff (1992) of the University of Illinois, Chicago, about his own initiation into the world of literary criticism and theory. Graff, one of America's most distinguished literary theorists and a former president of the Modern Language Association (the most prestigious professional association of university professors of literature), tells how his own performance as a student of literature was uninspired and disengaged until, in his junior year in college in an American literature class, he experienced what turned out to be a classic problem in the interpretation of *Huckleberry Finn*, the problem of an ending that imprisons and terrifies Jim while rendering him a humorous pawn in a fantasy game conducted by Tom Sawyer, with Huck's reluctant cooperation. Graff notes that he found himself suddenly interested in literature in a way he hadn't experienced before when he realized that his own response to the problematic ending of the novel put him and his classmates into a discussion that had troubled many leading critics and writers who found themselves at a loss over how to explain what seemed to many to be racist chapters, where Twain seems to treat Jim as a figure of ridicule rather than of sympathy and respect. Realizing that his questions and feelings about the novel were the topic of a body of critical essays and literary commentaries on Twain gave Graff a new respect for his own power to interrogate a text and to participate in an ongoing critical conversation about literature. High school students, too, might be inspired to appreciate the value of their questions and critical responses, if they are invited to get together in groups of three or four students to reread and try to make sense of a short passage like the one printed below from Chapter 38 of Twain's (1977) novel:

> But Tom thought of something, and says:
> "You got any spiders in here, Jim?"
> "No, sah, thanks to goodness I hain't, Mars Tom."
> "All right, we'll get you some."
> "But bless you, honey, I doan' *want* none. I's afeard un um. I jis' 's soon have rattlesnakes aroun'."
> Tom thought a minute or two, and says:
> "It's a good idea. And I reckon it's been done. It *must* a been done; it stands to reason. Yes, it's a prime good idea. Where could you keep it?"
> "Keep what, Mars Tom?"
> "Why, a rattlesnake."
> "De goodness gracious alive, Mars Tom! Why, if dey was a rattlesnake to come in heah I'd take en bust right out thoo dat log wall, I would, wid my head."
> "Why, Jim, you wouldn't be afraid of it after a little. You could tame it."
> "*Tame* it!"
> "Yes—easy enough. Every animal is grateful for kindness and petting, and they wouldn't *think* of hurting a person that pets them. Any book will tell you that. You try—that's all I ask; just try for two or three days. Why, you can get him so in a little while that he'll love you; and sleep with you; and won't stay away from you a minute; and will let you wrap him round your neck and put his head in your mouth."
> "*Please*, Mars Tom—*doan'* talk so! I can't stan' it! He'd *let* me shove his head in my mouf—fer a favor, hain't it? I lay he'd wait a pow'ful long time 'fo' I *ast* him. En mo' en dat, I doan' *want* him to sleep wid me."
> "Jim, don't act so foolish. A prisoner's *got* to have some kind of a dumb pet, and if a rattlesnake hain't ever been tried, why, there's more glory to be gained in your being the first to ever try it than any other way you could ever think of to save your life."
> "Why, Mars Tom, I doan' *want* no sich glory. Snake take 'n bite

Jim's chin off, den *whah* is de glory? No, sah, I doan' want no sich doin's."

"Blame it, can't you *try*? I only *want* you to try—you needn't keep it up if it don't work."

"But de trouble all *done* ef de snake bite me while I's a tryin' him. Mars Tom, I's willin' to tackle mos' anything 'at ain't onreasonable, but ef you en Huck fetches a rattlesnake in heah for me to tame, I's gwyne to *leave* dat's *shore*."

"Well, then, let it go, let it go, if you're so bull-headed about it. We can get you some garter-snakes, and you can tie some buttons on their tail, and let on they're rattlesnakes, and I reckon that'll have to do."

"I k'n stan' *dem*, Mars Tom, but blame' 'f I couldn' get along widout um, I tell you dat. I never knowed b'fo' 't was so much bother and trouble to be a prisoner." (pp. 205–6)

Students working on this passage in small groups and trying to make sense of it, sentence by sentence, will probably spend a good deal of time translating the dialect rendering of familiar words and clarifying the question of who is speaking line by line. They will surely notice that in this segment of text there is no narration. The entire text—after the first line—is spoken language, a dialogue between Tom and Jim. Students will certainly also wonder what Tom can possibly have in mind in his apparently crazy demands on Jim, and they may need some help, if they haven't already had it, in recognizing that Tom's imagination about how Jim ought to behave as a prisoner derives from Tom's experience reading literary romances and adventure novels that were especially popular in the nineteenth century. Thus, Tom is merely engaged in a game of fantasy adventure, much the way young boys play pirates or cowboys, requiring Jim, whose life seems to us to be in real danger, to treat his imprisonment as part of a game where he is pretending to be a young nobleman captured by political enemies. Most students will also find themselves puzzled, if not more deeply troubled, by the way in which Tom trifles with Jim's life and Jim's feelings, forcing a grown man to play out a game of pretend adventure, with ritualized gestures of sacrifice, suffering, and escape, when he is actually afraid that he will lose his life or be forced to spend it in a condition of brutal servitude. That Jim (as the reader will eventually discover) has already been freed by his owner, the late Miss Watson, in her will (though neither Huck nor Jim realize it) reduces the gravity of Tom's treatment of Jim, since Jim is not, in fact, in any real danger. But it doesn't finally excuse the cruelty and thoughtlessness of Tom's treatment of Jim, nor Huck's complicity. An attentive reader is likely to feel that he or she is missing something in this segment of the story, that the story has turned at once too cruel to Jim, and also too slapstick in its comedic treatment of him, dehumanizing him for comic effect in a way that seems unmistakably racist and entirely inconsistent with how we have come to feel about Jim over the course of the novel and how Huck—and with Huck, we ourselves—have learned to respect Jim as a man.

These puzzled and uncomfortable feelings about the story—if students are allowed to have them without being told in advance about how they will or are supposed to feel—are likely to be experienced by students who acknowledge them or come to discover them through their collaboration with classmates as evidence of some failure on their part as readers. In other words, they are likely to feel and think that something is wrong with their understanding of the narrative or that their distaste and confused emotional response to this segment of the story and their failure to appreciate the aesthetic or moral value of this narrative turn is evidence of some defect or insufficiency in their literary sensibility or intellectual sophistication. Some students might defend the narrative, however, and defend Tom as a boy whose literary imagination has overcome his good sense, seeing him perhaps as a figure of the author Twain, who might be said to be parodying himself and all writers in this segment of the story, in contrast to the more literal-minded and sensible Huck and Jim. Whatever position students take on the problematic character of the end of the novel, their experience of the novel and of its problems will be educative and formative for student readers to the degree that they are permitted to have their own experience without having it mediated by teacher talk about how one is supposed to experience the novel.

Only after students have had the opportunity to express their puzzlements and confusion, their resistance to the representation of Jim and to the character of Tom's treatment of Jim (or their defense of Twain and of the end of the novel), should a well-prepared teacher introduce information pointing to the fact that the problems troubling the students in the class have troubled generations of expert readers and critics, including Hemingway, who declared (in his nonfiction *The Green Hills of Africa*) that "All modern American literature comes from one book by Mark Twain called *Huckleberry Finn* . . . there has been nothing as good since," yet adding the advice that "if you read the novel, you must stop where . . . Jim is stolen by the boys. This is the real end. The rest is cheating." That judgment, though somewhat difficult to interpret, seems to have been confirmed by many critics who claim that the novel would be a better and a more coherent and less morally offensive one if its last twelve chapters had been cut.

My point here is not to suggest that teachers should introduce their students to the range of arguments advanced by various critics and scholars who have either defended Twain's novel or attacked it for its problematic ending, but merely to point out the importance of letting students know that their problems with the novel do not indicate any defect in their skill or sensibility as readers. Quite the opposite. Their problems in understanding the ending of the novel, the resistance they feel to the way Jim is represented, their disgust or puzzlement over the way Tom is treating Jim with no respect for Jim's feelings, Huck's failure to act on Jim's behalf, and his deference to Tom in the game being enacted—all of these feelings that invite student readers to perceive themselves as poor readers of this novel, are actually signs of the degree to which they are reading the novel well and critically. Their experience of the novel is mistaken or unsophisticated only to the degree to which they are inclined to ignore or suppress their own responses to the novel rather than articulate those responses as valuable starting points for a serious literary discussion of the merits and defects of the novel and the range of interpretive responses that are possible for its readers and worthy of elaboration and consideration in a classroom community of readers and writers.

References

Applebee, A. N. (1993). *Literature in the secondary school: Studies of curriculum and instruction in the United States* (NCTE Research Report No. 25). Urbana, IL: National Council of Teachers of English.

Blau, S. D. (2003). *The literature workshop: Teaching texts and their readers.* Portsmouth, NH: Heinemann.

Dewey, J. (1991). *How we think.* Buffalo, NY: Prometheus Books. (Original work published 1910)

Graff, G. (1992). Hidden meaning, or, disliking books at an early age. In *Beyond the culture wars: How teaching the conflicts can revitalize American education* (pp. 64–85). New York: Norton.

Hemingway, E. (1935). *Green hills of Africa.* New York: Scribner.

Marshall, J. D., Smagorinsky, P., & Smith, M. W. (1995). *The language of interpretation: Patterns of discourse in discussions of literature* (NCTE Research Report No. 27). Urbana, IL: National Council of Teachers of English.

Nystrand, M. (with Gamoran, A., Kachur, R., & Prendergast, C.). (1997). *Opening dialogue: Understanding the dynamics of language and learning in the English classroom.* New York: Teachers College Press.

Purves, A. C. (1993). Toward a reevaluation of reader response and school literature. *Language Arts, 70,* 348–61.

Twain, M. (1977). *Adventures of Huckleberry Finn* (Norton Critical, 2nd ed.). Ed. S. Bradley, R. C. Beatty, E. H. Long, & T. Cooley. New York: Norton.

Vygotsky, L. S. (1962). *Thought and language* (E. Hanfmann & G. Vakar, Eds. & Trans.). Cambridge, MA: MIT Press.

2 Reading between the Lines: Helping Teenagers Respond to American Literature

Carol Jago
California Reading and Literature Project, UCLA

Force-feeding has never been a successful instructional practice. It didn't work in the good old days—whenever those were—and it doesn't work today. The "Take this. It's good for you. You'll hate it now but thank me later" approach only sends kids to CliffsNotes/SparkNotes/tomorrow's version of shortcuts to reading. If we want students to read and respond to American literature, we will need to persuade them that what can be found between the lines in the stories of Mark Twain, John Steinbeck, F. Scott Fitzgerald, Rudolfo Anaya, and Toni Morrison is important and enduring. We also need to help students learn how to read between those lines for themselves.

Too often instruction in English classes has been an occasion for teachers who know and love literature to showcase what they love and show off what they know. Students come away from such classes—and this is when they are done well—in awe of their teachers but with little confidence in their own ability to read literature. Louise M. Rosenblatt (1983) asserts in *Literature as Exploration* that "[t]he problem that a teacher faces first of all, then, is the creation of a situation favorable to a vital experience of literature. Unfortunately, many of the practices and much of the tone of literature teaching have precisely the opposite effect" (p. 61). So what should we be doing differently? How can we help students respond to literature in authentic ways? What kinds of classroom practices foster "a vital experience of literature"?

Maybe I was just lucky. I came to teaching English reluctantly and without strong background in literature studies. I had always been a reader, but the need to waitress my way through college—I remember slipping out of my American Literature 202 classes early, outfitted in a

Heidi's Pies uniform, to make it to work in time for the lunch shift—meant that I began teaching with a Swiss cheese understanding of traditional works and literary periods. While my best friend could retrieve her notes from UCLA to help her prepare her lectures, I had only myself, the book, and my students to rely on.

I didn't have to pretend not to know what Dr. T. J. Eckleburg's eyes in *The Great Gatsby* (Fitzgerald, 1999) symbolized. I didn't. But I trusted that if we put our heads together, my students and I could make sense of F. Scott Fitzgerald's use of symbols. We read and reread, asked questions of one another, and talked our way into an understanding of passages that puzzled us. We took interpretive leaps. I never gave multiple-choice quizzes, because I wasn't sure of the correct answers myself. Instead we wrote about our emerging understanding and used that understanding to help us read on. Were these students short-changed? Probably. In fact, I am sure I owe them a refund. What is interesting, though, is that when students from my early years in teaching tell stories about their time in American Literature class, they use words like *fun* and *pleasure*. They tell me what they remember was how happy I always seemed, how much I loved the books, and how I made them feel smart. This unscientific sample of former students who find me online and send email messages to their old teacher may be an anomaly, but I truly loved American literature and loved reading it in their company.

Over the years, with help from scholars such as Rosenblatt and colleagues who were applying reader response theory to their practice, I learned techniques that help students have a vital experience with American literature. I'm still learning.

Question Papers

One technique that invites students to grapple with literature on their own is the use of question papers. The method is simple. Have students select a passage that puzzled them from the previous night's homework reading. Ask them to reread the passage and then to write for ten minutes nonstop, posing question after question on the page. I tell students not to worry about having answers to their questions, but if they find themselves thinking about something that feels like an answer, to write those down, too. They should let their minds range freely over the passage, speculating on meaning. It often helps to list the following sentence starters on the board:

- "I wonder if . . ."
- "Could it be that . . . ?"

- "What if . . . ?"
- "Maybe the author was trying to say . . ."
- "It seems to me that . . ."
- "I suppose it's possible that . . ."

I tell students to keep their pens moving nonstop. If they find themselves running out of questions, they should start copying the passage, trusting that a new question will soon pop into their heads. Students find this kind of exploratory writing liberating. They often surprise themselves with what they figure out for themselves. No questions of mine—and how many hours have I spent writing discussion questions that no one cared about!—have ever accomplished this half as well. Naomi Sanchez, an eleventh grader, wrote a question paper in response to the following passage from *The Great Gatsby:*

> But above the grey land and the spasms of bleak dust which drift endlessly over it, you perceive, after a moment, the eyes of Doctor T. J. Eckleburg. The eyes of Doctor T. J. Eckleburg are blue and gigantic—their retinas are one yard high. They look out of no face but, instead, from a pair of enormous yellow spectacles which pass over a nonexistent nose. Evidently some wild wag of an oculist set them there to fatten his practice in Queens, and then sank down himself into eternal blindness or forgot them and moved away. But his eyes, dimmed a little by many paintless days under sun and rain, brood on over the solemn dumping ground. (Fitzgerald, 1999, p. 16)

Student Question Paper
Who is this guy Dr. Eckleburg? And what is so special about his eyes? The narrator was talking about roads and cars in the paragraph just before this so it must be like a billboard. How can you have eyes with glasses but no face? Weird. And what is a "wild wag of an oculist"? Maybe it's an eye doctor or something and this is just how he was trying to get business, but what does this have to do with the place and the story? An eye doctor who goes blind? No, eternal blindness must mean the guy died. Are these eyes on the billboard supposed to be like an evil Big Brother watching over everybody? Or God? I suppose it's possible it's a reference to Nick who sees things the others don't. Well, he should if he's telling the story. Why does Nick describe the eyes as fading? Is he saying that God is getting tired of this world? But then why do the eyes "brood on"? I guess it could be that Nick is going to brood on over the story.

The question paper assignment invited Naomi to interrogate the text and the images in it with her own genuine questions. Her response was authentic and probing. Notice how she corrected her initial misunderstanding of "eternal blindness." Consider how she wrote her way out of a literal interpretation and into a metaphoric one. Naomi is well on her way to becoming a very good reader of American literature. How can I tell this? Because she is responding powerfully and personally to Fitzgerald's charged language.

You may be wondering why I didn't just begin the lesson on Chapter 2 of *The Great Gatsby* with an explanation of symbolism and walk students through the various examples of eye imagery in Fitzgerald's novel. Wouldn't it have been a more efficient use of classroom time just to tell them what they need to know? The problem is that my explanation would have been just that, mine and not Naomi's. What I try to do with the question paper assignment is to offer an alternative to the following scenario:

1. Teacher poses a discussion question to the class.

2. Students have no idea how to answer. They hope they won't be called on and hide behind their books pretending to reread the passage.

3. Teacher is made nervous by the silence and starts answering her own question.

4. Students breathe a sigh of relief. They go through the motions of taking notes while glancing up at the clock.

5. The bell rings.

A question paper can also be a springboard for classroom discussion, genuine discussion that isn't dominated by the teacher's voice. Have students highlight a question in their question paper that they feel they found a tentative answer to and then turn and talk with a partner about what they discovered. After a few minutes—I always give students a little less time than they need; it keeps them wanting more—open up the conversation to the whole class. Ask for questions that are still pending. Then comes the really hard part: *Resist answering these questions yourself.* Instead, turn to the class and ask if anyone can help. Wait patiently. Count to sixty in your head. Scan the room for promising visages, faces with ideas shining in quiet eyes or poking out from under heavy bangs. Gently, gently call on these students, not to put them on the spot but to invite them to enter the conversation.

The most thoughtful students are not always the ones who raise their hands first. Teachers need to find ways to reach beyond the ubiquitous waving arms of rapid-fire thinkers to the other thirty students in the room. The question paper activity gave everyone time to think. The time talking with a partner allowed students to practice their "answers" in an unthreatening environment. With a bit of gentle prodding, many are ready to speak up.

My students like writing question papers so much that they often ask to substitute them for essays. Don't fall for this. While question papers make an outstanding prewriting task, they should not replace the discipline of crafting a literary analysis paper. One reason students struggle with such writing is that we often ask them to analyze a text before they understand it. No wonder their responses seem one-dimensional and a limp restatement of what you told them in your introductory remarks. If we want students to write lively and original literary analysis essays, we need to make space in our classrooms for speculative thinking. This will never happen if all the questions are ours.

Show, Don't Tell

Everyone is familiar with the injunction to "show, don't tell" in writing instruction, but the same guideline applies to teaching literary analysis. Rather than telling students everything you know about a text, try showing them how you think. Make your thinking visible by reading aloud a passage and stopping to comment and question as you read. Pause to make connections. Demonstrate how even an expert reader rarely understands complex literature the first time through. When we offer students only our expert interpretations, interpretations that have been acquired through careful close reading and thinking, we inadvertently contribute to young readers' mistaken belief that there must either be something wrong with the text or something wrong with them. Neither is the case. As Walt Whitman said, "the process of reading is not a half-sleep; but in the highest sense an exercise, a gymnastic struggle; that the reader is to do something for himself" (qtd. in Triggs, 1898, p. 66).

Warning: Don't try to model the think-aloud process off the top of your head. Prepare the paragraph you plan to read aloud to students before class and be sure to include in your commentary the following:

- Questions about vocabulary or unusual uses of familiar words
- Comments that make connections to your life
- Observations about how a detail contributes to the effect of the passage
- Remarks about places in the passage that are unclear to you
- A question that is cleared up as you read on in the passage

Here is an example of a think-aloud of the first paragraphs of *Adventures of Huckleberry Finn*. The original text is in bold type. My comments and questions are in italics.

> **You don't know about me without you have read a book by the name of *The Adventures of Tom Sawyer;*** *Hmm . . . I did but years and years ago* **but that ain't no matter.** *Good, because I don't really remember it at all.* **That book was made by Mr. Mark Twain, and he told the truth, mainly.** *What's going on? Mark Twain is the author of this book.* **There was things which he stretched, but mainly he told the truth.** *Oh, I get it. Twain is having a bit of fun here letting his narrator comment on his writing.* **That is nothing. I never seen anybody but lied one time or another, without it was** *I'm not understanding this construction "without it was." Does it mean "except for"? That would work.* **Aunt Polly, or the widow, or maybe Mary. Aunt Polly—Tom's Aunt Polly, she is—and Mary, and the Widow Douglas** *Who are all these characters???* **is all told about in that book, which is mostly a true book, with some stretchers, as I said before.**
>
> **Now the way that the book winds up is this:** *So I guess Huck is giving readers a synopsis of what happens just before this book starts.* **Tom and me found the money that the robbers hid in the cave, and it made us rich. We got six thousand dollars apiece—all gold. It was an awful sight of money when it was piled up. Well, Judge Thatcher he took it and put it out at interest, and it fetched us** *The language seems folksy.* **a dollar a day apiece all the year round—more than a body could tell what to do with.** *A dollar a day sure wouldn't go far these days. Money must have been worth a lot more back then.* **The Widow Douglas she took me for her son, and allowed she would sivilize me;** *Why does he spell* civilize *this way instead of the right way?* **but it was rough living in the house all the time, considering how dismal regular and decent the widow was in all her ways; and so when I couldn't stand it no longer I lit out.** *It's interesting how Huck calls her both dismal and decent. I guess he recognizes that she means well even if it drives him crazy.* **I got into my old rags and my sugar-hogshead again, and was free and satisfied.** *"Lit out" must mean run away.* **But Tom Sawyer he hunted me up and said he was going to start a band of robbers, and I might join if I would go back to the widow and be respectable. So I went back.**

After I model my thinking aloud to students, I ask them to turn to a partner and to do the same with the next paragraph, taking turns sentence by sentence to pause and question, to stop and think aloud. The noise level in the room can get quite high with fifteen or more students reading and talking at once, but so is the energy level. It is such a low-stakes task that everyone feels comfortable participating. No one is worrying about wrong answers because everyone is too busy trying to make sense of the text with a little help from friends. Students are reassured to learn that their partner is struggling with the same word or phrase that is giving them trouble. They begin to see that reading literature—particularly the initial pages of a novel—requires serious thinking and work. But it is work they are capable of doing if they are willing to put their minds to it.

One of the things I like best about the think-aloud protocol is that it forces students to slow the pace of their reading. Teenagers spend a great deal of time reading online, skipping and scanning large volumes of text at an amazing rate. Many have lost, if they ever possessed, the habit of paying attention to every word. In *Proust and the Squid: The Story and Science of the Reading Brain,* Marianne Wolf (2007) explains how the invention of reading "rearranged the very organization of our brain, which in turn expanded the ways we were able to think" (p. 22). She goes on to discuss how our brains are changing as a result of our twenty-first-century reading habits, raising questions about what has been lost and gained as young people replace reading books with the multidimensional "continuous partial attention" reading that takes place online. Wolf's research suggests that the American literature we offer students—*Their Eyes Were Watching God, Of Mice and Men, Out of the Dust*—and the methods for reading literature that we teach students have the potential to change the way they think. Considered in this light, teachers play an important role in the development of the human race. I believe it is our responsibility to make sure students learn to linger over text, puzzling over its full meaning, musing on connections to their own lives. I want my students to be good readers of both literature and websites. I want them to know when it is effective practice to skip and scan and when to slow right down and ponder every word—sometimes a tortoise, sometimes a hare.

Rereading

The most commonly used reading strategy is so easy to employ that you might not think of it as a strategy at all. It doesn't require a fancy graphic organizer and doesn't have a cool acronym for a name. It's simply called rereading. Good readers instinctively reread when a passage in a procedural document doesn't make sense to us. We need to help students get into the habit of doing the same when a passage in the novel they are reading puzzles them. It can be a challenge to get students to revisit a passage they already read; it's hard enough getting them to read the text once let alone twice or three times. Yet, with rich literature such as the excerpt below from Harper Lee's *To Kill a Mockingbird* (1962), the full meaning only emerges after several readings.

To help students experience the power of rereading, begin by making copies of a passage chosen from the pages you assigned for homework reading. There is no need to retype the passage; just go to the online text and copy, cut, and paste. Ask students to reread the passage, underlining phrases or sentences that they found interesting and/or difficult to understand.

> Atticus was feeble: he was nearly fifty. When Jem and I asked him why he was so old, he said he got started late, which we felt reflected upon his abilities and manliness. He was much older than the parents of our school contemporaries, and there was nothing Jem or I could say about him when our classmates said, "My father—"
>
> Jem was football crazy. Atticus was never too tired to play keep-away, but when Jem wanted to tackle him Atticus would say, "I'm too old for that, son."
>
> Our father didn't do anything. He worked in an office, not in a drugstore. Atticus did not drive a dump-truck for the county, he was not the sheriff, he did not farm, work in a garage, or do anything that could possibly arouse the admiration of anyone.
>
> Besides that, he wore glasses. He was nearly blind in his left eye, and said left eyes were the tribal curse of the Finches. Whenever he wanted to see something well, he turned his head and looked from his right eye.
>
> He did not do the things our schoolmates' fathers did: he never went hunting, he did not play poker or fish or drink or smoke. He sat in the livingroom and read.
>
> With these attributes, however, he would not remain as inconspicuous as we wished him to: that year, the school buzzed with talk about him defending Tom Robinson, none of which was complimentary. After my bout with Cecil Jacobs when I committed myself to a policy of cowardice, word got around that Scout Finch wouldn't fight any more, her daddy wouldn't let her. This was not entirely correct: I wouldn't fight publicly for Atticus, but the family was private ground. I would fight anyone from a third cousin upwards tooth and nail. Francis Hancock, for example, knew that.
>
> When he gave us our air-rifles Atticus wouldn't teach us to shoot. Uncle Jack instructed us in the rudiments thereof; he said Atticus wasn't interested in guns. Atticus said to Jem one day, "I'd rather you shot at tin cans in the back yard, but I know you'll go after birds. Shoot all the bluejays you want, if you can hit 'em, but remember it's a sin to kill a mockingbird."

That was the only time I ever heard Atticus say it was a sin to do something, and I asked Miss Maudie about it. "Your father's right," she said. "Mockingbirds don't do one thing but make music for us to enjoy. They don't eat up people's gardens, don't nest in corncribs, they don't do one thing but sing their hearts out for us. That's why it's a sin to kill a mockingbird." (Lee, 1962, pp. 94–95)

Once students have finished rereading the passage, ask them to write for five minutes about the lines they underlined. Put the following questions on the board to help guide students' writing, but assure them that these are only suggestions to trigger their thinking.

- Why did you choose this line?
- What does it say to you?
- How did it make you feel?
- How does this line relate to the rest of the passage?
- What does this description remind you of?

Then put students into small groups and have one person in the group read the passage aloud. Following this rereading, have students take turns sharing their lines and thoughts about the lines they have chosen. It isn't necessary to have students read their quickwrites to one another. The purpose of their writing was simply to help prepare them for discussing the passage. The goal is to get students talking naturally about Harper Lee's novel. Writing about the lines helps students marshal their thoughts and have something to say about the lines they have chosen. Ideally, the group conversation will have a momentum and become more than simply a matter of taking turns to read and talk about lines from the passage. I encourage students to let their discussion of a single line grow into a discussion of the passage.

After about fifteen minutes in their small groups, I bring the whole class back together and ask students to read the passage again. Once we have done this, I instigate a full-class discussion by asking, "Who heard a really interesting comment in your group that would help the rest of us understand the passage?" We talk until the period is almost over, when I point out that they have now read this same passage four times. I ask them, "How did your understanding of the characters, of the idea of a mockingbird, of the novel change with each rereading?" We discuss how this reading strategy made a difference for us as readers until the bell rings.

Here is the rereading protocol set out as a series of steps:

1. Read the passage silently, choosing a phrase or sentence that strikes you.

2. Write for five minutes about this line.

3. In small groups, reread the passage aloud.

4. Share lines and comments in small groups.

5. Come together as a whole class and reread the passage.

6. Discuss the passage in large group with the teacher.

7. Discuss how rereading helped you understand the text.

The final metacognitive step in this protocol is extremely important. Students need to articulate for themselves how rereading a passage leads to deeper understanding. I want them to employ this simple, effective practice often when reading literature. For this to happen, they need to make it their own. One of the things I love best about being an English teacher is that it allows me to return again and again to luminous passages, pages that are so perfectly wrought that each time I reread them I see more. English teachers can't be so obsessed with getting students through a novel that we forget to design lessons that use rereading to draw them into the literature.

"Why are we reading this?"

It's a question my students pose often—and a question we need to have a good answer for. Our integrity depends on it. Here is mine: Great literature speaks to the human condition, offering readers solace in times of trouble, laughter in times of woe. It helps us see our own struggles in perspective by offering stories about others who like Huck Finn must fend for themselves in a cruel world. It invites us to measure our own mettle beside that of Scout and Atticus Finch. It takes us to places we could never travel outside the pages of a book. Few students come to class interested in visiting Yoknapatawpha County, but it is hard to resist a conversation about William Faulkner's *The Sound and the Fury* when the topic is Caddy's muddy drawers and what they might suggest about her natural sexuality. Students come to loathe her brother Jason, not because I told them to but because a close reading of the text persuades them of what a loathsome creature he really is. Along with the rest of the Compsons, they come to rely on Dilsey for her hard work keeping the family fed and being the only reliable narration in the whole story. My goal for students is that they learn how to read complex text with a measure of comprehension and—I hope—pleasure.

When making the argument for reading literature, I focus on my own love for the books I am inviting them to read. My first role is that of a cheerleader, drumming up enthusiasm in the somewhat lethargic crowd for the books themselves. "I think you are going to find this novel compelling. It's going to be a challenge, but I'm here to help you. We'll help one another. Don't worry if you don't understand everything. Neither do I. We're going to talk our way and think our way through it together. All questions are welcome. All honest responses are invited. My only plea is that you hold off judgment of the novel until you have read it."

It disconcerts me to hear stories of teachers dragging their students through books that they themselves hate. If you are unmoved by a novel or author, it is highly unlikely that you will be able to summon up enthusiasm for it in your students. It won't work. Kids see through us. They can tell when we are just going through the motions. While I recognize that many teachers do not have the luxury of choosing their own books, we sometimes have more power than we think in terms of shaping curriculum. Teach texts that speak to you, and you will find it much less of an uphill battle to bring your students along for the ride.

In his collection of essays *A Voice from the Attic,* Robertson Davies (1960) describes the kind of readers I hope my students become, "those who read for pleasure, but not for idleness; who read for pastime but not to kill time; who love books, but do not live by books" (p. 7). Davies defines a love of literature, "not as a manifestation of fashion, not as a substitute for life, but as one of the greatest of the arts, existing for the delight of mankind." I measure my success in the classroom by the intellectual delight my students take in their reading.

References

Davies, R. (1960). *A voice from the attic: Essays on the art of reading.* New York: Penguin.

Fitzgerald, F. S. (1999). *The great Gatsby.* New York: Scribner.

Lee, H. (1962). *To kill a mockingbird.* New York: Popular Library.

Rosenblatt, L. M. (1983). *Literature as exploration.* New York: Modern Language Association of America.

Triggs, O. L. (Ed.). (1898). *Selections from the prose and poetry of Walt Whitman.* Boston: Small, Maynard.

Twain, M. (2008). *Adventures of Huckleberry Finn.* New York: Puffin Classics.

Wolf, M. (2007). *Proust and the squid: The story and science of the reading brain.* New York: Harper Perennial.

3 Knowing and Becoming: Teaching and Reading Literature as a Process of Transformation

Jeffrey D. Wilhelm
Boise State University

I believe that the reading of literature offers all of us and all of our students a unique and powerful way of knowing that can lead to personal and social transformation (Wilhelm, 2008). It could be argued that at no time in history have we had a greater need for transforming how we lead our personal and corporate lives, and have never had a greater need for the problem-solving literacies and willingness to dialogue that are necessary to such transformations. And yet we are faced with many obstacles and constraints to using literature for this project. In this chapter I will explore how to overcome the conceptual obstacle of how English studies is construed, and then to address the practical issue of how we might teach literature in ways that will more powerfully foster engagement, meaning-making, dialogue, and transformation.

Response and Responsibility

In my study of adolescent literary response reported on in *"You Gotta BE the Book"* (1997, 2008), I argued that engaged readers operate on ten specific interdependent dimensions of response that can be categorized as evocative, connective, and reflective. On further consideration of these dimensions, I think that they offer the basis of my argument for this chapter: that we must philosophically deepen our notion of teaching, reading, and response to reshape English language arts around the moral idea of assisting students to become democratic citizens who are responsive to themselves, each other, and the world, and who take on responsibility to themselves, each other, and the world.

The evocative dimensions of response described in *"You Gotta BE the Book"* correspond to immersing and finding oneself in the world of others' creation—whether in literature or as we are enculturated into communal life. The connective dimensions correspond to putting the self in relationship to others and their perspectives—that of authors, characters, and others distant from our time, place, and experience. This is necessary to outgrowing oneself, to balancing responsibilities, to respecting other perspectives, and indeed to all understanding. The reflective dimensions are about using the prior dimensions to see the world differently and more largely, to achieve this outgrowing of the self. This is the essential cognitive, philosophical, and religious experience: to be taken to a new level, to achieve a new way of being and understanding by communicating and extending ourselves across our usual boundaries. This trajectory is the one I propose our teaching must take to work for the transformation of our students and of their future.

Taking on the Conceptual/Philosophical Obstacles

The year 2001 saw three watershed events in this country. The acts of 9/11 loom largely in our collective memories. The other two, the No Child Left Behind Act and the first and largest of the Bush tax cuts, have had tremendous effects on the conduct of education. The first had the functional effect of drastically reducing the substance of much education to the inculcation of mechanics and recalled information; the second drastically reduced the resources available to education, or at least to those domains unmeasured by standardized tests. Teaching expertise has likewise been reframed in reductive ways, by law, as simply possessing content knowledge and disseminating information, not as the ability to apprentice others into expert practice. As teachers, we must respond to impoverished notions of teaching, learning, reading, and composing, of assessment, and of literature itself—and all other attendant obstacles—with acts of imagination and courage.

Here is a brief proposal for what such a project might include:

1. **Take responsibility for whatever is under our control.** We must not let ourselves off the hook. We know that the most important factor to affect and improve student learning is quality teaching. (See, e.g., National Commission on Teaching and America's Future, 1996; National Writing Project and Nagin, 2003; etc.)

There are two distinct areas where important decisions about education are made. The first and foremost is in the classroom, made by teachers. Let us make those decisions that are open to us and make them in the most wide-awake way possible. These decisions should be justified by what we know, both from research and our reflective practice, for the end of benefiting our own students. Let us continually adapt our instruction, continually learning from our students how to best achieve this end of enhancing their experience, understanding, and application of what is learned.

The other area is in the policy arena, where decisions are made by elected officials or appointed leaders. These decisions have an undeniable effect, but they do not keep us from enacting motivating and appropriately challenging instructional activities with students. We must not use policies as an excuse not to do so. Additionally, these decisions do not preclude our capacity to speak against them and to give voice to our own concerns and those of our students.

2. **Rethink teaching as a personal and relational pursuit.** Many teachers I know profess to teach students; some argue that they teach content. In fact, as George Hillocks Jr. (1995) eloquently argues, teaching is a transitive verb. It requires a direct and an indirect object. We teach *something* to *somebody*. If we forget the something, and even worse, the "somebody"—those *specific human beings* in our classrooms—we miss the joy and power and purpose of teaching. And we will certainly accomplish very little. As we teach literature to students, we must relate to them as human beings in all their complexity, and we must help them to relate to the wonder and magic of literature, composing, ideas from science, history, and math, and we must encourage them in turn to relate what they are learning to the world. Teaching and learning are fundamentally relational pursuits. The major danger of standardized curricula and tests, in my opinion, is that they distract our attention away from our students as human beings, and away from the wonder, fun, and power of reading, writing, and learning as meaning-making pursuits that can stake one's identity and do amazing and transformational kinds of work out in the world.

3. **Reframe English language arts as personal studies and inquiries.** Some commentators have wondered (e.g., Bizzell, 1994; Pratt, 1990) whether English is in fact a discipline at all. It was inserted into school curricula rather late in the day, by Matthew Arnold in Great Britain toward the end of the nineteenth century. It does not have a community of practice outside academe but is instead what other disciplines use to do their own work. Nonetheless, I would argue that English language arts are a vital and unique part of educational experience because it is the

most natural place to explore personal and social issues of the most compelling nature. Literature is the most powerful tool I know for engaging in such explorations. By reframing ELA as personal studies into essential personal and socially significant issues, we could free ourselves from what students (and I) consider to be "schoolishly" (Smith & Wilhelm, 2002) narrow definitions of literature and an overemphasis on correctness and objectivity in reading and writing. Instead, such a reframing would encourage us to vitally connect students to texts and ideas that meet their needs to explore and extend their thoughts and feelings about important issues, and to write with voice and vigor as they explore and express their thinking to themselves and to others.

More on Reconceiving English

I have collaborated with my friend Bruce Novak on a book about creating a "wisdom curriculum" by using the humanities (and literature in particular) as tools to engage students in ongoing conversations that address our most pressing problems and concerns as individuals and as a community (Wilhelm & Novak, 2011).

Personally and here in this chapter I am greatly indebted to Bruce for his thinking about teaching English as personal studies (a fitting complement to the "social studies") and as a form of philosophical study. To this end, philosophy needs to be reconsidered in its original sense as "the love of wisdom." "Philosophy"—if it is to be a genuine *love* of living out personal *wisdom*, as its name implies—must go further than abstract theory to become an "essay" at living and helping others live a coherent and sustainable and mutually beneficial life within the particular life-world in which one finds oneself. Again, I propose that literature and the arts are our most powerful devices for such explorations, and for considering the various practical and ethical consequences of such attempts. Literature can serve as Kafka says as a way to "break the frozen seas within," as the means to awaken or reawaken us to our possibilities, and as tools and objects to think with as we attempt to actualize these possibilities.

Novak believes that Karl Jaspers is a philosopher whose thought can be applied to a project of educational transformation because of his understanding of (1) the history of philosophy as the story of the deliberate self-education of humanity; (2) the activity of philosoph*izing* as existential reasoning, which, if deliberately cultivated in educational institutions, can become the ground for the creation of more humane democracy and practical democratic problem-solving; and (3) the need to create transformational structures for attaining and exercising authentic personal and interpersonal freedom.

Lynn Jericho and Bethene LeMahieu (2003) call this transformation a striving for "a new ordinary life" in which each of us is encouraged "to find our way into ourselves, get to know who we are, get to understand what our instincts are, what our ideals are, what our personal truth is, to form pictures of possible futures" for ourselves and others.

In *The Soul of Education*, Rachael Kessler (2000) lays out the "seven gates to the soul" that can lead us toward a transformation to more wide-awake living: "meaning and purpose," "initiation," "deep connection," "creativity," "joy," "silence and stillness," and finally "transcendence." As I move to the practical proposals for implementing the philosophical proposal Kessler outlined, I will explore how a form of all seven gates can be opened through the mindful teaching of literature. (These seven gates correspond neatly with the evocative, connective, and reflective dimensions of literary response and some of the specific dimensions inside these categories [Wilhelm, 1997, 2008]).

Moving to the Practical

My proposal is that teachers of literature make three moves to promote meaningful engagements with texts: (1) frame the teaching of literature as inquiry (which will open the doors of "meaning and purpose" and "deep connection"); (2) assist students explicitly to create meaning ("initiation") and explore, express, share, and negotiate their own responses ("creativity" and "joy") during and after reading; and (3) lead readers to consider reading as an authorial transaction with an "intelligence" who created the text they are reading ("deep connection" and "silence and stillness" as reflection and the holding of various views in one's mind), and to consider how offered ideas must be embraced, adapted, or rejected in the real world, and how to act on this new insight ("transcendence" as an outgrowing of the self, as becoming a new, or a better possible self). Making these moves has the power to make classrooms into powerful sites for personal and social transformations.

Three Transformational Teaching Moves

1. Create inquiry contexts for teaching literature.

I would guess that many, if not most, English teachers came to the profession because of their love of literature. We know the good fun, the invigorating challenges, and the purposeful possibilities offered to us by a great book. Yet, in various studies of student reading, literacy, and lived-through experiences in school (Smith & Wilhelm, 2002, 2006; Wilhelm, 2008, forthcoming), I have found that even good readers tend to reject school reading as "schoolish" or a form of "busywork," often bifurcating "real reading" from "school reading." Real reading, in contrast to school reading, is purposeful, enjoyable, plays out personal connections and uses, is shared, thought with, and used to negotiate and implement meanings well beyond the actual reading of the text itself. For these students texts are seen in Freirian terms as means for reading oneself, others, and the world.

We can make school reading more like real reading when we use literature as a way of pursuing larger inquiries. News flash: Shakespeare did not write *Romeo and Juliet* to torture ninth graders. He wrote it to explore issues surrounding what makes and, especially, what breaks relationships. Teaching the play with this inquiry focus connects students to the text in a vital way, by making the reading purposeful and by connecting it deeply to their own concerns. To teach literature in an inquiry context we first identify a possible "essential question" that captures one of the problems that the book explores. In this way, *To Kill a Mockingbird* can be considered as an exploration of large questions such as: What are your civil rights and how can we best protect and promote them? And sub-questions such as: What is the best parenting? (witness the different methods of various parents or parent figures from Bob Ewell to Calpurnia, Aunt Alexandra, Atticus, et al.). What is justice and how can we achieve it? What does it mean to be "fair?" I have used all of these "essential questions" in my own teaching of this book at different times to good effect.

Likewise, all of the books considered in this volume can be framed by various essential questions such as the following:

> What are the costs and benefits of being an outsider/of fitting in? (*The Outsiders, The Great Gatsby, The Chocolate War*, etc.)

> How are people shaped/constrained by circumstance? To what degree can we determine the course of our own lives? (*The Outsiders, Their Eyes Were Watching God, The Great Gatsby, Huck Finn*, etc.)

> What is the most effective way of pursuing what you want? (*The Chocolate War, Huck Finn, The Great Gatsby*, etc.)

I have found that far from constraining interpretations, framing literature study with essential questions opens up interpretations. As David Perkins (1986) argues, knowledge is not a line but a network, so opening up one rich vein of inquiry necessarily leads to many related veins and sub-questions.

Asking an essential question gets after "the heart of the matter" and makes reading purposeful and personally connected to lived experience. While inquiry starts with this kind of problem-orientation, it culminates with a social project of some kind. This project could involve academic writing that explores an author's position on the essential question as well as one's own position (e.g., What does Shakespeare believe most threatens relationships and to what degree do you agree?). It could also involve other kinds of composing, such as individual or group multimedia presentations, parodies, public service announcements, or social action projects based on new understanding, and much more (see Wilhelm, 2007; Wilhelm, Wilhelm, & Boas, 2009).

Culminating projects for the civil rights question might include creating a museum of multimedia kiosks exploring the history of civil rights in America or in one's community. It might involve identifying and addressing civil rights issues in the school through public service announcements and social action projects (e.g., a mentorship or buddy program for new students, a writing center or tutoring program for new immigrant students, a problem-solution video documentary or news show, a petition, etc.).

Knowing that one is going to compose and create social projects makes literary study into a way of progressing toward deep understanding and transformed ways of staking one's identity and doing real work in the world. It takes teaching away from playing "guess what the teacher already knows" and makes teaching more into helping students with developmental and philosophical projects.

2. Use interactive strategies that meet kids' current needs for activity, engagement, personal relevance, and social as well as disciplinary significance—and that develop and use imagination.

Many studies show the importance of using engaging, interactive, hands-on techniques for developing new processes of meaning-making and deep conceptual understanding (Wilhelm, 2002, 2007, 2008). I would also make the case for the importance of developing and using imagination. Imagination is essential to all learning. We must be able to imagine what it was like to live in a different time or place, to imagine what might happen if we extrapolate data patterns, to imagine a story world or a mental model of how feudalism would affect us or how inertia works. Most importantly, perhaps, we must be able to imagine ourselves as the kind of person who would want and be able to use what is being learned when we are out in the real world, and we must imagine ourselves doing so. We must be able to imagine making a difference through who we are and what we are learning to become.

One technique that works toward all these ends is drama. Drama and visualization strategies that support imagination (as well as supporting many other reading, composing, and problem-solving strategies) are among the most underused and powerful techniques in our teaching repertoires.

The basic instructional features of drama strategies or action strategies put teachers in the role of facilitating student activity and student understanding (Wilhelm, 2002, 2008; Wilhelm & Edmiston, 1998). They help reframe instruction as these strategies foreground students' current state of being, their interests, and their engagement, but at the same time move them toward new and deeper understandings. Drama provides an imaginative rehearsal for living through problems and is a form of inquiry and problem-oriented play. Drama fosters different kinds of classroom interactions since we can speak as someone else and give voice to silenced perspectives. Drama foregrounds our personal human connections to studied material. Drama helps students to give personal voice to universal issues.

When teaching *Huck Finn*, for instance, Huck can be "hotseated" throughout the book to explore his inner motivations, e.g., why he played the trick on Jim on the island, fooling him into thinking he was a ghost, or why he decides not to turn Jim in, etc. If Huck is not going to tell the truth, but continue in his subterfuges, a student can stand behind him as his "inner voice" to tell what he is really thinking. He can be interviewed individually or on a panel with other characters such as the Duke and the King by the class in a kind of forum discussion drama. When faced with dilemmas such as whether to turn Jim in, a hotseat called "Good Angel/Bad Angel" could be used as different students make cases to Huck both for and against turning Jim in to a slave-catcher.

Like drama, visualization, thinking aloud, student-generated questioning schemes, and small-group discussion techniques can all work to engage students in exploring their responses; in contending with characters, authors, and their texts; and in arriving at deepened understandings.

Imagine thinking aloud for students early on in a reading of *To Kill a Mockingbird*. Not only can the teacher model particular strategies and ways of reading (e.g., inferencing is important early in the novel), but the teacher can also read aloud to students through the most challenging part of the text and embed substantive comments that provide necessary background information without resorting to lecture. In turn, students can take over thinking aloud for the modeled strategies later on in the book.

Likewise, think of using visualization strategies such as creating a map of Maycomb with the students (to help them create a mental model of the story world), creating tableaux or a graphic novel version of key scenes (to identify and visualize key details and events and how they work together), or creating a yearbook page for Boo Radley and layering on new information with tracing paper every time new data about him is revealed (to "trace" our evolving understandings as we read along textual indices and perceive complex implied relationships within the text).

All of these techniques focus on student activity and engagement, and they assist students to greater procedural expertise through a gradual release of responsibility that involves modeling, mentoring, and monitoring student readers into the use of specific interpretive strategies and their orchestration (Wilhelm, 2001, 2003, 2004). All of these techniques are interactive and focus on making meaning, not getting particular answers. But whether you use drama or these other techniques for inquiring into texts and how they work or not, the point is to continually experiment with and reflect on the use of various techniques for the purpose of improving students' engagement, response, and educational experience. This, after all, is the life work of a teacher, and worthy work it is. In your class, at this moment, many of your students may have their last best chance to engage, learn, and succeed. Grasp the moment. Pursue it. With *urgency*.

3. Teach toward expertise and authorial reading.

This kind of instruction should assist students through the phases of "authorial reading" (Rabinowitz & Smith, 1998; Smith & Wilhelm, 2009), i.e., respecting the author and the author's message as we work hard to discern the directly stated and implied meanings, and then moving beyond the stated and implied meanings of a particular text to evaluate its possible applications, to explore silences and other perspectives, including our own. In this final phase we ask: So what? What else is there? We imagine a more complex reality beyond the limited perspective and the limited description offered by our own experience or a particular text. We consider what part of a new perspective we may want to embrace, consider more deeply, adapt and transform, or even resist. We reflect on what the text or materials under discussion—and our critical response to it—should mean to us in specific and socially active ways in terms of our thinking and living.

It is the contention of authorial reading theory that reading is in fact a conversation with other perspectives and that to engage in this conversation we must posit and relate to an author. Readers must first deeply respect, consider, and discuss the constructed ideas of authors, then interrogate and reflect on these understandings so that we can choose to accept, adapt, or resist them. This kind of activity stands in sharp contrast to simple acceptance, to the simple restating of facts and officially sanctioned knowledge that typically occurs in school. In other words, the comprehension of an author's articulated message is the beginning, not the end, of knowledge construction and use.

In his wonderful book on the ethics of reading, *The Company We Keep* (1988), Wayne Booth famously proclaims that we can and do understand each other in both spoken and written conversation and therefore that we can learn from each other and from the texts we write for each other, but only if we learn how to listen carefully and respectfully before judging and using what we learn. Inquiry framing and the use of interactive strategies in the context of inquiry help students to pay this kind of respectful attention and then to move beyond respect to resistance, acceptance, adaptation, and the making of new meanings and applications. Imagine hotseating authors such as Hurston or Fitzgerald and asking these authors what they believe about the American Dream and if it is achievable. Imagine asking these authors about the fundamental fairness of American society, or writing from their perspective about this issue. Imagine asking students to create a power ladder of the characters in *Gatsby* and then asking Fitzgerald why women are at the bottom and how he feels about that.

> Meaningful interaction with others is an essential element of learning. Part of our apprenticeship to liberty must be to learn to listen to and understand the views of others, and to appreciate the values inherent in those views—even if, in the end, we may disagree with them.—John Goodlad

The religious scholar Karen Armstrong (2005) maintains that we can only have peace and justice when we create "dialogic spaces" where "we deeply consider the concerns and anxieties of others—of people who are truly different from us" as well as the rhetoric they offer us. She argues that this kind of dialogue is essential to democracy and to solving the pressing problems of the modern world.

This freewheeling kind of inquiry reminds me of Vygotsky's contention that the self is only the self in relationship. It follows that we can only become a "new self" through relationship—relationships with texts, the world, authors, characters, each other—by achieving "intersubjectivity" with another consciousness by taking on, however tentatively, a different point of view. It also follows that we need to communicate with others to be part of a community. But this kind of communal conversation and dialogue can be difficult to achieve in a classroom, or elsewhere. Teachers and students will need to be assisted to learn the skills and use the structures that lead to rich, open, and honest discussion and the learning that can be achieved through such dialogue.

We first respectfully interpret and enliven the text, bringing it to life in the way the conventions of language and texts allow us to believe it was constructed to be understood. Then we may operate on this textual meaning to resist, adapt, or transform it for our future use, always remaining open to future transformations.

Let's use the example of conversation as an analogy. If we are talking about an important issue, and I interrupt you and say, "This is what you should really be thinking . . ." or "a truly informed view of this issue would be . . ." you would think to yourself, and rightly so: This guy is a jerk. He didn't even pay me the consideration to try and figure out what I was trying to say.

But if I listen carefully and work hard to understand you, asking clarifying questions and rephrasing your ideas, conversing with you about your thinking, and checking to see if I fully understood, you would feel respected and attended to. Even if at the end I said, "I must respectfully disagree" or "though I respect your position, I would amend it for myself in this way," or "have you ever considered . . . ," you would still feel we had a meaningful and useful conversation. This is the point of authorial reading, to respect the author and the text, and after comprehending it to grant it the seriousness of reflection and evaluation so we make what we learn from that conversation our own.

The culture of the socio-constructivist, transactional, and learning-centered approach to teaching is that of learning from one another. I tell my students that "Every one here is a teacher and a student. We have thirty teachers and thirty students in this room. All of you and myself. And every author we read is our teacher. We don't have to accept what we learn from every teacher, but we must hear and attend to them."

Conclusion: Toward a Loving-Knowledge

I am currently pursuing a study on how students engage with texts that are not typically valued or used in school, such as video games, fanfiction, manga, fantasy, horror, etc. Astonishingly, many of these adept readers cannot identify a single engaging or meaningful text that they have read in school. I don't care how well these students read or how many personally enriching texts they read outside of school—these students are underserved by school. I would argue that any student who does not engage in meaningful activity, read stimulating texts, and write/compose something of intense interest and use to them *every day* in school is being underserved. A focus on ELA as personal studies and inquiries can help us to focus on these kinds of stimulating experiences that are at the heart of learning.

In school, we seem to privilege a particular kind of knowing and particular ways of demonstrating it. These ways are very limited, and I believe that students implicitly understand the shortcomings of schoolish ways of knowing and demonstrating knowledge, and the incompleteness and inadequacies of these.

Among powerful ways of knowing we might identify and name engaged knowing, loving-knowledge, self-knowledge, or even wisdom. I have studied the qualitative experiences of kids' lived-through experiences in school for many years and I must say without equivocation that it is typically of an abysmal quality. I am finding that the informants in my past and current studies are almost always seeking a more personal, intimate, different kind of more engaged, personal knowing and understanding through their out-of-school activity and personal reading. They seek the kinds of books that give them what they need *right now*. Their reading always provides evidence of engagement and almost always—not always, but almost—seems to provide evidence of a different way of knowing—of personal exploration, of archetypal energy, of a kind of loving-knowledge or wisdom seeking. Perhaps this pursuit takes the place of cultural myth and personal story-telling from more primordial and grounded cultures.

All of the literary works highlighted in this volume can be taught as cultural artifacts or sets of information. But they can all also be easily read as a way of inquiring into the issues that most compel us and our students. They can all be used as part of a project of transformation, of understanding and use for the purposes of leading more wide-awake and socially active lives. It is my argument that this pursuit should be our own classroom project, and that this project can easily be made entirely consistent with most curricula, with standards, and certainly with the true dimensions of the actual expertise of real readers, composers, and democratic citizens as they do their work. I hope that I have provided some help here in how we ourselves might fruitfully pursue this work.

References

Armstrong, K. (2005, October 4). *The battle for god* [Lecture]. Boise State University Distinguished Lecture Series, Boise, ID.

Bizzell, P. (1994). "Contact zones" and English studies. *College English, 56,* 163–69.

Booth, W. C. (1988). *The company we keep: An ethics of fiction.* Berkeley: University of California Press.

Hillocks, G., Jr. (1995). *Teaching writing as reflective practice.* New York: Teachers College Press.

Jericho, L., & LeMahieu, B. (2003). *Ground zero and the human soul: The search for the new ordinary life.* New York: Foursquare Conversations.

Kessler, R. (2000). *The soul of education: Helping students find connection, compassion, and character at school.* Alexandria, VA: Association for Supervision and Curriculum Development.

National Commission on Teaching and America's Future. (1996, September). *What matters most: Teaching for America's future.* Retrieved from http://www.teaching-point.net/Exhibit%20A/What%20Matters%20Most.pdf

National Writing Project, & Nagin, C. (2003). *Because writing matters: Improving student writing in our schools.* San Francisco: Jossey-Bass.

Novak, B. (n.d.). *A new guiding light for democratic education? Karl Jaspers' understanding of the universal educational history of humankind from a factually grounded cosmopolitan perspective.* Unpublished manuscript.

Perkins, D. N. (1986). *Knowledge as design.* Hillsdale, NJ: Erlbaum.

Pratt, M. L. (1990). Arts of the contact zone. In D. Bartholomae and A. Petrosky (Eds.), *Ways of reading: An anthology for writers* (2nd ed., pp. 528–42). New York: Bedford Books.

Rabinowitz, P. J., & Smith, M. W. (1998). *Authorizing readers: Resistance and respect in the teaching of literature.* New York: Teachers College Press.

Smith, M. W., & Wilhelm. J. D. (2002). *"Reading don't fix no Chevys": Literacy in the lives of young men.* Portsmouth, NH: Heinemann.

Smith, M. W., & Wilhelm, J. D. (2006). *Going with the flow: How to engage boys (and girls) in their literacy learning.* Portsmouth, NH: Heinemann.

Smith, M. W., & Wilhelm, J. D. (2009). *Fresh takes on teaching the literary elements: How to teach what really matters about character, setting, point of view, and theme.* New York: Scholastic and Urbana, IL: National Council of Teachers of English.

Wilhelm, J. D. (1997). *"You gotta BE the book": Teaching engaged and reflective reading with adolescents.* New York: Teachers College Press and Urbana, IL: National Council of Teachers of English.

Wilhelm, J. D. (2001). *Improving comprehension with think-aloud strategies.* New York: Scholastic.

Wilhelm, J. D. (2002). *Action strategies for deepening comprehension: Role plays, text structure tableaux, talking statues, and other enrichment techniques that engage students with text.* New York: Scholastic.

Wilhelm, J. D. (2004). *Reading is seeing: Learning to visualize scenes, characters, ideas, and text worlds to improve comprehension and reflective reading.* New York: Scholastic.

Wilhelm, J. D. (2007). *Engaging readers and writers with inquiry: Promoting deep understandings in language arts and the content areas with guiding questions.* New York: Scholastic.

Wilhelm, J. D. (2008*). "You gotta BE the book": Teaching engaged and reflective reading with adolescents* (2nd ed.). New York: Teachers College Press and Urbana, IL: National Council of Teachers of English.

Wilhelm, J. D. (in preparation). *Let them read trash.* New York: Scholastic. Manuscript submitted for publication.

Wilhelm, J. D., & Edmiston, B. (1998). *Imagining to learn: Inquiry, ethics, and integration through drama.* Portsmouth, NH: Heinemann.

Wilhelm, J. D., & Novak, B. (2011). *Teaching literacy for love and wisdom: Being the book and being the change.* New York: Teachers College Press.

Wilhelm, J. D., Wilhelm, P. J., & Boas, E. (2009). *Inquiring minds learn to read and write: 50 problem-based literacy and learning strategies.* Toronto, Canada: Rubicon.

4 Reading Fictions

Robert E. Probst
Professor Emeritus, Georgia State University

The past several years have suggested that there is little difference between reading our literature and listening to our politicians. Novelists want to draw you into the worlds they have created, convince you that they might exist, that events might transpire as they have related them, that characters might think as they have depicted them thinking and act as they have shown them acting. Politicians—who function as both creators of and characters in their own narrations—similarly want to draw you into the world as they see it and convince you that it works the way they say it works. Beyond that, the politicians want you to view the characters in the fictions they're creating—their opponents on the one hand and themselves on the other—in ways that will lead to their election and their opponent's defeat.

Reading Fiction—and Everything Is Fiction

And so the reader, whether sitting by the fire with the latest bestseller (or a classic neglected in high school English) or settled on the couch to watch a campaign speech, is entering a fiction, an imaginary world created out of words. One of those worlds is admittedly, unashamedly, fictional. The novelist doesn't pretend to be offering you a documentary, an accounting of events that have in fact taken place, with people who did in fact exist, speaking precisely the words that appear in his dialogues, behaving with exactly the motivation attributed to them, and obtaining just the results he presents. We grant the novelist that license, hoping perhaps that we'll find in this account of something that *did not* happen a truth about things that *do* happen, actually, in the world we live in. So we don't complain that J. K. Rowling is lying when Harry Potter wields a magic wand, confronts a Hippogriff, or plays Quidditch, and instead read on and think about fear and courage and accomplishment, or whatever else in human experience, actual human experience, the book might lead us to reflect on.

The other fictional world, the one we find in the political speech (or other political statement), is less forthrightly fictional and imaginary.

The politician either tries or pretends to be honest, informed, rational, and direct. His speech is purportedly based in fact. If we notice or later discover that it was not, we are disappointed that he was ignorant or misinformed and may lean toward skepticism. His intentions are, we are asked to believe, what he says they are. If we see or infer other—hidden—intentions, we may begin to suspect deceit and dishonesty. The politician does value, we are asked to accept, what he claims to value. We take offense (or should) if we learn that he is either too unreflective to know what he values or has simply lied to us about what matters to him. But whether skillful or clumsy, honest or dishonest, forthright or deceitful, what the politician gives us is a construct. He gives us a fiction. He offers us a representation of the world and of himself and we need to make sense, ourselves, out of that construct. We need to test his vision of the world against our own, see how well they match, evaluate them both, and draw the best conclusions we can.

Thus, when the novelist Rowling imagines a magic wand and tells us that Harry Potter has one, we smile and agree to pretend, for the duration of the story, that he has such a wonderful invention, and read on. We don't complain that she has lied to us, that she has deceived us. When she drapes Harry in a cloak of invisibility, we neither object that such cloaks don't exist nor do we go to eBay to search for one—we think wistfully that a cloak of invisibility could be very useful at times, and we keep reading. On the other hand, should a politician ever imagine magic wands, or weapons just as potent, imagine them in the hands of a foreign power, and then present that invention to us as hard, cold fact so that he can proclaim the foreign power to be our enemy, we do (or should) object. We complain that he has lied to us, that he has deceived us. In the one case, although that fictional magic wand may bring death and destruction, it will do so only to imaginary enemies and villains; in the other case, those fictional weapons might lead to real death and destruction for real people only imagined to be enemies and villains, and for many of us, as well. The one fiction yields excitement and pleasure; the other may mean that students sitting in your class today will be dying in the sand far from home tomorrow.

So we read novels and listen to speeches and respond in whatever way we have learned to respond. If by upbringing or training we have become inclined to seek out only confirmation for what we already believe, then that's what we'll do. If we are predisposed or trained to accept unquestioningly what we read or hear, we may immerse ourselves in the text and be easily persuaded by it. If we are inclined, or have been taught, to question and wonder, then we are more likely to pause and think. It is, of course, great fun to lose ourselves in a novel, and some we read just for that pleasant hour in which we become another person in another world. No child reads Harry Potter intent on producing the definitive critical essay about his place in British fiction of the late twentieth and early twenty-first century. You probably don't pick up a novel in the airport before a long trip hoping that it will become the subject for your dissertation. On the other hand, you probably don't want to become so immersed in the novel, so accepting of what it presents, that you absorb *unthinkingly* the values it presents or the conception of people it offers. To do so would be to allow what we read to mold us. If we are predisposed to lose ourselves in the novelist's world, to simply absorb it, we might lose opportunities to clarify and refine our vision of the world. Still, the novel invites us to pretend and to imagine, and that is much of its pleasure. We all love to get lost in a good story.

Political speeches often ask us to pretend and imagine, too. We're willing to do that, to an extent. We wouldn't want to dissect and analyze every word, every phrase, every sentence a politician utters. We'll allow a few rhetorical flourishes, a few exaggerations, a few emotional stories that may stretch the truth slightly. But in the end, although we may be amused, entertained, and enchanted by the language, we want to know if the political leader's statements are honest, based in fact, reasonable, and intended to promote the common good. An imaginary magic wand waved by Harry Potter is charming; an imaginary magic wand said to be waved by a foreign power so that he can be labeled an enemy is simply offensive, dishonest, corrupt, and dangerous.

Suspending Disbelief—or Not

The novel and the political speech, though they both offer us fictions, require us to bring slightly different attitudes to our reading. The novel expects us to be willing to suspend our disbelief, at least about some elements, and if we want to finish and enjoy the book, we agree. We accept the notion that this invented character is a real person, that this imagined city is a real place, that these concocted events actually do take place. Sometimes, the strain of suspending that disbelief is immense.

On an airplane one day, in the seat-back pocket in front of me, I found a science fiction novel about deep-sea rays that rapidly evolve, as a result of some environmental pressure, into savage predators not only able to swim but also to fly. *Unlikely*, I thought, but after all it was science fiction, and this was going to be a long flight, so I decided to see what this author could do with this idea. Once I had agreed to it, I was comfortable with the notion of flying, man-eating stingrays. Late in the book, however, the writer offered me a scene in which two men are fighting with one another in a helicopter that spins out of control and plunges toward the ocean. The hero finishes the fight, finds a parachute, slips his arms into the straps, buckles up the harness, and then leaps safely out the door. Having ridden in too many cabs over too many potholes in too many cities, holding on for dear life, I knew how absurd that scene was. Our hero wouldn't have been able to button his shirt, let alone struggle into a parachute in the backseat of that bucking, plunging cab, much less in the crowded cockpit of a helicopter spinning chaotically out of control. It was such an absurd image that I had to struggle to get through it, to forgive the author his carelessness, to hope that he found a more conscientious editor for his next novel, and to remind myself once again that this was science fiction and I had already agreed to accept some preposterous inventions. Even when we agree to immerse ourselves in the book, to suspend disbelief, and to accept the author's premises, a careless line or scene can be so jarring that it kicks us immediately out of the fictional world we have agreed to live in for the moment.

The same can happen with political statements. For instance, one politician in the recent presidential campaign asserted that "the Constitution established the United States of America as a Christian nation" (http://www.nytimes.com/2007/09/29/us/politics/29cnd-mccain. html?ref=politics). Such a statement would be jarring to anyone who had survived seventh-grade Social Studies with a grade of D- or better, but it is especially so coming from a candidate for the presidency, a position for which the oath of office consists of little more than a promise to uphold and defend that Constitution. Perhaps the writer, or in this case speaker, would like us to allow him this line, just as we allowed the novelist his giant, flying, man-eating, bat-shaped fish, but suspending disbelief in this situation is probably less appropriate and more difficult. The politician, after all, is talking about the real world in which we live all the time, not a fictional world that we will exit when we exit the plane. And so the reader, instead of suspending disbelief, acknowledges and investigates the disbelief. In the age of the Internet, this takes only three or four minutes—find a copy of the Constitution (http://www. usconstitution.net/const.html or any of several other sites), download it into a word-processing program, search the document for the word *Christ* (which will also locate the derivatives—*Christian* or *Christianity*), and, discovering that no form of that word appears at all, conclude with fair confidence that the politician is, to be generous, wrong. A conscientious reader might go so far as to actually read the document to see if in some subtle way the authors had contrived to establish a Christian nation without calling it a Christian nation. Taking the time to read the document will lead to the discovery that the word *God* is absent from the Constitution, and that the word *religion* doesn't appear until the First Amendment, in the phrase that begins "Congress shall make no law respecting an establishment of religion," ten words that fairly conclusively contradict the politician's absurd assertion.

So it's easy to see that this careless politician was wrong—any competent and curious seventh grader would demonstrate that in several minutes at the computer—what we can't know is whether the speaker was misinformed, ignorant, or lying. To decide which, we would have to go beyond this one statement to other events, other statements, other information—did the speaker pass seventh-grade history? I̲s̲ there any evidence that he has never had an opportunity to see the Constitution? Does he have a pattern of lying in public statements? All we know at this point is that he has offered us something as credible as the giant flying man-eating bat-fish.

Response and Responsibility

The point of this lengthy comparison is simple. Our primary job, our fundamental obligation, our central goal, is to teach readers to be responsible.

It's the solitary, lonely, independent reader who will ultimately have to decide what he does with any text. When he comes to the man-eating bat-fish, he has the option of saying either "This is interesting—let's see what happens" or "This stretches credibility too far—I'll look for another book when I land." When he struggles to imagine the hero putting on his parachute in a plummeting helicopter, he has the option of saying either "This has fractured the illusion of reality so badly that I can't go on" or "I'll blame the scene on careless editing and keep on reading." The consequences of his decision in this case aren't significant. When he comes to the statement about the Constitution, he can say, "It must be so" or "I trust him," or he might say, "This is surprising; I need to check on it." It's the individual reader who has to take the responsibility, who has to make the choice between those responses. The consequences in this case are likely to be more significant. Once our students leave our classes, they won't have the English teacher around to make the decision for them about what questions to ask or what line of thought to pursue.

They'll have to have, within them, probably instilled by parents and good teachers, the predisposition and willingness to think about what they have read. They'll have to be responsible.

One aspect of that responsibility is easy to cope with. It isn't difficult, when reading a novel, to decide to accept some illusion for the sake of the story, or, on the other hand, to decide that something is just too absurd for you to waste your time with it. It may be slightly more difficult to bring yourself to check on the accuracy or truthfulness of a politician's statements, especially if he or she is a politician you are inclined to favor; after all, this is the leader you have chosen or will choose to follow. For those significant issues, however, when we choose to accept statements with no questions asked, then we have to admit that, at best, we've fallen short of our civic duty.

The heavy burden is the reader's responsibility to question what he is not inclined to question, to question what he firmly and absolutely believes. In listening to that politician's claim, the heaviest burden falls on those who do believe that the Constitution established the United States as a Christian nation. First, they have the immense problem of simply noticing that it's a dubious assertion. When we hear or read something that we absolutely believe to be true, that we "know" to be true, we aren't inclined to doubt it. So the agreeing reader wants it to be true; believes that it's true; needs it to be true; may be badly disappointed if it isn't true. And, worst of all, if it isn't true it may challenge many of his other ideas about himself, the country, its political leaders, and the world in which he lives. Having our vision of the world and our place in it challenged is, well, unsettling. It would have been deeply disturbing to me if I had looked into the Constitution and found, to my shock, that it did indeed dictate that we were to be a "Christian nation." It would have left me with many questions about both the country and myself. Most important, it would have made me wonder how I could have lived for so many years in the delusion that our country offered religious freedom, and it would perhaps make me dread the intellectual labor of revising my conceptions, of changing my mind, of rethinking where I am, and who I am, and what my obligations now are.

It would have faced me with a challenge similar to that of a racist reader who comes to the passage in *Adventures of Huckleberry Finn* where Huck decides that he is going to treat Jim as a man instead of as a "nigger," that he is willing to take that stand despite the fact that—in his view of the world—he is going to go to hell as a consequence. That scene, as powerfully as any in all literature, challenges the assumptions that some readers may bring to the book. Huck is willing to, chooses to, determines to, fry eternally in hell simply to treat a man with respect. He decides that he will treat Jim with simple respect although almost none of his community do so, and although his society and his God will revile and condemn him for the indiscretion. *To Kill a Mockingbird* offers much the same opportunity to the reader, the chance to investigate assumptions, to rethink a worldview, to remake himself or herself. Doing so may not be easy and may not be comfortable. Perhaps all great literature offers us that opportunity, that challenge, that discomfort. Many—perhaps most—readers won't want to accept the challenge and suffer the discomfort, just as they avoid the discomfort of doing what's necessary to stay healthy, or to get in shape, or to accomplish anything else significant.

And that is why American literature is so important. It holds the world in which we live up to us, inviting us to look at it, think about it, question it, and in doing so question ourselves. We need responsible, discerning readers who are willing to face some of those questions and reflect on possibly troubling answers to them, or we will be stuck forever with what we've inherited, with no power to modify and improve it.

We've been able to accept the idea that life emerged from the primordial ooze, that life forms may have evolved from floating, to swimming, to lumbering around on dry earth, to flying, and so perhaps someday in the future giant, flying, man-eating batfish will emerge from the sea and I'll decide to move to Kansas or somewhere else far from the ocean. It hasn't happened yet and I'm not going to spend much time worrying about it, but I'll stay open to the possibility. And if a pilot comes along and tells me that it actually would be possible, in a dying helicopter, to finish up a fistfight, find a parachute, strap it on, write a letter to your kids, check your email, review your will, cancel weekend delivery of the newspaper, crawl to the door, and leap safely into space, then I'll admit that I was wrong, write a letter of apology to the novelist, and change my mind about what well-trained helicopter pilots can do. I'll stay open to the complex questions about what we have been given, good and bad, by all the religions that have influenced our country. And I'll hope that I, and our students, will have the courage to look for, in the books we read, the speeches we hear, the movies we watch—all the texts of our lives—the questions that we might not be eager to ask and perhaps the answers that, although we may not be comfortable with them at first, lead us to a clearer understanding of our country, our world, and ourselves, and then to the questions that we need to ask next.

5 Transforming Interpretation: Literary Theory and the Novel in the Secondary Classroom

John Noell Moore
The College of William & Mary

*Literary theory functioned in my education as a prism, which I could turn
to refract different spectral patterns of language use in a text, as one does
daylight. Turn the prism this way, and one pattern of color emerges; turn it
that way, and another pattern configures.*

        —Henry Louis Gates Jr., *Black Literature in America* (1971)

For teachers who have little experience using literary theory in
their classrooms, Henry Louis Gates Jr. provides a metaphor that
describes how he put theory into practice. His prism and the
multiple ways in which it refracts patterns of light/language in a text
offer a practical entry into the world of literary theory. Theory is not, as
some secondary teachers think, a huge monolith that they are power-
less to confront. It is not esoteric knowledge that belongs exclusively to
college professors and experts in literary criticism. It is not an excuse
for English teachers to continue traditional ways of teaching literature,
plodding day after day through the ritualistic analyses of New Critical
Formalism, processes that for half a century have brought comfort to
teachers and anxiety and frustration to many of their students. When I
started teaching high school English forty years ago, there were few, if
any, daily discussions among teachers about putting theory into practice,
discussions that are now common when teachers talk and conference
together. The purpose of this chapter is to offer a brief introduction to
literary theory and to point out some ways that it can offer secondary
English teachers and their students new entry points into the world of
literature and broader access to the power of our dynamic, ever changing, language.

    The word *theory* comes from the Greek work *theorein*, meaning
literally "to look at." In the simplest terms, literary theory offers multiple ways of looking into a text. No matter what theoretical approaches

teachers use, the goal should be to give students the tools to explore texts from multiple interpretive angles to achieve more complex understandings and, as a result, learn to become better readers, critical thinkers, and consumers of texts.

Since the 1950s, the concerns of literary theory have changed, and in large part the process can be described as a series of shifts—what the preeminent theorist Vincent Leitch (2003) calls "transformations"—from New Critical Formalism to cultural studies. These transformations have expanded dramatically the concepts of writer, reader, and text.

Literary Theory in Brief

A quick trip through the lenses/perspectives of selected literary theories is the best way to reveal how text, reader, and writer are connected or disconnected in the analytical process of reading. In the last half of the twentieth century new theories emerged in opposition to New Critical Formalism. The theories discussed here can be grouped into three categories: theories about structures (New Critical Formalism, archetypal theory, structuralism and semiotics, and deconstruction); reader response; and culturally based theories (feminism, black aesthetics, and cultural studies). Space does not permit the exploration of more recent theories, including post-colonialism, theories of whiteness, and queer theory.

New Critical Formalist readers work in the following way; they:

- Approach the written work as a complete, finished work of art
- Discover one best reading through a complex analytical process that highlights the unity of the text
- Use a sophisticated vocabulary for understanding literature
- Keep their feelings and emotions out of the analytical process (the affective fallacy)
- Keep the author and his intentions out of the process (the authorial fallacy) (Brooks & Warren, 1959)

Archetypal theory also seeks the unity in the text by moving outside the text to see it in the context of the long history of literary traditions. Readers explore the text to discover and interpret the following:

- Archetypal events (birth, initiation, loss of innocence, death)
- Archetypal patterns (journey, quest, transformation, and redemption)
- Archetypal characters (hero, villain, trickster)
- Archetypal images and symbols (paradisiacal garden, apple, darkness and light, snake, circle)

New Critical Formalists often use archetypes as part of their exploration of how literary elements unify the text, but they do not explore the significance of these characters, images, and symbols within the larger context of what Northrop Frye (1982) calls the "mythological universe," created by literary traditions and cultures worldwide.

Structuralism/semiotics takes a different approach to interpretation; readers focus specifically on the language system of the text. They

- Explore how a sign system (language particular to a culture) unifies the text;
- Decode the signs of the text; and
- Discover binary oppositions (night/day, love/hate) that contribute to meaning making.

Developing as a reaction to the structuralist approach and not to be confused with the destruction of the text, the deconstructionist/poststructuralist perspective finds readers admitting that the text has no unity. They:

- Enjoy the play of language in the text that dismantles the text
- Explore intertextualities—threads of earlier texts woven into the fabric of the text
- Understand that there can be no single author of a text
- View the text as "a tissue of quotations, drawn from the innumerable centres of culture" (Barthes, 2001)

Along with New Critical Formalism, reader response is the theory teachers most often use in today's public school classrooms. Unlike earlier theories that focused specifically on the text, reader response focuses on readers who:

- Bring their own experiences to the interpretation of the text
- Experience the transaction that takes place between reader and text
- Understand that interpretation of the text grows out of that transaction
- Understand that the text is incomplete and that it unfolds in time in the act of reading (Leitch, 1988)

Reader response does not mean that anything goes, that every reader's interpretation is correct or valid. The response is always to the text; the interpretation grows out of the experience with the language and ideas of the text.

Feminism and black aesthetics fall under the larger umbrella of Cultural Studies. Among other things, feminism invites readers to:

- Read the women (and men) in the text
- Read the female body in the text (gynocriticism)
- Read from gendered perspectives
- Investigate the traditions of women's writing (Walker, 1993)

Readers who use the black aesthetic contextualize the text in the wide expanse of black culture. Those who do not understand African American history and culture cannot successfully read texts by black authors. Readers from the Cultural Studies perspective discover the multiple disciplines and intertextualities in conversation in the text, as the approach to *The Outsiders* later in this chapter demonstrates.

The transformations of literary theory in the last half century invite us to teach students to use multiple approaches in discovering textual meanings and to learn that pluralistic readings do justice to the complexities of the texts they read.

Theory into Practice

How do we employ these approaches in our teaching of literature? What does a pluralistic reading look like? How is it constructed? We should always begin with reader response to explore what students bring to the text and how they construct meanings from the text in the context of their prior knowledge and experiences. From a reader response approach we can guide students to look at the text through the lenses of other theoretical perspectives. A brief reading of a short text demonstrates how the process works. Let's take a trip to the Chicago street that runs past The Golden Shovel Pool Hall, the location of Gwendolyn Brooks's poem "We Real Cool," her most anthologized poem.

In teaching from a **reader response** perspective, I suggest that teachers provide students the list of increasingly complex questions developed by Robert Probst, the leading proponent of the work of Louise Rosenblatt, who created the reader response approach to reading in the 1930s. Probst's questions guide readers from a simple gut reaction to an examination of their feelings as they read the text. Students' responses to visual images, associations with people, places, events, and memories in their lives, lead to more complex responses: evaluations of the quality of the poem, literary associations with other texts, and reactions to the responses of their classmates (Probst, 1988).

The obvious **archetype** in "We Real Cool" is the outsider; students will be familiar with some of the most famous young outsiders in literature: the Greasers in S. E. Hinton's *The Outsiders*; Jerry in Robert

Cormier's *The Chocolate War*; Holden Caulfield in J. D. Salinger's *The Catcher in the Rye*; and Piggy in William Golding's *Lord of the Flies.* These characters are all outside the dominant culture in some way, and for that they pay a price. Brooks suggests that her cool guys may pay the ultimate price for their juvenile nonconformity.

Working with **semiotics**, we can help students decode the sign system that operates in the poem by closely reading the language of Brooks's adolescents. In her choice of language she captures the implied smirks and swaggers of these dropouts. They are, as Brooks gives them speech, "cool" because they have "Left school"; they "Lurk late" and they "Strike straight," the phrases suggesting danger, violence, and, perhaps, gang connections. They wax poetic as the poem progresses: they "Sing sin" and "Thin gin," and they "Jazz June." In the final irony of the poem Brooks points out their likely fate: they will "Die soon."

The adolescents' language reveals their attitudes and reflects their existential/fatalistic worldview. Semioticians refer to *signs* rather than *words* because signs have no universal significance; they are particular to a culture in time. Brooks's signs and their meanings are particular to the street culture of the poem. Readers decode the text, something Hortense J. Spiller (1987) refers to when she describes the poem: "The simplicity of the poem is stark to the point of elaborateness. Less than lean, it is virtually coded." For a more detailed explanation and a demonstration of teaching and reading from a semiotic perspective see "Street Signs: Semiotics, *Romeo and Juliet,* and Young Adult Literature" (Moore, 1998).

A **cultural studies** approach offers students many rich interpretative opportunities. A recording of Brooks reading the poem is available at http://poets.org/view media/phpMID/15433, and her explanation of why she wrote the poem will intrigue students and help them understand how poetry can emerge from seemingly insignificant moments of everyday life. For example, Brooks explains what she meant by "Jazz June": it's a wonderful month, a time when people have fun and enjoy themselves. The word "Jazz" has generated controversy, leading to the banning of the poem in some places; she meant jazz as music, but others decode jazz as having a sexual connotation. In her reading of the poem, Brooks (2009) creates its music and tone by emphasizing the *We* at the end of the first seven lines, softly lifting the word into the air and inflecting it to convey what she has called the teenagers' awareness of "a semi-defined personal importance."

Using the **black aesthetic**, students can contextualize the poem with observations, personal experiences, research, and readings on the current educational and social status of young African American males.

The poem can serve as an introduction to the study of related, more elaborate texts. The novels of Walter Dean Myers offer insight into the world of teenage African Americans. A companion piece for the implied gang connection in "We Real Cool," Myers's *Scorpions* is a novel in which a middle school student is recruited to join a gang and experiences the power of having a gun; he rejects the gang when he escapes injury in a violent confrontation in which other gang members are killed. Myers's more complex psychological novel *Monster* uses a double narrative structure in dealing with the plight of Steve Harmon, a young black man who is on trial for murder. Steve's handwritten narrative about his incarceration is juxtaposed with a screenplay he is writing about the trial. An archetypal African American outsider is Bigger Thomas in Richard Wright's *Native Son*. Like Brooks's poem, Wright's novel is set in Chicago. Students can explore themes of violence, victimization, and social justice from the black aesthetic perspective in Ernest Gaines's *A Lesson Before Dying*, a novel about a young black man convicted and executed for a crime he did not commit.

Among other issues, a **feminist** literary critique addresses gender studies, which investigates how masculinity and femininity are constructed socially and culturally to empower men and subordinate women. This approach suggests a number of questions that students might explore. Are Brooks's adolescents the victims of patriarchal practices by the dominant white culture? How have the identities of young African American males been constructed by their families and their culture? What does it mean to readers that the poet is an African American woman of a different social class than the pool players? Taking her title from the first line of Brooks's poem, feminist scholar bell hooks (2003) addresses social dynamics, gender, and race in *We Real Cool: Black Men and Masculinity*. In chapters entitled "plantation patriarchy," "gangsta culture: a piece of the action," "from angry boys to angry men," and "waiting for daddy to come home: black male parenting" (2003), she explores feminist issues that readers can address in Brooks's poem and other texts written by African American authors.

The **new critical formalism** approach offers several useful entries into the poem. For example, the poem has an implied narrative to which three critical questions of the formalist approach can be applied: What happens? Male adolescents skip school and hang out in a Chicago pool hall. Who does it? Seven African American teenagers. What does it mean? Being cool today might not make you cool tomorrow; it may lead to violence, and someday it just might kill you. Formalist readers can also find rich layers of music in the language of the poem. Vince

Gotera (2009), for example, focuses his reading on alliteration, rhyme, and rhythm to show how these literary devices "contribute to the poem's meaning by providing sonic texture and unity—an impression that the poem is an interwoven whole of sound and sense." Consonants alliterate in "Lurk late," "Strike straight," "Sing sin," "Thin gin," and "Jazz June." Assonance sings in the vowel repetitions in "Sing sin" and "Thin gin." Pararhymes occur in the consonance of "lefT" and "laTe," and in the initial letter rhyme in "gin," "Jazz," and "June." Readers can hear rhythm in the musical power of enjambment in the placement of "We" at the ends of the first seven lines. In its structure, it seems significant that the poem relies exclusively on the couplet (Gotera, 2009).

Formalists typically investigate tone and irony as functions of language, and the first and last lines of Brooks's poem provide a good example of this approach. The word *cool* has connotations of self-control and calmness, often in the face of obvious difficulty; a cool character is detached, aloof. This is the connotation with which the poem opens, and all the lines that follow "We real cool" support that youthful bravado until the last sentence: "We / Die soon." What readers expect and what they get in the last line, that difference, is the essence of verbal irony: Words convey the opposite of what appears to be their literal meaning.

Such diverse, rich readings of Brooks's poem show how multiple theoretical perspectives can help teachers and students open up a text in ways that a single approach cannot. The literary language required in the formalistic reading can, we know, close down rather than open up the text and other, more complex texts for some secondary students. I do not mean to suggest that teachers abandon new critical formalism completely. After exploring the poem from these other perspectives, a Formalist reading can offer a deeper understanding of the language and structure of the poem. This is well demonstrated in seven interpretations of the poem from various perspectives available online at http://www.english.illinois.edu/MAPS/poets/a_brooks/werealcool.htm.

Critical Stances Open Up *The Outsiders*

Now I want to apply the perspectives of literary theory to reading one of our ten novels, S. E. Hinton's *The Outsiders*. I begin with **reader response** because some of my students respond initially that they don't like the novel because the female novelist overemphasizes the importance of hair and clothes; others are amazed that a sixteen-year-old girl wrote the book. Probst (1988) offers some useful reader response questions that might elicit some deeper personal response: "What image was called to mind by the text? Upon what, in the text, did you focus most intently as you read? How did you respond to the text emotionally or intellectually? Do you think this text is a good one? Why or why not?"

Females seem to play a minor role in the novel, so a **feminist** approach might focus on the relationship of female characters to the patriarchal construction of the society presented in the novel. The adolescent girls include Cherry Valance and her well-to-do friends who date the Socs, as well as Sylvia, Sandy, Evie, and the loud, tough girls who, as Pony Boy says, are "the only kind of girls that would look at us" (Hinton, 1995). Only two adult females appear: Pony's deceased mother, remembered for her kindness, and Johnny's abusive mother who, as he lies near death in the hospital, reveals her callous attitude toward her son: "But I have a right to see him. He's my son. After all the trouble his father and I have gone to raise him, this is our reward" (p. 108).

The abusive mother's language represents one of the ways of talking in the novel; such talk makes the novel a rich site for **semiotic** study. The language of the street rewards study. Other elements for semiotic study include, for example, hair styles, clothes, and cars. *The Outsiders* is truly a rich cultural deposit. From a **new criticism** perspective, the circular structure of the novel is crucial to our understanding of plot, character, and theme. As the novel ends, readers learn that the story we have experienced has been told by Pony Boy, and this revelation invites a closer look at character: how it is revealed through plot and how plot and character contribute to meaning making in the novel. Character study can lead, as well, to considering one of the major **archetypes** in literature, the outsider, and open up discussions about what happens to some nonconformists in Hinton's story. They suffer the same fate, although by different means, as Brooks's outsiders.

Cultural studies have clearly transformed literary investigation. A cultural studies reader would consider the historical, political, and literary context before and after reading *The Outsiders* (see Figure 5.1). In this stance the reader takes into account what's happening contemporaneously with the writing of the novel and events happening at the time period during which the novel is set. Or, a cultural studies reader may begin with multidisciplinary texts related to the novel and, as a consequence, explore how these multidisciplinary connections contribute to a deeper understanding of the novel (Belsey, 1988).

The first sentence of *The Outsiders*, for example, sets up a link to the world of film: "When I stepped out into the bright sunlight from the darkness of the movie house, I had only two things on my mind: Paul Newman and a ride home" (Hinton, 1995). The reference to Paul

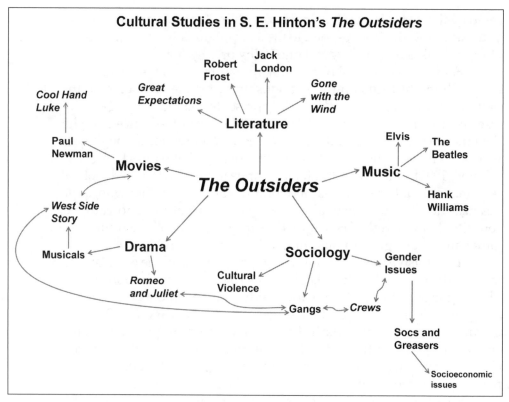

Figure 5.1. Cultural studies in S. E. Hinton's *The Outsiders*.

Newman calls to mind the film *Cool Hand Luke*, which premiered in 1967, the same year Hinton's novel was published. The film reference reinforces Hinton's title, sets up the outsider theme, and suggests an archetypal approach: Luke Jackson, like the Greasers, is a noncon-formist, an outsider, who suffers because he insists on being different. References to well-known literature also contribute to the construction of meaning in *The Outsiders*. Pony Boy identifies with Pip in Dickens's *Great Expectations*, a young boy who is also an outsider in social class and who is consequently rejected by the wealthy Estella. The connection highlights class differences between the Greasers and the well-to-do girls with whom these lower-class guys are unpopular. *Gone with the Wind* also figures into the narrative, but the most memorable text, the one most popular with young readers, is Robert Frost's "Nothing Gold Can Stay." Quoted in its entirety in the novel, this brief poem underscores an archetypal theme: the fate of innocence. Pony Boy remains on the borderline between childhood and adolescence throughout most of the novel, but the narrative shows how "Eden sank to grief" for him in the deaths of Bob, Dally, and Johnny. In his death bed letter to Pony Boy, Johnny interprets the poem in the context of their lives: "that guy that wrote it, he meant you're gold when you're a kid, like green" (Hinton, 1995, p. 154). Just before the big rumble, Pony Boy is "reminded of Jack London's books—you know, where the wolf pack waits in silence for one or two members to go down in a fight" (p. 125). Although Pony Boy does not name the novel, it is clearly *White Fang* in which London's fiction deals with the struggle of an individual to survive in a harsh, sometimes unforgiving, environment. This theme emerges in *The Outsiders* in the struggle between the gangs, in Johnny's abuse by his parents, and in Dally Winston's admonition to Pony Boy: "You'd better wise up, Pony . . . you get tough like me and you don't get hurt. You look out for yourself and nothin' can touch you" (p. 128). Sadly, Pony Boy later watches his reckless friend gunned down by the police.

Contemporary music plays a role in defining character in the novel and setting the historical context. The Beatles arrived in the United States in the 1960s and the in-crowd, the Socs, dig their music; the Greasers are fans of country music idol Hank Williams: The contrast in their musical preferences highlights the class differences between the two gangs. The rumble in the novel calls to mind the climactic scene in Leonard Bernstein's *West Side Story*, where multiple disciplines—story, music, and dance—combine to represent a world where class and ethnic differences clash to bring tragedy to the young Anglos and Puerto Ricans who populate the ghettos of New York City. A sociocultural approach might look at the growing violence in American culture found in Bernstein's 1950s musical and Hinton's 1967 novel and that of the present day. The interviews with gang members in Maria Hinojosa's nonfictional *Crews* present the reality of gang life in New York City in startling detail.

A Teacher's Guide to Theory

The first text that set me on my odyssey into literary theory, a book that dramatically transformed my life as a reader and teacher, was The Norton Case Studies in Contemporary Criticism edition of Joseph Conrad's *Heart of Darkness* (1996). I highly recommend the books in this series to teachers who want to explore literary theory and introduce it to their students. Each book in the series offers the complete text of the novel, interpretations from the perspectives of multiple literary theories, a selected bibliography, and a useful glossary of critical and theoretical terms. The series includes familiar texts in the secondary canon, among them *Frankenstein, The Awakening, Emma, Great Expectations, The Scarlet Letter, Wuthering Heights,* and *Adventures of Huckleberry Finn.*

Others have made strong cases for the power of literary theory in the secondary classroom. In *Critical Encounters in High School English: Teaching Literary Theory to Adolescents* (2000), Deborah Appleman focuses on the application of various theories to the reading of familiar high school texts, including *Native Son, Hamlet,* and *The Awakening.* Her book is particularly helpful to teachers new to theory because her applications come from her work with classroom teachers and their students. *Critical Encounters* presents theory in action; the book is both practical and inviting.

In my own *Interpreting Young Adult Literature: Literary Theory in the Secondary Classroom* (Moore, 1997), I focus on the genre of young adult fiction. I offer an overview of the key ideas of eight literary theories. For each theoretical perspective, I give a reading of a young adult novel to demonstrate the application of that perspective, subsequently suggesting other young adult texts to which that theory can also be applied.

Electronic resources on literary theory and critical theory abound, among them a basic introduction is available online where, in fifteen pages, Vince Brewton (2006) addresses the question "What is theory?" and provides accessible definitions and concepts related to New Criticism, Marxism, structuralism, poststructuralism, new historicism, and ethnic and postcolonial criticism, as well as gender studies, queer theory, and cultural studies. For a more detailed introduction online, see *Introductory Guide to Critical Theory* by Dino Felluga (2009).

Since I began working with literary theory in the early 1990s, one of the most helpful books for me has been David H. Richter's *Falling into Theory* (2000), a volume of essays by well-known literary critics. At the outset Richter demystifies theory, contending that it is a natural phenomenon; we are always unconsciously putting theory into practice, "falling into" it, whether expressing our pleasure or displeasure about the ending of a movie or exploring literary and nonliterary texts. Richter organizes the essays around three topics always of interest to English teachers: "Why We Read"; "What We Read"; and "How We Read." Among the intriguing titles are Stanley Fish's "How to Recognize a Poem When You See One" and Annette Kolodny's "Dancing through the Minefield."

Putting It Together

The diagram that follows summarizes a major transformation in literary theory over the last half century and how these central approaches have changed the ways we view the author, the reader, and the text. The explanations that follow serve to pull together the theories and practices suggested in this chapter.

New Critical Formalism	Cultural Studies
Aesthetics	Ideologies
Work of art	Text, context, and intertext
The work centered	The text decentered
Author as artist	Who is the author?
Reader as audience	Reader as cowriter
One correct reading	Multiple valid readings
Canon of great works	Exploded canon; everything is a text
Microscopic vision	Telescopic vision

New Critical Formalism considers the piece of literature aesthetically as a *work*, an art object to be admired and read on its own terms without reference to its author's life, the cultural issues that surround the text, or the reader's emotional response. In contrast, cultural studies views the text in the context of ideologies contemporary with its production, as well as intertexts that appear within it, what Roland Barthes (1981/1994) refers to as "quotations without quotation marks." That is, all texts are fabrics woven of multiple cultures and texts; consequently, there can be no single, definitive author of a text. The author is, as the poststructuralists/deconstructionists say, dead.

From the perspective of New Critical Formalism, the reader looks at the work, not as the person strolling through an art gallery but as a critic with a specialized language for understanding the arts of language. Through careful exegesis or explication, what the New Critical Formalists call a close reading, the reader discovers that the text has one correct reading, knowable to readers with well-developed analytical skills and a specialized vocabulary for describing its structures and formal elements. The New Critical Formalist reader is an outsider who studies the text as if under a microscope, while the cultural studies reader, both insider and outsider, takes a panoramic view, as with a wide angle telescope. For New Critical Formalist readers, the objects of their interest are most often short texts, poems that are part of the Western literary canon. In contrast, the cultural studies reader understands that everything from *The Odyssey* to the modern shopping mall to clothing and hair styles constitutes a text to be read and interpreted. Consequently, no elite literary canon exists, and cultural studies readers investigate the whole world from a number of perspectives to create multiple, valid possible readings; no single "correct" reading exists.

Questions to Use in Teaching

Given this array of literary theories, what questions about acts of reading might teachers explore with students? The following provide useful entries into the reading process and textual interpretation:

- What constitutes a text?
- What is reading? Is it synonymous with interpretation?
- How do we read? What happens when we read a text?
- How many different ways can we approach a text as readers? Are some approaches more appropriate for some texts and not for others?
- What is meaning? Do we receive meanings from a text or do we make meanings as we read the text? Or both?
- How is a text constructed and how does that construction direct and affect our reading of it?
- How does a text connect to other texts that have preceded it?
- What are intertexts and what effect do they have on how we interpret a text?
- Are we conditioned to read by what we have read before?
- What is the language system of the text and how does that system affect the way we read and make meaning of the text?
- What is the relationship between the author and the text? Between the author and the reader? Between the reader, the text, and the world? How do these questions affect our reading and teaching of texts?

As teachers work with theory, their students will realize that these questions can have different responses for each literary theory. They will see that a single approach limits their imaginative and intellectual responses to texts as well as their interactions with other readers of texts.

References

Appleman, D. (2000). *Critical encounters in high school English: Teaching literary theory to adolescents.* New York: Teachers College Press and Urbana, IL: National Council of Teachers of English.

Barthes, R. (1981). Theory of the text (I. McLeod, Trans.). In R. Young (Ed.), *Untying the text: A post-structuralist reader* (pp. 31–47). London: Routledge. (Quoted in *A concise glossary of contemporary literary theory,* by J. Hawthorn, 1994, London: Edward Arnold)

Barthes, R. (2001). The death of the author (S. Heath, Trans.). In V. B. Leitch (General Ed.), *The Norton anthology of theory and criticism* (pp. 1466–70). New York: Norton.

Belsey, C. (1988). Literature, history, politics. In D. Lodge (Ed.), *Modern criticism and theory* (pp. 399–410). London: Longman.

Brewton, V. (2005). Literary theory. In J. Fieser & B. Dowden (Eds.), *Internet encyclopedia of philosophy*. Retrieved from http://www.iep.utm.edu/literary/

Brooks, C., & Warren, R. P. (1959). *Understanding fiction* (2nd ed.). New York: Appleton.

Brooks, G. (n.d.). On we real cool. *Modern American poetry*. Retrieved from http://www.english.illinois.edu/MAPS/poets/a_f/brooks/werealcool.htm

Brooks, G. (1972). *Report from part one*. Detroit, MI: Broadside Press.

Brooks, G. (1983). We real cool [Audio clip]. Retrieved from http://www.poets.org/viewmedia.php/prmMID/15433

Conrad, J. (1996). *Heart of darkness.* In R. C. Murfin (Ed.), *Heart of darkness: Complete, authoritative text with biographical and historical contexts, critical history, and essays from five contemporary critical perspectives* (2nd ed., pp. 17–95). Boston: Bedford/St. Martin's Press.

Coppola, F. F. (Director). (2005). *The outsiders: The complete novel* [DVD]. Burbank, CA: Warner Home Video.

Felluga, D. F. (2011). *Introductory guide to critical theory.* Retrieved from Purdue University, College of Liberal Arts website: http://www.cla.purdue.edu/academic/engl/theory/index.html

Frye, N. (1982). *The great code: The Bible and literature*. San Diego: Harcourt.

Gotera, V. (1999). Craft of poetry: Rhyme and music. Retrieved from http://www.uni.edu/~gotera/CraftOfPoetry/rhyme&music.html

Hinton, S. E. (1995). *The outsiders*. New York: Dell.

Leitch, V. B. (1988). Reader-response criticism. In *American literary criticism from the thirties to the eighties* (pp. 211–37). New York: Columbia University Press.

Leitch, V. B. (2003). *Theory matters*. New York: Routledge.

McLaughlin. T. (1991). Theory as equipment for (postmodern) living. In J. M. Calahan & D. B. Downing (Eds.), *Practicing theory in introductory college literature courses* (pp. 261–70). Urbana, IL: National Council of Teachers of English.

Moore, J. N. (1997). *Interpreting young adult literature: Literary theory in the secondary classroom.* Portsmouth, NH: Heinemann Boynton/Cook.

Moore, J. N. (1998). Street signs: Semiotics, *Romeo and Juliet,* and young adult literature. *Theory Into Practice, 7*(3), 211–19.

Probst, R. E. (1988). Dialogue with a text. *English Journal, 77*(1), 32–38.

Richter, D. H. (2000). *Falling into theory: Conflicting views on reading literature* (2nd ed.). Boston: Bedford/St. Martin's Press.

Spiller, H. J. (1987). Gwendolyn the terrible: Propositions on eleven poems. In M. K. Mootry & G. Smith (Eds.), *A life distilled: Gwendolyn Brooks, her poetry and fiction* (pp. 224–35). Urbana: University of Illinois Press.

Walker, V. (1993). Feminist criticism, Anglo-American. In I. R. Makaryk (Ed.), *Encyclopedia of contemporary literary theory: Approaches, scholars, terms.* Toronto, ON, Canada: U of Toronto Press.

II Teaching John Steinbeck's *Of Mice and Men*

Bonnie Ericson
California State University, Northridge

John Steinbeck's *Of Mice and Men* was published in 1937, a slim volume widely read and reviewed. Most reviewers of the time praised its moving portrayal of the harsh lives of migrant farm workers, although a few criticized what they viewed as offensive language and coarse characters. *Of Mice and Men* was also a work bound for the theater. The stage play featuring Wallace Ford and Broderick Crawford opened in 1937 in New York and received the New York Drama Critics Circle Award. The 1939 movie with Lon Chaney as Lennie and Burgess Meredith as George, supported by Aaron Copeland's musical score, was nominated for several Academy Awards, although both *Of Mice and Men* and *The Wizard of Oz* lost out that year for best picture to *Gone with the Wind*. Gary Sinise directed a 1992 version of the movie and played the role of George, with John Malkovich as Lennie; they had appeared together in a theatric production of *Of Mice and Men* in the 1980s.

Additionally, allusions to *Of Mice and Men* have appeared widely in American popular culture. If you are of a certain age, for example, you may recall the 1940s Warner Brothers cartoons with the ubiquitous line, "Which way did he go, George; which way did he go?" Even recent television programs and movies regularly allude to *Of Mice and Men*. Readily found online, my favorite is an episode of *CSI: New York* in which Gary Sinise interacts with a suspect who is trying out for an *Of Mice and Men* stage production. All these references suggest that the reading of this work is seen by many as a shared cultural experience.

Indeed, *Of Mice and Men* became a mainstay in high school and college English classes as a work that could bring the suffering of the Great Depression to life, inform our notions of friendship and tragedy, or illuminate discussions on the American Dream. But the novel has also been a target for censors and has been commonly challenged as an inappropriate text for reading by adolescents, largely because of its language and George's mercy killing of Lennie. However, in my informal polling of groups of southern California high school English teachers and in examining core literature lists for area schools, it appears that *Of Mice and Men* is no longer as commonly taught as in the past.

That's unfortunate. With the exquisite power of Steinbeck's language, the poignant friendship and dream of George and Lennie, the characters' bleak lives, and the relentless movement to a tragic ending, this is a book that engages high school and college readers and their teachers. It is a choice that opens the possibilities for the types of reading proposed in the beginning chapters of this book, a choice that lends itself to teaching approaches that make possible students' "authentic knowledge" (Blau) of a text and their "personal and social transformation" (Wilhelm), based on their unique experiences (Jago). Yes, there are challenges in its teaching: Some clarification and discussion of vocabulary and word choices are required, along with background information on the Great Depression and 1930s California. But the potential is strong for connections to students' lives, issues in contemporary society, and other texts. Perhaps with the teaching ideas for *Of Mice and Men* included in this section, you will be inspired to include it for whole-class reading or recommend it as an option for group reading at your school.

Additional Texts to Pair with *Of Mice and Men*

When we authors and a wonderful group of teachers initially came together in a fishbowl discussion at an NCTE Annual Convention, the teacher talk was so compelling that we had to be reminded to leave the room for the next group! Each idea stimulated another, and we did not want the conversation to end. Therefore, to extend that conversation with you, we suggest a few other texts you may want to consider pairing with *Of Mice and Men*. After reading both, students can engage in a Socratic seminar as they find comparisons, contrasts, and connections.

Healey, Michael. 2008. *The Drawer Boy*. Playwrights Canada Press. ISBN: 0-88754-814-8.

> *The Drawer Boy*, a play that won four Canadian Dora Awards, including Outstanding New Play, premiered in Toronto in 1999. Angus and Morgan, both in their fifties, live on an Ontario farm in the early 1970s. Angus has severe memory problems and suffers

from terrible migraines, although he's a whiz with numbers, and Morgan is clearly the more responsible and down-to-earth of the two. They are joined by Miles, a college student who asks if he can stay with them to learn about farm life so he can write a play. When Miles overhears Morgan relating to Angus their history together, an obviously oft-repeated story (not unlike George's dream of the farm with rabbits and a cow and living "offa the fatta the lan"), Miles turns the story into his play. As events transpire, however, we discover that the truth, connected with events in World War II, is quite different. Alternately hilarious and touching, the play closes with Angus's recitation of a portion of Gerard Manley Hopkins's poem "At the Wedding March."

Rylant, Cynthia. 1994. *Something Permanent*. Walker Evans (Photographs). Harcourt. ISBN: 0-15-277090-9.

Published in 1994, Rylant's poems are paired with Walker Evans's photographs from the Great Depression; together they tell compelling stories of the era.

Of Mice and Men. 1939. Lewis Milestone (Director). Lon Chaney Jr., and Burgess Meredith (Performers). Image Entertainment. Video and DVD.

Of Mice and Men. 1992. Gary Sinise (Director and Performer). John Malkovich (Performer). MGM. Video and DVD.

Selected poetry also pairs well with *Of Mice and Men*. For example, in Stephen Dunn's wonderful "The Sacred," a teacher asks students if they have a sacred place, and one student responds with a description of being in his car. Others in the class recognize the truth in this and also begin sharing, in ways akin to Lennie and George's conversations about their farm.

By selecting novels such as Steinbeck's *Of Mice and Men* and by using teaching approaches that promote students' authentic reading as described here and in other chapters, I believe that our classrooms can be places where truths are discovered and spoken.

6 Analyzing *Of Mice and Men* through Creative Writing

Mary Adler
California State University, Channel Islands

Purpose

In the following lessons, I seek to help students step into an author's shoes, to try walking in them awhile, and in so doing to gain new understandings of the text, new tools for analysis, and a new perspective. After all, it is only in putting on someone else's shoes that we feel the high arch, notice the slight lean toward the left side, or appreciate the springing sole. But there is more to be had than appreciation. I would also like students to explore particular areas of the writing and use those areas to contribute to an overall analysis of the text that benefits from the knowledge raised by the creative writing experience. Specifically, I want students to explore how characterization is developed through dialogue and setting; identify potential choices writers make and explore how those choices affect the resulting text; and articulate the logical and emotional connections between the reader and the story.

Materials

To accomplish the full version of this lesson, including all optional elements, I use the following materials:

- Copy of initial dialogue with narration removed (Figure 6.1)
- Questions/prompts on an overhead, PowerPoint, handout, or whiteboard for discussion
- T-Chart tracing personal character allegiances (optional; Figure 6.2)
- Follow-up writing assignments (see assessment section, below)
- "To a Mouse, on Turning Her Up in Her Nest with the Plough" (optional, Robert Burns, available on the Internet at http://www.robertburns.org/works/75.shtml)

Introduction

To draw students into the character dynamic between Lennie and George that is at the heart of the novel, we explore those characters before reading. Working only with the initial conversation between Lennie and George, students design the scene that contains this dialogue. Along the way, they decide what kind of man each is, inferring from word choices, responses, punctuation, imagined pauses. They determine where these men are, what they are doing as they talk, how they stand or sit, what gestures they make. Is Lennie sitting, looking up at George? Are they side by side on a bus? Walking down a city street? After writing their own scenes, students compare passages—this is the important bit—generating discussion that helps them to reflect on the choices they made as writers and the allegiances they made to characters. It also helps them hear the effects of these choices on their audience of peers and to see how different choices create sometimes wholly opposite effects, despite the same foundational dialogue.

Now, primed with their characterizations and settings resonating in their minds, students enter Steinbeck's text, reading and discussing the choices he made with the same character, and focusing particularly on his use of setting. I use responsive writing prompts along the way to help focus students on particular areas of the text and to help generate new thinking. After the explosive scene in the final chapter, students may return to scene writing again, taking the understated final dialogue between Lennie and George and reimagining it.

Connections

Clearly, I am making a major assumption that there is something about actively writing fiction that engages and instructs students in the study of literature. As such, I build on Sheridan Blau's thinking in Chapter 1 about the power of discovery that happens when students are challenged to work with a text in an authentic experience of reading. In writing their own scenes, students learn, in some small way, what it is to be a fiction writer. They wrestle with the characters, test settings, try on relationships, and in doing so closely revisit the original text for support. Their writing illuminates Steinbeck's novel, and his text in turn opens up the pleasurable and stimulating world of imagination for them.

In asking students to recognize their allegiances to characters and to follow those emotional connections during the reading of the text, I also draw on John Moore's concepts in Chapter 5 of interpretation, using a reader response approach to guide students in articulating the understanding—the poem—that results from the transaction between reader and text. In this context, I hope to make the author's choices behind the scenes more visible, opening the text to critique. Finally, Jeffrey Wilhelm (Chapter 3) reminds us that literature instruction is not only about analyzing the author's role and technique in constructing the text, but that it is also foundationally about finding supportable ways, such as the visualization employed in these activities, for students to raise their voices in response as readers, writers, and fellow human beings.

Activities

Before students enter the text, they receive the dialogue in Figure 6.1 (excerpted from the opening of the novel). The class reads it aloud a few times using different dramatic readings to interpret characterization and sources of conflict. Then, each student crafts the dialogue into a fully realized narrative scene, incorporating into their narration whatever setting, internal thoughts, and behaviors they feel are appropriate. (This activity is adapted from one by B. K. Loren at the University of Iowa Writer's Workshop Summer Festival, July 2005.)

After students write their scenes, I ask them to read the scenes aloud to each other in small groups. After reading each scene, students talk about the choices they made as writers, using the following questions to guide their discussion.

- What choices did you make as you wrote the characters into the scene?
- What personality or attitude did you try to convey for George and Lennie? How did you reveal these attitudes?
- Who did you sympathize with in the scene? (Which character would you have been more friendly with?) Why?
- What setting did you choose and how did that affect the scene?

Volunteers read their scenes to one another and discuss these questions. I like to circulate and listen to the discussions, making mental notes on different versions of the scene. After the small-group discussions are complete, I call on several students to read their scenes to the whole class—those who have made varied choices or who have aligned themselves with different characters. The contrast between these scenes is excellent fodder for discussion and for the following quickwrite: "Which choices of setting and characterization seemed particularly effective to you? Why? What did you learn from them?"

Lennie [to himself]: *I ain't gonna say nothin'* . . . *I ain't gonna say nothin'* . . . *I ain't gonna say nothin'*.

George: O.K. An' you ain't gonna do no bad things like you done in Weed, neither.

Lennie: Like I done in Weed?

George: Oh, so ya forgot that too, did ya? Well, I ain't gonna remind ya, fear ya do it again.

Lennie: They run us outa Weed!

George: Run us out, hell, we run. They was lookin' for us, but they didn't catch us.

Lennie: I didn't forget that, you bet.

George: God, you're a lot of trouble. I could get along so easy and so nice if I didn't have you on my tail. I could live so easy and maybe have a girl.

Lennie: We gonna work on a ranch, George.

George: Awright. You got that. But we're gonna sleep here because I got a reason.

Lennie: George—why ain't we goin' on to the ranch and get some supper? They got supper at the ranch.

George: No reason at all for you. I like it here. Tomorra we're gonna go to work. I seen thrashin' machines on the way down. That means we'll be bucking grain bags, bustin' a gut. Tonight I'm gonna lay right here and look up. I like it.

Lennie: Ain't we gonna have no supper? (pp. 7–8)

Figure 6.1. Initial dialogue with narration removed.

If this activity is completed for homework, the next class session opens with a sharing of the quickwrite responses, as students tell what they know about the characters (and what they have inferred from the text so far). Any questions and predictions lead directly into a reading of the first chapter of the novel.

After reading the first chapter, I ask students to return to Steinbeck's use of the same dialogue. Some questions they consider in discussion and/or in responsive journaling are the following:

- What choices does Steinbeck make in his use of setting and characterization in this scene? What role does setting play?

- Where do you sense tension in this scene? What are the sources of this tension? What predictions does this lead you to make?

- How does this tension position you in relation to the story? (How do you feel about these characters? Where are your allegiances? Why?)

First chapter: How do you feel about these characters? Where are your allegiances? Why?	Last chapter: How do you feel about these characters? Where are your allegiances? Why?

Figure 6.2. T-chart tracing responses to the text.

The last question is particularly useful for a journal response, because students keep their writing and refer to it later, when their allegiances may be changing. They may write this response on the left side of a T-chart, anticipating that later in the story (perhaps just after Curley's wife is killed) they will answer the same question on the right side and trace any differences (see Figure 6.2).

During the reading of the text, the conversation continues about the interplay between setting, dialogue/characterization, and conflict. After reading the final scene, students discuss the impact of the novel as a whole and wrestle, in discussion, small groups, or writing, with the implications of Lennie's and George's respective actions. Some questions they consider include the following:

- What images stand out to you in the last chapter, at the river? Why?
- What is the effect of these images on your thinking about the plot? About character? About theme?
- Is the setting—the natural world around Lennie and George—affected by what happens? Why or why not?
- What do you notice about the dialogue between Lennie and George at the end of the story? In what ways is it similar to the opening scene? What has changed?
- Based on your reading of the characters in the opening scene and following, do you find the final outcome inevitable?

To extend the activity further, students try their hand again at writing a scene, using fiction as a tool to explore the final dialogue between Lennie and George in which so much is left unsaid. Students take up the challenge to rewrite this scene in such a way that the characters actually say what is on their minds. The same sharing in small groups follows, in which students discuss the choices they made and how well their readers feel they have captured the motivation and characterizations of Lennie and George. As a whole group, I ask several students to read their pieces aloud and then return to Steinbeck's version with a critical eye, asking,

- What is said (and unsaid) in the published version of this scene?
- What choices does Steinbeck make about how much he's willing to have characters reveal aloud? What is gained (and lost) by such choices?

Assessment

Assessing creative writing is sometimes a thorny issue. I use it here not as a piece of crafted fiction, to be graded on how well it reflects elements of the genre, but rather as a means to understanding and analyzing the writer's experience. Rather than assessing the original scenes, I am more comfortable grading the quality of the reflection on the scenes in which students describe their choices and what they learned about characterization. As a summative evaluation for the whole unit, I ask students to apply the knowledge they have gained to a larger issue, such as one of the following projects.

1. I review the settings used in the book by making a chart that briefly describes the events of each scene and lists the setting in which each scene takes place. I ask students to write on the following prompt:

   > Your school's drama teacher is thinking of re-staging *Of Mice and Men* in an urban setting, with Lennie and George as twenty-first-century firefighters working in New York City. The teacher is holding an open after-school meeting to discuss the staging idea. Write a carefully reasoned speech to read at the meeting, either arguing for or against this choice. Provide specific evidence that shows how the new setting would affect the characterization, plot, and theme of the novel—positively or negatively.

2. As a class, we read and discuss the poem from which the novel's title comes, "To a Mouse, on Turning Her Up in Her Nest with the Plough" (Robert Burns). We then discuss how it relates to the characters in the novel. I ask students to use their thinking, writing, and notes about the characters, setting, plot, and theme to write an analytical short essay on the following prompt:

   > The original title for this book was *Something That Happened*. What does that title suggest about Steinbeck's intentions for the novel and characters? What does *Of Mice and Men* suggest? Which is more appropriate, and why? Support your answers with specific evidence from the book.

Considerations

There are many valid reasons to teach this book, but the one I like best is the remarkable quality of the story: Despite the impersonal, removed narration, it has power to connect and challenge the reader at a deeply human level. All the better, then, to have students enter the novel as humans and as writers, exploring the intersection between. In taking up the characters and placing them in scene, we make an initial connection with both the story and its author. Students jump, temporarily, into Steinbeck's mind. From there they take a leap into the characters' minds, deciding how they move, talk, think, feel. This initial resonance keeps them in the story as readers but also gives them the support to step back into the writer's perspective when they sense a dissonance. As such, they gain the tools to connect, read closely, analyze, and appreciate the text. They also have the potential to gain voice and confidence as writers and thinkers.

7 *Of Mice and Men*: Rules, Laws, and Disenfranchisement

John Gabriel
DePaul University

Purpose

Among the many possible ways to approach teaching *Of Mice and Men*, a focus on the disenfranchised characters, the rules of the card games they played, and the laws that governed them as American citizens provide intriguing opportunities for students. The main purposes of my lessons, then, are to engage students in research to learn the rules of the card games (euchre, rummy, solitaire) and to learn about several laws and legal cases that relate to various characters in the book. By learning the rules of the characters' leisure pursuits, their card games, and laws of California and the United States that affected their livelihoods and access to their dreams, students identify with and understand the characters. They also evaluate the laws, how they have changed over the years, and reflect on the extent to which they offer American citizens—then and now—equity and justice under the law. By learning rules and laws, students come to understand the personal, social, cultural, and legal contexts of the characters' lives in *Of Mice and Men* and of Americans who lived during the time of the novel and to deepen their understanding of various current laws that govern us in the United States. The lessons here are about knowing the letter and spirit of rules and laws that promote equity and justice and in so doing increase students' chances of "winning" in the different domains of games and laws. Knowledge of rules and laws is power.

Materials

Students need the following to complete the lessons.

- Decks of cards

- Access to the Internet to obtain the rules for euchre, solitaire, and rummy
- Access to the Internet for photographs by Dorothea Lange, Ansel Adams, Walker Evans, and others
- Access to the Internet or a library for various legal documents and/or their summaries and commentary, including The California Civil Code of 1905, which Crooks reads; The Nineteenth Amendment, which gave women the right to vote; The National Origins Act, which effectively eliminated immigration from Asia, particularly Japan; The Americans with Disabilities Act, which provides protections for those with disabilities; and several Supreme Court decisions related to racial equality
- Disposable or digital cameras (optional)

Three of the laws, the California Civil Code of 1905, the Nineteenth Amendment ratified in 1920, and the National Origins Act of 1924, predate the novel's 1937 publication; the Americans with Disabilities Act comes much later in 1992. The *Dred Scott* Supreme Court ruling of 1857 denied citizenship to African Americans; the *Plessy v. Ferguson* case of 1896 established the doctrine of "separate but equal"; and the *Brown v. Board of Education* case of 1954 reversed the "separate but equal" ruling.

Introduction

Of Mice and Men portrays "the lower depths," to borrow from Gorky, of American society during the 1930s. Destitute characters dream of better lives but can do little to leave the misery of their existence behind. Even the characters who have a chance at a better life—George and Slim—have little hope of achieving their dreams. The Great Depression has taken its toll on countless working-class men and women. Jobs are scarce, and pay is dirt poor. Many Americans eke out an existence.

Further, the novel shows women, blacks, Japanese, and the disabled further cut off from their dreams, from the discrimination they face in a largely patriarchal white society, and from laws that further restrict their full participation in American society and pursuit of the American Dream. A reading of the novel in the twenty-first century invites us to look again at the social, cultural, racial, and economic forces that should always be part of our national conversation. President Obama is our first African American president. We are currently in a deep economic recession. What has changed in America since the 1930s? What issues predominate today? What games do people engage in for leisure? How have our laws changed to address social, economic, and racial discrimination?

These are some of the questions you and your students might address in reading *Of Mice and Men*.

Connections

In presenting these lessons for teaching *Of Mice and Men*, I have drawn on Wilhelm's (Chapter 3) belief that we need to deepen our notion of teaching to include evocative and connective dimensions of response. In the introductory writing prompts, for example, students write about incidents similar to those of the novel's characters. Or, in playing euchre or solitaire students experience the leisure behavior of the book's characters. Wilhelm's "use of various strategies such as drama, think-alouds, visualization, and other interactive strategies" is also part of my framework for the teaching of Steinbeck's novel and the related readings I have included, as in the courtroom presentations and the gallery walk of photographs.

Activities

Prior to entering the text, students write responses to one or both of the following journal topics:

- Describe a game you enjoy playing with friends and family, e.g., board games, card games, a computer game. Which do you enjoy most and why? Discuss the differences in your personal or social interactions when playing an actual card game—with real cards, for example—versus a computer game. What are the rules of the game? How did you learn them? What happens if you decide not to follow the rules?

- Write about an incident in which you or someone you know was treated unfairly—discriminated against. What happened? Who was involved? What was the outcome? Do you know of any laws that might have been related to the incident? What was the effect of a law or laws on the outcome?

Students then share and compare their responses in a group, followed by a whole-class discussion that touches on games that are part of our leisure time and the impact of discrimination in today's society. This discussion serves as an introduction to the reading of the first chapter of the book.

During reading, students keep a dialectical journal. The journal is divided into four activities:

1. Observation and exploration of texts: Students record quotations from the novel and comment on each quotation—why

they chose it, its significance to the scene or the novel as a whole, questions, or other reactions. Students may also select a photographic "text," particularly during their reading of early chapters, by searching for photographs by Dorothea Lange or Walker Evans of migrant life in California during the Great Depression. I model "visual literacy" by choosing a photograph and conducting a think-aloud about what is happening in the photograph, what stands out in it, what questions it evokes, and what the photographer might be trying to say. Students try out the think-aloud process with one another and different photographs. Finally, students may also quote from and comment on the texts of laws and legal cases with connections to *Of Mice and Men*, when research on these is introduced in the lessons.

2. Need-to-know questions: Students write questions they have about their reading; they explore possible answers in their writing. Again, I model or share an example with students.

3. Dialogue with another person: Students choose several of their journal entries to share and discuss with another student. These discussions allow them to reconsider texts and to share questions and insights. A whole-class discussion follows so that students can share highlights of their discussions with other class members.

4. Think again: At a couple of points, including the end of the book, students return to earlier entries to see if and how their thinking has changed from what was said in previous entries. They comment on both changes and places where they stand by earlier understandings.

When card game rules or connections with laws/Supreme Court cases arise during reading, students research the rules or legal connections online or using library resources. The first time we encounter the playing of euchre, for example, I have students research the rules and print out or make a copy of them. In groups of four, they attempt to play several hands of the game and learn the rules. The groups discuss various interpretations of the rules and strategies for the game and consider who among the characters in *Of Mice and Men* would be the best players of this card game, and why.

At points in the book where characters appear relegated to second-class citizenry, I ask students to locate information on laws that pertain to the characters' social and legal standings and their places in society. For example, Crooks states at one point, "Maybe you guys better go. I ain't sure I want you in here no more. A colored man got to have some rights even if he don't like 'em" (90). Students or a group of students use the Internet or library resources to locate the California Civil Code of 1905, which Crooks has mauled from reading so often. The code reads in part:

"The Ralph Act," Civil Code sections 51.7 and 52 . . . provides that it is a civil right for a person to be free of violence or its threat against the person or his or her property, because of a person's race, color, religion, ancestry, national origin, political affiliation, sex, sexual orientation, age or disability or position in a labor dispute, or because a person is perceived to have one or more of these characteristics—(bases of discrimination are illustrative, rather than restrictive).

Students make sense of the law and then discuss and consider connections among the law, the characters, and current issues in society. This and other legal topics for research and discussion during the reading of *Of Mice and Men* include the Nineteenth Amendment (the nameless wife of Curley or "old Susy"); the National Origins Act ("Jap cook"); the Americans with Disabilities Act (Candy, Crooks, Lennie); and the Supreme Court decisions related to Crooks: *Dred Scott, Plessy v. Ferguson,* and *Brown v. Board of Education*. Reading legal text or even summaries of legal cases may challenge some high school readers, so I find it useful to bring the Supreme Court cases to life by having students develop arguments for both the plaintiff and the defendant and reenact the court case and decision. In their dialectical journals, students ask important questions about these laws and Supreme Court decisions and relate them to current issues of justice and equity.

After reading the book, to extend students' thinking on the disenfranchisement of the book's characters—especially the "lesser" characters—and the connections they see in current American society, I believe it is valuable to take students visually to another difficult time in US history where they might again consider how rules and laws had an impact on the lives of Americans. Students search online for photographs of the Japanese internment at Manzanar or another "relocation center" during World War II. The stunning photographs by Dorothea Lange and Ansel Adams are particularly effective. In pairs or small groups, students select two or three photos that resonate with them. They can then discuss questions such as the following for each, mirroring the earlier think-alouds with California Great Depression photos, or respond in a quickwrite:

- What detail stands out most to you in the photograph?
- What is happening in the photograph?
- What do you think the persons in the photograph are thinking or saying to each other?
- What would daily life be like if you were this person/one of these persons?

- What comment do you think the photographer is trying to make?
- Create a caption for the photo.

The pairs or small groups of students then write the caption and a description of one of the photos they have discussed. All the photos and captions are then displayed in the classroom where students participate in a gallery walk. Finally, they discuss as a class any links they see between the settings, people, and issues of social justice in *Of Mice and Men* and the relocation camp photographs.

Assessment

During the unit I use the dialectical journal as the main focus of assessment, collecting it at two or three points. For the court case enactment, I focus on students' understanding of the issues and the logic of the arguments they present. For the relocation center photographs they select and write about for the gallery walk, I note students' descriptions, captions, and insights about the setting, people, and issues described.

Considerations

I realize that I have not focused a great deal on much of what happens in *Of Mice and Men*. Indeed, my interest is less on characters such as George and Slim and instead on those characters who are so clearly disenfranchised in the novel: Curley's wife, Crooks, Candy, Lennie. Though they face similar economic woes as George and Slim, by their gender, race, or disability they are pushed to even lower depths of society. It is the main goal of several of the activities to target the discrimination these characters experience and to bring to light some of the long and dark aspects of US history. Though we have come a long way in our social relationships, and in bringing equity and justice to those who have historically been the targets of discrimination, we still have far to go. By knowing more deeply the rules of the game and the laws of the land, we invite ourselves to redress the grievances—and the inhumanity—of the past. We invite ourselves to get to know each other better, to see that underlying gender and skin color, we have much we share in common. Living in California provides me and my students with one perspective, but the universal issues in *Of Mice and Men* are provocative for all students.

8 Geometric Characters and *Of Mice and Men*

Anna J. Small Roseboro
Calvin College

Purpose

I assign the activity I call Geometric Characters when I want to assess the depth and breadth of what students understand about characterization, symbolism, the relationships among characters, and, perhaps, the theme(s) of a novel we have finished reading and discussing. I particularly like this assignment with *Of Mice and Men* because the visual, written, and oral components of the activity elicit authentic responses that increase students' understandings of its characters—Lennie and George, but also Crooks, Curley, Curley's wife, Candy, and even Candy's dog—in ways difficult to achieve with teacher-led discussions. The assignment requires students to think creatively and symbolically; they demonstrate this thinking in art and writing. More importantly, these artistic and spoken responses expand understandings of their classmates. Students discover different ways to see the same work of literature.

Materials

The materials needed for this assignment include the following:

- Construction paper in a variety of colors and shades (I precut the construction paper into four or six small squares and rectangles of different sizes to reduce waste and increase the number of colors from which each student can choose.)
- Glue sticks, scissors, 8 ½" □ 11" white paper
- A kitchen timer
- Copies of *Of Mice and Men*
- Access to computers either at home or in school

Introduction

Of Mice and Men, coupled with *To Kill a Mockingbird*, is required summer reading for incoming ninth graders at my high school. The grade 9 English course is designed to focus on the themes of diversity, tolerance, and perseverance. In preparation for the first weeks of school, students are asked to read and annotate *To Kill a Mockingbird* by Harper Lee and *Of Mice and Men* by John Steinbeck. Both books establish a solid jumping-off point and provide a common reading experience with connections to reading and writing across the curriculum for the rest of the year.

While initially attracted by the length of *Of Mice and Men*, students find themselves enthralled with the storytelling. They begin to "feel for and with the characters." The students are moved by the variety of characters who speak so passionately of their longing for a better home. As to be expected, these young teens are appalled when George kills Lennie, thus killing his friend and his dream. An equal number are upset that they "understand" why George shoots his friend because this empathy seems to indicate that they approve of mercy killing. All these responses provide fodder for deep thinking and discussion.

Since *Of Mice and Men* is a text used to set the tone for the school year, the opening assignments that accompany it are relatively open-ended, inviting students to show their understandings about the times and people of the book and to articulate what they believe the book is saying to us today. I often use the Geometric Characters assignment in which students use shape, color, and size to represent three to four (or more) characters. On a standard sheet of white paper, they cut out and arrange these shapes to comment on the qualities of each character and to show the relationships among the characters. Students then write a short essay explaining their choices, citing quotations and specific references in the text from their annotations.

Connections

In Chapter 5 of this text, Moore recommends that teachers keep in mind that there is no "single correct interpretation of a text." This lesson invites students to show graphically and artistically what *they* think the personality of each main character is and through arrangement of the shapes to portray the relationships *they* believe exist among these characters. Sheridan Blau urges teachers to allow students to "discover the pleasure and exhilaration of their own discovery by working on texts themselves and mining them for meaning" (Chapter 1). This assignment

sends students back to the text, mining it to determine and then justify
their choice of colors, shapes, sizes, and arrangement of geometric shapes
to represent the characters and these relationships.

Wilhelm, Chapter 3 in this text, argues that it is necessary to offer
students opportunities to respond to texts "in ways that embrace, extend, adapt, and resist textual meanings in some way." This assignment
includes an oral component during which students meet in small groups
to explain to their peers the reason for their particular geometric depiction of the characters and the relationships among them. Deciding the
colors, shapes, sizes, and arrangements based on their understanding
of the novel forces students to embrace the text in some way; reflecting
on the texts and considering the passages that influence their choices
extend the students' experience with that author's work. Sharing their
artwork, seeing the artwork and hearing the explanations of their peers,
may cause some students to adapt their understanding to what they see
and hear; it also may cause some students to resist the interpretation of
their peers.

Because "struggling with a text does not mean there is something
wrong with the reader or anything wrong with the text" (Jago, Chapter
2), varying responses may simply mean that the prior knowledge and
experience of readers cause them to see different things in the text.
Students reveal these differences through their artistic response to
the reading. Struggling with this assignment and having their efforts
affirmed by their peers can be the confidence builder that will flow across
to subsequent activities and assignments.

Activities

Part 1

In class, I introduce Geometric Characters with a discussion on symbolism—something concrete standing for something abstract—and review
literary terms with which students may be familiar, but not confident,
such as *motivation* and *characterization*. Because the assignment requires
them to choose colors, shapes, and sizes for several characters, we spend
time talking about the symbolism of colors. Writing on the board, overhead transparency, or computer, we could create two columns—one
marked positive and the other negative—and then call out a color and
ask the students to state a positive and a negative emotion or incident
each one could represent. For example, red could mean love or anger;
black could represent power or evil; depending on the culture, white
could stand for the joy of marriage or the sorrow of mourning. We do the

same for geometric shapes. Some students see a square as something to represent firmness; others see it as dull or old-fashioned—or unwilling to change. Some with science or math leanings see the triangle as a delta meaning change. The circle could mean complete, confident, ready to roll; others could suggest a closed group, such as a clique.

The size and position of the shapes need little explanation. By the time we get to these two parts of the assignment, the students know that they will be portrayed in an artistic way. The size and proximity of the shapes indicate the relationship of one character to another and among them all.

I distribute the assignment (Figure 8.1), review it with the students, entertain questions, and send them on their way. Most leave eager to make their choices and look forward to assembling their designs. For homework, students review their annotations and preplan the diagram. They complete Steps 1 through 3 and bring these notes to the next class meeting.

Part 2

At this point, students are ready to create the artwork and a simple legend (the characters' names and several of their qualities) to accompany the illustration. In class, students cut the shapes and arrange the geometric characters on a single sheet of white paper and draft the legend to accompany it. They often choose to sit on the floor in small groups with the stacks of paper in the center. I set the kitchen timer to ring about five minutes before the end of the period to give us time to put away the supplies, throw away the curly scraps left from cutting out the shapes, clear up the room, and to review the next step in the assignment. Because the assignment requires the students to come to class with the first three preplanning steps completed and they only do the cutting and assembling in class, I provide used envelopes available to store partially completed assignments. These I send home for students to complete the art portion.

I do not give the entire assignment for homework because I learn by listening to student talk as they work. As they sit on the floor, choosing colors, discussing these choices, cutting the shapes, then discarding and cutting a different one, laying out the shapes to reflect the relationships, then rearranging them when a classmate looks over and asks why they have spaced the shapes in that way, I watch and listen. I observe them returning to the text to assure themselves that they are right. I hear them justifying their choices, and I get a glimpse into their thinking. I begin to understand what they know and what they need to know before I

Geometric Character Analysis

(Adapted from Lauren May and David Panenheimer)

Carefully re-read your annotations and journal entries on *Of Mice and Men* by John Steinbeck. Be prepared to complete the following assignment.

1. Draw several geometric figures on your paper (circle, triangle, rectangle, square, blob, etc). Decide what type of personality each shape suggests.

2. Choose three or four (or more) of the main characters from *Of Mice and Men* and along the side of a blank piece of paper, devise a shape to represent each of these characters. Write the character's name next to the shape.

3. Use the middle section of the paper to group the shapes you have devised, keeping in mind that the placement and size of the shapes should show the relationships of the characters to one another.

4. Decide on color for each shape, cut it out of construction paper and arrange them all on a piece of paper (preferably 8 ½" x 11"). Place the figures so they represent ways the characters relate to one another. Use arrows, dotted or jagged lines, varying shades, to better explain these relationships. Add a legend. (TO BE COMPLETED IN CLASS)

5. Finally, write a two-three-page essay explaining what your geometric design represents about each character. Be sure to explain color, shape, size and placement. Back up your interpretation with specific details and quotations from the play. Include parenthetical citations. Don't forget an introduction and a conclusion.

6. Use the rubric to check your project before submitting it for evaluation.

7. Be prepared to meet in small groups to show your artwork and to explain to the members of your group your reasons for your choice of colors, shapes, sizes, and arrangement .

Figure 8.1. Geometric characters analysis assignment.

proceed to the next lesson. I can see who is bold enough to challenge a classmate and who is confident enough to stand by his or her decision; I discover who uses the text with ease and who struggles to find support for his or her choices.

For me, this activity is a form of no-stress assessment and also an insight into the social dynamics within the class. Acquiring this information early in the school year is so valuable that it is worth allotting class time. The students are relaxed, thinking they are doing easy work, not realizing the sophisticated higher-order thinking skill it takes to make the complex decisions in an assignment they think is simply creating cutouts to represent fictional characters.

At this point, for many classes, I ask students to complete a prewriting activity as their homework assignment. They make a list of the characters they selected and jot down the reasons for their choices of

---

Rubric for Evaluating Art and Writing about *Of Mice and Men*

I. Visual Presentation

- Three or more characters are represented in ways that can be justified by the text of *Of Mice and Men*.
- Written legend briefly explains decisions for color, shape, size, and position.
- Student name appears on the front.
- Design is neat.

II. Written Explanation

Introductory paragraph

- includes title and author of literary work
- identifies characters
- has a thesis statement.

Body

- is an explanation of choices
- uses quotations to support decisions about color, shape, size, position.

Conclusion

- is a summary of the process
- is a reflection on the characters and choices.

Conventions

- is edited for mechanics, usage, and grammar.

Figure 8.2. Scoring rubric.

shape, color, size, and arrangement on the page. They choose references and quotations from *Of Mice and Men* that justify these choices, including page numbers in parentheses. Students may complete an essay draft as homework, or we schedule time in the computer lab for students to draft and revise their essays. It is also important to review the scoring rubric (Figure 8.2) with students when giving the assignment (Figure 8.1).

Part 3

Students meet in small groups to describe their artwork and explain their choices. I set up a chart where students meet with three different groups during the class period so that over half the class gets to see what their peers have done. Because the students will have talked informally about their choices on Day 2 as they assembled the artwork, they usually can write competent essays. And because they have written their explanations, citing excerpts from the literature, they are ready to talk with confidence to their peers. Each assignment builds toward the next. Students then submit their artwork and essays.

Assessment

The final products are consistently remarkable, so I create a patchwork bulletin board, filling the board with as many pages of artwork as possible. These pieces demonstrate the myriad ways one assignment can be done right. I score their work using the rubric. Perhaps the strongest reason I use this assignment is the wealth of information garnered just by seeing students' artwork and listening to their oral explanation in the small groups. Finally, reading the essays helps me better understand students' thinking and creativity.

Considerations

Parents have sometimes challenged my use of art in English language arts classes, accusing me of dumbing down the course or giving students elementary school assignments. My response is this:

> Come visit my classroom and see the students' work. You'll see the depth of understanding required to complete the project. You'll see the quality of writing students produce once they've figured out what colors, shapes, sizes, and arrangements best represent the characters and their interactions with one another.

A number have taken up the challenge and see that, when the students confirm their choices with direct references to specific passages from the text, they know they are on the right track. Most are pleased at the high grades they earn. Furthermore, parents see how much students can learn from one another when they view the work of their classmates. This kind of assessment increases both confidence and competence in literary analysis.

The graphic depiction of characters in this assignment can be a way to put the book back together again after weeks of analysis, deconstruction, and close reads of small parts of the book. Fran Claggett suggests in her book *Drawing Your Own Conclusions* (1992) that tearing apart a book without giving students an opportunity to look at it as a whole leaves the students unfulfilled. It is unfair to the author to leave the books in pieces—each of the elements of the fiction disaggregated, separated, in its own column of a spreadsheet. To do so would be like the scrambled pieces of a puzzle stored in a box: Until the parts are reassembled, the beauty of the picture is unseen or distorted. The parts need to be pulled back together to see the whole picture, the puzzle re-assembled, the column of individual entries summed up. This goal the Geometric Characters assignment addresses quite well.

When students have choices about what they do, they tend to give more time and effort to the assignment. When I see what students choose, I have more accurate insight into their understanding. From their work, I can determine what they have learned and if I need to reteach concepts, give further practice in mastering the skill, or if I can move along to the next topic. Art proves to be an effective way to engage students in showing what they know, expands their understanding and extends the experience for the whole class, and helps me to plan subsequent instruction.

Reference

Claggett, F. (with Brown, J.). (1992). *Drawing your own conclusions: Graphic strategies for reading, writing, and thinking.* Portsmouth, NH: Boynton/Cook, Heinemann.

III Past and Present in *Out of the Dust*

Sheryl Long
Chowan University

Carol A. Pope
North Carolina State University

Karen Hesse's *Out of the Dust* is easily distinguished from the other American novels in this collection. Written in blank verse, each chapter of this work can stand alone as an individual poem. As a whole, these poems work together to present the poignant first-person narrative of Billie Jo, a thirteen-year-old girl struggling to survive the desperation of the Oklahoma Dust Bowl.

Published in 1997, *Out of the Dust* received much critical attention, including the 1998 Newbery Medal, the most prestigious award for American children's literature. Like many great works of children's literature, this novel speaks to readers of all ages. Its narrative is simple enough to be understood by readers as young as elementary school, yet this same simplicity speaks powerfully to older readers. Hesse's deliberate, parsimonious use of language holds us in place; there are no extra words, no unnecessary explication, no opportunity to look away. We, like Billie Jo, are trapped in this unyielding world. Our only way out of the dust is to pass through it.

The lessons presented in this section offer diverse approaches to teaching *Out of the Dust*. They address the structure, content, and context of Hesse's novel and suggest ways to lead students into thoughtful exploration of the text. Bowen (Chapter 9) focuses on the structural features of the text, Hesse's use of blank verse and the impact of an author's stylistic choices. Katzmarek (Chapter 10) guides students to examine the narrative structure of the novel by first creating narratives based on interviews with community members. By going outside the classroom, students discover how a complex text is created and how it can be read in the same way that Jago (Chapter 2) challenges students not to back down from just such a text.

Goodrum (Chapter 11) addresses the importance of students' acquiring background knowledge and grasping the cultural context of the text. Stover's lessons (Chapter 12) prod students to examine *Out of the Dust* through comparison with another piece of American fiction and then to draw connections between the works

These lessons stimulate experiential learning and provide a way for students to interact with the text in a meaningful way. None asks students to adopt someone else's interpretation of the text, but each empowers them to explore, question, experiment, and interpret. Collectively these lessons illustrate how sound instructional practices can encourage students to examine a text from multiple perspectives and for varied purposes while always leaving them free to own their personal experience with the text and to share their pleasure and discoveries.

9 Author's Craft in *Out of the Dust*

Kimberly C. Bowen
Metametrics, Durham, North Carolina

I never attempted to write this book any other way than in free verse. The frugality of the life, the hypnotically hard work of farming, the grimness of conditions during the dust bowl, demanded an economy of words. Daddy and Ma and Billie Jo's rawboned life translated into poetry, and bless Scholastic for honoring that translation and producing OUT OF THE DUST with the spare understatement I sought when writing it.

Karen Hesse, Newbery Medal Acceptance Speech, 1998

Purpose

This series of lessons engages students in a close examination of the author's craft in *Out of the Dust*. As they carefully examine Hesse's use of language, students begin to develop an understanding of free verse. By analyzing the connections between meaning and style, they deepen that understanding. The lessons culminate with a free-verse writing assignment that allows students to experiment with free verse as they transform a piece of prose writing into poetry. This process-centered activity guides students through the drafting, revising, and sharing stages of writing.

Materials

For this study, I use four poems concerned with seasons of the year; three of these poems are Shakespeare's Sonnet 18, Nikki Giovanni's "Winter Poem," and E. E. Cummings's "a leaf falls." Building on ideas learned in the Capital Area Writing Project, I wrote a fourth poem, "Blue Spring," to be stereotypically bad (see Figure 9.2). I provide students with three other handouts that I have also created. I begin with the Defining Poetry handout (Figure 9.1), which asks students to respond to the four poems. The *Out of the Dust* Journal Poetry handout (Figure 9.3) offers students specific directions for creating a free-verse poem, while ReVIEWing Your

Poem (Figure 9.4) guides students through the revision of their poems. I model this revision process by using a computer and LCD projector to display changes to my poem.

Introduction

Studying *Out of the Dust* provides an excellent opportunity for middle school and high school teachers to focus on author's craft, specifically on the stylistic choices that authors make as part of writing. This deceptively undemanding novel contains relatively simple diction, few pages, and a focus on a young girl's grief, making the story approachable. At the same time, this moving story may be students' first experience with a verse novel and perhaps the first time they have ever explored free-verse poetry.

We begin in my class with a focus on poetry, defining and understanding what poetry is to get beyond the stereotypes of sappy rhyming verse so many students envision when we mention poetry. I give students the Defining Poetry handout (Figure 9.1). Then on an overhead or LCD projector, I share four examples of verse one at a time, not reading them aloud, while students independently respond to each on the handout. If the poems have titles, I include those on the slide, but I remove authors' names. I start with Shakespeare's Sonnet 18, then move to one I created to be stereotypically bad (see Figure 9.2). These are followed by Nikki Giovanni's "Winter Poem" and E. E. Cummings's "a leaf falls," poems that may challenge students' stereotypical views of poetry. It is important to let the students complete both columns of the Defining Poetry handout—they need opportunity to explore definitions apart from personal preferences. Moreover, the "Do I like it?" column provides a precursor to later activities with style. Students discuss their responses in pairs or small groups; I facilitate the discussions, especially explaining Cummings's poem to any group necessary. Groups draft definitions of poetry that we then post and discuss as a whole group, eventually creating a class definition and identifying characteristics.

Like *Out of the Dust*, these poems move through the seasons. We spend some time discussing the different images in the poems that help the reader appreciate the season portrayed. Focusing on the Cummings and Giovanni poems as examples of free verse, we discuss how form complements the meaning.

	Is it a poem? Why or why not?	Do I like it? Why or why not?
#1 Sonnet 18		
#2 "Blue Spring"		
#3 "Winter Poem"		
#4 "a leaf falls"		

Group definition of poetry:

Class definition of poetry:

Figure 9.1. Defining Poetry handout.

Blue Spring

Everyday we have showers,
But I see no flowers,
Only blue.
I think of you
In the night
Longing for the sight
Of you.
Days were too few
Before you had to go.
I miss you so.

Figure 9.2. Deliberately bad poem.

Connections

This novel study focuses on critical understanding of author's craft. Because the content is accessible, I emphasize the stylistic challenges in discussions and activities. Through the study of *Out of the Dust*, students experiment with language and learn that authors make conscious choices. In its thoughtful and structured focus on Hesse's poetic form, use of language, and narrative structure, this lesson supports the philosophies outlined by Moore, Jago, and Wilhelm earlier in this book. Students give the text the careful attention that Jago advocates and in doing so, focus on the useful knowledge that Moore says will help them become better interpreters of text. Wilhelm calls for a greater appreciation of the author's construction of the text, and certainly this intentional exploration of craft helps students draw conclusions about Hesse's authorial choices.

Through the stages of developing topics, drafting, and revising their poems, students begin to see themselves as authentic writers making their own thoughtful choices. Such an approach clearly aligns with Blau's call in Chapter 1 for "learning through experience, not learning about experience." Students engage with the language; they play with their words and reach conclusions about how they structure those words to convey their intended meanings. Writing is not about merely putting words on paper, but about experiencing the effect of those words.

Activities

While students are reading the novel, we have journal responses, some related to content and some to style. For example, students write about stories they have heard in their families about their births or some event early in their lives. We use this writing as a bridge to the novel's opening poem in which Billie Jo tells us of her birth. We discuss why Hesse began the novel this way: What do our own stories mean to us? What do they suggest about the characters? Also with that first chapter, we discuss the importance of strong ending words in free-verse poetry, having students underline the last word of each line and do a class "rap," with one student at a time reading aloud just that final word.

Other journal responses focus on the style of the "On Stage" chapter that resembles keys on a piano, repetition (as seen in "Breaking Drought"), disappointments, first crushes, and forgiveness. I encourage students to relate to the story even as we focus on the author's craft. Moreover, the more personal connections serve as possible content for the students' final projects.

Another writer's craft activity that we use with this novel focuses on determining line breaks. Students can be both excited and over-whelmed when they have the freedom of breaking lines at any point. I take an unfamiliar excerpt from the novel and reconstruct it as a sentence. I place each word on a sticky note; then we work together as a class to break it down. "Apple Blossoms" works well, with its first line of "Ma has been nursing these two trees for as long as I can remember." I use each suggestion for a line break to spur discussion of meaning—what does it suggest to break it down that way? Then we compare our version to the original one and talk about differences in emphasis. Students work in groups to do the same with other sentences taken from this chapter and the next two. At the end of the class, students present their poems, and we compare them to Hesse's originals.

We continue reading the novel together. When we reach the chapter/poem "The Path of Our Sorrow," I share an excerpt from an interview with Hesse:

> Q: Reviewers rave about your novels in blank verse and praise your "poet's eye for telling detail." The spareness of your poetry seems to be almost more about what's left out. How do you decide what to leave in and what to throw out as you're trying to capture the essence of your story?

> A: Anything that doesn't move the story forward, anything that doesn't contribute to the reader's understanding of the character does not belong no matter how juicy the tidbit, how beautiful the writing. (http://www.karenbeil.com/hesse-interview.html, 11/10/05)

We discuss what this poem adds to the story and why its history lesson about the Great War is positioned so far into the book.

To have students apply the process of selecting events and details, I take an excerpt from an informational book or news story related to our topic and have students consider what to leave in, take out, or add to make the given excerpt into a poem. For example, the Public Broadcast System program *American Experience* features online selections from the memoir of a Kansas wheat farmer who experienced the difficulties of the Dust Bowl (see http://www.pbs.org/wgbh/amex/dustbowl/sfeature/eyewitness.html). These nine short excerpts provide vivid content for the class exercise of selecting aspects for the poem and conveniently lend themselves to groups' crafting verses for different parts of the poem.

As we finish the novel, we return to the content-related journal en-tries. Each student selects one journal entry to transform from freewriting to free verse. (See Figure 9.3.) Just as Hesse presents some poems focused

Review your journal entries for our study of *Out of the Dust*. Select one entry to transform from your prose freewrite into a free-verse poem. (Note: Other students will be reading your selected journal entry and your poem, so don't choose one you wouldn't want to share with your classmates.) Just as Hesse had some poems focused on information, others on images, and still others on events, you are free to select any of these types for your original poem. Through the process of writing and revising your poem, you will add, delete, and change many things, so your poem will be quite different from your original.

Once you have selected your journal entry, complete the **focus sentences** below in PENCIL (these responses will help me assess the effectiveness of your stylistic choices, so you may be revising them as we progress through the assignment).

This piece is about _____ .

It is important to me because _____ .

If someone else read this, I would want them to understand _____ .

I already know I want to add / take out _____ .

Type your draft poem into MSWord. Print and save your draft poem (*namepoemdraft*).

Turn on *Track Changes* (MS Word tool). Save your poem again as a new file (*namepoemchanges*). Then, using ideas from the ReVIEWing Your Poem handout, revise your poem. You don't need to make all of the changes you noted as possibilities; you may also make other changes if you wish. Make at least one change from each category (Imagery, Diction, Structure).

Once you have made your changes, choose the most significant or effective change in each category, explain the change that you made using the MS Word *Comment* feature. If you have decided you don't like any of the changes you tried in a certain category, that's OK. Use your comment to explain why you think your original version was most effective. Be sure you save this version again as well. Print your poem with the changes highlighted and your comments visible.

Save your poem under a third file name (*namepoemfinal*). Using *Track Changes*, accept or decline each change in your draft according to your final decisions. Save again and then print your final copy.

Be sure to **attach three versions** *of your poem—original, draft showing revisions (using highlight changes) and comments, and final (after changes have been accepted).*

Checklist:

____ Journal entry (copied) attached, marked up based on peer assessment

____ Original poem attached, marked up based on self-assessment

____ Revision draft attached and shows consideration for

     ____ images that show rather than tell

     ____ images developed with detail

     ____ diction (word choice) more specific

     ____ vivid, precise verbs

     ____ appropriate line lengths and stanza breaks

___ Explanation of changes shows thoughtfulness

___ Final poem

     ___ reflects understanding of characteristics of free verse

     ___ shows improvement through revisions

     ___ contains no careless errors

     ___ neatly presented

Figure 9.3. *Out of the Dust* Journal Poetry assignment.

on information, others on images, and still others on events, so students are free to select any of these types for their poems. We talk about how some words or details might be added and others taken away and how the poem version might look very different from the original freewrite.

To help students with their poems, we return to "Blue Spring" (Figure 9.2) and use it as a model through the stages of their writing. Together, we reread the poem and complete the same focus sentences that are on the assignment handout. Because that poem is vague, we discuss each item quite a bit and make decisions that can shape the poem's revision. I ask them to reread their journal entries and complete the focus sentences themselves.

Using copies of their original journal entries, students swap papers and read through the entry. With the authors' responses to the focus sentences in mind, the peer responders circle effective images, underline important events, and write questions or requests for more information in the margins. Now that they have defined their foci and have some input from an audience perspective, students draft their poems and bring them to class for further work.

Again, we discuss "Blue Spring," completing the ReVIEWing Your Poem handout (Figure 9.4) together. Then using a computer attached to an LCD projector, we revise the poem by implementing some of the changes suggested in the discussion. Through this process, I model how to use the Track Changes features in MS Word. Students benefit from seeing the revision and the think-aloud process as we accept some suggestions and put others aside. We decide on three to five changes that are most important or effective. For those, I add MS Word comments paraphrasing the students' explanations.

Then students use the ReVIEWing Your Poem handout (Figure 9.4) to guide their individual revisions. Students submit three versions of their poems—an original draft, a marked-up version with comments, and a final draft.

Assessment

Much of the assessment in this unit is formative. Students receive feedback and credit for each completed activity. I review students' journals to note the connections they make with the novel and how their understanding of the author's craft is developing. I monitor class and small-group discussions to assess student understanding. Peers respond to each other's journal entries at least once in the unit. Students also self-assess their poem drafts.

Examine your draft *stylistically* by following the steps below. Remember to keep your focus questions in sight (and in mind) during the review. All of your **imagery**, **diction**, and **structure** should emphasize or complement the focus you shaped through your responses to those questions.

Imagery

To help readers experience your poem, you want to **show, not tell.**
   Circle any words or phrases that appeal to senses (smell, touch, taste, sight, sound) and note which sense is used in the margin.
   • Are you appealing to more than just sight?
   • Are you using any action (leaf falling, snow gathering, hand reaching)?
Note at least two ways you could improve the imagery in your poem.

Word Choice

To make your images vivid pictures, you want to be **specific** (Is that flower a tulip, a sun-flower, or a rose that you smell?), **include details** (Is it a yellow rose bursting with petals or a cream-white rosebud with blushing pink tips?), and **use precise verbs** (Does that rose wilt, wither, bounce, stretch, linger?).
   Underline your nouns in blue and your verbs in red.
   • Are your nouns specific?
   • Are your verbs precise?
   • Are you including details?
Note at least two ways you could improve the diction in your poem.

Structure

To shape your free-verse poem, make thoughtful, not random, choices about line and stanza breaks.
   Double underline the final word on each line. Count the syllables on each line and write the number in the margin. Draw a line underneath each stanza.
   • Are the words strong (not vague or empty)?
   • Does line length (in syllables or words) appear random? Or does it help the poem flow naturally and/or emphasize your meaning?
   • Do your stanzas indicate shifts in focus, perspective, topic, or events?
Note at least two ways you could improve the structure of your poem.

Figure 9.4. ReVIEWing Your Poem assignment.

Final assessment of the students' poems focuses primarily on process. Through the students' drafts, marked areas of revision, and comments about their reasons for at least some of their changes, I find evidence of their knowledge of free-verse poetry, their willingness to experiment with their writing, and their thoughtfulness in making their choices. I keep anecdotal notes on their process, checks for completion, and a final grade for the entire unit.

Considerations

Students enjoy *Out of the Dust* and are engaged in our discussion of the novel's content. This unit has been a successful approach to discussing style in a way that adolescents of all ability levels can understand. Too often students are reluctant to write and/or revise poetry. However, through this unit we have worked on so many aspects of the novel's verse that students begin to see poetry as a craft they can explore. When my students begin to discuss the merits of changing specific words or line lengths, I can see them becoming thoughtful poets indeed.

Reference

Hesse, K. (1998). The 1998 Newbery Medal acceptance speech. *Journal of Youth Services in Libraries, 11*, 341–45.

10 Reading Our Lives

JoAnne Katzmarek
University of Wisconsin–Stevens Point

Purpose

This lesson cycle explores the power of life story, of narrative, to help students learn more about their life experiences. It also looks at the productive context narrative provides for integrating language arts and social studies with early adolescent readers. Through the use of interviewing as a tool for primary research (and a form of place-based writing through inquiry), role playing, note taking, student-constructed discussions, and narrative and expressive writing, students recognize the rich connections of text to personal experience, text to events in history, and text to primary sources used to create historical fiction.

Materials

Community members are an essential resource for this lesson as students conduct interviews that become the basis of future activities. Other resources needed include oversized chart paper, sticky notes, and computers with Internet access. Depression-era photographs are useful for the extension activity.

Introduction

In Karen Hesse's novel *Out of the Dust,* the narrator, Billie Jo, suffers through incredible adversity: extreme poverty in the Dust Bowl years in the Oklahoma Panhandle, a deadly fire that maims her and eventually contributes to the deaths of her mother and newborn brother, and a father who subsequently grows distant and despairing. By the end of the account, however, she has learned that these adversities have actually made her stronger and more determined to find happiness in her life and what it offers. To be able to see how life's experiences help to shape characters is a worthy achievement for any reader. In teaching this novel, I focus on activities that help students understand the importance of life story, of narrative, to help each of us learn more about our life and our experiences.

Connections

Essentially, this lesson series demonstrates the power of connecting literature to the students' lives and to the larger community. It also makes use of student writing, inspired by the literature, to deepen understanding of self as well as an appreciation for the work of an author creating fiction. These goals align with Blau's (Chapter 1) and Wilhelm's (Chapter 3) calls for instruction that emphasizes personal meaning. Additionally, this lesson adheres to Wilhelm's desire for teaching in an inquiry context. The interviews with community members allow students to ask questions that interest them. As they work to shape their interview notes into a narrative and a Found Poem, they have the freedom to focus on what interests them most; thus, the experience remains highly personal.

The interview process culminates with students' examining Billie Jo's lessons learned and making connections to what they learned from their interviews and experiences. In addition to being the type of personal, authentic learning described by Blau and Wilhelm, this activity also illustrates how, as Probst (Chapter 4) explains, American literature can be used to help readers examine themselves even as they are examining the text.

Activities

Before reading the novel, my students spend time interviewing self-selected residents of the community about their life experiences. To prepare for the interview and its use as a language tool for learning, students brainstorm questions that they can use during their interviews. Working together, they create interview questions that yield specific details and interesting information. They delete any questions that can be answered with one word. We pay special attention to constructing questions that help the interviewees explain how they learned something important from the experience(s) they recount. Next, the students prepare index cards with the questions and then sequence the questions effectively. In preparation for the actual interview, students role-play interviews with their classmates. They practice taking notes during the interviews, and they sometimes decide that, with the permission of the persons they are interviewing, they will audiotape the discussion.

The focus of the actual interview is for the community members to share personal events, ideally when they themselves were adolescents, and what they learned from the events. The interviewees are made aware of this focus in advance. Following the interviews, students share in class the results of their interviews and discussions.

Following these interview activities, students create a narrative of the events they learned about during the interviews. This writing activity relates to previous work done in language arts class on narrative structure. Students focus on sequence, connecting phrases, and providing moments of insight. As students write their narratives, they consider how the interviewees themselves presented the information and learn that their notes come from oral narrative. This emphasis on spoken language helps them use narrative structure. Additionally, students have multiple opportunities for writing process activities, with much interaction with their classmates and me, and many chances to revise and improve their narratives.

The final step, creating a Found Poem from the narrative, helps students appreciate the poetic power of *Out of the Dust*. We create Found Poems by selecting words from other sources (in this case their narratives and perhaps their notes) and then arranging those words to make a poem. It is no accident that Karen Hesse researched her material extensively before writing the novel, so I use actual examples from the novel to illustrate how these words and phrases could have come from a text about the Dust Bowl years. For example, the novel's poems "Fields of Flashing Light" in which Hesse describes in vivid detail the combination of a lightning and dust storm and "The Path of Our Sorrow" in which she traces the agricultural and economic policies that actually culminated in the Dust Bowl dynamic match historical writings that can be easily found through Web searches about the period.

As the students work on creating Found Poems from their narratives, the chances for authentic discussion about research techniques, expressive writing, and writing process are rich indeed. Modeling the writing process of a Found Poem provides the best help for students, and it is always wonderful for students to see their teacher writing for expressive purposes.

These preparatory steps may seem time consuming, but through them we address academic standards and provide an integration of literacy experiences with social studies skills. The most important consideration for these preparations, however, is that they help the students read the novel with an added awareness of the narrative genre, especially one written as poetry.

As a final anticipation for reading the novel, students brainstorm what is important to them in their daily lives. They respond with such topics as friends, money, fun, family, sports, and safety. I record the ideas on chart paper or on the board as students offer them. Then I lead the students in a class discussion. Can the ideas be grouped or classified?

Can they be prioritized? Should anything be added? Do they speak to people of all ages, or are they age-specific? I post these recorded ideas, and they remain visible as the students read about Billie Jo's experiences from 1934 to 1935 in the panhandle of Oklahoma. Students are often amazed at the universality of the events in the novel and of their own experiences.

Following their reading, which does not take more than a few days and usually requires relatively little support from me, students redirect their attention to the ideas and experiences they have brainstormed. Students often use sticky notes to mark places in the text where Hesse addresses these issues. I use such questions as "How many of these are apparent in the novel? Which are the important ones?" to stimulate discussion. These conversations always prove productive because students easily remember the vivid details from the novel, and they have the experience of previously applying these ideas to their lives. An important focus of the discussion addresses the lines from the poem "Music," where Billie Jo values the hardships she has had to endure because they have made her "good enough." Students easily bring their own "lessons learned" as well as those from their interviews into this discussion.

Assessment

I asses student learning in an ongoing fashion through the writings they have generated during the lesson activities. These writings include interview questions, narrative writing, and a Found Poem. Students receive feedback and guidance as they revise or complete these pieces. I also assess student learning by monitoring student participation in constructivist activities such as the sticky note posting for the data chart and contributions to class discussions as they relate their ideas to the text. Students receive full or partial credit for all products and one grade for participation.

Considerations

Possibly the most appealing element of this novel is that readers of almost all abilities can read and enjoy it. At the beginning of a school year, a few seventh-grade girls read the book and created some excitement among the other girls, who then read it themselves. By Thanksgiving at least one boy had read it, and by January every student in the class had read it. They were enticed by its seeming simplicity (not to mention its generous white space on so many pages) and vivid descriptions and in no time were captured by the many adversities Billie Jo faces. Even though the protagonist is a girl, the middle school boys had no trouble being drawn into the story. These qualities recommend the book especially for a full-class reading as I advocate here.

This lesson cycle can also be extended to incorporate additional writing opportunities. Following the process they used with their interview narratives, students can write a memoir of an event they experienced and then create a Found Poem from the memoir. Another possibility is for students to use photographs of the Depression and/or the Dust Bowl (Walker Evans's photos are especially effective) and create first-person narratives about the stories they imagine from the photographs.

11 Weaving Background Knowledge into a Study of *Out of the Dust*

Shayne G. Goodrum
North Carolina Department of Public Instruction

Purpose

Out of the Dust takes place in a window of time that is often unfamiliar to middle school and high school students. They may be aware of the Great Depression and know about the stock market crash of 1929, but the Dust Bowl is typically less familiar to them. The idea of "black blizzards" is difficult to imagine, even for adults. For many students, even snow blizzards are not part of their practical weather knowledge. Activating their background knowledge and building connections to their lives help students make connections to this era so that when Hesse's sparse poetic style alludes to events, these references have a place to stick in students' minds, and they have the confidence to explore the ways Billie Jo tells her story.

Materials

To complete the "Now and Then" activity, students need chart/poster paper and markers. The attached handout (Figure 11.1) provides students with suggested topics to address in their groups. This guide helps to shape their collaborative discussion and ensures that they are prepared to make wide-ranging connections between the setting of *Out of the Dust* and their lives today.

This lesson cycle also requires a large timeline, which I create from poster paper. For the research portion of the lesson, students need computers with Internet access and a list of suggested websites. The PBS documentary *Surviving the Dust Bowl* and its companion website (http://www.pbs.org/wgbh/americanexperience/films/dustbowl/) are excellent resources for helping students understand the historical context of the novel. Other possible online resources can be found through the

Library of Congress American Memory Collection (http://memory.loc. gov/ammem/index.html).

Introduction

Literature and writing are the center of my teaching, and my key goal is for students to develop identities as readers and writers. My students read what other authors have written in both fiction and nonfiction, and they also hear their own voices emerge from their personal writings. To develop effectively as readers and writers, my students need to feel confident in their knowledge of content and to build connections to the historical and practical world in which they live.

Out of the Dust is a powerful novel that offers challenges because of its poetic style, but that style also provides a rich path to explore the differing ways that authors tell their stories and how these choices shape the impact of the content. The novel's poetic style provides comfort to some of my students because there is more white space on each page, making the text seem less intimidating than novels with every page covered in print. This apparent "easiness" makes some reluctant readers more willing to take on the reading task.

Throughout the year, I anchor learning to students' lives and their future aspirations. We work in collaborative groups that continue for varying periods of time ranging from a few days to several months. These groups provide security while fostering development of skills for interacting supportively and collaboratively. I often remind students that the skills they use for collaborating in their groups are the same skills they will use as adults working in business, on teams, and in communities. Working together, these groups become the experts who help us understand Billie Jo's life.

Connections

This series of lessons reflects the inquiry-based context Jeffrey Wilhelm describes in Chapter 3 in this book. He suggests using inquiry as a means for students to engage in personal explorations. These activities assist students in understanding the historical context of *Out of the Dust*, but they also allow students to pursue their interests in social studies, science, and the arts.

As the students connect Billie Jo's experiences with their lives and as they delve more deeply into elements of the novel that interest them individually, they are able to experience the novel on a personal level. They do not depend on me to tell them what to think, but they are free to draw conclusions based on their understandings. As Blau has explained in Chapter 1, this type of learning is the most authentic form of knowledge and should always be the goal of reading and language instruction.

Activities

Now and Then

To anchor the novel study to my students' lives, we begin with their present experiences. Using work groups, I ask each team of students to draw one of four topics (home life, school, life in the community, work/occupations) from a hat to be their specialty for the study. These topics are open ended, and more than one group may have the same topic. Groups begin by discussing life today and creating a poster to describe their current experiences with the assigned topic. I frame a few basic subtopics to help each group hit the aspects I want to ensure are covered (see Figure 11.1). For example, I make certain the "Life in the Community" group responds to a prompt about getting groceries, so that when Billie Jo goes to the store, there is material to form a comparison.

After completing their small-group assignments, students have a chance to share their posters with other groups who have worked with the same topic, and together they present their findings to the whole class. Their posters are displayed in the classroom so that students can use them as a resource. As we read the book, students continue to work in their same groups. At this point they prepare a similar poster for Billie Jo's life with quotations from the text that support their points. They follow the same procedures for sharing with other groups and the class.

Framing the Era

Before we begin reading *Out of the Dust*, I use a modified KWL process and elicit a list of what students know about how people lived during the late 1920s and early 1930s. I follow this activity with a short, basic overview of the Dust Bowl years. We then post on the wall a blank timeline from 1850 to 1950 and begin to fill in the timeline as we talk about what they know. Students are generally familiar with the era of the Civil War and World War II, so we frame the timeline with these years. In addition to the timeline, we post a map of the United States and mark the Dust Bowl area.

While reading the novel, we continue adding to the timeline as events and places are mentioned in the novel. I use the PBS documentary

I limit the number of topics that each group addresses to maintain the focus, limit the time needed, and ensure connection to the novel.

Home Life
  - o Housing
  - o Eating
  - o Sleeping
  - o Families
  - o Chores

School
  - o Daily schedule
  - o Classes
  - o Teachers
  - o School lunches
  - o Getting to and from school

Life in the Community
  - o Shopping for food and clothes
  - o Social events
  - o Medical care
  - o Religion
  - o Entertainment

Work/Occupations
  - o Jobs
  - o Employers
  - o Hours
  - o Wages/Salaries
  - o Banking

Figure 11.1. Now and then activity topics.

Surviving the Dust Bowl to provide a visual context, and the companion website has a wealth of resources to use with or without the film. Other resources from the Internet, particularly the Library of Congress American Memory Collection, also provide visual images of the era.

Becoming an Expert

To provide research and interdisciplinary connections, students discuss what they have seen about this era and select a topic that they would like to explore in greater depth. Some may look at science, history, arts, music, or literature. Using online and library resources, I help students prepare a base set of materials to consult as they explore their topic. I ensure that each group has Internet, print, and auditory sources that include primary source documents. As our unit progresses, students have a designated time to share the results of their exploration. When Billie Jo's teacher discusses the impact of farming in "Rabbit Battles," students who have worked on science or ecology present their findings and make connections to the novel. When Billie Jo listens to Mad Dog on the radio, students who have worked with music share. The result is that throughout our study, I become a director and facilitator rather than the sole authority. As the students take responsibility for bringing content to our learning community, our mutual commitment to learning together is reinforced.

Assessment

Because each of these activities has a product or presentation attached to it, students have ample opportunity to show what they have learned. Therefore, I do not give a test on this entire unit. Students instead complete a summative writing project and receive credit for each completed assignment.

Drawing on the work the learning groups have done documenting their lives and Billie Jo's, students individually write a comparison/contrast essay on one aspect of life today as compared to life in the Dust Bowl years. I check that students are only addressing one small aspect of life so that they have the opportunity to focus their ideas in approximately two to three pages. If the topic is too large, the essays tend to become diffuse and give way to summary, rather than providing the opportunity to hone the expository writing skills of comparison/contrast. The essays are not "one-draft wonders" but evolve through a process so that the learning about writing is as solid as the learning about the Dust Bowl years.

Considerations

Out of the Dust provides many opportunities to integrate learning. While much of the novel-based discussion and writing are based on a reader response approach, the historical backdrop provides a rich tapestry of connections to social studies and science content as well as to literature and the arts. Understanding the historical placement of the novel builds students' capacity to tackle this text with confidence. This lesson makes space in our study for each of the other content areas and helps students who are naturally inclined to those subjects gain purchase as they address a writing style quite different from most of the fiction we have read. I find that these activities and lessons adapt for my heterogeneous classes at both the middle and high school levels.

12 Teaching *Out of the Dust* as an American Novel: Using a Jigsaw Approach to Define "American Fiction"

Lois T. Stover
St. Mary's College of Maryland

Purpose

Using *Out of the Dust* as part of a unit on American Fiction, this lesson plan is designed to enlarge students' knowledge, skills, and experience with the novel. By the end of the unit, students are able to participate in multiple "ways in" to the novel—through personal connections and through bridges to the history and societal issues framing the narrative. They also connect their personal world to larger themes and concepts present in fiction. By participating in a jigsaw activity, students connect this novel to other American young adult novels by an inductive exploration of the concept of "American Fiction."

Materials

The introduction to this lesson cycle calls for actual dust (I collect dust from my driveway) and photographic images from the Dust Bowl era. For the jigsaw activity, students need access to another work of American fiction. I provide students with a list of suggested adolescent literature (*Lyddie* by Katherine Paterson, *Jacob Have I Loved*, also by Paterson; *Staying Fat for Sarah Brynes* by Chris Crutcher; *Hush* by Jacqueline Woodson; *The Year of the Gopher* by Phyllis Reynolds Naylor; *A Solitary Blue* by Cynthia Voigt; *The Land* by Mildred Taylor; and *Heroes* by Robert Cormier). I provide chart paper for group activities. We also need laptops or a computer lab with Internet connection.

Introduction

This lesson works well with a wide range of students, from middle school to high school students and even with college-age students. The adolescent novels that I use appeal to students of all levels, but teachers may choose to substitute books they have available or ones that match students' reading levels. For instance, I know that Gary Paulsen's *Hatchet* and Virginia Euwer Wolff's *Make Lemonade* both work well, but other classic literary works may also work well for the individual reading.

I introduce *Out of the Dust* early in a semester-length course in American literature. I begin by showing the students dust from my driveway, and we feel it with our hands, describing its physical properties, as a way to prompt responses for a structured web on "dust." The classroom gets noisy as students call out terms and phrases that come to mind, definitions of dust, synonyms for dust, and personal reactions or associations to dust. Typically, responses include the biblical phrase "Ashes to ashes, dust to dust," and many negative associations with dust relating to allergies, chores, and chalk. Interestingly, the Harry Potter books are also often referenced in our conversations as the image of the phoenix crying as it dies, melting into ashes.

Then we talk about the Dust Bowl. I show pictures of the landscape of the southwest in the 1930s, and we use the Internet to find out which states were most affected, why the dust storms happened, and what life was like for families living in the Dust Bowl. After this set of bridges and discussion, I ask students to read the novel on their own, responding by using the questions identified below, and to come to class having completed the book.

Connections

The easy and effective "bridge," using actual dust that students can see and touch, brainstorming their own experiences with dust (emotional ones such as having allergies), and their prior knowledge of historical events relate clearly to Blau's (Chapter 1) and Wilhelm's (Chapter 3) emphases on personal experiences with text. Additionally, the journal response topics allow readers to respond to events and characters in a personally meaningful way, to connect emotionally and intellectually to the text by asking questions of it. Using class activities such as tableaux, described below, provides students with a kinesthetic opportunity to explore character relationships and themes and offer another type of experiential learning.

As someone with more experience and knowledge of American literature and history, I help students to make sense of *Out of the Dust* and the supplementary novels in deeper, richer ways by asking questions about how the texts create meaning. Blau believes that students need to discover the pleasure and the exhilaration of discovery by working through texts and mining them for meaning. This philosophy means not submitting to lectures or teacher-directed analyses that alienate students from the experience of literature, but engaging students directly through authentic problems in the interpretation and criticism of literature. Wilhelm advocates creating inquiry contexts for teaching literature and for using diverse techniques to foster inquiry and response to textual meaning. The jigsaw approach in this lesson helps students form intertextual connections and generate personal definitions of "American literature," processes that are consonant with Wilhelm's ideal.

Activities

Responding to *Out of the Dust*

After I introduce the text, students read Hesse's beautifully nuanced book independently; while they read, they keep a journal in which they react to the book in several ways. These journal writings include the following:

1. Responding to the plot and characters of the novel on a personal level

2. Posing questions to the author about anything that puzzles, delights, frustrates, or concerns them

3. Making connections of any sort—about plot, theme, characterization, characters and motivations, settings, narrative voice, tone—with their chosen title from the supplemental book list

4. Highlighting any passages or themes that seem particularly "American"

We do not define "American" at this time, but I ask the students to reflect on the attributes they believe define characteristics of American literature. I ask them to draw on their experiences reading American literature. How does *Out of the Dust* resonate with the American classics they know that are typically part of the high school curriculum, such as *The Scarlet Letter, Adventures of Huckleberry Finn, Death of a Salesman, Of Mice and Men,* or *The Crucible*?

Several weeks later, as we begin to discuss *Out of the Dust*, we participate in several class activities as a whole group. Students brainstorm categories of characters and then argue about who goes into which category. For example, some of their character category suggestions have included gritty vs. helpless, courageous vs. timid, able to change vs. hardened, sympathetic vs. not sympathetic. They work in groups to portray, in tableaux, a scene they view as either reflective of the relationships within the book as a whole or as a turning point in some way for the plot or character of Billie Jo.

Continuing to work in groups, students skim either the notes on the author and an interview with her or the excerpts from her Newbery Award speech, both of which appear at the end of the Apple *Signature* teacher's edition of the novel; as they read, they look for information that adds to their appreciation or understanding of the novel as a whole. Then we make a big chart on which we list those traits that we can agree as seeming to define a body of literature as "American." Typically, we arrive at themes such as the importance of individuality, the exploration of frontier, identity formation, forgiveness, and the power of choice. Our list of traits often includes a tone of optimism in the face of great hardship or the use of an expansive canvas and setting.

Independent Novel Reading

To explore the concept of American literature, I present students with the list of American novels provided in the Materials section. Students individually select a novel and work to complete their reading by the designated date. Each student provides a *brief*, three-to-five-sentence plot overview and states both the theme and thesis of the work. Students also write a short, two-to-three-sentence description of what they liked/ disliked most about the book. My goal for this part of the activity is to ensure that students come to class prepared to work collaboratively. I ask students to post these responses on Blackboard, but in the absence of such a system, students may send their response by email or turn in a written response.

The Jigsaw Activity, Phase I

Once the students have read *Out of the Dust* and their companion novels, I introduce our jigsaw activity. I begin by grouping students who have read the same novel in "expert groups." As a group, they review the plot and theme/thesis insights and then answer a series of questions—using either chart paper and markers or a computer program such as Inspiration to collect responses that can then be projected for other groups to see and use. See Figure 12.1 for the list of questions used to guide this group work.

As you work together in your group, you should answer the following questions about the novel that your group members have read.

1. Who are the major characters in the work? What are some adjectives you would use to describe them? What, if any, are the predicaments the characters bring on themselves?

2. How do individual characters use their strengths to deal with these predicaments? What do they learn in the process of addressing them?

3. What generalizations can you make about your author's style? What aspects of her or his use of language did you, as a reader, most enjoy? What kinds of literary devices did she or he often use? What was the effect on you, as reader, of specific kinds of imagery or other literary devices? How would you say the author's style is or is not connected to the kind of themes she or he investigates, and/or the kind of mood created? [One way of getting at the abstract concept of style is to think about such comparisons as *Out of the Dust* and *The Chocolate War*, so students can compare/contrast these authors' use of language with that of the author of their book. Another option might be to think about pieces of music or art that somehow seem analogous to the author's style in some way.]

4. To what age group, or to what kind of reader, do you think your book would most appeal and why? Are there readers who might not respond particularly positively to the work? Would you choose to use the book as an in-common reading for a whole class? Why or why not? If yes, in what grade, given local curricular content and goals, might you place it? How could you use your book in conjunction with a title typically taught in an American literature course?

5. What is your personal response to the book—and what is it about the style, the craft, the themes, settings, character development, and so forth that cause that response?

6. Students post their responses [either on the discussion forum, if we are using laptops with wireless connectivity, or they create posters that are hung around the room]. The idea is to have a resource available for everyone to use as we move into the next phase of the activity.

Figure 12.1. *Out of the Dust* jigsaw activity, phase I.

The Jigsaw Activity, Phase II

At this point, I mix students into new groups so that each group has representatives who have read at least four of the seven different titles. Having completed the first task, individual students have an easy time being the "expert" in this new group. Each participant is charged with providing a brief overview of the key aspects of his or her individual title. The rest of the group has, as their "purpose for listening," trying to find patterns and commonalities among the books. Specifically, the groups consider assigned questions (see Figure 12.2); they record their responses on a discussion forum, allowing for future reference by

Your group includes "experts" for each of the novels from our suggested list. Each of you should begin by giving a brief overview of your novel. Then working as a group, answer the following questions. You should connect your individually read novels to each other and to Hesse's *Out of the Dust*.

1. What are the dominant themes of these works, given your admittedly limited knowledge base? Paterson says, in various essays in *Gates of Excellence* (1981), that she writes about "love" and "hope." Do you think these two themes are important attributes of American literature? Of young adult literature? Why or why not? Love of what sort? Hope in what sense?

2. Most of our authors also say that they write to comfort a childhood self who was always an "outsider." In what sense were the main characters "outsiders"? How does the environment in which the characters are living contribute to the creation of their personalities? Can we make any generalizations about the nature of the American landscape and the concept of pushing back frontiers of all sorts and the way characters develop in these titles? Do the writers share any stylistic commonalities? If so, is there any way these could be said to be "American"—or are they more likely to be shared characteristics of literature written specifically for and about young adults?

3. In her Newbery speech, Hesse says that *Out of the Dust* is, in the end, a novel about forgiveness. Is she telling the truth? How does forgiveness— or a lack thereof—play a role in the other novels you have read?

4. Some of these novels we have read have come under attack by censors. What objections can you imagine someone might voice about these books? Given what you know about the authors and their work, how would you argue for teaching these books?

Figure 12.2. *Out of the Dust* jigsaw activity, phase II.

everyone in the class. To process this discussion, I first ask different reporters to share responses to a specific question; that is, not every group reports on each topic, though everyone is invited to give examples and elaborate on what an individual reporter might say.

Assessment

The group presentations give me a chance to informally assess students' understanding of their novels, their cooperation in the groups, and their higher-level thinking abilities. Their journals provide an artifact I can use to assess their reflective skill and personal connections to *Out of the Dust* as do their responses to the self-selected novel.

For closure, students write two paragraphs; in the first, they discuss what title they now most want to add to their reading list after hearing about it from their peers and why it sounds most compelling. In the second paragraph, they describe the pros and cons of the jigsaw approach, focusing on what they learned about themselves in terms of collaborative skill through their participation in the process.

Considerations

As a result of these experiences, my students report that they gain a deeper appreciation for Hesse as a writer and for the ways novels can "speak to each other." They add titles to the list of books they want to continue to read after the course has ended. They say they better understand the jigsaw strategy—how it holds individuals accountable for their part of the task, uses questions that help all group members collaborate and draw on their individual knowledge to make generalizations, and holds individuals responsible for using the collaboratively constructed knowledge in some individual way. Furthermore, they often report that they have at least begun to think about how to tie together works read across their study of American literature.

The approach described here works best if students have practice working as experts and in mixed jigsaw groups with shorter tasks earlier in the year, and if they are accustomed to assessing their own and their peers' contributions to such groups. What seems to be important in the high school classroom is that students, especially those who are less sophisticated readers and may not be considering college, are able to think about larger thematic issues relevant to the typical junior year American literature curriculum in ways that help them see the connections among texts often perceived to be dry and not personally engaging. Using easily accessible young adult novels helps students see themselves in the larger societal context and to think on a personal level about what it means to be an "American." This structured lesson gives them a scaffold on which to build a deeper understanding of self, others, important texts, and our nation.

IV Teaching F. Scott Fitzgerald's *The Great Gatsby*

Elizabeth A. Kahn
James B. Conant High School, Hoffman Estates, Illinois

The Great Gatsby is frequently studied in high school English language arts classes as an exploration of the American Dream, the Jazz Age, and the 1920s. The story of the fabulously wealthy Jay Gatsby is narrated by Nick Carraway, a midwesterner who rents a small bungalow in West Egg, Long Island, in the spring of 1922. Jay Gatsby throws extravagant parties at his enormous West Egg mansion and seeks to win back his love Daisy, who married the wealthy college football star Tom Buchanan while Gatsby was overseas fighting in World War I.

The intriguing plot, setting, and characters of *The Great Gatsby* appeal to high school students; however, F. Scott Fitzgerald's language and imagery make it a challenging novel. The lessons in this section focus on engaging students in interpreting Fitzgerald's complex language, imagery, symbols, character development, and exploration of the American Dream—with the goal of helping students learn how to become sophisticated readers of complex literature.

The teachers who created the following lessons, like the theorists who open this book, seek to approach literature in ways that will help students learn how to make meaning for themselves. Like Moore (Chapter 5), they want students to learn that there is no single correct interpretation of a text and that they may "combine various reading strategies to construct pluralistic interpretations." To achieve this goal of creating classrooms in which students are actively engaged in thinking through and responding to the meanings of texts, the authors of these lessons use the kinds of interactive strategies advocated by Blau, Jago, Wilhelm, Probst, and Moore (Chapters 1–5). They involve students in generating questions, creating graphic representations, analyzing film, writing, discussing, and debating issues in small-group and whole-class formats. The lessons focus on teaching students "to discern the constructed ideas of authors" and then "interrogate and reflect on these understandings . . . to accept, adapt, or resist them" (Wilhelm).

While it would probably be too much to try to teach all of these lessons together in one unit on *The Great Gatsby*, a few of them could be effectively combined into a unit. Each of the lessons is rich enough that any one could be worked into a focal or guiding framework for a unit on the novel.

Wilhelm (Chapter 3) makes the argument that in addition to promoting meaningful engagements with texts through teaching toward expertise and authorial reading, we can make "school reading more like real reading when we use literature as a way of pursuing larger inquiries." He provides several examples of essential questions for inquiry that would be appropriate for *The Great Gatsby*. One way I have used an essential question to frame the teaching of literature as inquiry is to have students grapple with a specific case or scenario before they begin reading *The Great Gatsby*. I ask them to work in small groups and then compare their ideas in whole-class discussion.

> Sunny Skye starred in five hit movies that made her a multi-millionaire by the time she was thirty-five years old. Raised by a single mother who worked cleaning office buildings twelve hours a day, Skye grew up in poverty. She worked hard in high school to receive a scholarship to a local state university. She received good grades but dropped out of the university after two years to pursue an acting career. Skye had three marriages that all ended in divorce. Several tabloid magazines have published stories about Skye's stints at rehabilitation facilities to deal with alcohol and drug abuse issues. Should Sunny Skye be considered a success? Has she led a successful life? Support your viewpoint with specific evidence.

As students discuss these questions, they debate if wealth equals success, if there is a difference between a successful career and a successful life, and if one has to fulfill the stereotype of a "perfect life" to be called a success.

Using a specific case that is accessible to students stimulates their thinking about the essential concept, prepares them for reading the novel, and makes it more relevant to their own lives. Students often return to the case and their views about it as they read. As an alternative, creating a set of five to eight cases, or scenarios, like these can increase the depth of the discussion and debate (see McCann, Thomas M., Johannessen, Larry R., Kahn, Elizabeth, & Flanagan, Joseph M. 2006. *Talking in Class: Using Discussion to Enhance Teaching and Learning*. NCTE. ISBN: 0-8141-5001-2). The lessons in this chapter could easily be embedded within a larger inquiry that, in Wilhelm's terms, makes students more likely to view their school reading as "real reading."

13 Illustrating and Illuminating Gatsby's Transformation

Sherry Medwin
Truman College

Purpose

This lesson series, which invites students to visually illustrate Gatsby's transformation from James Gatz to Jay Gatsby, will jumpstart an exploration of some of the novel's central problems as students mediate concrete particulars and complex abstractions, ultimately judging whether Gatsby is indeed "great." By exercising students' imaginations in addition to their analytical skills, the artistic interpretation taps into the novel's celebration of imagination—the capacity to wonder, invent, create.

Materials

Materials needed include newsprint, poster board, or blank paper, and markers; if computers with drawing/painting software are available, one for each of six small groups. Handouts include six copies (one per group) of the artistic interpretation task (Figure 13.1) and several copies of each of six M. C. Escher drawings. The drawings that I use are from the M.C. Escher website (www.mcescher.com), which posts a downloadable form for copyright privileges. They are taken from Escher's "Metamorphosis I 1937 woodcut printed on two sheets," "Metamorphosis II 1940 woodcut in black, green and brown, printed from 20 blocks on three combined sheets," and "Metamorphosis III 1967–68 woodcut printed from 33 blocks on six combined sheets." I make enough copies of the six Escher drawings so that each student can record a copy of one of the drawings.

Introduction

Navigating the first five chapters of *The Great Gatsby* is smooth sailing for many eleventh-grade readers who are drawn into the story of Nick's dubious introduction to the Long Island "eggs" and his often bizarre entanglement in the affairs of the "pursued" and the "pursuing." Invariably, though, they get stuck on the opening of Chapter 6, when Nick announces that "Jay Gatsby, of West Egg, Long Island, sprang from his Platonic conception of himself." In the past, my students' blank faces often prompted a brief lecture about Plato's philosophy of ideal forms, sometimes accompanied by an excerpt from the philosopher himself. But while the metaphysical side trip interested a few inquisitive readers, the foot-tapping and yawning sent me scrambling for a more accessible path, one that put students at the helm and steered a familiar course, channeling their creative energy into critical inquiry. After they have read the first six chapters of the novel, I invite my students to explore the transformation of James Gatz to Jay Gatsby, first by drawing it, then by debating it, and finally by writing about it.

To a seventeen-year-old, what is not captivating about change? Change is also the plot of adolescence, with students trying on the identities of different groups as they begin to pen their life script.

Avoiding mechanistic approaches that students can complete in front of the television—hunting for symbols, researching allusions, filling out study guides—the drawing assignment generates considerable enthusiasm ("Really?" "We get to draw?" "During our *English* period?"). At the same time, it compels students to confront some of this novel's most complex questions, including the mystery surrounding the colorful central character. "Even Gatsby could happen, without any particular wonder," Nick muses about the man who "came alive . . . delivered suddenly from the womb of his purposeless splendor." Fitzgerald baits the reader to trace the origins of the West Egg Wonder, heightening interest by having Gatsby say he is from San Francisco, which is part of the "Middle West." Riding Nick's rollercoaster of skepticism and faith, the reader cannot help but join in the fun of unraveling the mystery.

"Do you think Gatsby is a phony?" I asked one group who seemed to be arguing unproductively about some detail of their drawing.

"That's a no-brainer," they replied. "The question we're stuck on is whether he's a good phony or bad phony."

That Fitzgerald compresses the core of Gatsby's transformation into one chapter makes it easy for students to focus on the problem, read closely the illuminating details, and then, with broader brushstrokes, connect to the more general themes in the novel: the rags-to-riches archetype, the self-made man, the corruption of the American Dream, the confusion of idealism and opportunism.

Connections

Like Blau (Chapter 1) and Wilhelm (Chapter 3), I regard my classroom as a laboratory where students collaborate to solve a problem and test hypotheses through natural inquiry. The artistic interpretation at the heart of this assignment turns the classroom into just such a laboratory as students grapple with the problem of Gatsby. But it also adds a dimension of the art studio, since their transactions with Fitzgerald's text are invigorated by their need to create an artwork. That this work will soon be on public display in the classroom raises the stakes even higher.

After they have committed their ideas to their canvas, students eagerly read ahead, hoping to confirm their conceptions. One year, a student whose perfectionism often triggered anxiety episodes asked me to remove her group's pictogram—a cleverly designed game-board schematic depicting the moves Gatz made to become Gatsby. It featured the crooked roadblocks he had to cross, a "Get-out-of-jail-free" square occupied by Wolfsheim, and "elite" cards that he collected on his journey. After this conscientious student had finished reading the novel, she decided that her group was "way off" in representing Gatsby as a white-collar criminal. "He wasn't a bad guy," she told me before class began. "He was a victim." Although I sympathized with her change of heart, I refused to take down the picture. I reminded her that interpretation is fluid and tentative, an evolving and often recursive dynamic, a dance between the reader and writer that continues late into the night, long after the reader has put down the book. Giving students three approaches to the same problem—drawing, debate, and in-class writing—encourages the testing and revision of earlier hypotheses, letting students take the lead.

Activities

Phase I: The Drawing

As students walk into the room, I hand them photocopies of M. C. Escher drawings, each depicting one of six metamorphoses that will determine the groups to which they are randomly assigned. Infinitely intriguing, the drawings become conversation pieces, as students vie for status by arguing that their graphic is cooler than their classmate's.

I direct students to form their groups by teaming with those holding the same drawing. Each group then takes a few minutes to discuss its graphic before describing it to the rest of the class. Specifically, the students describe the objects in their picture that transform, the means of transformation, and the positive, negative, or neutral outcome of that transformation. For example, in one design a set of lines morphs into a chessboard and then a city, prompting students to evaluate whether the city represents progress from the initial line configuration. Most say it does, arguing that it is both more sophisticated and more practical than the line set. But the line-lovers also offer rigorous challenges. I recall one who pointed out that the infinite potential of the lines held greater promise than the finite city. Ah—a Gatsby protégé in the twenty-first century!

Beginning with a visual activity helps prime the pump for the visual representation of Gatsby they will be creating as well as introducing students to the idea that any transformation begs an evaluation. We then go on to discuss briefly other transformations, generating examples from popular culture. Latching on to the literal, students mention *Transformers* (robots in disguise), later volunteering such science fiction transformations as those featured in *The Fly* and *The Incredible Hulk*, or realistic dramas such as *Catch Me If You Can*, the story of a con artist who impersonates successful professionals, and *Boys Don't Cry*, the painfully brutal account of a young woman who pays dearly for her decision to live as a man. In each case we discuss what prompts the transformation (craving power, seeking love, fulfilling one's true identity) and the consequences of donning a disguise, assuming a new identity, and/or meddling with Mother Nature.

We end this discussion by considering how transformations are fueled by the power of wonder and imagination—either the author's or character's or both. To reinvent herself as the male Brandon Teena in *Boys Don't Cry*, for example, the female Teena Brandon harnessed an extraordinary imagination, as did Gatsby, who, as narrator Nick observes in Chapter 4, "could happen, without any particular wonder."

In the final minutes of the period, I read aloud the first two pages of Chapter 6, through the paragraph ending with "So he invented just the sort of Jay Gatsby that a seventeen year old boy would be likely to invent, and to this conception he was faithful to the end." For homework, as students finish reading Chapter 6, they are asked to highlight information relevant to Gatsby's transformation.

The next day, students reconvene in their groups, and I distribute copies of the group task (see Figure 13.1). I encourage students to communicate as much as they can through visual images but allow them to add small bits of text to clarify any part of their illustration. To hold individual group members accountable and to maximize the cooperative learning benefits, I suggest the following roles for group members: one illustrator, two fact-finders/evidence-checkers (who verify that every

> Based on your reading of the first six chapters of *The Great Gatsby*, and with particular attention to the details illuminated in Chapter 6, illustrate in a drawing or pictogram the transformation of James Gatz to Jay Gatsby. Your drawing should highlight the following:
>
> 1. The essential differences between James Gatz and Jay Gatsby
> 2. The cause(s) of the change
> 3. The characters and circumstances that influenced his transformation
> 4. The consequences of the transformation, especially the gains and losses
> 5. Other characters' reactions to the transformation
> 6. An evaluation of the change: Was it for better or for worse? Is Jay Gatsby a better man than James Gatz was?

Figure 13.1. Artistic interpretation.

interpretation informing the drawing can be backed up by the text), and one discussion director, who mediates between the illustrator and fact-finders as well as facilitates discussion. Students typically take a full class period to complete their illustrations, which range from scratchy stick figures to stunning Picasso-inspired portraits.

Phase II: The Debate

On Day 3, students hang their drawings on the wall (or computer monitor) and, after taking a ten-minute museum walk around the room to examine every group's work, they prepare a response to the following debate prompt:

Resolved: James Gatz never should have become Jay Gatsby. Agree or Disagree?

After writing on the topic for five minutes, students choose whether to sit on the Affirmative or Negative side of the room, no longer tied to their groups. As they debate the issue, they refer to the illustrations on the wall (or computer screens), often pointing directly to some feature on the drawing to clinch their point. For example, if a group has represented Jay Gatsby as a mobster in its drawing, a debater could exploit that image to support an affirmative position. If students run out of ammunition during the debate, the teacher can always play devil's advocate or toss in a few incisive questions (e.g., Is one better off for having loved and lost than never to have loved at all? Did he change just to win the woman, or was the woman merely his means of reaching another goal? To what extent was Gatsby a victim of his society? What side would Nick Carraway take in this debate? And does his point of view matter?). Because students have already staked a position in their graphic interpretation, the debates often become heated.

Over the next week, students finish reading the novel, actively seeking new evidence that would support or overturn the position they took in the debate and the interpretation they represented in their drawing.

Assessment

Group Assessment

Using a simple rubric, I evaluate each group's drawing for the effectiveness (not artistry) of its design and thoughtfulness of its visual interpretation (i.e., Have they attended to key details relative to the central problem of Gatsby's transformation?).

Self-Assessment

After the debate, students reconvene in their groups to complete a self-assessment of their drawing. Now that they have seen the other five groups' graphic interpretations, heard multiple perspectives in the debate, and finished reading the novel, they are ready to revisit their drawing and reflect on the following questions: What features of your drawing are most consistent with your understanding of the novel? If you could revise your drawing at this point, what features would you add or change? Why? In what ways did this artistic challenge facilitate and/or distort your understanding of the novel?

Individual Written Assessment

The final assessment is an in-class essay on the following question: Is Fitzgerald's title meant literally or ironically? Is Gatsby truly "great," or is Fitzgerald poking fun at his "greatness"? Directed to draw evidence from their books, from the illustrations on the wall, and from their notes from the debate, students have a full period in which to compose a thoughtful, well-organized argument defending their claim. I will often give them an extra day to revise the essay, if time permits.

Considerations

Year after year, this assignment proves to be among students' favorites. To be fair, most eleventh graders enthusiastically read *The Great Gatsby* anyway, compelled by its romantic trysts and understated violence, intrigued by its anything-can-happen possibilities. Many admire Fitzgerald's style, and all appreciate the novel's brevity. Perhaps because students' imaginations have been flattened by an army of Venn diagrams, study guides, vocabulary lists, and selected-response tests, they jump at any opportunity for invention. A blank piece of paper, a few markers, and a group of peers—what could be more inviting?

Ideally, students should be turned loose with the open canvas and the task directions, free to generate questions about Gatsby's transformations. When I tried this approach one year with an accelerated class, however, most groups finished their drawing in fifteen minutes, disappointingly content with a literal depiction of a farm boy morphing into a polished preppie. The next year, I added the prereading activity with the Escher drawings to help build a schema for transformation. And what a difference that made. The illustrations were a bit more chaotic but far more nuanced as students began to incorporate causes and effects of Gatz's conversion. One group even featured Nick in the centerfold and Gatz / Gatsby off to the side, demonstrating that the reader understands Gatsby's transformation only through Nick's perception. A couple of groups a few years apart, determined to get right the notion of Gatsby "springing from his Platonic conception," looked up the term and asked me for clarification. They then proceeded to draw an adult-sized Gatsby hatching from a dinosaur-like egg that lay in a nest over which sat farm boy James Gatz. Although Plato and Fitzgerald surely stirred underground, I saw this as a golden opportunity.

Reluctantly, I added the six guiding requirements a few years ago when students—and parents—came to expect meticulous rubrics to ensure students' successful completion of a task. This presented a bit of conundrum for me, as it usually does, since anticipating every facet of the final product will necessarily constrict kids' imaginations. Still, when they know what matters in the final analysis, they are less likely to ask, "Is this good enough?" In keeping the requirements open-ended, I tried to maintain some quality control over students' work without choking their creativity.

14 Analyzing F. Scott Fitzgerald's Diction and Word Choice in *The Great Gatsby*

Asra Syed
James B. Conant High School, Hoffman Estates, Illinois

Purpose

At the beginning of Chapter 2 of *The Great Gatsby,* narrator Nick Carraway offers an unflattering description of Myrtle's sister, Catherine: "Her eyebrows had been plucked and then drawn on again at a more rakish angle but the efforts of nature toward the restoration of the old alignment gave a blurred air to her face." Year after year, I find the description absolutely hilarious. Phrases such as "rakish angle" and "the restoration of the old alignment" help me enjoy Nick's complex, roundabout way of saying how ridiculous Catherine looked because she had penciled on fake eyebrows without regard to where her own eyebrows were growing back. After first noticing it for its humor, I also recognized that this description shows Nick's judgmental, haughty character and his penchant for details and highlights the recurring problem of phoniness.

Most students skip over this minor detail during their first read. However, they tend to be amused by it when I share with them my enjoyment of Nick's subtle, arrogant humor. Consequently, they too start to pick up on such details for themselves.

Through interpreting Fitzgerald's diction and word choice while reading independently, students have their own experiences with the novel and grasp the text for themselves. By approaching the text in this way, students hone their literary analysis skills.

Materials

I use two handouts, "Analyzing Fitzgerald's Diction" (Figure 14.1) and "Final Assessment" (Figure 14.2).

Introduction

When students first approach the concept of diction, they typically have some difficulty. They often want to think of diction as simply a literary technique that an author uses, similar to a metaphor or personification. They fall into the trap of saying, "The author uses diction in this passage when he describes Daisy's eyes," just as one may say, "Fitzgerald uses a metaphor with the broken clock on Nick's mantle," or "The author uses personification when describing how the Buchanans' lawn was 'jumping over sun-dials.'"

Another problem students have is oversimplifying an analysis of diction, thinking it is simply any words the author employs, using "diction" and "word choice" interchangeably: "Fitzgerald's diction is significant with his use of the word 'imitation' to describe Gatsby's house." They do not understand that diction involves understanding the complex tone that an author achieves through a pattern of intentionally chosen, related words and phrases.

Teaching students how to analyze diction is not merely a path to getting students to understand literary jargon. Learning to analyze diction helps them to read *The Great Gatsby* incisively and interpret the complex meaning of the text. Perhaps even more significantly, approaching a piece of literature this way makes them more capable of independently analyzing and enjoying the depth of other literature.

Connections

In designing this lesson series, I wanted to "assist student readers to master techniques for thinking through and responding to the meanings of texts, first by respecting the author and how [he] constructed the text" (Wilhelm, Chapter 3) and to engage students "in the more serious intellectual enterprise of thoughtfully unpacking a difficult text or constructing a meaningful interpretation of what they have read" (Blau, Chapter 1). I share Moore's belief (Chapter 5) that students must learn that there is no single correct interpretation of a text, so I want my instruction to allow for pluralistic interpretations and to value students finding their own interpretations. By introducing my favorite elements (such as Nick's description of Myrtle's sister, Catherine), I attempt to lure students into the enticing parts of the text that go beyond the surface level.

Activities

Before assigning independent reading of the novel, I read and discuss with students the first two pages of Chapter 1, which could be described as Nick's prologue. We look at only those pages for an entire class period, picking apart every sentence and deciphering what it tells us about our narrator. We especially look at the words he has chosen to introduce himself and Gatsby. This process does require some simple summary: Nick found himself the recipient of unsolicited information about his classmates during his college years, and to avoid further revelations, he often pretended to be asleep or annoyed with them as they tried to divulge their secrets. But I encourage students not to merely summarize; I ask them to thoroughly consider the phrases Nick uses to tell us this information. For example, students sometimes point out how he "feigned sleep, preoccupation or a hostile levity." Also, immediately after telling us, "I'm inclined to reserve all judgments," Nick calls his classmates "curious natures" and "veteran bores," comparing the "abnormal mind" of his classmates to himself, "a normal person." Some students recognize Nick's unintended display of arrogance and hypocrisy, which he somewhat admits later when he says he "snobbishly repeats" advice given to him by his father.

I also have students examine Nick's description of Gatsby. Why would Nick put forth that Gatsby "represented everything for which I have an unaffected scorn" and still say "there was something gorgeous about him"? A few students realize that Nick introduces Gatsby with contradictory and ambiguous descriptions. He does not say he found Gatsby likeable or endearing; instead, he clarifies that Gatsby's "personality is an unbroken series of successful gestures," which students note is a more confusing yet revealing description of the title character. They initially conclude that this description is meant to depict Gatsby as a phony, someone who gives off the right impression, but may be trying too hard. Yet they also note the reverent diction Nick uses to describe Gatsby throughout this passage, such as his possessing "an extraordinary gift for hope, a romantic readiness such as I have never found in any other person and which it is not likely I shall ever find again." Dissecting the novel's first segment gives students a good grasp of the title character, of the narrator, and of the narrator's strong feelings toward the title character. Moreover, this discussion demonstrates for the students the depth at which they will be considering diction and word choice throughout the novel.

After this discussion, I give them the assignment "Analyzing Fitzgerald's Diction" (Figure 14.1), which accompanies their nightly independent reading. While they read the novel independently, I expect students to do this assignment for every chapter, which is feasible since

---

Analyzing Fitzgerald's Diction

F. Scott Fitzgerald's diction is anything but accidental. Therefore, pay attention to the words he chooses and his desired effect. As you read each chapter, write two paragraphs analyzing examples where you find the word choice particularly noteworthy. Incorporate the specific word(s) smoothly within your paragraph. Make sure you explain the significance and Fitzgerald's intended effect and do not merely summarize plot.

Remember to use the word *diction* when you are writing about similar clusters of words and phrases, not just a word choice.

Here are examples that might help you as you think about writing an analysis of an author's diction and word choice.

Sample #1

Nick's condescending diction in describing his response to others' secrets shows his true character. Nick says that "frequently I have feigned sleep, preoccupation or a hostile levity when I realized by some unmistakable sign that an intimate revelation was quivering on the horizon" (5–6). Especially by indicating that he acts with "hostile levity" he expresses how arrogant yet cowardly he can be. With "hostile" behavior, he manages to express his true nature to the reader while hiding it from his peers behind his "levity," a jokingly mean demeanor. He's cruel, but he's careful not to let them know, which means he doesn't offend people whom he doesn't seem to like anyway. His criticism of his peers is obvious when he says "an intimate revelation was quivering" instead of "near" or "coming." With the word "quivering" Nick indicates sarcastically that these secrets he found so annoying seemed crucial to the person exposing them.

Sample #2

When Nick explains his father's advice to reserve judgments, his haughty nature comes forth. Nick expresses the idea that "a sense of the fundamental decencies is parceled out unequally at birth" (6). His choice to use "fundamental" in describing "decencies" makes Nick appear contradictory. He makes a point of describing these decencies as essential, but he says people aren't equally moral. This phrase makes Nick appear overly critical of others who don't have decency even as he discusses his attempt to not be judgmental.

Figure 14.1. Analyzing Fitzgerald's Diction handout.

the book has only nine chapters. This assignment offers a more meaningful alternative to pop quizzes or other ways to check that students are keeping up with the reading. My feedback on each paragraph they complete yields different levels of improvement. On a mechanical level, they get much better at incorporating evidence smoothly into their writing, by better punctuating and inserting partial quotes into the writing. On a deeper level, instead of merely explaining the evidence they include—which at first is often little more than plot summary—we work on expressing *how* the evidence makes a meaningful commentary. For example, if a student chooses the lines, "The truth was that Jay Gatsby,

of West Egg, Long Island, sprang from his Platonic conception of himself
. . . . So he invented just the sort of Jay Gatsby that a seventeen year
old boy would be likely to invent, and to this conception he was faithful to the end," she would not simply explain that this passage shows
how Gatsby was a self-created man. She would also note the effect of
Fitzgerald's repetition of the words "conception" and "invent." With
these words, Fitzgerald emphasizes how the character formulated a
specific notion of what he intended to become and perhaps that he in
fact conceived this idea. This proves that Jay Gatsby is not merely a man
trying too hard or changing himself in some way or another, but that
Gatsby is an entirely new entity separate from who he was previously.

This nightly independent reading and writing assignment enhances the class discussions because students' choices of passages lead
to exploration of important themes. It works whether I assign group
presentations comparing and contrasting the different homes and parties Nick visits; or if students are engaging in Socratic seminars on time
and weather symbolism in the novel or on the failure of the American
Dream; or if they are acting out and discussing the intense hotel scene.
Through this method, they become close readers and notice subtle details
of the text, thereby developing their own analytical abilities.

Assessment

After completing our work on the novel, to assess students' growth in
their ability to analyze diction, I give them the final assessment (Figure
14.2). At this point students have completed the assignment nine times
and also applied the skills during in-class discussions. I look for growth
in their ability to discuss diction and word choice by comparing their
writing early in the sequence to their writing at the end. Most students
become more sophisticated in their ability to identify and explain the
effect of the author's diction and to support their viewpoint with specific
evidence from the text.

Considerations

I have successfully used this approach with both "average-level" juniors
in American Literature and juniors in AP Language and Composition.
Students have told me that it is because of this experience they develop much greater confidence in their ability to analyze texts without
guidance from me. Although we tackle diction and word choice with

---

Final Assessment

Choose <u>one</u> of the following passages. Write a well-constructed paragraph with a solid assertion explaining the significance of Fitzgerald's diction. You shouldn't merely explain/analyze the passage. Instead, make sure to consider the specific words the author chooses and the effect produced by those choices. Identify diction through the pattern of intentionally chosen, related words and phrases.

1. "If personality is an unbroken series of successful gestures, then there was something gorgeous about him, some heightened sensitivity to the promises of life. . . . This responsiveness had nothing to do with that flabby impressionability which is dignified under the name of the 'creative temperament'—it was an extraordinary gift for hope, a romantic readiness such as I have never found in any other person and which it is not likely I shall ever find again" (6).

2. "No—Gatsby turned out all right at the end; it is what preyed on Gatsby, what foul dust floated in the wake of his dreams that temporarily closed out my interest in the abortive sorrows and short-winded elations of men" (6).

3. "There must have been moments even that afternoon when Daisy tumbled short of his dreams—not through her own fault but because of the colossal vitality of his illusion. It had gone beyond her, beyond everything. . . . No amount of fire or freshness can challenge what a man will store up in his ghostly heart" (101).

4. "The truth was that Jay Gatsby, of West Egg, Long Island, sprang from his Platonic conception of himself. . . . So he invented just the sort of Jay Gatsby that a seventeen year old boy would be likely to invent, and to this conception he was faithful to the end" (104).

5. "[Gatsby] was left with [Dan Cody's] singularly appropriate education; the vague contour of Jay Gatsby had filled out to the substantiality of a man" (101).

Figure 14.2. Final Assessment handout.

a fictional text, they easily translate this skill to the nonfiction they encounter in later units and on the AP exam. The process enables them to improve their ability to analyze many of the author's rhetorical choices, not merely word choices.

15 The Great American Novel Is Not the Great American Film: Using Film Excerpts to Teach Visual Literacy

M. Elizabeth Kenney
Stevenson High School, Lincolnshire, Illinois

Purpose

The Great Gatsby is perhaps the most widely taught novel in American literature classrooms, and with good reason: lyrical beauty, compelling characters, a complex exploration of the American Dream—all that and it's short! However, the aspects that make the novel teachable are not always the same qualities that make the novel worth teaching. Students are fascinated by the outsized characters, the potboiler of a plot. However, the aspects that have earned the novel its place in the canon—the elegiac tone, the ambivalent dissection of the American Dream—are not as easy for young readers to access.

The novel has presented a similar problem for those who have tried to adapt the story for film. At least four versions exist on film, beginning with a 1926 silent film made scarcely a year after Fitzgerald's novel was published; followed by a mostly forgotten 1949 film with Alan Ladd as Gatsby and Shelley Winters as Myrtle; the much-ballyhooed 1974 production directed by Jack Clayton based on a script by Francis Ford Coppola and starring Robert Redford, Mia Farrow, and Sam Waterston; and a made-for-TV version in 2000 that featured Paul Rudd as Nick. Few people even know that the 2000 adaptation exists. (As I write this, *Variety* reports that Australian director Baz Luhrmann, known for flamboyant films such as *Moulin Rouge, Romeo + Juliet*, and *Australia*, has acquired the rights to the novel and is planning his own adaptation. Stay tuned!)

These films are mostly mediocre: They faithfully depict the pulp-fiction plot and render the 1920s fashion and the extravagances in gorgeous detail. But the films fail because, in the end, it is not the plot and characters that make this novel a classic, but rather Fitzgerald's evocative language, and this is much harder to translate into a visual medium.

The 1974 and 2000 film adaptations of *The Great Gatsby* are readily available to teachers. Although neither film is particularly successful as a film, both can be useful in the classroom for helping students grasp the wealth of the main characters and the scale of their extravagance, as well as to explore the purpose of the opening, the meaning surrounding Gatsby's death, and the tone of Fitzgerald's novel. What follows are several distinct activities that can be used separately or together to enrich students' understanding of the novel and to develop their visual literacy.

Materials

Teachers will need copies of two film versions of *The Great Gatsby*: the 1974 film directed by Jack Clayton and starring Robert Redford, Mia Farrow, and Sam Waterston and the 2000 production that aired on A&E.

Introduction

As literature teachers, we are often ambivalent about using film in class. We recognize that today's students live in a media-saturated world and that they need our help to become savvy consumers of the visual media, and we know the powerful effect film can have in the classroom. Students respond to the power of the visual medium: sometimes a two-minute clip from a movie can do more to make a setting come alive than ten pages of expository prose (or ten minutes of our explication of that prose). And yet, we worry that the film is doing the hard work for our kids. If students have access to a film adaptation of our text, what will motivate them to read? Furthermore, we realize that, as powerful as film is, it is impossible for a ninety-minute feature film to contain all of the complexity of a 300-page novel, and so we are almost inevitably disappointed with film adaptations. They rob us of the pleasure of creating our own vision of the characters and settings, and they almost always leave out something we consider essential to the novel.

Too often, then, film has been used as "dessert," a treat to offer students *after* doing the hard work of reading a novel. This approach leads to passive viewing, doing little to improve students' visual literacy and even less to help them understand the novel. Even when teachers want to make the study of film worth the class time it takes, it can be difficult to create meaningful assessments. We do not want our class to be reduced to simplistic "Which did you like better?" or even "How faithful was the movie to the novel?" (I would dread reading a stack of those essays!)

Connections

As Wilhelm points out in this text (Chapter 3), many students who regularly engage with popular texts such as video games, fanfiction, manga, fantasy, and horror "cannot identify a single engaging or meaningful text that they have read in school." He argues that we need to "use interactive strategies that meet kids' current needs for activity, engagement, personal relevance, and social as well as disciplinary significance—and that develop and use imagination." One way to meaningfully engage students in a complex text such as *The Great Gatsby* is to create classroom activities that take advantage of the power of film to orient students in an unfamiliar world but bring them back to the novel, not away from it. We want our students' experience with film to deepen their experience with the source text, not simplify it.

Activities

Activity 1: Using the Opening to Establish Tone

Probably the best part of the 1974 film is the opening montage. On the screen we see large, gorgeous rooms, all empty; on the soundtrack we hear music and the sound of parties, as if heard from a distance. The contrast between the visuals and the sound creates a dissonance, suggesting a remembrance of something that has been lost. The camera then finds a scrapbook with pictures of Daisy and pans over several beautiful and beloved objects. Among these lovely objects is a half-eaten sandwich with a fly resting on it. It is a subtle image, one that you might miss on first viewing, but is fascinating once you notice. The 2000 version uses a different approach, combining Nick's narration with images of Gatsby floating in his pool. From an underwater camera we see a shadowy figure walk up to the edge of the pool; we hear a shot ring out, and then another. The camera holds for a long time on an abstract shot of the water, and then we move into a flashback that constitutes the bulk of the movie. I use one or both versions to explore the peculiar way Fitzgerald opens his novel.

- I begin by leading a discussion: What is the author's task in the opening pages of a book? What is a filmmaker's task in the opening minutes of a movie? How are the two tasks similar? How are they different?

- Then we view the first four minutes of the 1974 film. I tell the students we will watch the clip twice; the first time they just watch, not take notes. The second time through, they list images they see on screen.

- After watching for the second time, students consider the following questions: Close your eyes: Which image do you recall most vividly? Open your eyes: In your notes, select two or three particularly vivid images and describe what you remember about them.

- I then lead a discussion about which images were vivid and what made them so. If students do not bring up the image of the half-eaten sandwich, I point it out to them. Why has the filmmaker included this image? How does its placement with the other objects alter our understanding of them?

- Now we discuss what we *hear* in this sequence. What distinct sounds are included on the soundtrack? How has the sound been manipulated, and what effect does this have? What is the connection between what we see and what we hear? What is the effect of the contrast? Imagine someone going to the movies in 1974, someone who has not read the novel. What sort of movie would they expect after this opening? What tone does the opening montage create?

- Students then reread the first two pages of Fitzgerald's novel, up to the break after Nick declares that "Gatsby was all right in the end." To what extent is this a conventional one for a novel? Does it give us the information we expect to get in the first two pages of a novel? What is the tone of this passage? What sort of book does it lead us to expect? To what extent has the opening of the film captured the tone of Fitzgerald's opening?

Optional variation: After screening the 1974 opening montage and discussing the first two pages of the novel, I show the first two minutes of the 2000 version and compare the two versions. (Remember: The opening sequence of the A&E version constitutes a spoiler for those who have not yet finished the book, so this version should only be used if students have finished reading the book.)

- The following questions provoke class discussion: To what extent does this sequence "give away" the ending of the movie? To what extent does Fitzgerald "give away" the end of the novel in his opening? What effect does this hint have on the readers and viewers?

- The openings of the two movies are very different, and yet both of them combine images of beauty with something that disrupts this beauty. Which opening is closer to the tone of Fitzgerald's opening?

Activity 2: Depicting Tragedy

Perhaps the most artful sequence in the 2000 film depicts Gatsby's and Wilson's death. Interestingly, this is a scene in which Fitzgerald's prose is relatively straightforward. This contrast can lead to a discussion of the importance of Fitzgerald's language.

- Before screening, students reread the passage in which Fitzgerald narrates Gatsby's (and Wilson's) death, beginning with "At two o'clock Gatsby put on his bathing suit" and ending at the end of the chapter with "the holocaust was complete." Students then write about what is essential about this scene. What would be important for a filmmaker to "get right" if adapting this for the screen? Which elements would be easy to translate to a visual medium? What would be challenging to film?

- Students receive a brief list of film techniques that would be available to them as filmmakers, and I then ask which of these they might use to film this sequence. These terms might include the following:

  - Light tells us where to look. Contrast between light and dark can create a mood.

  - Color can be saturated or de-saturated. Color creates emotional associations and sometimes symbolic meaning.

  - Arrangement refers to the physical relationships between objects and people in a shot.

  - All objects exist in a frame. When there is a frame within a frame, our eye is drawn into the frame and emphasis is created.

  - Placement refers to the position of the camera relative to the subject. A high camera angle makes the subject look small and vulnerable. A low camera angle can make a subject look big and powerful and can elevate the importance of an object. A close-up emphasizes the importance of an object or can help us feel the emotion of a character. Medium shots emphasize relationships between characters. Long shots are used to establish a setting.

  - When the camera moves, it usually reveals information that we did not have. When the camera moves in closer to a subject, we notice details we did not notice before. When the camera pulls away from a subject, we may discover people or objects are present that we did not know were present. The camera can pan left and right, it can tilt up and down, or it can travel through space on a dolly or on a crane.

  - Voice-over is a technique in which we hear the voice of a person who is not on screen. This may be a character in the story, or it may be an anonymous narrator. Voice-over can reveal the inner thoughts of a character or provide an objective point of view.

- Flashback is a technique in which we see images or a scene that we understand to have happened at some point in the past.

■ I then screen the three-minute scene that begins with a close-up of the phone. A crane shot moves back from the phone to survey the whole scene of Gatsby's pool, followed by a flashback montage of Gatsby and Daisy's relationship. There is a long shot, a spinning camera, and close-ups of cufflinks and blood falling through the water. There is a lovely moving camera shot that travels from Gatsby's foot up to his body, revealing the fatal wound, then travels to reveal Wilson's lifeless body, then captures Nick running onto the scene and discovering the tragedy. We then cut to a high overhead shot (a bird's-eye view) that offers an extremely unnatural perspective. (Teachers can tell curious students that the cufflinks are a leitmotiv in the film, a gift given to Gatsby by Daisy in a dance scene that has no counterpart in the novel.)

■ Students watch the scene twice, once without taking notes, the second time jotting down whatever techniques they notice. I then lead a discussion about the techniques students noticed and their effect on the viewer. Students sometimes struggle to explain *why* a filmmaker made a particular choice but are able to discuss what *effect* the choice has on us as viewers.

■ We then discuss the extent to which both the novel and the film offer the same perspective on Gatsby's death, and to what extent each offers a distinct impression of his death.

■ Optional: I sometimes screen the same scene in the 1974 film (which runs approximately four minutes, is a little more graphic, but is a little less abstract than the 2000 version). Students then compare the two scenes.

Assessment

I assess students' understanding of the relationship between text and adaptation either informally (collecting and evaluating the responses to the activities above) or I may use a more formal writing assignment, such as the following.

> To what extent are the writer and the filmmaker using the tools of their medium to convey the same idea? To what extent are they using their art forms to convey different ideas about Gatsby and the meaning of his life and death? First, decide whether you think the book and film are expressing the same or different ideas about

Gatsby. Then discuss each separately, identifying specific stylistic choices made by the writer and filmmaker to convey these ideas.

Considerations

Most of our students spend much more time watching movies and other visual media than they do reading books. And yet they lack the practice and vocabulary to analyze the visual media with which they are so familiar. By giving students a basic vocabulary for describing filmmakers' choices, I find students can readily learn to analyze the effect of these choices. By harnessing the natural appeal of film, I help students learn to analyze complex works of literature.

16 Analyzing Symbols and Motifs in *The Great Gatsby*

Sarah Rosas
Oak Park and River Forest High School, Illinois

Purpose

The purpose of this lesson series is to improve students' close reading skills and to increase students' facility in analyzing literary motifs and symbolism. *The Great Gatsby*, with its themes, stylistic grace, and intriguing characters, offers a rich context for this study and the development of student skills.

Materials

Required materials include sheets of blank paper, an assortment of colored pencils and markers, and two handouts, "Example of a Motif Web" (Figure 16.1) and "Example of a Double-Entry Journal" (Figure 16.2). Computer access facilitates some of the activities.

Introduction

I find that my students can relate to Jay Gatsby's story: They have tremendous dreams for themselves and root for Gatsby despite his flaws. After all, he is the underdog, and they want to see him succeed. As a result of their empathy, students become critical of social stratification and the American Dream; they begin to question their places in society and what is possible for them and others. Through their close examination of the text, students also see beyond the plot to the beauty and complexity of literature. They develop a deeper appreciation of the author's craft and understand what Fitzgerald meant when he proclaimed, "I want to write something *new*—something extraordinary and beautiful and simple and intricately patterned." Perhaps most important, they see literature as accessible to them, not reserved only for adults or teachers or academics.

The Great Gatsby is a story for everyone, and my students feel a sense of accomplishment when they have finished the novel.

This lesson engages students in close reading and examination of a symbol or motif in *Gatsby* by having them create a double entry journal. Close reading can be difficult for high school students because they can become lost in the text. There is so much in the text that they have difficulty zeroing in on significant and relevant passages. Using a double entry journal helps them to focus on salient passages and better enables them to draw connections among those passages.

Connections

Blau in his essay (Chapter 1) laments that students typically come to literature classes expecting their teachers to provide them with interpretations that they can record in their notebooks and draw on later as they write papers and exams, and that far too often teachers fulfill these expectations. He calls this result "false knowledge" and argues instead for methods that foster authentic learning. This lesson is designed to help students acquire what Blau calls direct knowledge through activities that support them as they learn to unpack a difficult text and construct thoughtful, meaningful interpretations of what they read.

Activities

Before we begin reading the novel, I assign each student one symbol or motif. I use a list that includes poor driving, window views (looking out and looking in), Gatsby's car(s), pearl necklace, the letter, lights, water, white, yellow, red, blue, green, crème, silver and gold, pink, grey, Airedale puppy, Owl Eyes, Doctor T. J. Eckleburg, Meyer Wolfsheim's cufflinks, the green light/the green card, shadows, clocks, East Egg, West Egg, Valley of the Ashes, downtown New York, kissing. I make these assignments based on students' reading level, interests, and frustration level. I want all the students to find success and challenge in this assignment, so I spend a good amount of time deciding on appropriate matches. An alternative, however, is to let students select the symbol or motif that catches their interest.

After students have their symbol, they brainstorm for a few minutes in class everything they can think of regarding that symbol. I often model the process by using the fire motif and asking the students to contribute while we make a list on the board. Usually the list includes "flames," "fireplace," "hearth and home," "warmth," "destruction,"

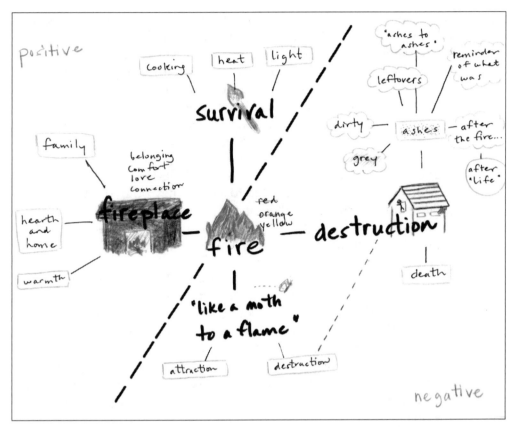

Figure 16.1. Student example of a Web motif.

"danger," "smoke," "ashes," "forest fire," "smoldering," and other related topics.

Next, students use their brainstorm list as a springboard for creating a graphic web. I remind the students that authors play on the reader's background knowledge. They count on us to bring our experience to reading. Therefore, this activity helps them activate their prior knowledge and their associations with the symbol before they delve into the novel and look for connections as they read. For this assignment, students organize and add to the ideas they generated from the previous day's brainstorming. I also ask them to incorporate color and images. This activity is a good way to get them thinking about imagery and to prepare them for analyzing the multiple ways Fitzgerald incorporates his motifs. I also provide my students with a sample—again, using the fire motif—to get them started (see Figure 16.1).

Students who have Doctor T. J. Eckleburg or Meyer Wolfsheim's cufflinks, for example, may ask how they can come up with anything for these motifs without having read the novel. I suggest that they use their imagination and focus on associations with "doctor" or "cufflinks" and also associations they have with the sound of the names.

It is at this point that we begin reading Chapter 1 together. As we read and discuss, I remind students that part of their active reading includes keeping track of references to their respective motifs/symbols. As a class we look for those that appear early in the text. For example, students often notice the "foul dust" that floats in the wake of Gatsby's dream and wonder if it is related to ashes. They point out the "red and gold" volumes on Nick's shelf and Nick's statement that "life is much more successfully looked at <u>from a single window</u>." Most students recognize the "bizarre and not a little sinister contrast" between West Egg and the "white palaces" of East Egg.

After about three chapters, I introduce the double entry journal, which consists of two columns so that students can make dual entries. In the left-hand column, they record passages that refer to their symbols of study. On the right, they explicate, each time drawing a conclusion about what they think the symbol may represent (see Figure 16.2). The right-hand column is a place for them to think—in writing. There they pose questions and make connections to the brainstorm and web from the beginning of the unit, as well as connections among the quotations they have chosen.

While the double entry journal could certainly be kept in a notebook, I have found it is easier and more beneficial to teach the students to create tables on the computer. Keeping a Word document enables students to add to their journals at any time, freeing them from that "final draft" feeling. After all, the goal is for their thinking to change and evolve as they progress through the novel.

As we continue reading *Gatsby*, I collect the students' journals in progress. These regular checks keep them on track, enable me to gauge their understanding, and provide an opportunity for quick and specific feedback. I also like to schedule some time in the computer lab so that I can watch their thought processes unfold and have discussions as needed.

Finally, based on their double entry journals, the students lead a whole-class discussion once we have finished reading the novel. I set aside a class period so that they can talk about what they have learned and ask each other questions. Each student has become an expert, and

Quotation	Explication
"The lawn started at the beach and ran toward the front door for a quarter of a mile, jumping over sun-dials and brick walks and **burning gardens**—finally when it reached the house drifting up the side in bright vines as though from the momentum of its run" (Fitzgerald 11).	In this description of Daisy and Tom's home, their lawn starts at the beach and jumps over "burning gardens." If the gardens burn, there must be some sort of destruction; there can be no life in a burning garden. It is significant, however, that their lawn jumps over this. Perhaps they will be safe from any destruction. Their lives will remain intact.
"'Why *candles*?' objected Daisy frowning. She snapped them out with her fingers" (17).	This only reiterates the idea in the previous quotation. Not only are the Buchanans safe from fire, but it also seems that Daisy is able to put out fire without burning herself. Does she control the fire? Can she save people from the fire?

Figure 16.2. Example of a double-entry journal.

during the class discussion, they explore the interconnectedness of their study and inevitably leave with a greater understanding of their symbols and motifs.

Assessment

I assess students in three ways: their completed double entry journals, their contributions to our whole-class discussion, and a final essay in which they explain what they have learned through their study and how that amplifies a theme of the novel. As an alternative to an essay, I may ask students to rework their initial webs to reflect Fitzgerald's use of the symbol or motif in the novel and its relationship to a theme. The completed journals—which they have added to and revised over the course of our study—are finished with a cover page. The cover must include an image that represents the symbol/motif of study, one with significant meaning about the text. I am always stunned by some of the covers I receive. It serves as a great place for the students to use their creativity and talents, while demonstrating their knowledge. For example, one student who focused on the color red filled the cover page with an intricate design of different words related to *red* printed in a variety of fonts and sizes—all in red ink. Students receive a grade based on the completion of all the assignment parts and the quality of products.

Considerations

This lesson series works because it encourages students to be responsible for their learning, while still providing the support they need. Rather than my making meaning of the students' reading, the double entry journal serves as a mechanism through which they can test their ideas. Because it is always a work in progress, it frees the students from feeling as if they "have to get it right." Instead, they rely on the skills we have practiced in reading previous texts and apply them to *Gatsby*. It also provides me with ample opportunities to support student learning in both group and individual settings, and in the end it builds student confidence and skill.

That said, some students feel daunted for part of our study. They look to me for answers, and when I insist that they will find answers as they read and reflect, they feel at a loss. They do not yet trust themselves, thinking that understanding great literature is reserved for a few and certainly not for them. It can be difficult for them to depend on themselves and each other to make meaning, but they always prevail and become better, more confident students as a result of engaging in these activities.

V Lesson Plans for *Adventures of Huckleberry Finn*

Elizabeth A. Callahan
Chapel Hill High School, North Carolina

The never-ending controversy over Mark Twain's *Adventures of Huckleberry Finn* is sufficient reason to keep the American classic in the repertoire of the American literature classroom. Our first words about the novel should be: "Students! The book we are about to read has offended many, been banned in numerous schools, burned, and created heated arguments across our nation!" Without a doubt, heads will come off desks, spines will unfurl, and brains will flicker on.

If parents, religious leaders, politicians, and teachers have a wide array of opinions about the novel, we can guarantee that high school students will be drawn into this debate. As any teacher knows, a controversial topic generally means students will become engaged; each student will want to make his or her opinion heard. Developmentally, secondary students are learning to formulate ideas and are eager to argue about these ideas. Their newly acquired skill in argumentation is fun, compelling, and, therefore, should be harnessed in the classroom. Huck Finn's journey can become the ideal vehicle for discussing and digesting social expectations of the present and past, understanding literary elements such as satire, and exploring the breathing, personal lives of both characters and our students.

The lessons in this section focus on engaging students in real, self-directed learning. Each teacher presents lessons that engage, encourage, challenge, and inspire young students. Echoing the book's five literary theorists, the contributing teachers want to transcend the mundane by broadening the weaponry of language arts teachers. They offer lessons that incorporate screenplay writing, contemporary films and literature, formal letter writing, and oral debate. The pedagogical stances of the teachers clearly create interactive and energetic classrooms through their strong lessons.

Jago (Chapter 2) encourages us: "If we want students to read and respond to American literature, we will need to persuade them that what can be found between the lines in the stories of Mark Twain, John Steinbeck, F. Scott Fitzgerald, Rudolfo Anaya, and Toni Morrison is important and enduring." The ingenuity of Mark Twain is abundantly clear in creating Huck Finn, a lasting character. Huck is totally relatable; he is the early embodiment of present, discontent teens. His actions, thoughts, dilemmas, and decisions mirror the lives of our students, creating the ideal platform to springboard our students into real, self-directed learning. As Wilhelm argues (Chapter 3), learning should be personal; in fact, *real* learning can only occur if it is personal. If students are "expecting their teachers to provide them with a sense of the meaning of what they read" then there is no real process of engagement. The students are simply spouting others' thoughts. You will find the following lessons do just what Jago and Wilhelm suggest, discovering literature and life.

17 The Journey Is the Destination: Self-Realization in *Adventures of Huckleberry Finn*

Amy Fitzgerald
R. J. Reynolds High School, Winston-Salem, North Carolina

Purpose

Teenagers are strange and complicated human specimens. Discontent with the wagging fingers of their parents, many of them thrive on the instinct to break away. They soon realize, however, that breaking away means they have to find themselves, and that finding oneself requires a great deal of effort. Many may abandon the arduous process of true self-realization for the simpler, more immediately gratifying path of social conformity. This is why they need Huck Finn in their lives.

Huck Finn does what most every young person dreams of doing: He gets fed up and runs away. And yet, Huck is not intimidated by the self-discovery that such an action entails because it is disguised as an adventure. As he sets off with Jim down the Mississippi River and endures various trials, he unwittingly shows his readership how to steer around conformity, through self-discovery, and toward self-realization.

For many, the appeal of running away lies not in the destination but in the action itself. While the idea of self-discovery may frighten us, the idea of a road trip is enticing. The journey of Huck Finn gives students a language, a framework with which they can discuss the instincts that they themselves may have. The main purpose of my unit on *Adventures of Huckleberry Finn* is to help students use this framework to guide them as they make their own decisions and engage in their own process of self-realization.

Before we can use literature to affect students' lives, we must first help them to understand it. Thus, I have a second purpose that supports the first: to aid students in summarizing the main events of the novel and identifying the patterns of change throughout particular scenes. To do so, I encourage them to think like filmmakers making adaptations of the novel. Filmmakers are often forced to read and analyze a text critically, pulling out the most significant events and presenting them in an understandable and entertaining way. By adopting the role of the filmmaker, students can come to a better understanding of the novel's message of self-realization, and then use it as an inspiration for their own self-realization.

Materials

For the activities in this unit, I use a PowerPoint presentation (Figure 17.1) to review the Hero's Journey, an example of screenplay writing, and sticky notes to mark the identification of beats in the screenplay.

Introduction

To begin my unit on *Adventures of Huckleberry Finn*, I ask my students whether any of them have ever been on a road trip before (sometimes in a journal entry, sometimes just in discussion). Being only recently licensed drivers, they usually have not, although some of them surprise me. In addition to drawing on their own experiences, I ask them to name examples of road trips from movies they have seen. They may shout out things like *Little Miss Sunshine*, *Dumb and Dumber*, or *The Motorcycle Diaries*. Once students exhaust the possibilities, I ask them to give some reasons why people go on road trips. First, they may instinctively suggest that the reason to go on a road trip is to get somewhere, and even offer their own suggestions for places to go ("Warped Tour!" or "To see the world's biggest ball of twine!"). Acknowledging these as possibilities, I challenge them to think of other reasons to go on a road trip besides just wanting to get somewhere. Pretty soon, they pick up on the fact that, sometimes, we just need to get *away*. And what do we need to get away from? Our parents. Drama. Boyfriend/girlfriend problems. School. You name it. So, often, people who go on road trips are somehow discontent. Is seeing the world's biggest ball of twine going to make them content? Not necessarily. But all the adventures they have on their journey to see it—will those help make them content? Quite possibly.

Hopefully, by this point, students have had at least some exposure to the Hero's Journey of Joseph Campbell. If they have not, I use a PowerPoint presentation (Figure 17.1) to remind them of the pattern the journey follows: After getting some kind of Call, a Hero goes on a journey into a new realm, where he encounters many trials before achieving his final task. To achieve that task, though, he has to learn some kind of lesson from his trials. For this reason, the true purpose of a journey is not the destination, but the process it takes to get there. It's the process that makes it possible for us to even complete our final task, and ultimately helps us grow as people. The journey *is* the destination.

By this point, students should have read the first seven chapters of *Huck Finn*, so I ask them to do a writing exercise where they explain the reasons why they think Huck decides to run away, and then draw parallels between those reasons and the problems in their own lives. I ask them: Have you ever wanted to run away from home? Have you ever wanted to escape from something? Why? What are some things about your life that make you unhappy? In this manner, the stage is set for students to begin their own journey.

Connections

The task of understanding a text, much like the process of self-discovery, can be overwhelming for some students. As Blau suggests (Chapter 1), they are often able to avoid the ardor of having to hash out the meaning for themselves when their teachers simply dictate the meaning to them. What they do not realize, however, is that this dictation is dangerously akin to the parents or other significant societal figures who stand above them, wagging their fingers and telling them who to be. It is just as necessary for us to avoid conformity in understanding texts as it is to avoid conformity in living our lives, for to truly understand a text is to learn something about your life. As Wilhelm argues (Chapter 3), the study of literature is a personal endeavor, and the process should be as personal as the outcome.

To avoid preaching meaning to my students in this unit, I bypass most of the traditional language used in discussing literature in favor of the language of film. Perhaps one reason teachers are tempted to explain texts to students is because they are so used to explaining them a certain way. When the language of literature is complemented by the language of film, it becomes ripe for the personalized analysis of a new generation of readers.

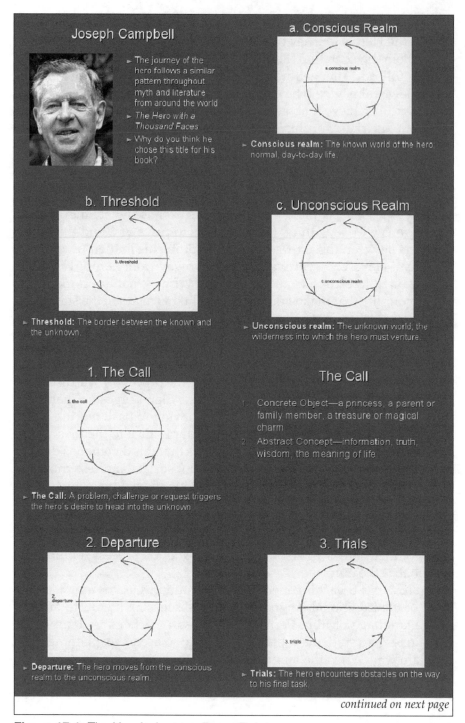

continued on next page

Figure 17.1. The Hero's Journey PowerPoint.

Figure 17.1 continued

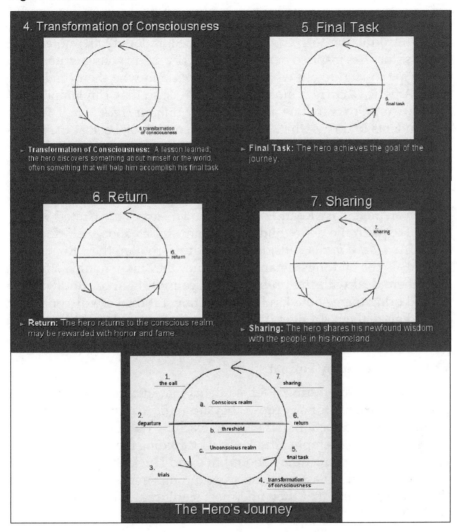

Activities

Phase I: Bildungsroman

In an introduction to *Huck Finn*, George Saunders (2001) noted that Huck's story has inspired derivative works by many young writers who are trying to "figure out what their River is, and who their Jim is, and what America's current most noxious trait is, so they can lampoon it" (p. xiii). As an overarching activity for my unit on *Huck Finn*, I prompt my students to do just that. First, I ask them to look back at their journal entries from the day I introduced the unit. After discussing their answers as a class, I ask them to imagine that they really did run away from home. That, I tell them, is going to be their assignment. As they read about Huck's escapades on the Mississippi River, they are going to plan an imaginary Road Trip of their own, across the United States.

I explain the genre bildungsroman: stories about self-development. As *Huck Finn* is considered a bildungsroman, their Road Trips should also be bildungsroman. The journey they take should somehow help them deal with the problems that caused them to run away—it should bring them some kind of contentment if they are discontent, it should make them stronger if they are weak, it should help them to see some aspect of the world in a different light.

Phase II: Screenplay Format

To keep things interesting, I tell students that instead of writing their bildungsroman in ordinary prose, they are going to write it in screenplay format. I spend a section of the lesson teaching them about screenplay writing and then exemplify the concept by guiding the class through the composition of a screenplay about Jim's and Huck's first meeting and conversation. First, I ask students to go through and pull out aspects of this initial meeting that they find most significant. Then, together, we write these out as a screenplay on the overhead, making sure to describe the setting and action.

A filmmaking concept that I find fascinating is the *beat*—an event, decision, or discovery (usually occurring every five minutes or so) that alters the way the protagonist pursues his or her goal. In teaching about screenwriting, I introduce this concept to students to show them that the self-development they find in a bildungsroman will not be characterized by one sudden "aha" moment where everything makes sense; instead, it will be a constant, gradual process, a series of tiny circumstances that alter characters' viewpoints, strategies, and attitudes and lead them toward maturity. As a class, we work together to identify the beats in the scene we have just developed. I give students sticky notes and ask them to place them on their own papers wherever a beat occurs in the scene, writing out a brief explanation of how this event, decision, or discovery has affected Huck's approach to his adventure *and* his life.

Once this activity allows the class to come to an understanding of Jim and Huck's relationship, I ask them to make predictions about how their developing friendship may help Huck develop as a person. After students discuss the ways this new acquaintance may give Huck new insights about the common values of the society in which he lives, I challenge them to apply the dynamic potential of this relationship to the decision that they, too, have to make about *who* will accompany them on their own Road Trip. I challenge them to select someone who is not necessarily a close friend, someone with whom they would not normally associate, but someone who has the potential to change them, influence them in a positive way. The journey becomes more internal if it involves a developing relationship.

Phase III: Using Film Language to Unlock the Text

Throughout our study of the novel *Huck Finn,* I ask students to get into groups of three or four and use the screenplay-writing format to write their own brief screenplays of various stages of Huck's journey. It works best to break each chapter into smaller scenes and assign each scene to a different group. Depending on time constraints (and the maturity of the class), I sometimes allow students to act out the scenes they write. This helps to give the class a visual representation of the text, in addition to showing them what lines and events resonated with them the most. I always require them to identify the beats in each scene, using sticky notes to explain how each beat represents some sort of change.

Depending on the type of class, I either give them time during the class period to work on the screenplays for their own Road Trips or just have them complete them at home. Either way, I remind them to include trials throughout their journey that help them to grow as people and gradually teach them some sort of lesson, possibly helping them solve whatever problem inspired them to run away in the first place. I also instruct them to follow the same pattern as the in-class screenplays we work on for *Huck Finn,* including the identification of beats using sticky notes.

Phase IV: Evaluating Text and Self

At the end of the unit, I ask students to evaluate the ending of *Huck Finn.* Since it turns out that Jim was free all along, was the journey pointless?

My hope is that students will not find it so, and instead recognize the value of the trials Jim and Huck endured together. Reminding them of the process of the Hero's Journey (Figure 17.1), I ask them to determine what kind of lesson Huck learned from his trials, and then ask them to mirror this process in their own Road Trips. What lesson did they learn as a result of the imaginary trials they endured while traveling across the United States? Hopefully students will come out of this unit with an enlightened, positive outlook on an issue that previously troubled them, having learned something about themselves along the way.

Assessment

Journal Entries

Depending on the type of class, any of the questions posed for discussion may be preceded by a journal entry. I score any journal entries students write throughout this unit using a check scale: a check-minus signifies a one-sentence, underdeveloped response; a check represents a response that elaborates but could still be more detailed; and a check-plus signifies a response that is well-written, well-developed, and detailed.

Screenplay Rewrites

When I score the screenplay rewrites that students compose for the various scenes in *Huck Finn*, I look for three things: their selection of significant excerpts, their identification and explanation of various beats, and the quality of writing, including technical adherence to screenplay format.

Road Trip Screenplay

When I score students' individual Road Trip screenplays, I examine the creativity of their trials, the relationship development between the characters on the road trip, and the quality of writing, including technical adherence to screenplay format. Overall, I determine whether the Road Trip qualifies as a bildungsroman. Does it show evidence of some kind of self-development? Is that development the gradual result of the trials the characters experienced on their journey?

Considerations

For teachers who feel uncomfortable adopting the filmmaking thread of this unit, it is entirely possible to have students simply write about their Road Trips in prose. I do, however, recommend that you incorporate the concept of the *beat* into your lessons, as it fits perfectly with the idea of gradual change and development presented in the bildungsroman. If you do decide to use the screenplay approach, you can easily find resources online and adapt them to whatever level of complexity you think will work for your students. Also, when helping your students to plan and execute their Road Trip screenplays, be sure that you encourage them to take it seriously. It's okay for them to have fun with it—indeed, Huck Finn seems to take a lighthearted and carefree approach to life, himself—but continuously challenge them to frame their trials in a manner that promotes self-development. When students are planning their trials, some of them may feel the need to do research on activities, locations, and events that they may encounter on their journeys. While it is perfectly reasonable for them to do so, remind them that these imaginary trials can come in many forms that do not necessarily require research: they could be robbed, their car could break down, they could run into some interesting character along the way. They may also feel compelled to have some sort of destination for their Road Trip. While I do not discourage them from having one, I always remind them that the destination should not be the focal point of their stories. The journey itself—both internal and external—is the true destination.

Reference

Saunders, G. (2001). Introduction. *Adventures of Huckleberry Finn*. New York: Modern Library.

18 Student as Expert: Working within and Going beyond a Framework in Mark Twain's *Adventures of Huckleberry Finn*

Chad E. Harris
West Forsyth High School, Clemmons, North Carolina

Purpose

This lesson prompts students to take on the role of expert, moving from student to teacher. Students are equipped with a framework to model their executive decisions but ultimately must engage in the text to an extent that they are discerning what is valuable. The provided framework offers a variety of ways to engage students and, hopefully, spark enthusiasm for the classroom and Twain's *Huck Finn*. Ultimately students are asked to find, interpret, and expertly teach concepts, themes, motifs, and other important literary elements.

Materials

At all stages of the lesson students will need class notes to direct their literary decisions and study guides from previous texts (Figure 18.1) to offer a framework for their final product. Students will work individually, in small groups, and as a class. Individual work will require students to have a copy of *Adventures of Huckleberry Finn*, paper, and pen. Small groups will need transparency papers and transparency pens. The whole-class discussion will utilize individual and small-group work.

Introduction

As a teacher of eleventh-grade students, I find my biggest blockade is the students' preconditioned mindset. At sixteen or seventeen, students come to class with fixed ideas of how to approach literature, and often those ideas do not involve the best pedagogical practices. Students *ask* for worksheets, preferring to "get it over with" rather than spending time engaging with the text. I often hear, "but if you don't give us a worksheet how will we know what is on the test?"

If I cannot steer the students from the safety net of worksheets, then I'll adapt the worksheet to fit my hopes for them. I start by simple guides for students' reading of the text; however, it is not simply a matter of copying notes and passively answering questions. Each point along the way asks students to provide an array of different answers: illustrating, defining, interpreting, and even summarizing. In the end my questions become starting points for class debates and, most importantly, for challenging the teacher's ideas and expertly defending their own. One guideline states: "tattoo scene—illustrate and explain." Students must artistically interpret the scene through a sketch, emblem, or some sort of visual representation. Visual and kinesthetic learners enthusiastically engage in interpreting the scene without the restraints of written defense. Other points on the guides are written to encourage students to search for passages to find the information needed to answer my questions. For example, the ninth bullet point in Figure 18.1 reads, "IRONY p. 193. What is the <u>significance</u> of this?" When providing answers, students must first read the passage. The act of reading for discernment ensures that they are deeply processing the text. At other points True/False items are even included. All types of questions are fair game, because they add variety to the lesson and engage more learning styles. I have found that a variety of questions creates a spark of energy as students search for answers and attempt to show their literary prowess.

As more years pass, I realize the importance presentation plays in creating the right, most invigorating environment. I encourage students to challenge my choices in making the guiding questions. For example, one particular student felt the ending of Chapter 28 did not deserve an exclamation point (Figure 18.1) because she did not find it exciting. When such a challenge is offered the class awakening is visibly apparent! The one contingency to the right to challenge is that students must defend their grievance with valid, text-proven evidence. The students enthusiastically devour the text with the demands of becoming an expert to challenge the teacher.

Connections

Louise Rosenblatt (1994) states, "taking somebody else's reading as your own is like having somebody else eat your dinner for you" (p. 86). Providing broad guiding questions gives students a starting point and offers

(The rest of) *Huck Finn* Chapters 27–29. Be the first to answer/explain each item.

- Why does Huck want Mary Jane to leave?
- True or False: Huck tells Mary Jane where he left the gold.
- Awww! (186)
- Huck thinks he is "bad." Explain why. (186)
- lies (187)
- end of Chapter 28!
- Who is Hines?
- Who isn't gullible? 3 people.
- IRONY p. 193. What is the <u>significance</u> of this?
- handwriting
- tattoo scene- illustrate and explain
- foolishness of the people (196)
- greed and Huck's escape
- *Excitement and Disappointment*
- lies about escape (199)
- king and duke argue
- duke stands up for himself
- "thick as thieves"

Figure 18.1. Teacher-created outline.

them the freedom to interpret the text for themselves. Furthermore, the Students as Experts activity gives students the freedom to lead the class's exploration of the text, putting full power in their hands. The teacher is no longer the single expert in the room; instead, each student is expertly navigating the text. My students come back to me saying my classes made them feel smart because they were not asked to simply recall my interpretation of a text, a similar experience to what Jago (Chapter 2) recalls. When given such freedom, students will begin to explore texts in ways that are rich and full of agency. The role I strive to fulfill is one of guidance, providing the framework for students and then allowing them to go beyond.

Activities

Phase I: Providing the Framework and Setting the Stage for Challenges

I ask students to read Chapters 27–29 in class or as a homework assignment and provide the guiding questions for the chapters (Figure

18.1). This prompts students to thoroughly defend their answers and develop challenges for the teacher. The following day students meet in small groups to discuss their answers and any grievances they want to present to the class. These questions are used as leads for debates and whole-group discussions. We spend as much time as needed on each point but allot twenty minutes at the end of class to introduce the collaborative learning assignment and give students time to get started.

Phase II: Students as Experts

At the conclusion of the discussion (Figure 18.1), I assign groups and inform students they will be creating their own guiding questions for Chapters 30–32. They should have read those chapters the previous night and determined what is valuable in the chapters. I encourage them with, "You are now the expert; you must decide how the class will proceed with these chapters. I'm no longer in charge, but you, as expert, will determine what we learn!" Students work for the rest of the period and have the following class period to complete the assignment. The guides provide a framework but students have the liberty to diverge. Students are encouraged to come up with creative ways to engage their classmates. The rules are simple: (1) include something about the climax of the novel that occurs in this set of chapters and (2) provide, on the back of their sheets of paper, the answers to all of their clues/questions as well as page and paragraph numbers for each. Once students decide what to include they transcribe the information on a transparency to present to the class the following day.

While students work in their groups I move around the room and prompt all members to participate. Students spend the next class period working in their groups, polishing their outlines, and turning them in for grading. The next class period is spent discussing Chapters 30–32 using the students' own work (Figure 18.2). Each group presents its guiding questions and the class decides which questions to include in the final version. Students must decide which questions are most worthy of inclusion, which are worded best, and which are most challenging. Using student work to lead class puts the students in the role of expert; I find students love seeing see their work displayed and feel more inclined to question each other and defend their arguments.

Assessment

To assess student learning for this lesson I use class participation and the concrete outlines. Teachers can evaluate student effort and participation

Huck Finn, Chapters 30–32
<u>Chapter 30</u>
- Title of Chapter 30
- Huck lies
- Duke defends Huck (200)
- Relationship between king and duke (shift?)
- Why does the king admit to hiding the money?
- "thick as thieves again"

<u>Chapter 31</u>
- days and days . . .
- Success of king and duke (203)—what do they try?
- Secretive talk
- JIM IS GONE! (Huck's conversation with boy—civilization or natural instincts?)
- CIVILIZATION VS NATURAL INSTINCTS! (205–206)
  - How does Huck make himself feel better after Jim is sold?
    - Represents :
  - Huck starts to think about . . . (207)
  - CLIMAX!
    - Huck is forced to . . .
  - IRONY (207)
- Huck sees duke
  - Duke's attempts to trick Huck

<u>Chapter 32</u>
- An indirect message about equality (212)
- Tom? (213)
- T F Huck is Silas and Sally's nephew.
- Realistic Racism (213)
- Satire in Chapter 32?
- Haha! (end of chapter)

Figure 18.2. Compiled student-made outlines.

during the individual, small-group, and whole-class work. Circulating during the group-work time, I can assess student understanding of the novel and listen to their thought processes when deciding what to include in guides. Additionally, student-created guides provide a concrete means of measuring student comprehension.

Considerations

The idea of introducing concepts and having students trace them throughout the novel provides an important framework that gives them the stability to embrace the idea of student experts. Students can find examples of what they know will recur in the novel but also add new insights, ask and answer new questions, and formulate fresh ideas. Enabling structures are there to guide them, but they are always encouraged to go beyond the framework. Additionally the freedom to create validates student ideas and opinions as experts of the text. Students are free to experiment with creative ways to cover important material in individual, small-group, and class environments.

Reference

Rosenblatt, L. (1994). *The reader, the text, the poem: The transactional theory of the literary work*. Carbondale: Southern Illinois University Press.

19 Helping Students Recognize Stereotypes and Understand Satire in Mark Twain's *Adventures of Huckleberry Finn*

Emily Houlditch
Reagan High School, Pfafftown, North Carolina

Purpose

Students have no shortage of opinions on the value of reading *Adventures of Huckleberry Finn* in school, and I generally encourage this debate to become the centerpiece for my class's study of the novel. Emotion and conviction can run high when it comes to the discussion of racist language or stereotypes in the novel. Yet, in my experience, students engage in a more in-depth debate about the novel after a lesson that highlights its historical context and Mark Twain's interest in satire. In this lesson, students first review the concept of satire through contemporary examples. Students then identify particular instances of satire in *Huck Finn* and analyze the features of nineteenth-century America that Twain satirizes. After breaking down Twain's use of satire, students return to the central debate over the value of the novel with a better understanding of the author's intent. Ultimately, the class will address the question of whether or not the satire in this social critique justifies its use of racist language and stereotypes.

Materials

Each student needs an unabridged copy of *Adventures of Huckleberry Finn*. Additionally, give students a page of notes defining satire and other useful literary terms (Figure 19.1). The teacher needs a specific example of modern satire to share with the class. For this lesson, I chose a clip from the TV show *The Simpsons* (Season 20, Episode 4). Each student will need two copies of "The Tools for Analyzing Satire" (Figure 19.2).

Introduction

My class's study of *Huck Finn* begins with a candid discussion on the topic of racism and racist language. It is a teacher's responsibility to preface this novel with an explanation about the context of the language and to gauge students' comfort level with that language. Often, I present students with articles written by critics on both sides of the debate (of the value of Twain's use of racist language in the text). I have found the essay "The Struggle for Tolerance: Race and Censorship in *Huckleberry Finn*," by Baylor University professor Peaches Henry (1992), useful for outlining the arguments of those in favor of teaching the classic and those opposed. If this essay is not accessible to less able students, there are news articles about challenges to the novel that can provide an overview of the debate. Once students hear experts from both sides, they have an easier time forming their own arguments for or against reading the novel in school.

Discussing Twain's use of satire and stereotypes enhances the debate on the value of the novel. While some students instantly pick up on Twain's satire and tongue-in-cheek tone, those who struggle just to interpret the dialect and to follow the plot need guidance. Recognizing and understanding satire requires knowledge of the culture and time period in which the piece was written. At some point, I realized that I was asking students to engage in a debate that requires an understanding of literary elements such as tone, satire, and stereotypes without explicitly teaching about any of them. By teaching students about Twain's techniques for creating satire, I offer a tool they can use to advance their own exploration and opinion of the novel.

Connections

Probst (Chapter 4) posits that the central role of any English teacher is to teach students to be thoughtful, discerning readers. He states, in unequivocal terms, that, "Our primary job, our fundamental obligation, our central goal, is to teach readers to be responsible." That obligation, in my opinion, is especially important to uphold when teaching a powerful and controversial text such as *Huck Finn*. For a modern-day student to read this text without critical thought about the author's satirical tone and intent is a dangerous thing. Any superficial or unguided reading of the text can lead to those unfortunate instances, often cited by opponents of the novel, in which immature students use the story to justify their own racial prejudice or use of hurtful language in the classroom. With such consequences in mind, Probst's requisite for teaching responsible reading becomes imperative. He writes, "If we are inclined, or have been taught, to question and wonder, then we are more likely to pause and think." This lesson plan teaches students to ask questions of the novel and discourages them from accepting Twain's writing at face value.

Contributors Blau, Jago, and Wilhelm (Chapters 1–3) all promote the idea of explicitly modeling literary analysis for students. This process can encompass the think-aloud strategy in which the teacher makes internal dialogue as a reader evident to the class by commenting and questioning publicly. All of these educators propose that modeling this critical process encourages students to become more active and inquisitive readers. By first modeling an analysis of satire in *The Simpsons* (or any other contemporary example), I give students the opportunity to hear my thought process. They hear me speculate about what aspect of society each character represents and guess, rightly or wrongly, about how the writers or artists mock or criticize society. I may do the same think-aloud analysis for an early passage in *Huck Finn*. Hopefully, students see that while I do not know as much about the culture of nineteenth-century America as twenty-first-century America, I do not hesitate to question and speculate meaning.

Activities

Phase I: Modeling Analysis of Satire

Most eleventh-grade students have been introduced to satire and related literary terms such as irony and parody. However, I find that it never hurts to offer a refresher before the start of this lesson, which I usually teach at the mid-point of the novel. Figure 19.1 offers a useful glossary of terms for the study of satire. Teachers may present students with these definitions or require that students search for the definitions on their own.

In terms of modeling an analysis of satire, clips and characters from *The Simpsons* are easily accessible and fun examples. South Carolina teacher Junius Wright has an excellent lesson on the NCTE website readwritethink.org about using *The Simpsons* to teach satire. If you are not familiar with the show, follow Wright's lead and simply show the opening credits as an example of satire. The opening offers great caricatures of the stereotypical American family. Beyond the opening credits, I recently used a clip from the first two minutes of Episode 4, Season 20, in which Homer tries to vote in the 2008 election. After viewing the clip with the class, I used the talk-aloud method to guide students through

Satire: The literary art of ridiculing a folly or vice to expose or correct it. The object of satire is usually some human frailty; people, institutions, ideas, and things are all fair game for satirists (Example: the *Saturday Night Live* skits that offer "fake news" and ridicule politicians).

Authors can employ many techniques when it comes to creating satire:

- **Parody:** A humorous imitation of another, usually serious, work. It can take any fixed or open form, because parodists imitate the tone, language, and shape of the original in order to deflate the subject matter, making the original work seem absurd (Example: *Austin Powers* mocks old spy movies by imitating them).

- **Irony:** A literary device that uses contradictory statements or situations to reveal a reality different from what appears to be true (Don't forget the difference between verbal irony, dramatic irony, and situational irony!).

- **Hyperbole:** A figure of speech using deliberate exaggeration or overstatement. Hyperboles sometimes have a comic effect; however, a serious effect is possible.

- **Understatement:** The ironic minimizing of fact, understatement presents something as less significant than it is. The effect can frequently be humorous and emphatic. Understatement is the opposite of hyperbole.

- **Wit:** In modern usage, wit is intellectually amusing language that surprises and delights. A witty statement is humorous, while suggesting the speaker's verbal power in creating ingenious and perceptive remarks.

- **Sarcasm:** From the Greek meaning, "to tear flesh," sarcasm involves bitter, caustic language that is meant to hurt of ridicule someone or something. It may use irony as a device, but not all ironic statements are sarcastic. When well done, sarcasm can be witty and insightful; when poorly done, it's simply cruel.

- **Juxtaposition:** Placing dissimilar items, descriptions, or ideas close together or side by side, especially for comparison or contrast.

These notes were adapted from the following sources:

Murfin, R. C., & Supryia, M. R. (2009). *The Bedford glossary of critical and literary terms* (3rd ed.). Boston: Bedford St. Martin's.

Swovelin, B. V. (2008). *English language and composition* (3rd ed.). Hoboken, NJ: Wiley.

Figure 19.1. Literary terms useful for the study of *Adventures of Huckleberry Finn*.

the satire. I also put a copy of Figure 19.2 on the overhead to record my thoughts about the guiding questions (see italics):

1. What character or scene are you analyzing? *The clip in which Homer tries to vote.*

2. What is the general subject of the satire? *Corruption in politics and the election process. The naiveté and oblivion of some American voters.*

3. Describe the character or scene as presented. *Homer walks into a gymnasium and demands to vote for "President, Governor, and anything that will take money away from our parks and libraries." After trying unsuccessfully to fit into the standard voting booth, the attendant tells him to use the "double-wide." Once in the booth, Homer marvels at the electronic voting machine. He enthusiastically pushes the button for Obama, but the machine registers a vote for McCain. After frantically pushing the button for Obama but being told he voted for McCain, Homer is eaten alive by the machine as he yells, "This doesn't happen in America, maybe in Ohio, but not in America!"*

4. What comment or criticism about society is being made? *Well, both the voter and the election process seem to be ridiculed. Homer shows that he really has no interest in the public good with his first comment. We also get the same old representation of Homer as the overweight, unhealthy American when he can't fit into the booth. The clip seems to reference the 2004 debacle with the voting machine in Florida when Bush was reelected. I think he yells about Ohio, because there were a lot of questions about their elections in 2004?*

5. What method is used to create this satire? *Exaggeration and verbal irony.*

I explain to students that I did not use the election clip to make any kind of political statement; rather, I chose the clip because understanding its satire is so dependent on the viewers' knowledge of politics and current events at a specific period in America's history. Viewers of the clip 100 years from now may have a tough time picking up on the satire and humor ("Who was John McCain, anyway?"). Similarly, many readers today do not immediately recognize the satire or critical tone in *Huck Finn* because we were not around 125 years ago to experience the culture and political climate—which included growing support for the abolitionist movement and an unpopular public opinion of the ways of the Old South.

Phase II: Students Find and Analyze Modern Satire

After modeling an analysis of satire with the class, I ask students to brainstorm their own satire example for homework and to answer the guiding questions (Figure 19.2) about their chosen example. My only requirement is that their examples satirize something specific to twenty-first-century American society. The next day in class, I assign small groups to compare examples. The examples students bring may include movies such as *Clueless, Not Another Teen Movie, Scary Movie, Shaun of the Dead,* or *Fight Club.* They could also name TV shows such as *The Daily*

Use these guiding questions to analyze each example of satire:
1. What character or scene are you analyzing?
2. What is the general subject of the satire?
3. Describe the character or scene as presented.
4. What comment or criticism about society is being made?
5. What method is used to create this satire?

Figure 19.2. The Tools for Analyzing Satire handout.

Show, 30 Rock, South Park, Family Guy, or *Saturday Night Live.* Some bring print examples such as *The Onion* or various political cartoons. Each student should share answers to the guiding questions with the group and discuss any similarities between examples.

Phase III: Students Analyze Satire in *Huck Finn*

By the third stage of the lesson, students' attention should turn to analyzing satire in *Huck Finn.* I usually question students before this activity, asking: "Why was it so easy to see that Homer represents the stereotype of the lazy, overindulgent American? Why was it so easy to see that Bart represents the apathy of American teens?" Through this questioning, I hope to reiterate that recognizing stereotypes and satire depends on cultural familiarity. I reassure them that it is understandable that twenty-first-century teens would not immediately recognize the stereotypes of Southern antebellum society, but that it is important to use what we do know about this time period to make educated guesses about the satire and Twain's message. At this point, I model one more think-aloud analysis for the early chapter "The Hair-Ball Oracle," which is filled with many of the minstrel-show stereotypes that recur in other chapters about Jim. In this way, I offer students a little background about the time period and model my analytical process.

At this point there is the option of letting students find scenes that they believe are satirical, or posting a list of suggested scenes on the board to guide students. Students should work together in small groups to read selected passages and talk through an analysis of the satire or stereotypes. The groups should appoint a recorder to keep notes on the guiding questions (Figure 19.2). However, I emphasize to students that there are no right or wrong answers in their analysis. The activity is simply designed to encourage a dialogue about why Twain used the language and images that he did. Assuming that students are halfway through the novel (Chapter 21), they should be able to discuss the following characters and scenes:

1. Tom Sawyer—in "Our Gang's Dark Oath" and "We Ambuscade the A-rabs"
2. Jim—in "I Spare Miss Watson's Jim" and "Fooling Poor Old Jim"
3. Pap Finn—in "Pap Struggles with the Death Angel"
4. The Grangerford Family—in "Why Harney Road Away for His Hat"
5. Emmeline Grangerford—in "The Grangerfords Take Me In"
6. Colonel Sherburn—in "Why the Lynching Bee Failed"
7. Duke and King—in "What Royalty Did to Parksville" or in "An Arkansaw Difficulty"

Assessment

To assess student learning for this lesson, I review the groups' notes about satire in *Huck Finn* and engage the whole class in a discussion about the message behind the satirical scenes. I also require that students take what they have learned about stereotypes and satire back to our debate on the value of the novel. Ultimately, I want students to return to the question of whether or not Twain's efforts at satire justify his use of racist language and stereotypes. Does Twain make a clear point through his satire? Did ridiculing the prejudices of Southern society require using the language of the day? Who exactly does Twain ridicule? Did Twain use satire for his own amusement or was he truly concerned about pointing out the problem of racism? All of these questions can lead to another lively debate on the novel. After this final discussion, students record their responses in a reflective journal entry that I then collect for a grade.

Considerations

The novelty of this lesson is its availability to tailoring, taking the interests and needs of any class into account. Struggling students may need guidance through more examples of satire before thinking of their own or delving into Twain's. Upper-level students may be able to brainstorm and dissect their own examples of satire right off the bat. Additionally, the initial examples of satire that I discuss with the class vary depending on their interests and exposure. Every year I teach about satire the list of contemporary examples grows and changes with the times.

Additionally, the class's analysis of satire in *Huck Finn* often varies based on their exposure to the history of the time period. I have had the greatest success with this lesson when I coordinate my unit on *Huck Finn* with their studies in US History. Students pick up on the stereotypes and satire in the novel all the better when they have studied the Romantic and Victorian periods or, most importantly, the culture surrounding slavery in the South.

Reference

Henry, P. (1992). The struggle for tolerance: Race and censorship in *Huckle-berry Finn*. In J. S. Leonard, T. A. Tenney, & T. M. Davis (Eds.), *Satire or evasion: Black perspectives on* Huckleberry Finn (pp. 25–48). Durham, NC: Duke University Press.

20 Wisdom from the Unexpected in Mark Twain's *Adventures of Huckleberry Finn*

Tiffany A. Jones
Creekside High School, Fairburn, Georgia

Purpose

An oracle, sage, elder, and nature have all been considered sources in finding wisdom, a most sought treasure. But wisdom that comes to us in humble forms are all the more valuable. In this lesson, students will confront their ideas of wisdom: What is wisdom? Where and how can someone gain wisdom? In addition, students are asked to, at the very least, *listen* to counter ideas of wisdom from an individual who adheres to ideals that fall outside their personal convictions. The class will journey through the process of exploration, consideration, connection, and application through class discussions, formal letter writing, and journal entries. Following Huck, students will begin or continue to become valuable members of a democratic society that allows them to hold on to their personal convictions but also to respectfully listen to and wrestle with the ideas of others.

Materials

The materials necessary for this lesson include class copies of the following: *Adventures of Huckleberry Finn*, any copied materials for Phase I, and any of the questions in handout form used from Figures 20.1–20.4. Phase I's materials will vary depending on which stories you decide to ask your students to explore; materials may include some but not all of the following: any movies and DVD player used, Internet access and speakers if listening to NPR clips; copies of excerpts from comparative texts. Phase II's project will require students to have access to a computer and printer from which they can type their business letters. Additionally, highlighters, pencils, and paper can be used as students interact with the text.

Introduction

High school students are obsessed with relationships: "Did you hear Joe is dating Hannah now? Oh! Tara and Cynthia aren't talking anymore? Did you notice how those two teachers always hang out together?" The teen obsession with relationships then makes it natural for teachers to focus on relationships within literature. The relationship between Huck and Jim now becomes a focal point to explore concepts of wisdom. Do Huck and Jim gain wisdom in their river adventure? From where and whom, expected and unexpected, does this wisdom come? How does the wisdom change the two characters and their relationship with each other?

To prep students for our exploration of wisdom, we must first create a working idea of their conceptions of wisdom. I have students write a paragraph in their journal about a person in their life they consider to be extremely wise. Each student is to answer why he or she feels this person is wise and to question how this person has influenced his or her own ideals. After five minutes, we discuss the students' journal entries to establish an idea of what they, as students, value as wise and how that wisdom plays out in each life. Students are to keep the journal entries on wisdom and will come back to reconsider the definitions proposed.

The lesson begins at Chapter 14; therefore, students should feel confident in their previous exposure to and understanding of the relationship between Huck and Jim. I have found that Jago's (Chapter 2) seven-step discovery process is a fine tool for digging deeper into Huck and Jim's relationship, launching into the study of wisdom. First, use Jago's seven-step discovery process to dissect Huck and Jim's discussion of Solomon in Chapter 14. As laid out by Carol, the steps are as follows:

1. Reread the passage silently, choosing a phrase or sentence that strikes you.

2. Write for five minutes about this line.

3. In small groups reread the passage aloud.

4. Share lines and comments in small groups.

5. Come together as a whole class and reread the passage.

6. Discuss passage in large group with teacher.

7. Discuss how rereading helped you understand the text.

Additionally, I use questions from Figure 20.1 to guide my interaction with the students as they explore Huck and Jim's discussion of
Solomon. Figure 20.1's questions lead students to focus on the unusual
relationship between the two characters and in particular to highlight
Jim's imparting wisdom to Huck. Ultimately I want students to transfer their considerations of Jim as wise to their interactions with others.
Where can I, as a student, gain wisdom from an unexpected source?
The teacher can further the discussion to include Huck's relationships
with other characters and what he learns from their wisdom and/or
folly (Figure 20.2).

Connections

As teachers, we do not want to tell students *what* to believe but use our
time to teach them how to question and re-question so as to affect "personal and social transformation" (Wilhelm, Chapter 3). Having been in
the classroom during the times of debate in our nation's last election, it
has been interesting to hear students so staunchly defend their beliefs
(and many times their parents' beliefs) without even a small consideration for each other's ideas. The activities of this lesson, therefore, seek
to help students put aside a stubborn resolve to cling to their ideas, their
wisdom, at any cost "as it becomes itself an obstacle to further learning"
(Blau, Chapter 1).

This lesson plan directly incorporates the philosophies of Jago,
Probst, Wilhelm, and Blau (Chapters 1–4). First, the precursor to the lesson is the exploration of Chapter 14 using Jago's proposed seven steps
to help students reread and interact with Jim's imparting wisdom to
Huck. As all four authors suggest, the study of literature should be about
discovering humanity. The activities prompt students to discover not
only Jim and Huck's humanity or that of someone much unlike themselves, but also their own humanity as they hopefully identify and begin
to overcome some of their misconceptions of those unlike themselves.
As Probst suggests, this lesson asks each student to "question what he
is not inclined to question, to question what he firmly and absolutely
believes" not only in the novel but in his or her own community as well.

Activities

Phase I: Connections

After discussing the relationship between Jim and Huck with the seven-
step discovery process and Figure 20.1, transition into Phase I is natural.

1. Compare and contrast Jim's family situation with others from the novel. Consider how you believe family is defined and what constitutes the ideal family.
2. How do you define wisdom? Who do you consider wise in your own life? Is Jim wise? If so, in what way?
3. How are Jim and Huck's situations similar? Provide examples.
4. Why do you think Huck is hesitant to even consider Jim's values and ideas as valuable/plausible? What tends to make *you* hesitant to consider others' beliefs and ideas?
5. Many of the adults in Huck's life are trying to "sivilize" him. How would you describe a civilized person? Do you believe that Jim offers Huck a good example of how to conduct oneself in a civilized manner?
6. Make a rough list of Jim's superstitions. Do some of Jim's superstitions prove to be true? Give specific examples of superstitions and how they are proven true. Does this make you more prone to believe in superstitions? Why or why not?

Figure 20.1. Questions about Jim.

1. Is he or she wise? Why or why not? (Use examples from text and tie to your own idea of what wisdom is and how it is displayed interpersonally and within society.)
2. Does he or she offer Huck a good example of family values? Use examples and tie them to your own ideas of family.

Figure 20.2. Questions about other characters.

This phase offers students other relationships in literature, film, and/or real life in which a character gains wisdom from an unexpected source. I regularly use an excerpt from *Tuesdays with Morrie* (Mitch and Morrie) and/or a clip from *Finding Forrester* (Jamal and Forrester), but there are many texts/films to choose from that highlight peculiar relationships where one character learns unexpected lessons from another character. Other sources are the novels *She's Come Undone*, *Ender's Game*, *Malcolm X*, *Great Expectations*, and *Pride and Prejudice*; the films *Driving Miss Daisy*, *The Power of One*, and *UP*; the play *Oedipus the King*; and the following recordings from NPR:

> http://www.npr.org/templates/story/story.php?storyId=104979771 (marriage story)

> http://www.npr.org/templates/story/story.php?storyId=89164759 (mugger story)

> http://www.npr.org/templates/story/story.php?storyId=111091624 (millionaire story)

Homeless man Leaves Behind Surprise: $4 million

1. Who taught whom what in this story?
2. In what way was the wisdom of these parties unconventional, both to you and to the other individual(s) in the reading?
3. Compare and contrast this relationship to (1) a relationship in your life, (2) to that of Jim and Huck.
4. Can you recall other examples of peculiar relationships where wisdom comes from unexpected sources in literature, film, or real life?

Figure 20.3. Questions about relationships in Connections (Phase I).

Figure 20.3 offers general questions that can be used to engage the reading/viewing of these excerpts/clips and then to compare these examples with the relationship between Huck and Jim. A modified form of Jago's seven-step process can also be used. Before starting Phase II, I ask students to recall their working definitions of wisdom arrived at through the initial journal entry and I remind students to keep their views of wisdom in mind as we begin Phase II of the lesson.

Phase II: Unconventional Wisdom in My World (Project/Assessment)

Distribute the handout from Figure 20.4. The business letter handout (Figure 20.4) directs students to write a formal business letter to the teacher about a person they know and consider to have opposing ideas on life and wisdom from themselves. The letter should include a list of ten student-generated questions that each student believes the interviewee would love to answer. (While I go over the handout I harp on the idea that they are to ask questions that their interviewee would *love* to talk about rather than questions that are driven by their own desire to show the interviewee that he or she is "wrong" or misguided.) For homework, they type the final draft of this letter in the format provided. The next day I collect the letters and inform students that within the next week they need to interview their chosen person. I most often collect the letters on a Thursday or Friday so that I can read them over the weekend and return them the following Monday. We continue with the discussion and reading of the novel while students embark on the interview project mostly outside of class time.

In one week's time the typed transcript of students' interviews, including both their ten questions and the answers, are due. In class, students use the transcript to write a first-person monologue from the point of view of the interviewee describing his or her worldview. I find having students take on the voice of the interviewee helps them

This is an activity that will benefit you in other areas of your education and life in general. Knowing how to write a business letter is important in establishing a favorable image of yourself to people you have never met. If, for example, you are applying for a job and have to write a cover letter to explain more about yourself, it will not look favorable if you do not follow correct formatting or misspell every other word. Whether you like it or not, people do judge you by the way you write and talk. Some rules to remember when writing your letter are:

1. The letter needs a one-inch margin.
2. The body of the letter is single-spaced, with double spaces between each paragraph (each at least four sentences in length).

Your assignment is to write a final draft of your letter of intent. Be very careful with your spelling and grammar. The following page is a formula for the letter of intent to help you remember what you need to address in your letter.

Format of Letter of Intent

YOUR STREET ADDRESS
YOUR CITY, STATE AND ZIP CODE

DATE

TEACHER'S NAME
SCHOOL NAME
SCHOOL STREET ADDRESS
SCHOOL CITY, STATE AND ZIP CODE

DEAR (TEACHER'S NAME):

PARAGRAPH 1:   Give an introduction explaining the assignment, the person you have chosen to interview, as well as your feelings about the assignment itself.

PARAGRAPH 2:   Give a brief description of your own values and beliefs.

PARAGRAPH 3:   Compare and contrast yourself with your interviewee and expound on why you have chosen him or her to interview.

PARAGRAPH 4:   Pledge that your ten questions are intended to genuinely inquire into the ideas and beliefs that your interviewee holds to be true and valuable, rather than an attempt to prove to your interviewee that his/her worldview is wrong or strange. Include your ten questions.

Sincerely,
Your signature (four spaces between Sincerely and your typed name)
YOUR NAME TYPED

Figure 20.4. Business letter of intent to teacher.

to understand the humanity of and honest human experience of that person. In years past, we have recorded these as podcasts (we change the names of those we are representing) or class recordings; we've also performed the monologues in class. Hopefully through the interview and monologue the students gain a different perspective. It is important to encourage students to relate their own experience with the interviewee to that of Huck and Jim. In a class discussion I ask: "Did Huck see Jim as imparting wisdom? Why was Jim's perspective valuable in Huck's development as a person? Has the experience with your interviewee changed your 'wisdom,' and if so, how?"

The final part of the project is to bring an addressed, stamped envelope to class. We then make thank-you cards for those we have interviewed. I let students know before their interview that they must acquire an address so as to send the thank-you card. If the interviewee would prefer an email or to put their letter in a homeroom teacher's box rather than give out a street address, we make accommodations. I usually borrow laptops from the library this day for students who will need to email. You can also make them copy the email to you for home-work that night if you do not have the luxury of having computers in your classroom.

Assessment

To assess student learning teachers can easily use the activities of the lesson as concrete barometers and can use class discussions as a measure-ment of comprehension. Collecting the initial journal entry, the business letter, typed monologue, and final thank-you letter offers gradual forms of assessment at various points in the lesson. Furthermore, teachers can use the discussions to gauge student comprehension and enthusiasm. In past years I have used an essay prompt as a final form of assessment (Figure 20.5).

Considerations

Depending on the students that make up your classroom, this lesson may offer unique challenges; however, those of us whose populations make us the most tentative to embark on the lesson may find the most rewards through the adventure. Teachers can choose to have the stu-dents reflect on the process in their writing journals or as a take-home assignment as reflection often forces the student to consider the caliber of participation and effort he or she offered to the process. There are

In Chapter 14, Huck reflects to himself that Jim "had an uncommon level head for a nigger." We have wondered about and discussed in-depth Jim's impact on Huck. In a convincing five-paragraph essay, discuss Jim's wisdom, no matter how unconventional in Huck's mind or your own, and its impact on Huck. A stellar essay will include a convincing assertion in thesis form, textual evidence and analysis thereof to support the thesis, as well as overall coherency of the essay. Remember that any assertion can be "correct" if backed sufficiently by textual evidence.

Figure 20.5. Unit test essay question.

many parts of the process outlined above that teachers can modify and shorten as necessary for their curriculum and professional learning community (PLC) demands.

VI *To Kill a Mockingbird:* Characterization, Historical Context, and Technology Integration

Jane C. Brocious
North Carolina State University

Harper Lee's *To Kill a Mockingbird* is near the top of every list of commonly read and taught novels in American public schools. Its appeal is universal in part because of Lee's accessible prose and engaging parallel plots, but probably more because of its memorable characters and its significant commentary on social injustice, racism, and individual heroism.

Set in fictional Maycomb, Alabama, during the Great Depression, this book affords adolescent readers opportunities to reflect on themselves and their place in their environment. The narrator is the adult voice of the child Scout, the daughter of Atticus Finch, a prominent attorney in Maycomb. Atticus is gentle and nurturing; in his quiet, confident way, he teaches Scout and Jem to be tolerant, compassionate people. Scout is observant and intelligent, a willing "student." Atticus teaches Scout that "You never really understand a person until you consider things from his point of view. . . . Until you climb inside of his skin and walk around in it." What sets Atticus apart from many other adults in Maycomb is his sincerity and his honesty in words and actions. He is able to pass on to Scout and Jem his belief in the basic goodness of humankind.

It is easy to see why students and many adults answer "*To Kill a Mockingbird*" when asked their favorite book in school. The lessons in this section offer a variety of activities designed specifically to engage students in meaningful reading and response to the text. Viewed together, the authors open *To Kill a Mockingbird* with students through dramatization, a study of historical context, and the value of technology as a tool for exploring the culture and time of the novel. The activities push students to "construct their own understanding and interpretation of the text" (Blau, Chapter 1) through verbal, kinesthetic, interpersonal, and intrapersonal learning strategies.

But the teachers here do not shy away from a close examination of the text or from the discomfort that comes from considering issues of social justice. They provide opportunities for "interactive inquiry . . . speculative thinking . . . and linger(ing) over text, puzzling over its full meaning, musing on connections to their own lives" (Jago, Chapter 2). These teachers embrace their responsibility to provide a student a "chance to investigate assumptions, to rethink a worldview, to remake himself. Doing so may not be easy, and may not be comfortable," as Probst (Chapter 4) reminds us. Particularly for the study of *To Kill a Mockingbird*, it is critical that students see themselves as "democratic citizens who are responsive to themselves, each other and the world."

Each of these three lesson series calls for active involvement of the students with the text. The use of technology and contemporary supplementary resources, in addition to students' close reading of text, and careful reader response interpretive exercises insist the students be active, rather than passive, learners.

21 Role-Play with *To Kill a Mockingbird*

Leigh Ann Lane
East Wake High School of Arts, Education, and Global Studies,
North Carolina

Purpose

In this lesson series role-play engages students in making connections with various characters through creative strategies. They take Atticus Finch's advice and "step into someone else's shoes" to experience the story from a character's perspective, thus deepening their understanding of characters' lives, motivations, and the characters themselves. Through various role-play strategies, students interact with the text and extend their knowledge beyond surface meaning. They become one of the characters and view the story through that character's eyes. This strategy challenges students to question their initial judgments, interpretations, and criticism of the text and its characters.

Materials

Students each have a copy of *To Kill a Mockingbird.* Before beginning the novel and then throughout the reading of the novel, students complete role-play scenarios. In pairs or groups, students each take on different roles and interact in that role in a given scenario. These roles and scenarios are projected for them using an LCD projector, or groups choose a paper strip that contains the given scenario from a bowl (Figure 21.1). Students also complete various writing assignments from the perspective of a character. The prompts are projected for them, and they complete the assignments in their class journals (Figure 21.2). Students engage in talk show skits and follow questions designed to assist them in preparing for the performance (Figure 21.3). The final role-play activity is a culminating assignment in which students prepare responses from their assigned character's perspective and then complete a bio poem for that character (Figure 21.4).

Introduction

To Kill a Mockingbird is a wonderful novel to use for role-play activities. The characters elicit strong opinions from students: some loathe Mayella Ewell for falsely accusing Tom Robinson of rape; others champion Atticus Finch for standing up for the victim, no matter the cost. At this point in the semester, students are familiar with characterization and how to describe the various ways a character is revealed in a story. However, role-play activities allow the students to delve deeper into understanding the character as they are given the opportunity to become a character through writing, oral scenarios, and dramatizations. Through engagement in role-play activities, students create their own understandings of the text and creatively respond through writing and drama, instead of rote memorization of details to complete a worksheet.

Connections

Role-play connects to Blau's theory (Chapter 1) that engaging students directly with the text enables them to discover it for themselves, create their own meaning, and to experience the literature in a satisfying manner that may lead to lifelong reading and learning. Taking a character's perspective also reflects Moore's suggestion (Chapter 5) that a repertoire of reading strategies assists students in constructing various interpretations of the text. Reader response theory emphasizes the importance of readers connecting with the text and building relationships with the characters. Role-play activities allow students opportunities to discover the various characters and interact with the text in scenarios and dramatizations.

Having students engage in role-play also enacts Wilhelm's focus (Chapter 3) on using various strategies to encourage the reader's inquiry of the text through think-alouds, questioning strategies, and drama. He stresses the importance of gaining an initial understanding of the text and then extending beyond to agree with, question, or resist it in a creative way. Role-play activities allow students to move beyond this initial understanding of the text by examining characters' actions, motivations, personalities, thoughts, and decisions.

Activities

To prepare students for some of the novel's situations, I begin the unit by pairing them or grouping them and letting them act out a general scenario (see Figure 21.1). They have fun doing this, while also taking

---

Role-Play Scenario Skit

Task: Your group should create a skit based on the scenario below. Show the scenario itself along with a possible solution to resolve the situation in a positive way. In order to accomplish this, your group must brainstorm possible peaceful solutions to the situation.

Scenario: A teacher accuses and punishes you for something but you did nothing wrong.

Role-Play Scenario Skit

Task: Your group should create a skit based on the scenario below. Show the scenario itself along with a possible solution to resolve the situation in a positive way. In order to accomplish this, your group must brainstorm possible peaceful solutions to the situation.

Scenario: Someone insults you and your parent/guardian.

Role-Play Scenario Skit

Task: Your group should create a skit based on the scenario below. Show the scenario itself along with a possible solution to resolve the situation in a positive way. In order to accomplish this, your group must brainstorm possible peaceful solutions to the situation.

Scenario: You discover someone who was your absolute most positive role model is actually a hypocrite.

Role-Play Scenario Skit

Task: Your group should create a skit based on the scenario below. Show the scenario itself along with a possible solution to resolve the situation in a positive way. In order to accomplish this, your group must brainstorm possible peaceful solutions to the situation.

Scenario: Someone who is rumored to be a mean, nasty drunk threatens you and your family.

Role-Play Scenario Skit

Task: Your group should create a skit based on the scenario below. Show the scenario itself along with a possible solution to resolve the situation in a positive way. In order to accomplish this, your group must brainstorm possible peaceful solutions to the situation.

Scenario: You have been invited by a friend to his or her church, which is populated by a race of which you are not a member. One of your friend's fellow church members makes a scene about your being there and says you are not welcome.

Figure 21.1. Role-play scenario skits.

on various characters' roles without realizing it. Once students have begun reading the novel and are introduced to the main characters and some of the more memorable minor characters, they complete writing assignments from various characters' perspectives (see Figure 21.2). These writing prompts engage them in the lives of the characters and force them to view the text from a different angle. The reader only gets the story from Scout's point of view. What about the others' views?

Journal Entry Assignment

Choose either the character of Walter Cunningham Jr. or Burris Ewell. Write a journal entry assignment from his perspective about his first day of school. Please review Chapters 2–3 of the novel if you need to refresh your memory of that day.

Letter Assignment

Imagine you are either Scout or Jem. Write a letter to an adult (Atticus, Aunt Alexandra, Calpurnia, Uncle Jack) in which you explain why you think a recent situation was handled inappropriately. Give a detailed explanation and a suggestion for how you can both proceed from now into the future.

Diary Entry

Write a one-page entry from Mayella Ewell's point of view. To prepare for this assignment, review the description of the Ewell yard and her testimony during the trial.

Thank-You Note

Pretend you are Boo Radley writing a thank-you note to the Finches for the way the final situation of the novel was handled. Include anything you think Boo might have wanted to say to Atticus, Scout, or Jem but was unable to the night of the incident.

Figure 21.2. Writing assignments for characters' perspectives.

After Chapter 3 of the novel, students draw a character's name from a bowl. The students take detailed notes about this character for the remainder of the novel. Students then have an opportunity every few days to meet in their character groups to exchange notes and discuss questions posed for each group to consider about its character. For example, "Why is Jem so angry with Atticus when he catches Jem with the fishing pole?" or "Give three reasons to feel sorry for Mayella Ewell." At the end of the novel, these character groups are mixed so that groups have each character represented. Students receive a handout (see Figure 21.3) that assists in preparing them for the talk show role-play activity. I usually play the role of the talk show host, and each member of the group interacts as the assigned character during the skit. This activity is fun for the students yet challenging as they have to truly place themselves in the mindset of their character to respond in an appropriate manner. They must also dress the part for the performance.

For the final role-play activity, students provide information regarding a character's behaviors in a Maycomb County social gathering. Then, students write a bio poem for their assigned character (see Figure

You have met in your common character groups twice now to collaborate on details, actions, and descriptions of your character. You will now extend that information one step further. You will be grouped with other classmates to make a group that contains other characters from the novel. Together you will participate in a talk show skit in which you will play the role of your assigned character. You will need to play the role of your character and respond in ways in which your character would respond. You will also speak, act, and react in the role of your character. I will play the role of the talk show host. I have eight questions from which I will randomly choose to ask you four. All characters must respond. In groups, you should prepare your answers and ways you plan to act and respond. Write your answers to the questions below based on your assigned character. Then, you can rehearse responding as a group with your answers.

1. How has your life changed in the past few weeks?
2. What has been your biggest challenge?
3. Describe how the past three years have made an impact on you.
4. What is the biggest lesson you have learned throughout this whole ordeal?
5. Tell me about your relationship with the others. Who is the most important to you and why?
6. Predict the future for Maycomb County.
7. Debate the pros and cons of the Tom Robinson trial.
8. Make a statement about the future in regards to prejudice, race relations, and social injustice.

These talk show skits will be performed in front of the class. You will receive a group and individual performance grade and a grade for your individual written responses to these questions. Please take your role seriously but have fun with it!

Figure 21.3. *To Kill a Mockingbird* character skits.

21.4). To create an impressive bio poem, students must truly examine their characters. They provide information about what their character feels, needs, and fears. To accomplish this task, students must delve deeply into the text to get past just surface information.

Assessment

Student assessments are formative rather than summative. All of the assignments are shared with the class and evaluated based on knowledge of the chosen or assigned character. Grades for these assessments are based on the degree to which students assume the "voice" of the character and display their grasp of the character's personality, living conditions, desires, fears, and intentions. For the talk show skits, students receive a guide outlining the expectations for the performance. Students use this guide to evaluate each other and themselves. I can take these

Character Activity

You have been assigned the character _____ from *To Kill a Mockingbird*. Consider everything you have learned about this character based on your reading of the novel and our class discussions to complete the assignments below.

Maycomb County Social Gathering

Imagine your character were to attend a Maycomb community social gathering. Based on your knowledge of your character, give the following information and/ or answer the following questions.

1. What would your character wear to the party? (Describe his or her typical outfit.)

2. List three other characters your character would speak to or interact with at the party. (Note the conversation does not have to be pleasant.)

3. Give three questions your characters would ask another character or topics of conversation your character would have with another character.

1.

2.

3.

Bio Poem: Complete a bio poem for your character based on the format below. You may complete the poem on the back of this handout.

Line 1: Your character's first name only,

Line 2: Four traits that describe your character,

Line 3: Sibling of . . . (or son/daughter of),

Line 4: Lover of . . . (3 people or ideas),

Line 5: Who feels . . . (3 items),

Line 6: Who needs . . . (3 items),

Line 7: Who gives . . . (3 items),

Line 8: Who fears . . . (3 items),

Line 9: Who would like to see . . . (3 items),

Line 10: Resident of (the town of the novel); (your character's road name—you can make this up but make it realistic to the novel),

Line 11: Your character's last name only.

Character Bio Poem

(1)_____

(2)_____, _____, _____, _____,

(3) Sibling or Son/Daughter of _____

(4) Lover of _____

(5) Who feels _____

(6) Who needs _____

(7) Who gives _____

(8) Who fears _____

(9) Who would like to see _____

(10) Resident of _____, _____

(11)_____

Figure 21.4. *To Kill a Mockingbird* character activity and bio poem.

peer and self-assigned evaluations into consideration when assigning the final evaluation. This method gives students clear expectations for the performance yet encourages them to adopt the persona of their character as they know their peers will evaluate them as well as the teacher. The role-play scenarios receive a participation grade, while the written assignments and character activity with the bio poem receive a letter grade.

Considerations

Role-play activities allow us to use differentiated instruction. For example, when assigning characters, I may choose the more discreet characters for higher-level students and the main characters chosen for struggling readers. I display the scenarios and writing assignments on an LCD projector, overhead projector, or distributed in a handout. If time is an issue, the talk show skit performances can be videotaped and viewed by the teacher instead of the class watching each separate group's performance. Certainly not all of the activities have to be used.

22 Connecting the Past to the Present through Human Rights Discourse in *To Kill a Mockingbird*

Jessica Conley
Consultant

Purpose

This lesson series contextualizes *To Kill a Mockingbird* historically and sets out to connect its themes and messages to the students and to the United States. We address these two goals by reflecting on the concept of human rights and social injustice as a theme that is of particular value to our American identity. Through this sequence, students learn about a time period that may be unfamiliar to them. The lesson creates a space for the students to assess injustices of the past and juxtapose those events to their experiences and knowledge of contemporary society.

Materials

I often use a visual presentation such as a PowerPoint to deliver the minilesson on lynching (Figure 22.1). *The Great Debaters* movie (media equipment required) provides substance for the second phase of the lesson (Figure 22.2). Copies of Paul Laurence Dunbar's poem "The Haunted Oak," the accompanying handout (Figure 22.3), and the writing prompt (Figure 22.4) provide the assessment portion of the lesson.

Introduction

While *To Kill a Mockingbird* rightfully finds itself in the American canon, the contents of the novel are directly tied to a complex era in US history that is frequently overlooked. In addition to African American literature and history often being neglected or misrepresented, contemporary society's view of itself as a colorblind society brings many students to our desks with a limited understanding of how racism and social injustice permeate the fabric of American history. Therefore, students can easily fail to see the relevance, power, pleasure, or significance of Harper Lee's novel regarding both civil and human rights.

This novel becomes relevant to our students through reflecting on the concept of an American identity that is ever-expanding as we traverse new boundaries, spaces, and voices. By surveying American literature, students enter spaces beyond the limits of their neighborhoods, friendships, and communities. Teaching works from the American canon helps us think about who and what is American and how these diversified authors, as well as our distinct American voices, constitute a complex body of knowledge, experience, humanity, and culture.

This text affords students the opportunity to connect with a people, a past, and multiple voices that are both different from and similar to their own. I find that students enjoy exploring the open-ended questions about taboo topics in a setting that is controlled, informed, and safe. As students advance through adolescence, their childhood ideals are often crushed by the ambiguities of life. Students become passionate and energetic when responding to such essential questions that tie them to the text as, "When have you been accused of something you didn't do, and what tools did you have to get yourself out of the situation?" Students begin to exchange their experiences with each other, and their stories personally connect them in a small way to Tom Robinson. By tying the novel to an era and a group of people whose rights were violated, the questions and activities push students to step into the shoes of others, as Atticus suggests. When teaching this novel, I tend to center on activities that inform students of what life was like for different people from this time period and contrast that with how life in the United States has changed or remained the same.

Connections

This lesson employs the literary theory, or more specifically the cultural studies method of unlocking texts, as outlined earlier in this text by Moore (Chapter 5). Grounding the events of the novel in African American history and culture allows students to rethink and expand their notions of US identity. The open questions, essential questions, and journal entry approach cultural studies through the reader response lens that Moore recommends. When thinking about race, human rights, and social injustice, it is necessary for students to respond and express their feelings. The open style of instruction exposes conflicting experiences and thoughts, ultimately leading students to think dynamically about the text. This is not to say, as Jago states (Chapter 2), that any and all interpretations are permissible. I guide and make sense of the diversified experiences that students present. The questions and close reading strategies, supported by Jago, teach students that they have the skills to find meaning and to develop a relationship with literature. Finally, by enabling students to think more deeply about the human experience, this series satisfies Wilhelm's notion (Chapter 3) of quality instruction.

Activities

I. Lesson Placement

This lesson occurs in the middle of the novel; because of the novel's length and syntax, students enjoy engaging with an accessible concept such as human rights and social injustice. As we move into this series that extends pieces of the novel, students have previously read Chapter 15 in which the mob has come to the jail to kill Tom Robinson prior to his case being tried. This close reading of the chapter focuses on open questions that allow readers to respond. Questions include the following:

- Why are the men coming to the jail?
- Why do they wish to take matters into their own hands?
- Would it be problematic to let the men deal with Tom Robinson? Explain why or why not.

II. Historical Context

A minilesson addresses the historical facts of lynching in the United States. I use a PowerPoint presentation (Figure 22.1) that is meant to both guide and inform student responses to the topic. I introduce the slide with questions that allow me to assess student knowledge of the topic. By the end of the lesson students can define lynching, understand why lynching was an accepted practice, and know basic facts about the lynching that occurred in the United States. The minilesson provides a backdrop for the mob's intentions and ties the Tom Robinson scene to the Jim Crow era. With this knowledge, students can better critique this historical time period and these events.

III. Pairing Texts

Great Debaters is a provocative and moving film. Viewing selected clips offers another medium to access content to respond, understand, and

Slide 1

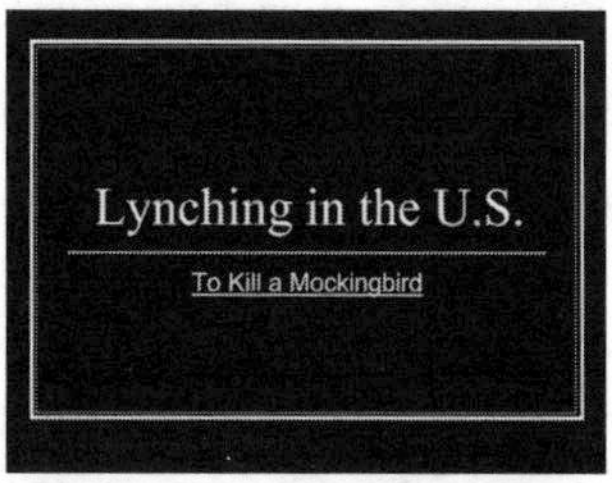

Slide 2

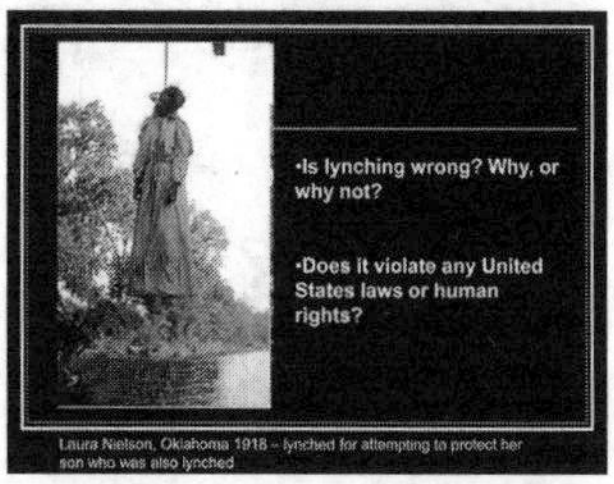

Slide 3

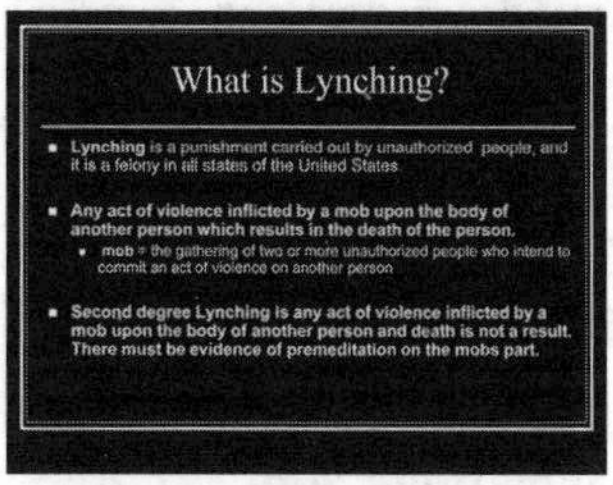

Slide 4

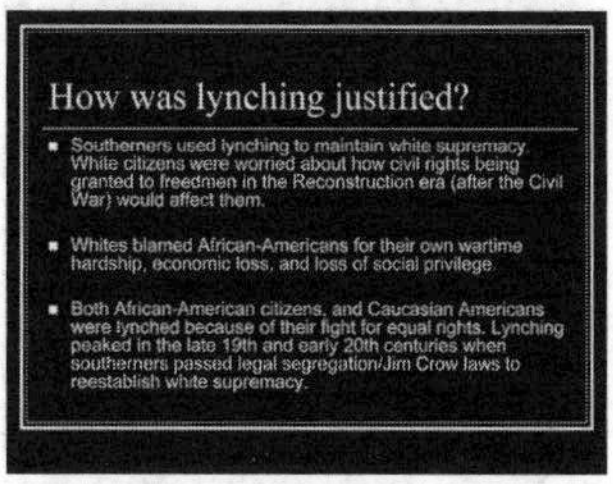

Slide 5

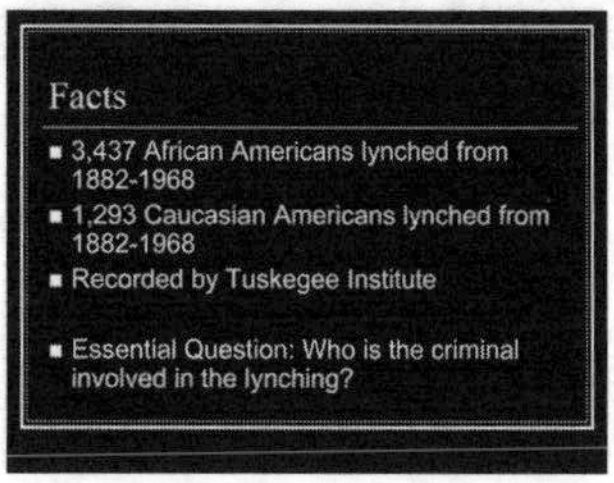

Figure 22.1. Lynching PowerPoint presentation.

---

1. Introduce the movie clip
2. First clip: Lynching Scene: Scene 17 (1:14:23–1:17 = 2.5 minutes)
   - What did you notice about the lynching scene?
   - Why were there so many people present?
   - Why did the man in the passenger seat want to cut the lynched man down?
   - How did the people in the car feel? Should they be scared? What can we assume would have happened if they wouldn't have gotten away?
   - Were they protected by the law?
3. Second clip: Debate (1:52–1:55:13 seconds = 3 minutes)
   - "What was this Negro's crime that he should be hung without trial?"— What was the Negro's crime?
   - How would you feel if you could be killed at any moment for no reason at all? How would you feel if you were not protected by the law?
   - "The mob was the criminal"—Do you agree, and why? Who is the criminal involved in the lynching?
   - "Nothing that erodes the rule of law can be moral"—What does this phrase mean? Was the law just during this era?
   - "An unjust law is no law at all"—St. Augustine. If the law is wrong/unjust/immoral, what rights do we as people have to change/resist it?
   - If people would not have protested these laws back then, what would our society look like today?

Figure 22.2. *The Great Debaters* lesson plan.

critique the statements that the film and the novel make about segregation's violations of human rights. The clips stimulate students' response through the use of open-ended questions (Figure 22.2). They consider the mood of the scene, why the mood is tense, why lynching occurred, and how it was justified. They also consider what it would be like to live in fear with limited resources to resist the systems of oppression. Because US segregation is an era that inhumanely violated the rights of a group of US citizens, students have experiences that can be used to connect them to the Tom Robinson case. The clips move students to a level of analysis and understanding that must accompany the novel and its contents; students begin to contextualize this novel within the greater American experience.

Assessment

There are two portions of assessment for this lesson series; a close reading activity first tests whether students can identify how African Americans'

- Read the poem two to three times.
- Circle the three most important words and in two or three sentences explain your choices.
- Underline two things that are confusing and in two or three sentences explain your choices.
- What is the significance or meaning of the title?
- Illustrate the poem.
- What is the main idea of the poem?
- Would you reorganize the stanzas in any way? Would you put stanzas together or break stanzas apart? Explain your choice.

Figure 22.3. Reading directives/strategies.

human rights were violated. Students receive a copy of Paul Laurence Dunbar's poem "The Haunted Oak" and a list of seven directives (Figure 22.3). The directives are strategies that are frequently used to give students a framework to understand that reading is a process; these directives illustrate that reading and unlocking texts is accomplished through the development of a set of skills. Through the close reading of the poem, students explore the heart of Dunbar's poem whereby an inanimate object, a tree, is personified and given a voice; the human being hanging from his limbs becomes the inanimate object. Students work through the poem individually and then share in small groups; we transition from small groups to a larger group discussion. Students realize through the small-group work that poetry rarely has one answer; with this realization students become more confident in their interpretations. The larger group discussion greatly benefits from the small groups because students feel more comfortable. Students receive a class work grade for the completion of the assignment; the assignment is worth 100 points, and each task is equally weighted. Students receive full credit for the completion of each task.

Finally, the journal entry provides a formative assessment where students enjoy connecting to the literature (Tom Robinson's case) by identifying how the topics of human rights and social injustice present themselves in their own lives (Figure 22.4). Students keep a journal that is composed of responses to essential questions, creative writing prompts, and entries that students choose; students receive credit for each journal entry and at the end of the year do a reflective assignment on their journal. The journal is a dialogue journal where I engage with the students

Have you or anyone you know been accused of something that you didn't do? What feelings did this situation evoke? Were any of your rights violated? If so, which ones? How did you handle the situation?

Figure 22.4. Journal prompt.

by posing questions and making comments to guide them to think and articulate themselves more clearly, deeply, and dynamically. In some cases, I ask the students to rewrite the entry after having reviewed my comments or if the topic has been discussed further in class.

Considerations

To Kill a Mockingbird is dynamic in its accessibility and connectivity to a diverse audience. While we can choose to highlight many different aspects of the text, it would be doing Harper Lee, African American history, and civil rights activists a disservice if students walk away from the novel believing that Tom Robinson was merely a fictional character, or that *To Kill a Mockingbird* was simply a sad fictitious story. Discussing cultural and racial topics can be uncomfortable; however, if we fail to engage and better understand these topics, we are simply putting up blinders and ignoring the complexity of the American experience both past and present.

23 Integrating Technology, Inquiry, and Personal Connections through a Study of *To Kill a Mockingbird*

Angela M. Woods
Garner Magnet High School

> *"First of all," he said, "if you can learn a simple trick, Scout, you'll get along a lot better with all kinds of folks. You never really understand a person until you consider things from his point of view—"*
> *"Sir?"*
> *"—until you climb into his skin and walk around in it."*
> —Atticus Finch to Scout in *To Kill a Mockingbird*

Purpose

While students come to enjoy *To Kill a Mockingbird* by the end of the unit, they often have a difficult time relating to some of the characters and events in the first part of the novel. Through this interdisciplinary experience, students not only become more personally engaged with the novel, they also make thematic connections between the novel and our global society. A group study of the historical and cultural background in which *To Kill a Mockingbird* is set provides students with the framework to begin understanding important themes and characters' reactions in the novel. Through careful examination of characterization, students respond personally to the text in character blogs. The blogs also offer opportunities for students to practice writing narratives, establish rules for blog etiquette, and engage in dialogue with each other about the characters' actions and reactions in the novel. The essential question, "How does the environment in which we live affect us?" guides the focus of the unit and provides a lens through which students can interact with the novel. The final assessment asks students to examine the society in which they live, identify an area of social concern, and prepare a publication that presents their findings and offers solutions to effect positive change.

Materials

The primary materials required for this lesson are computers with Internet access. The technologies used are available on most home and school computers or are from trusted websites and are free downloads. Voice-Thread (www.voicethread.com) is a free program where students can create interactive and collaborative documents to share with classmates about the historical and cultural background in the novel. Headphones with attached microphones are an option if students are creating VoiceThreads at school, but they can also type text directly in the thread, so microphones are not required. Because different websites offer blogs (e.g., Blogger, WordPress, and EduBlogs) I choose one appropriate for me, my students, and my school, and one that they are comfortable using. Chart paper and sticky notes are also useful for brainstorming. The characterization chart (Figure 23.1) assists students in analyzing the various characters in the novel before they choose a character to follow in their reader response journals and blogs. A data projector connected to a laptop computer with Internet access is also helpful to use when modeling how to use the various technologies.

Introduction

One primary theme in the novel *To Kill a Mockingbird* is that understanding, appreciating, and empathizing with others' points of view is a necessary life skill if we are to be successful, productive, caring adults. This interdisciplinary unit of inquiry asks students to follow a character and his or her actions and reactions to events in the novel by considering how the historical and cultural environment of the time might have affected that person. Students understand that the purpose of our activities is connected to examining and attempting to answer the essential question guiding our unit. The historical and cultural background they research provides students with a solid foundation for understanding the context of the novel before they begin reading. This background allows students to activate prior knowledge when analyzing characters and responding to the literature.

Another important method for engaging students is using technology to foster student reflection and dialogue between students. As students make connections to the characters they follow, they become more comfortable and confident sharing ideas and analyzing texts both in their blogs and in class discussions.

Connections

This lesson is designed around an inquiry approach that asks students to make personal connections to the literature. Using an essential question to guide the direction of our reflections, blog dialogues, and in-class discussions gives students a clear purpose for our inquiry-based activities. An inquiry-based approach aligns with Wilhelm's goals (Chapter 3) to "reframe English language arts as personal studies and inquiries." Framing the lesson around an essential question not only helps students connect the literature to their own lives, but it also encourages them to consider other people and to actively seek positive changes to make the world in which we live a better place.

The reader response journals and blog posts encourage students to engage with the characters, the text, and with other students, an approach advocated by Jago (Chapter 2) and Blau (Chapter 1). Jago encourages students and teachers to ask questions in their reader responses; the blog dialogues foster questions and challenge students' thinking as they consider others' point of view. The reader response journals, blog posts, and in-class discussions also support Blau's approach that students of literature must "construct a meaningful interpretation of what they have read" rather than "expecting their teachers to provide them with a sense of the meaning of what they have read."

Activities

I begin the *To Kill a Mockingbird* unit by placing students in new literature groups of mixed ability and multiple intelligences. As a class, we read a short introduction to the novel before I give students a list of possible historical, social, economic, cultural, and political background topics to research with their groups. The topics include Jim Crow laws, the Great Depression, the Scottsboro trials, Southern culture in 1930s, racial prejudice, education in the 1930s, women in the 1930s, and headlines of the 1930s. Each group chooses one topic to research and creates a VoiceThread that is accessible from any computer with Internet access. Students begin researching and designing their group VoiceThread in class, working cooperatively; but the features of VoiceThread allow them to work individually on the presentation so it can be finalized outside of class without students' having to meet personally.

Before students begin researching their chosen topic, we have a class discussion on reliable and unreliable sources. I have found that, rather than giving a worksheet explaining how to evaluate websites, it is more effective and engaging if I research a topic with them. I ask students to suggest topics, select one of their suggestions, and using my data projector and laptop computer, I search for websites using Google. As a class, we survey the results of the search, and they choose which websites they want me to select. While exploring these websites, I show students how they can uncover more information about the sites so they can determine their reliability. We locate the author, the creation date, and latest update of the pages. We also discuss common extensions in domain names: commercial (.com), educational (.edu), organizations (.org), government (.gov), and networks (.net). Extensions tell Web users what type of group owns and publishes the domain name. This information is often helpful when determining the site's reliability. To illustrate unreliable Web sources, I find examples that might be hosted by groups with an ulterior motive.

Next, I show students the VoiceThread website and several examples of interesting, interactive documents others have created. Finally, I show students how easy VoiceThread demonstrations are to create. Because VoiceThread is similar in function to a slideshow, each group member locates at least two images related to their group topic and annotates those images with written text or a voiceover.

I give students two class periods to conduct their research and set aside at least fifteen minutes at the end of each research session for students to discuss their findings in their group. During these discussions, students plan how they will divide the research, provide updates on their research, and finalize the content that will appear in their presentation. After two days of research, students strategize how they will finish their portion of the presentation and document whether or not they will finish at home or using one of the computers in the media center. Students have two more days outside class to finalize the VoiceThread before they present their demonstrations. The final product is similar to a slideshow presentation, and I link the VoiceThreads to the class website so all students in class can access the research projects later in the lesson when they are responding to the novel.

After the research presentations, students have a clearer understanding of the historical, social, economic, cultural, and political setting of *To Kill a Mockingbird*. Before we begin reading the novel, I give students a brief character sketch of the main characters. In previous units, we have brainstormed ways readers personally respond to literature, and I remind students of the list we generated that they have in their reader response journals.

One of the ways readers respond to literature is by making personal connections to the literature, often through the characters, so I ask students to share personal examples of when in their past reading they have connected to characters. I then explain that throughout the study of To *Kill a Mockingbird* they will choose one character they will follow while reading the novel. I ask students to choose one character for each member in their group to prevent overlap and to choose from Scout Finch, Jem Finch, Atticus Finch, Miss Maudie, Boo Radley, Aunt Alexandra, Mayella Ewell, or Tom Robinson.

I remind students that we will guide our study of *To Kill a Mockingbird* by using an essential question as we delve into the themes and characters in the text while making connections to our own communities. The essential question is, How does the environment in which we live affect us? This broad essential question provides opportunities for students to think about how historical, social, economic, cultural, and political environments shape us as individuals and our decisions. It prompts us to consider life from the perspective of others and provides opportunities for students to have enriching discussions on tolerance and our personal responsibilities to an increasingly global society.

While reading *To Kill a Mockingbird*, students keep a reader response journal where they respond in two ways: a personal response to the text and a response through the eyes of the character. In their personal response, students describe their thoughts and feelings, ask questions, make inferences, predict events, draw conclusions, explain what they like and dislike, and make personal connections to the characters and thematic events in the novel. When responding through their character's voice, students consider the historical and cultural environment and provide an honest reaction to events in the novel. Students use their reader response journals to create their own character blog for the character they are following throughout *To Kill a Mockingbird*. I provide a unit reading calendar with character blog post directions and due dates. Creating a posting calendar is essential so students are responding to the same events in their posts. In their blogs, students create one new post every week and comment at least one time a week on each of their group members' weekly character posts. Before we begin blogging, we brainstorm blogging etiquette and create a list of rules for us to follow. Also, students meet in their blogging groups to complete the *To Kill a Mockingbird* characterization worksheet (Figure 23.1) to analyze the characters before blogging starts.

Characterization is used to describe the qualities of a character by (1) showing the character's appearance, (2) displaying the character's actions, (3) revealing the character's thoughts, (4) letting the character speak, and (5) getting the reactions of others. Examine the characterization of the different townspeople in *To Kill a Mockingbird* by completing the chart below.

Character	Physical Description (Appearance and Clothing)	Character's Actions	Personality Traits	Reaction of Others
Scout				
Jem				
Atticus				
Miss Maudie				
Boo Radley				
Aunt Alexandra				
Mayella Ewell				
Tom Robinson				

Figure 23.1. *To Kill a Mockingbird* characterization worksheet.

In the beginning, it is helpful to have short in-class group discussions and allow students to meet with others who have chosen the same character so they can share their personal responses and character responses. Students are successful at brainstorming possible blog topics, and the blog posts are more reflective when students have the direction. I also frequently remind students to consider our essential question when posting and commenting, and I encourage them to challenge what other posters in their group have said. Sometimes I also provide possible topics or questions students can reflect on in their posts, but I try to remove these scaffolding techniques at the midpoint of the unit to ensure their character responses and the dialogue are reflective and authentic.

Throughout our work, we have several seminars where we make thematic connections between the novel and contemporary social issues. Some topics we consider are the economy, racism, prejudice, discrimination, classism, sexism, religious intolerance, harassment, slavery, famine, and genocide. I pull from current local and world events to make the discussions more relevant. However, I also ask students to consider these topics from other points of view and to comment on their own personal responsibility to social concerns.

The final assessment for this lesson requires students to work in their blogging groups to identify an area of social concern either local or global, research their topic, and prepare a publication, in a format of their own choosing. They present their findings, provide reasons why everyone has a personal responsibility to improving the larger community, and offer solutions to effect positive change. Groups have chosen many formats in which to present their information: brochures, posters, public service announcements, websites, and VoiceThreads.

Assessment

I assess student work in a variety of ways throughout the study of *To Kill a Mockingbird*. Each student presents research findings on the historical and cultural setting of the novel in the group VoiceThread. They are assessed on the validity of their research, the appropriateness of the images they selected to represent their topic, and the quality of the VoiceThread produced. Since the VoiceThread project is a demonstration presented to the class and my expectations are high, this assessment counts as a test grade.

Periodically during the unit, I collect reader response journals and evaluate them for thoughtful, reflective, personal responses and assess students' evaluations of the character responses. I ensure that students are focused in the right direction and are authentic before they post their character blogs. When grading the reader response journals, my goal is to ensure that students are responding to the assigned readings by the due dates and that their responses are appropriate; therefore, most students receive full credit for a class work grade on their journals. Student blogs also show evidence of personal connections to characters, themes, and events in the novel, while also illustrating appropriate blog etiquette, writing style, and proper grammar. However, since the blogs are formally published for others to read, students are given a combined quiz grade for each group of postings and responses. The seminars provide another assessment tool and require students to examine their own personal responsibility to the global community. Preparation for and participation in seminar discussions also counts as a quiz grade.

The final assessment is a test grade that culminates with students illustrating their greater understanding of how the environment in which we live not only affects us as individuals, but affects us as a community. Through this greater understanding, students think more globally about how social issues affect the larger society and how we all have an investment and personal responsibility to bring about positive change.

Considerations

This interdisciplinary lesson series integrates English language arts, social studies, and technology to provide students with multiple opportunities to be responsible for their own learning while making connections to the text, their local community, and the global society. My students especially enjoy the technology integration as I meet them in an environment where they are comfortable and allow them to showcase their technology skills. The online dialogue among classmates keeps my students engaged in the novel as they challenge their own thinking and that of their classmates. They have been successful in gaining a deeper understanding of the points of view of others, and this connection transfers to other texts we read.

Incorporating some of these technology tools can be challenging. Therefore, it is important, when planning, to ensure that the tools are available to students in school and at home, or provide alternative ways for students to access the technology. Although I heavily integrate the novel study with technology, there are ways it can be adapted if technology is limited. Students could present their historical and cultural research findings in a PowerPoint presentation or any other overhead projection rather than a VoiceThread. Exchanging reader response logs with other group members is also a low-tech alternative to blogs.

VII Talking Back to *The Bluest Eye*

KaaVonia Hinton
Old Dominion University

My copy of *The Bluest Eye* is worn with frayed edges and dark, tan pages. It looks like someone decided to take a bite out of the front cover, and it smells like it has been packed away with a batch of chocolate chip cookies. I bought it at a used bookstore, but the stamp on the spine says it belonged to a local university bookstore at some point. I do not know how many owners it had before me, but I was the first to mark it up. The novel was assigned reading in my college African American Novel II class.

The Bluest Eye is Toni Morrison's first novel. Claudia MacTeer, the nine-year-old narrator, looks back at her eleven-year-old friend Pecola Breedlove's demise, beginning with being raped and impregnated by her father. Pecola prays for blonde hair and blue eyes, symbols of beauty she hopes will bring her love, and when they do not, she goes insane. Set in the 1940s in Lorain, Ohio, the novel's major themes surround internalized racism, beauty aesthetics, and stifling oppression. Passages from a *Dick and Jane* reader serve as chapter headings throughout, reinforcing and juxtaposing characteristics of mainstream US society, such as the narrow definition of family and beauty aesthetics.

It was one of the hardest texts I read in college, if I do not count the huge book of collected Shakespearean plays assigned that semester. At the time, I thought *The Bluest Eye* was a much needed respite, since it is so thin. I still have both texts, but *The Bluest Eye* is filled with marginalia, though the collection of the bard's plays is not. My copy is filled with questions: "How does Pecola first learn she is ugly? Did Morrison read Brooks' *Maud Martha* (1953)? Ellison's *Invisible Man* (1952)? How does Claudia know what society is up to? Why is he called Cholly and the mother is called Mrs. Breedlove? Why didn't Cholly hate the white men who humiliated him? Is colorism to blame too? Gender? Poverty?" It is also filled with notes. On the title page where I summarized the text, I wrote, "Pauline cannot show love nor demonstrate affection or concern for her children or husband." On page 11, I wrote, "A few run together sentences describe Dick and Jane's pretty house. The Breedlove's house is a converted store with beaverboard panels providing the only inner walls."

Questions and notes often fill the margins of a difficult text, a text that makes one uncomfortable and maybe even afraid. Issues of racism and poverty are explicit and raw, the rape scene cruel and unthinkable. The lessons featured in this section tackle these tough issues and argue that identity is socially constructed and constantly changing. Under the guidance of professional educators, students can make sense of the world in the text and the one around them.

Where was *The Bluest Eye* in my teen years, I wondered during my twenties. The television and magazine ads had nearly gotten the best of me, too. Being beautiful was impossible. Terms such as "good hair" and "bad hair" plagued me. Where I grew up, someone with "good hair" had hair that was straight and silky while a person with "bad hair" had hair that looked like mine. As a young girl running around slinging my toweled head from side to side, perception and the urge to develop my own understanding of beauty became important. In fact, one lesson that follows (Chapter 24) asks students to wrestle with those deeply seated opinions about beauty and self. Other lessons confront issues of identify formation, examine Morrison's craft, and lead students to question be-haviors and values in texts and society. Together, the lessons encourage reading, writing, speaking, listening, viewing, and evaluating. Don-ning multiple lenses, manipulating graphic organizers, tinkering with technology, and applying real-world connections are a few of the best practices at the heart of these plans. Instruction around *The Bluest Eye* requires a focus on how the characters respond to multiple oppressive forces such as racism, classism, and sexism, topics pursued forthrightly here. Finally, the lessons move beyond an analysis and critique of the novel toward acting against social injustice. The plans critically embody the concepts and guidance of our introductory essayists.

24 Beauty and Identity in *The Bluest Eye*

Chelsey Saunders
Needham Broughton High School, Raleigh, North Carolina

Purpose

The Bluest Eye is an ideal text for incorporating different epistemologies and metacognitive strategies. The goal is to help students read and re-read the text while effectively utilizing reader response and other lenses, theories, or methods of looking at words, context, voice, and other textual factors. Pecola's life exposes both the journey for acceptance and the adverse effects of heartache and rejection. Literary theory pushes students to expand their critical thinking skills in the midst of Pecola's extreme emotions and moments of self-awareness.

Toni Morrison's text may be students' first exposure to literature from the point of view of the perceived "other" or marginalized voice. Therefore, the following lesson is an effort to introduce students to a few basic, yet problematic, concepts that affect all who are searching for identity, particularly those marginalized by race or gender.

Through the unit experiences, students examine and differentiate methods of perception as well as analyze representations of beauty in our culture as not merely arbitrary and esoteric but unavoidably fictitious and hyper-real while creating a new way of perceiving beauty, describing identity for the twenty-first century. They also identify and contest the power of language as well as explore the powerful language used to describe characters and notions of identity.

Materials

- *The Bluest Eye,* LCD projector, computer with Internet, Figure 24.1 (4-2-1 worksheet), Figure 24.2 (Close Reading Practice worksheet), Figure 24.3 (list of quotations), and a series of articles help articulate the concepts of beauty / gender / race / reader response theory:

- Cheng, Anne. "Wounded Beauty: An Exploratory Essay on Race, Feminism, and the Aesthetic Question." *Tulsa Studies in Women's Literature*, 19.2 (2000): 191–217.

- Sekayi, Dia. "Aesthetic Resistance to Commercial Influences: The Impact of the Eurocentric Beauty Standard on Black College Women." *The Journal of Negro Education* 72.4 (2003): 467–77.

- Soublis, Theoni, and Erik Winkler. "Snapshots: Transcending Bias through Reader-Response Theory" *English Journal* 94.2 (2004): 12–14.

Introduction

Using literary theory to approach the novel may strike students as, well, novel. Many are not exposed to literary theory and may cower behind complaints that these concepts are useless and complicated. However, this approach examines why many students may resist *The Bluest Eye* because it is written by someone who does not look, think, or experience a familiar lifestyle or because it starkly reveals the grotesque realities that hit too close to home.

Theory, as it applies to Toni Morrison's texts, gives validity to several perspectives and forces students to deliberate and ponder why they react to texts with such distaste or disinterest. In addition, it guides students to engage with the text and the never-ending questions it evokes, both with personal fervor and critical distance. In fact, by dealing with realistic ideas and problems, such as beauty, identity, friendship, and loss, students evolve in self-awareness while learning to embrace different perspectives and "historical" viewpoints simultaneously.

Connections

One way to engage student minds into multiple, critical readings of a text is to consider several perspectives and interpretations of the same text. Literary theory not only diminishes authoritative dictums of interpretation but also, in a digital age when everyone has an opinion, delineates multiple pathways for the twenty-first century student to discern how opinions may or may not be valid. Today, students are unaware that the latest gossip blog is a censorious reader response essay, which interprets pop culture as a text. Literary theory, as Moore (Chapter 5) reminds us in his essay, helps facilitate discussion about concepts such as beauty, identity, perception, and context in the "high" and "low" texts. Reading

The Bluest Eye opens the minds and hearts of students to the awareness of how to read and interpret the world.

Activities

Activity 1: First Thought, First Word: I am beautiful.

As soon as the bell rings, I ask the students to respond to the statement above on a blank sheet of paper. They consider the following questions: Do they agree? What do they believe about beauty? (Fun add-on: Students repeat the statement aloud several times and stand up to strike a pose every time they use the word *beautiful*. This technique helps student engagement if it is brief and quick and energetically suggested.)

After five minutes, students respond to the Essential Question displayed on the board: How do you know what is beautiful? They write how they know what is beautiful, creating a bulleted list, fragments, run-on sentences, or other form. I encourage them to use specific examples of things, people, and places they believe are beautiful. Then, they write about the most beautiful thing they have ever seen and explain why it was so beautiful. After discussing the aesthetics of art, culture, landscapes, and other ideas they may have listed in their answers, I shift the conversation to "beauty" as it applies to people. How do we know/decide someone is beautiful? How do we decide whether I/you/we are/were beautiful? This discussion leads them to describe the ideally beautiful person.

They reflect on their freewrite and find reasons for their opinions by identifying a specific instance/experience that led them to a specific conclusion about beauty.

Opinion	Experience
1.	1.
2.	2.

Debrief: Do we all find the same things beautiful? What does that word really mean?

Activity 2

Part 1: What are beauty and identity?

To begin this activity, I write my own definition of "time" on the board and explain why I think it is valid. Next, students write quickly a definition of "love" on a note card and pass it to the front. As I read them aloud, I discuss my thought process as I compare and contrast the given definitions. Students then combine two or three of the best definitions and explain why they find them to be the most valid. For example, love may be a feeling of excitement to one student, but a large group of students may disagree and say that it is more of a commitment that increases in worth and value over time, regardless of feelings. The class members argue, dispute, and eventually agree on what their experience and lives "tell them" is the best definition of love.

Using the 4-2-1 worksheet (Figure 24.1), each student receives either the word *identity* or *beauty* and writes four definitions of the word in the first four boxes. Students then have two minutes to find someone else with the same word and collaborate to create two possible definitions; then two students meet with two more students (to total four) to agree on one definition. Each group writes this definition on a giant piece of paper and tapes it on the board. They stand and defend the definitions they created using their experiences; as a class, we vote for the best one. Finally, students answer the following questions individually:

> Identity: What is identity? How do you know?
>
> Beauty: What is it? How do you know if you are beautiful?

Summation: Students explain how they answered these questions based on their perception (of experience) and context.

Part 2: What roles do perception and context play in our understanding?

I begin this activity by asking students the following questions about their definitions of beauty and identity: Would my next class create the same definition? Would a class in California? In Australia? In Africa? Would you create the same definition for identity and beauty five years from now? Why or why not?

Next, I use the following minilesson.

1. I create a bubble map on the board with "context" in the middle and label all the factors that change context of situations, reading, and understanding. I do the same for "perspective" and take some time to show how our eyes play tricks on us using the following website: Illusions and Paradoxes: Seeing Is Believing? (www.scientificpsychic.com/graphics/). Students discuss

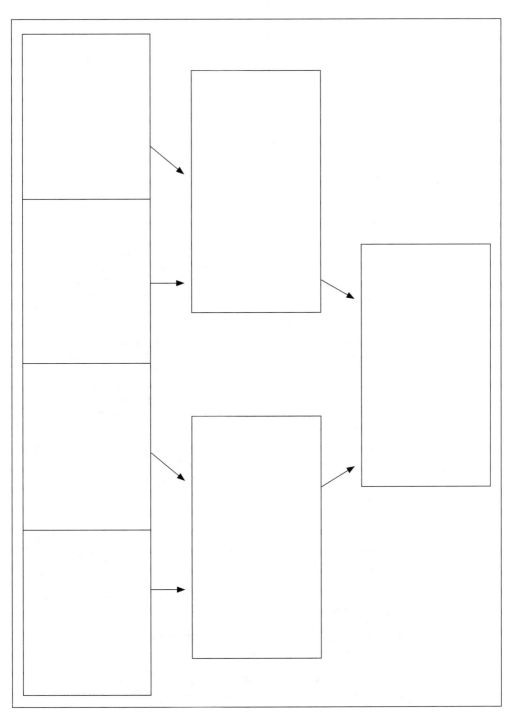

Figure 24.1. 4-2-1 worksheet.

briefly the way these tricks happen on the way from the eye to the brain and are scientifically fascinating and engaging.

2. I ask students to imagine a beautiful flamingo in a Sprite Zero bottle. I follow with the questions, "Can you imagine it? Can it really exist?" Students explore how the flamingo can exist in the mind, but not in reality. I follow with, "What do these two ideas [perception tricks and flamingo in the mind] show us about the validity of perception?" We then review how context can be one of the many factors that shift perception by referring back to the bubble maps.

3. For the next step of the activity, I ask students to complete the following sentences: "Discuss how beautiful you think ____ is to you. (It can be a type of stuffed animal, a pet, a place, and so on.) Explain how throughout your life and since childhood it has meant ____ and made you feel ____. Show how these experiences with ____ were affected by the context and your perception." Students proceed to tell a partner about someone who would fit their ideal of a beautiful person and discuss the reasons and experiences they used to validate their opinion. They take notes on their partner's reasoning to share with the class.

   Other questions I use to guide an expanded discussion: What factors may affect or de-validate students' opinions? Does a person exist who fits the criteria for beautiful? Did you know about the person in advance, or was it the other way around? In other words, why did you choose those characteristics? Or, why did the person next to you have different words and a different image of beauty?

4. In the next part of the activity, students write an argument in response to one of the following statements.

   Perception: How do you know that what you see is truly what is?

   Context: What are the factors that shift our understanding and perception of words and meaning?

   The follow-up discussion explores how we can be aware of these concepts as we read a text.

Part 3: What are textual examples of the nuance of context and perception as they influence beauty and identity?

With the entire class, I conduct a close reading exercise using the following quotation from *The Bluest Eye*:

> It had occurred to Pecola some time ago that if her eyes, those eyes that held the pictures, and knew the sights—if those eyes of hers were different, that is to say, beautiful, she herself would be different. (46)

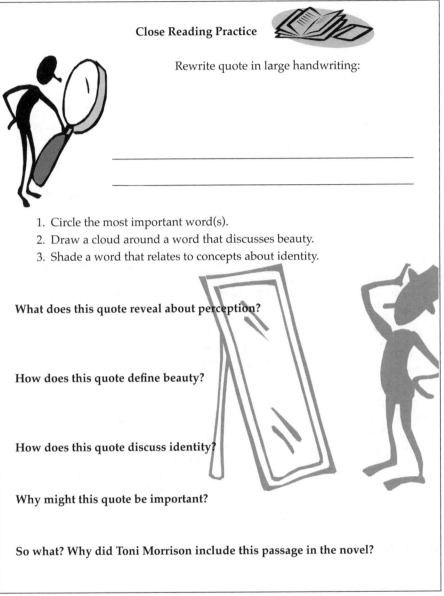

Figure 24.2. Close Reading Practice worksheet.

We explore the questions, "What point of view is the quotation arguing? Predict what the context might be for Pecola. What is her perception? What is she saying about perception?" Students discuss these ideas as they complete the Close Reading Practice sheet (Figure 24.2).

"We stare at her, wanting her bread, but more than that wanting to poke the arrogance out of her eyes and smash the pride of ownership that curls her chewing mouth." (9)

❖ "Adults, older girls, shops, magazines, newspapers, window signs—all the world had agreed that a blue-eyed, yellow-haired, pink-skinned doll was what every girl child treasured. 'Here,' they said, 'this is beautiful, and if you are on this day "worthy" you may have it.'" (20–21)

❖ "Long hours she sat looking in the mirror, trying to discover the secret of the ugliness, the ugliness that made her ignored or despised at school, by teachers and classmates alike." (45)

❖ "Dandelions. A dart of affection leaps out from her to them. But they do not look at her and do not send love back. She thinks, 'They are ugly. They are weeds.' Preoccupied with that revelation, she trips on the sidewalk crack. Anger stirs and wakes in her; it opens its mouth, and like a hot-mouthed puppy, laps up the dredges of her shame. Anger is better. There is a sense of being in anger. A reality and presence. An awareness of worth." (50)

❖ "It was their contempt for their own blackness that gave the first insult its teeth. They seemed to have taken all of their smoothly cultivated ignorance, their exquisitely learned self-hatred, their elaborately designed hopelessness and sucked it all up into a fiery cone of scorn that had burned for ages in the hollows of their minds—cooled—and spilled over lips of outrage, consuming whatever was in its path." (65)

❖ "In equating physical beauty with virtue, she stripped her mind, bound it, and collected self-contempt by the heap. . . . She was never able, after her education in the movies, to look at a face and not assign it some category in the scale of absolute beauty, and the scale was one she absorbed in full from the silver screen." (122)

❖ "I thought about the baby that everyone wanted dead, and saw it very clearly. It was in a dark, wet place, its head covered with O's of wool, the black face holding, like nickels, two clean black eyes, the flared nose, kissing-thick lips, and the living, breathing silk of black skin. No synthetic yellow bangs suspended over marble-blue eyes, no pinched nose and bowline mouth. More strongly than my fondness for Pecola, I felt a need for someone to want the black baby to live—just to counteract the universal love of white baby dolls, Shirley Temples, and Maureen Peals." (190)

Figure 24.3. Other quotations to consider.

The Bluest Eye contains numerous other references to beauty and identity that I use for further experiences with close reading (Figure 24.3). Students practice with new quotations independently. I provide Figure 24.2 on the front and back of the sheet, so they can practice once with the class and once individually.

Summation: Students consider the following questions independently, in groups, or in whole-class discussion. "How do you know what is beautiful? How do you think Pecola decides what is beautiful? What do you predict is her identity? What do you predict is her context? What sort of things do you think shift her perception throughout her story?"

Activity 3: I am beautiful.

I show pictures of celebrities with and without makeup (check out http://seehere.blogspot.com/2006/08/celebrities-without-makeup.html) and ask students to rethink their standard of beauty and where it originates. I then ask them to think twice when they read the world around them, to think about why they believe people, places, and ideas are or are not beautiful. Is beauty in the eye of the beholder, or is it both perception and beauty that are more than skin deep?

Assessment

The number-one topic of conversation for high school adolescents begins with "I think." Therefore, when students express themselves and find new ways to relate to the world, it allows for endless teachable moments, especially with Toni Morrison's text as the inspiration. Using these activities as a catalyst, students write daily reflection papers of no more than a page as they read. These papers lead to an extended dialogue, where I ask students further open-ended questions to guide their thinking. Students receive credit both for their participation in these activities and for their papers.

Considerations

With several possible layers and questions embedded in the plot and in the relationships among the characters, students can be overwhelmed with the trauma and miss the nuances of *The Bluest Eye*. Even though civil rights is a well-covered topic in high schools, rarely are the effects of slavery and segregation shared from the black, female perspective. It is because the text is challenging and complex and comes from a marginalized voice that secondary students should read it. The issues of identity and beauty are still relevant. The harsh events that Pecola and her friends experience are still realities for teens today. It is important to consistently point out the atrocity of the moments and the reality that these are not just fictional plot points. This lesson allows for chaos and unbridled limits of thought and direction, so it may be useful to take the discussions to online discussion boards.

25 American Naturalism in *The Bluest Eye*

Roger S. Baskin Sr.
Lake Braddock Secondary School, Burke, Virginia

Purpose

By building on students' prior knowledge of issues of social justice, this lesson enables students to develop a deeper understanding of the literary tradition of American naturalism and how the novel *The Bluest Eye* represents the technique in characterization, theme, and plot structure. Because naturalism relies on social science to explain the phenomenon of social stratification, the lesson also introduces students to Abraham Maslow's hierarchy of needs.

The activities in this lesson series guide students to read and analyze relationships among American literature, history, and culture while also using a variety of informational materials. In this process they write in a variety of forms, with a particular emphasis on persuasion and research. They also explore the philosophical underpinnings of naturalism to interpret *The Bluest Eye* from that perspective.

Materials

- LCD Projector, computer, Internet access, Blackboard, and Figure 25.1 (PowerPoint)
- Internet sites:
    - Naturalism in American Literature: http://www.wsu.edu/~campbelld/amlit/natural.htm
    - From "Novel Expert Evidence in Federal Civil Rights Litigation" by Gordon Beggs: http://varenne.tc.columbia.edu/class/common/dolls_in_brown_vs_board.html
    - Maslow's Hierarchy of Needs: http://honolulu.hawaii.edu/intranet/committees/FacDevCom/guidebk/teachtip/maslow.htm
- Novels:
    - *Adventures of Huckleberry Finn* (Twain)

- *The Bluest Eye* (Morrison)
- *The Handmaid's Tale* (Atwood)
- *Woman at Point Zero* (Wright)
■ Short stories:
  - "The Man Who Was Almost a Man" (Wright)
  - "Roselily" (Walker)

Introduction

According to *Classroom Instruction That Works: Research-Based Strategies for Increasing Student Achievement*, "Questions are effective learning tools even when asked before a learning experience. We generally think of questioning as something teachers do *after* students have been engaged in a learning experience. . . . Teachers, however, can use questions *before* a learning experience to establish a 'mental set' with which students process the learning experience" (Marzano, Pickering, & Pollock 2001, 114). This lesson begins with a question—"Why do we need literature that shows *how* people fail to overcome certain obstacles?"—to encourage students to think about *The Bluest Eye* in light of a larger purpose and to encourage them to create their own rationale for the importance of reading the novel.

Following the initial question, students view a picture of a rat being lowered into a terrarium with a snake whose mouth is wide open as if poised to strike. The image is a powerful one and is indicative of the experience of protagonists in naturalist novels in general, and of Pecola Breedlove, the main character of *The Bluest Eye*, in particular. With Pecola's existence—surrounded by poverty, violence, racial discrimination, and dysfunctional adults—Morrison portrays a young girl who will not overcome obstacles. The task of the reader, then, is not to search for the happy ending but to critique the degree to which the author is true to the portrayal of Pecola's loss of sanity. Is this really how it happens? Are these the forces that drive people mad? Hence, students leap into the realm of literary criticism and evaluate the author's attempt at an authentic depiction of how social stratification contributes to psychological frailty.

Connections

In the introductory essays of this text, both Jago (Chapter 2) and Moore (Chapter 5) focus on American literary history and critical reading strategies that are born out of an understanding of the philosophical underpinnings of American naturalism. The study of American naturalism, in general, and *The Bluest Eye*, in particular, lends itself to psychoanalytic criticism, Marxist criticism, and historical criticism.

Activities

Activity 1: American Naturalist Literature

I begin the lesson by displaying Figure 25.1 (PowerPoint), a picture of a rat and a snake, and I ask the students to respond orally to the following questions:

> Given the rat's current environment, does it have a chance to survive and live a long life? What barrier exists?
>
> Can this rat's reality mirror the reality of some people?

Next, students respond to the following question either in writing or orally:

> Given a person's environment at birth, can their future be predetermined, assuming there is no intervention? Explain in detail.

Students offer examples to support their position on the topic.

Extension: Students may keep a journal as they read the novel to determine if their response to the prior question changes over time.

Activity 2: Dick and Jane

Students read the novel's opening Dick and Jane story. Then students draw a picture of the characters and events in the Dick and Jane story. Next, they read the italicized section at the beginning of the novel and draw a picture inspired by the passage. Once the drawings are complete, students write about the contrast between both environments using the drawings as a guide. Students should also use excerpts from the text to support their written response.

Extension: Students write about how Toni Morrison creates this contrast by responding to the following question:

> What effect is created by juxtaposing the two passages, and how does the author create this effect (e.g., symbols, archetypes, imagery, and so on)?

Activity 3: The Plight of the Protagonist

In this activity students research interventions that could change Pecola Breedlove's story, and they develop recommendations for a plan of action to remedy Pecola's situation.

Figure 25.1. Oral response activity.

Suggestions:

- Students identify specific quotations and instances in the novel where a particular problem occurs. For example, students find excerpts and examples of economic problems that impact the life of the main character either directly or indirectly. Then they identify a research-based approach for resolving the issue—connection to an agency, an existing program, or pending legislation.

- Students work in groups of no more than five to focus on one of the specific intervention areas: psychological, economic, educational, media.

- Students research organizations that work to address issues presented in the novel.

- Students make a group oral presentation on instances of the problem in the novel and recommendations for solutions.

The following organizations and sources provide helpful information.

- Psychological: American Counseling Association, local school counselor

- Economic: National Urban League, NAACP, Children's Defense Fund

- Educational: Office of Student Achievement, National Alliance of Black School Educators
- Media: National Association of Black Journalists, Black Actors Guild

Activity 4: Comparative Analysis of Literature

Students read excerpts from one of the following texts and note how these selections compare to *The Bluest Eye* in terms of effect, form, characterization, theme, and atmosphere:

- *Adventures of Huckleberry Finn*, a novel by Mark Twain
  Students may find similarities in the characterization of the fathers in both texts.

- *Woman at Point Zero*, a novel by Nawal El Saadawi
  Students may find similarities in the environment of the protagonists and the author's close observation of cultural views of beauty and femininity.

- "The Man Who Was Almost a Man," a short story by Richard Wright

  Students may find similarities in the symbolic significance of the gun and its connection to the blue eyes in Morrison's novel.

- "Roselily," a short story by Alice Walker
  Students may find similarities in the use of italics and the deconstruction of the institution of marriage.

- *The Handmaid's Tale*, a novel by Margaret Atwood
  Students may find similarities in the conflicts of the protagonists and the point of view of the narrator.

Suggested guiding questions throughout the exercise are the following:

> In what ways do both Morrison and the other author have a similar effect in some part of their writing? How do they establish that effect? Do they use the same technique to create the same effect or are different techniques used to create a similar impact on the reader and story? Explain.

After considering these questions, students write a comparative essay in which they explore some specific similarity between *The Bluest Eye* and one of the other texts.

> Extension: Students may also give an oral presentation.

Activity 5: Technology and the Study of Literature

Students read and post comments on Blackboard concerning each of the following links.

- Naturalism in American Literature.

  http://www.wsu.edu/~campbelld/amlit/natural.htm

  This link explains the characteristics of naturalistic literature and mentions famous writers of the genre.

  Discussion board question: What characteristics of naturalism are evident in *The Bluest Eye*?

- "Novel Expert Evidence in Federal Civil Rights Litigation" by Gordon Beggs.

  http://varenne.tc.columbia.edu/class/common/dolls_in_brown_vs_board.html

  This link discusses the experiment conducted by Dr. Kenneth Clark that exposed the damaging effects of segregation on the self-image of African American children.

  Discussion board question: How does this information help you to understand the development of Pecola's character?

- Maslow's Hierarchy of Needs.

  http://honolulu.hawaii.edu/intranet/committees/Fac DevCom/guidebk/teachtip/maslow.htm

  This link discusses Dr. Abraham Maslow's hierarchy of needs. This serves as a valuable resource in the discussion of character development.

  Discussion board question: How does this information help you understand the conflicts encountered by the protagonist?

Extension: Students may write a fictional story in which they demonstrate the findings of Dr. Clark or Dr. Maslow.

Assessment

Forms of assessment I employ include oral presentations that require students to compare a literary aspect of the novel to that of another work read during the unit. For example, students may decide to discuss the similarities and differences between the quest of the protagonist in *The Bluest Eye* and that of a protagonist in another work of realism such as *Woman at Point Zero*. Students are also assessed by reading a passage from the text and explaining why the text is indicative of naturalism. Other assessments include responding to questions posted on Blackboard and conversing with classmates online.

Considerations

The approach I use in teaching *The Bluest Eye* helps to make it among the most popular novels students read at my school. It affords them the opportunity to learn conceptual frameworks that equip them to answer difficult and complicated questions concerning systemic injustice and symbolic violence. Further, the incorporation of social sciences in the evaluation of the author's characterization of the protagonist encourages students to stretch their thinking and make connections between the text and real life. These activities enable students to gain valuable exposure to the art of critical analysis and ideas related to challenging the status quo and providing seeds for possible solutions.

References

Atwood, M. (1994). *The handmaid's tale.* New York: Anchor Books.

The Dolls in *Brown vs. Board of Education.* (2004). Retrieved from http://varenne.tc.columbia.edu/class/common/dolls_in_brown_vs_board.html (excerpt from Novel expert evidence in federal civil rights litigation by G. J. Beggs, *American University Law Review, 45,* 1–76)

El Saadawi, N. (1983). *Woman at point zero.* London: Zed Books.

Marzano, R. J., Pickering, D. J., & Pollock, J. E. (2001). *Classroom instruction that works: Research-based strategies for increasing student achievement.* Alexandria, VA: Association for Supervision and Curriculum Development.

Maslow's hierarchy of needs. (n.d.). Retrieved from http://honolulu.hawaii.edu/intranet/committees/FacDevCom/guidebk/teachtip/maslow.htm (excerpt from *Psychology: The search for understanding* by J. A. Simons, D. B. Irwin, & B. A. Drinnien, West Publishing Company, New York, 1987)

Naturalism in American literature. (2009). Retrieved from http://www.wsu.edu/~campbelld/amlit/natural.htm (from Naturalism in American literature, by D. M. Campbell, Department of English, Washington State University)

Twain, M. (1953). *Adventures of Huckleberry Finn.* London: Puffin Books.

Walker, A. (1973). Roselily. In *In Love and trouble: Stories of black women* (pp. 3–9). Orlando, FL: Harcourt.

Wright, R. (1996). The man who was almost a man. In *Eight men: Short stories* (pp. 3–18). New York: HarperCollins. (Original work published 1940)

26 *The Bluest Eye* and the Power of Culture Scripts

Darlene Russell
William Paterson University, New Jersey

Purpose

As a practitioner of critical teaching and social reconstructionism, I believe that it is imperative for educators to adopt transformative curricular practices that precipitate critical thinking and problem solving in the classroom. As such, teachers must be nontraditional in their practices to foster and encourage students to become increasingly inquisitive about the importance of accurately reading the written word and the world to better the human condition (Freire, 1970). The activities included here encourage students to think critically about themselves, others, and societal issues. They learn to understand how cultural scripts are performed in fiction and reality and shape how one thinks, sees oneself, and sees the world. They are then able to juxtapose their cultural and personal scripts with the protagonist, Pecola.

Materials

- *The Bluest Eye* (Morrison, 1970)
- *Nappy Hair* (Herron, 1997)
- *The House on Mango Street* (Cisneros, 1984)
- *Twilight Zone* (1960) episode titled "The Eye of the Beholder" (Serling, 2006)
- *I Am Not My Hair* (Arie, 2005)
- Newspapers
- Chart paper
- Figure 26.1 (The Abuse Wheel)
- Figure 26.2 (Cultural Scripts Chart)
- Figure 26.3 (Beauty and the Beholder's Eye)

Introduction

I have been making chocolate chip cookies since I was twelve years old. Over the years, I have made modifications to the recipe, but I always make it a point to clean the bowl. I try not to leave even a moist crumb of batter behind. This is one of my metaphors for teaching. I believe that effective teachers get the maximum mileage out of all classroom activities, not necessarily by employing a plethora of activities. Instead, it is important to clean the bowl for every activity while thinking anew.

Teachers need to groom students into individuals who are intellectually charged, exposed to the sociopolitical problems of the world, and committed to making the world a more inclusive, pluralistic, human, and democratic place to live. It is this type of human rights curriculum that transforms students into independent critical thinkers who are in tune with themselves and others in this changing global society.

The activities here invigorate and challenge students' thinking through literacy and real-world connections. They incorporate technology and multiple intelligences and can be modified to differentiate instruction.

Connections

As Probst (Chapter 4), Wilhelm (Chapter 3), and Blau (Chapter 1) indicate in the opening essays of this text, literature is a vehicle to study history, language, humanity, and societal and cultural practices. These activities for *The Bluest Eye* offer myriad approaches to teaching the text. Reader response, through reader-text-world connections, is at the nucleus of all the lesson's activities. Each activity is student-centered and allows students to use different lenses to view the text. These lenses call for movement in students' thinking—analyzing characters and deconstructing how characters see themselves and the world, how the world sees them, and why—to participate in critical discourse and be able to organize thinking into creative writing (Moore). This chapter invites critical inquiry and creative thinking through the use of multiple literacies; the literacy constructs activate prior knowledge and metacognition. It is important for English teachers to use a cultural studies criticism framework for teaching literature to augment critical thought in students. Cultural studies criticism summons students to juxtapose their behaviors, values, and perceptions with societies in the text and the world by asking critical and complex questions: Who am I? How does my cultural background shape the essence of who I am and how the world sees me? What are the societal norms and values that confront characters in modern American literature and those who people the world? How are these norms and values embraced or negated? Who created these norms and what power do they have? This lesson series showcases some activities that support a human and pluralistic curriculum that encourages students to be innovative critical thinkers in the twenty-first century.

Activities

Activity 1: The Abuse Wheel

This activity prods students to think about a social problem that has plagued the universe since the beginning of time: abuse. Studying how both society and people serve as perpetrators of abuse, students engage in social activism by utilizing artistic and technological skills to convey messages against abuse.

I begin this activity by defining and discussing the types of abuse that exist. Excerpts from newspapers and broadcast news serve as sample texts of abuse and how abuse is reported. After reading *The Bluest Eye*, students work collaboratively to discuss how one of the following characters has been abused by another individual or society: Pecola, Pauline Breedlove, Cholly Breedlove, Sammy Breedlove, Maureen Peal, and Geraldine. Each group uses "the abuse wheel" to plot or track (complete with page references from the book) how a selected character has endured physical, emotional, and psychological abuse (see Figure 26.1). Each group writes its sentences around the perimeter of the respective area on the wheel. As a culminating activity, each group creates a public awareness message on abuse. The public awareness message focuses on abuse of a specific population (e.g., senior citizens, females, children, etc.) and includes ideas to help eradicate abuse. The message can be expressed in (1) a T-shirt design; (2) a bookmark; (3) a video; or (4) a webpage. The goal is for students to create a product that reaches a real audience.

Extend: Students seek opportunities to market their announcements. Perhaps the T-shirts and bookmarks can be marketed and sold at a store in the community or school, and the videos can be used on a local public television network.

Activity 2: Understanding and Charting Cultural Scripts

I begin the lesson by asking students to respond to the following questions in their writer's notebook: "What is culture? What are your values and beliefs?" Next, I draw a mammoth circle on the board so students can post their responses to the first question (What is culture?) outside

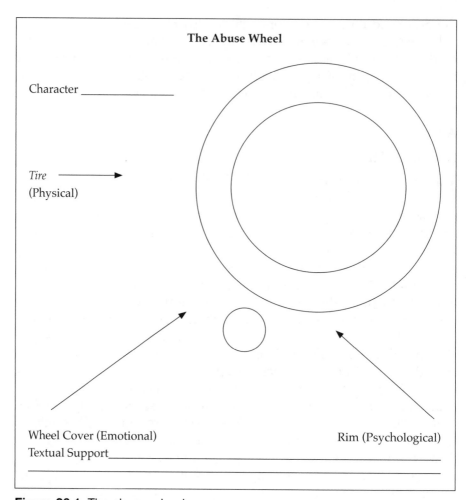

Figure 26.1. The abuse wheel.

the circle. I illustrate how culture is both constant and evolving by drawing a semicircle with arrows inside the circle on the board. Then I guide
students toward connecting their values and beliefs—as indicated by
the definition on their paper—with the definition of culture already on
the board.

I then explain that cultural scripts are sayings—repeated sayings—
that govern or contribute to daily practices and outlook on self, others,
and life. Some movies with salient cultural scripts include *Mississippi
Masala, The Scarlet Letter,* and *Boys in the Hood.* Cultural scripts are the
compilation of what one has been taught to act like, to believe in, and to
practice by family and community (James & Jongeward, 1996).

In *Boys in the Hood*, the prevailing cultural script for young African American males consists of selling and using drugs, becoming entangled in gang activity, spending time in prison, and living lives absent of direction and purpose. This script, which is shaped by the local community and macro-society, is clearly evinced in the character Doughboy and other neighborhood boys. There is, however, one character, Tre Styles, whose father counters this cultural script that permeates the "Hood." Tre's mother sends him to live with his father, Furious Styles, when he begins to have some problems in school. Throughout the movie, Tre's father creates, shapes, and fosters a cultural script of hope, discipline, and dignity for his son.

To reinforce the cultural script concept, I ask a volunteer to read *Nappy Hair* by Carolina Herron, a picture book that explores self-image and affirms a little girl's feelings about her hair. Then, I read "Hair" from *The House on Mango Street* by Sandra Cisneros and encourage students to listen to popular neo-soul artist India Arie's song titled "I Am Not My Hair." The class holds a mini-discussion about the three eclectic works and the cultural scripts they suggest. The following questions expand students' thinking: "Why aren't there books about loving your straight hair? Why are books such as *Nappy Hair* written?" Since hair is the focus of these works and is an obvious part of outward appearance, students think about their own cultural script for hair and the episodes in their lives that generate or perpetuate the script. Students then complete the cultural scripts chart (see Figure 26.2), using evidence from *The Bluest Eye* to complete the episodes for Pecola.

Using the chart as a springboard, students write a draft of an essay juxtaposing how they practice their cultural script and how Pecola practices hers. For example, one of the lines in Pecola's script is the absence of love. As students write about cultural scripts, they think about whether stereotypes are present in cultural scripts. Stereotypes can become embedded in the crevices of cultural scripts. If students write about how their cultural script is practiced, they can examine their script and decide what the script, silently or loudly, echoes about their racial, ethnic, social, and gender identities.

Activity 3: *Why* Questions

Classrooms should be high-traffic areas for weighty *why* questions, the cornerstone of an inquiry-based classroom. This activity catapults students to think about *why* questions while placing themselves in the shoes of Pecola and pondering what matters.

Cultural Scripts Chart	
Self	Pecola
On Hair: Episodes:	
On Education: Episodes:	
Other Physical/Personality Traits: Episodes:	

Figure 26.2. Cultural scripts chart.

Students begin the lesson by listening to "Why" by Traci Chapman and discussing the speaker's intention, tone, and word choice. I then read the following passage aloud: *"There is really nothing more to say—except why"* [Italics in original] (Morrison p. 9). Students create a *why* question for every season of Pecola's life; they pose questions from Pecola's perspective and as an outsider looking at her circumstances. Since the entire text is arranged by four seasons, this activity is ongoing and can lead to creating a *why* poem.

Activity 4: Beauty and the Beholder's Eye

Students create word webs for *beautiful* and *acceptance*. Then I lead them in a discussion about "Beauty is in the eye of the beholder." To explore these words and ideas associated with them, students watch the *Twilight Zone* episode titled "The Eye of the Beholder." This episode explores the notion of beauty and what it means to look "normal." Next I arrange the students in groups and tell them to research how beauty is perceived in a particular country. (Each group can brainstorm a list of countries and select one.) The goal is to expose students to countries that are considered eclectic, receive poor or inadequate media coverage, or have a host of stereotypical views attached to it. Some key words to discuss are *beauty, perception, icon, societal,* and *norm*. Students use as many primary resources to inform their research as possible.

Each group completes a mini-research project on their assigned country (see Figure 26.3). The research questions (RQ) stimulate students to explore beauty from various perspectives. Once students have responded to the research questions, they construct a large eye on a poster board.

To create eyelashes, students use long strips of paper to write each one of their findings about the country's view on physical beauty (RQ#1). Next, students plot words on the pupil that capture how the societal view of beauty negates or confirms women's actual appearances (RQ#2). Then students create a repetition of a ring of words around or inside the iris that reflect their opinions of all of the characteristics that capture the inner beauty of the people in the studied country (RQ#3). Students then write a reflective summary of the research process and findings at the bottom of the poster board. The following questions guide this reflection: "What did you learn about yourself as a researcher as a result of this assignment? What did your findings reveal to you about the word *beauty*? Who really defines beauty and why? Discuss how your views on beauty have shifted or solidified as a result of your research." Following the group-work assignment, students work independently on an essay juxtaposing the prevailing societal notions of beauty in the world where Pecola lives and their researched country.

Activity 5: Characterization through Wikipedia

Many students use, and perhaps overuse, the online encyclopedia Wikipedia, created by the public. This activity intertwines students' knowledge of the characters in *The Bluest Eye* with technology, giving students license to critically and creatively illustrate characters with

Research Questions:

Your group will collaboratively respond to the following research questions (RQ) for your assigned country and cite sources.

RQ#1. What is the prevailing societal view on the physical beauty of women?

RQ#2. How does the societal view of beauty compete with or affirm women's actual appearance?

RQ#3. In your opinion, what might be the inner beauty of the people in your assigned country?

Poster Board Presentation:

Your group will create an artistic eye and plot your responses to the research questions in the appropriate places in the eye on a poster board. The *pupil* will represent the country's views on beauty and women's actual appearance. The *lashes* will capture the country's perceptions of beauty in a broader sense. The *iris* will reflect women's inner beauty concluded in research of the country. Your group will craft a collective reflective summary under the graphic representation of the eye. The reflective summary should report the group's research process and reactions to the research findings.

Figure 26.3. Beauty and the Beholder's Eye mini-research project.

words. After reading the autumn and winter sections of the text, students work in groups to create a descriptive overview for all of the major and minor characters in the text, which will be loosely based on Wikipedia entries. Each group includes the following to create their own Wikipedia character descriptions: (1) adjectives for internal and external descriptions; (2) meanings of characters' names; (3) a song that best reflects each character; and (4) a motto that best suits the character. Students are encouraged to use colloquial expressions as well as different languages to define characters. The teacher can consider publishing each group's definitions on the Wikipedia website or the school's webpage.

Assessment

The activities are assessed through reflective journals and critical discourse. The writing activities and research project are peer evaluated on the basis of content, creativity, and delivery. The criteria are designed and decided by students to aid student-centered learning and student ownership. Ongoing classroom observation, critique notes, and quality of work produced on the unit activities provide me with further assessment data.

Considerations

These activities for *The Bluest Eye* confront the school-student disconnect by revolving around issues that are relevant to students and incorporating their interests and skills. Each activity beckons students to engage in critical and creative thought to examine identity through various frameworks. It is necessary for *community* to exist in the classroom to get the maximum mileage from activities cited in this lesson. The Abuse Wheel activity requires an awareness of many kinds and manifestations of abuse. The teacher also needs to be prepared to respond to any possible disclosures by students of abuse. In addition to the activities calling for the engagement of critical and creative thinking skills, they also call for sensitivity. Through critical and creative thought and sensitivity, these activities present students with the possibility to explore language, culture, and societal issues within and outside US borders.

References

Arie, I. (2005). I am not my hair [CD Single]. New York: Motown.

Chapman, T. (1988). Why. On *Tracy Chapman* [CD]. New York: Elektra.

Cisneros, S. (1984). *The house on Mango Street*. New York: Vintage.

Freire, P. (1970). *Pedagogy of the oppressed*. New York: Continuum.

Herron, C. (1997). *Nappy hair*. New York: Knopf.

James, M., & Jongeward, D. (1996). *Born to win: Transactional analysis with Gestalt experiments*. Boston: Addison Wesley.

Serling, R. (Writer). (2006, December 31). The eye of the beholder [Television series episode]. In *The twilight zone*. New York: SciFi Channel, NBC Universal. (Original air date 1960)

VIII Teaching S. E. Hinton's *The Outsiders*

Carl A. Young
North Carolina State University

Before there were middle schools, there were only junior highs, an educational landscape in which I struggled to survive given the push to mold me into an obedient and productive future high schooler. In my case, this situation was even more pronounced as my school became a junior high from a high school, and we faced a faculty of seasoned high school teachers ready to whip us into shape. One of the most striking memories I have of junior high is reading S. E. Hinton's *The Outsiders*, probably because it mirrored so well the sharp division between the jocks/preps and prevocational students (or "prevos" as they were called), and because it offered hope for me—a student from a broken home who still managed to value school and succeed despite economic hardship and family conflict. I connected with Ponyboy's ability to see multiple perspectives, to communicate with Cherry while still remaining loyal to his gang, to value Robert Frost while also understanding keenly what it means to survive on the streets.

The Outsiders was published in 1967, the year I was born, while Hinton was a first-year student at the University of Tulsa. However, she began the novel while in high school, motivated by the clashes of two rival gangs. I have had the fortune of not only being affected by the novel's universal message of portraying the adolescent outsider in such a compelling way, but also seeing its effect on students both as a teacher and a teacher educator. When I taught seventh grade in a small inner-city school system, my students were completely engaged with Ponyboy's narrative. As a teacher educator, I have had the fortune of hearing from former students who are now teachers just how compelling Hinton's novel is for their own students. Even now, I have had the incredible experience of seeing how preservice teachers and middle school students partnering together can bring *The Outsiders* to life through emerging technologies in the work of my North Carolina State colleagues Carol Pope and Candy Beal. Together, they facilitate a partnership between our middle grades preservice teachers and seventh graders from a local middle school that results in community research presentations, dynamic skits, and digital music videos all related to their work with *The Outsiders*.

Hinton's novel has sold more than fourteen million copies and continues to be a popular part of the young adult canon. As Denitia Smith (2005) of the *New York Times* explains, *The Outsiders* "transformed young-adult fiction from a genre mostly about prom queens, football players and high school crushes to one that portrayed a darker, truer adolescent world" (par. 1). Francis Ford Coppola brought this darker, truer adolescent world to the big screen. His film adaptation, released in March 1983, was received with mixed to positive reviews. Perhaps the adaptation is best known for launching or further establishing the careers of many current stars, including C. Thomas Howell, Emilio Estevez, and Rob Lowe, as well as Patrick Swayze, Matt Dillon, Tom Cruise, Ralph Macchio, and Diane Lane. Howell earned a Young Artist Award for his role as Ponyboy, and Diane Lane was nominated for one for her portrayal of Cherry Valance. Coppola and the movie itself were also nominated. In 2005, Coppola rereleased the film on DVD, editing it further but also adding twenty-two minutes of additional footage and rescoring it with songs from the sixties to give it a more authentic feel. In fact, he titled the rerelease *The Outsiders: The Complete Novel*.

One of the songs that remained, "Stay Gold" co-written by Carmine Coppola and Stevie Wonder and performed by Wonder, captures the theme of Hinton's coming-of-age novel, paying homage to Robert Frost—that "nothing gold can stay" reflecting the challenges of "staying gold" and hanging on to the wonders and innocence of childhood. *The Outsiders* still resonates with today's youth through Ponyboy's story, one that reveals the power of narrative, of writing your life into being, into existence, for others to experience and learn from—a compelling message today when many students publish online for authentic audiences willing to provide instant feedback. The novel also provides a strong historical lens for studying the sociocultural aspects of the sixties and for making connections to modern-day culture.

The lessons that follow offer ideas for teaching *The Outsiders* that engage students in authentic reading, inquiry-based learning, hands-on activities, and reflective meaning making. Each plan draws on the teacher's classroom experience and forges connections to the opening essays of the book. Students in these classrooms create meaning for themselves, connect with the characters' moral choices, and analyze responsibly from their own perspectives.

It is our hope that these teaching ideas for *The Outsiders* will serve as inspiration for exploring identity, coming of age, and the power of narrative with students. Rather than blueprints, consider them as possible bridges for engaging in the timelessness of Hinton's classic with students and, ideally, erasing misconceptions and building tolerance.

Reference

Smith, Dinitia. (2005, September 7). An outsider, outside of the shadows: An interview with S. E. Hinton. New York Times. Retrieved from http://www.nytimes.com/2005/09/07/movies/MoviesFeatures/07hint.html

27 Building Classroom Community through Film and *The Outsiders*

Robert Prickett
Winthrop University

"All Socs aren't like that," she said. "You have to believe me, Ponyboy. Not all of us are like that."

"Sure," I said.

"That's like saying all greasers are like Dallas Winston. I'll bet he's jumped a few people."

I digested that. It was true. . . .

"I'll bet you think the Socs have it made. The rich kids, the Westside Socs. I'll tell you something, Ponyboy, and it may come as a surprise. We have troubles you've never even heard of. You want to know something?" She looked at me straight in the eye. "Things are rough all over." (*The Outsiders* 33)

Purpose

The purpose of this lesson is best articulated through what students will learn. First, students investigate *The Outsiders* through the lens of issues related to cliques, gangs, and "collective self-esteem." Second, students connect their personal identifications, relationships, and experiences with various cliques to the novel's interactions between the two main character groups, the Socs and the Greasers. Finally, to promote the understanding between different cliques/groups/gangs and their tendencies toward creating inclusive communities, students engage in a variety of activities.

Materials

- Figure 27.1: Potential Film Bibliography
- Figure 27.2: Film and Literature Analysis: Characterization (modified from *Reading in the Dark: Using Film as a Tool in the English Classroom* by John Golden [2001])

■ Southern Poverty Law Center: Teaching Tolerance: Mix It Up website (http://www.tolerance.org/mix_it_up/)

Introduction

By starting with a simple brainstorming activity and then expanding it to include a film/literature comparison activity, students immediately become "experts" by plumbing their own knowledge and experience base—both in the real world of their school and the fictional world of the novel and film. Students engage immediately with the texts through familiar experiences and relationships both real and vicarious. Thus, the introductory activity is a whole-class brainstorming activity in which students identify, categorize, and organize the many, varied cliques found within school settings.

Connections

This lesson connects to both Blau's (Chapter 1) and Wilhelm's (Chapter 3) approaches to teaching literature. According to Blau, teaching literature should "[engage] students directly in the experience of literature and in authentic problems in the interpretation and criticism of literature." Students can find one of the "authentic problems" in the interpretation of *The Outsiders* connected to the dichotomy presented by the relationship between the Greasers and the Socs—both within the text and also in students' perceptions of cliques in their high school. That the characters are separated into the two gangs through action, placement, and fighting sets up the "opposing views." The other connection is with Wilhelm's issues of communication and response, particularly as media representations (i.e., films) play a key part in this lesson. Wilhelm writes about "drama and visualization," specifically, that "much of what we teach when we teach literature (plot, theme, setting, character) misses the point about how meaning is communicated and responded to." Film can open this two-way communication.

Activities

I use this lesson as a culminating activity, but slight modifications could make it usable as an introductory activity for the novel.

Brainstorming Activity

The introductory activity is a whole-class brainstorming activity identifying, categorizing, and organizing the many, varied cliques found within students' school experiences. As a class, we generate a list of the various cliques within the school on the board. After the students have created an exhaustive list for the class to work from, I break students into smaller groups to create an organizational flowchart or hierarchy of the cliques at the school (e.g., Who can "run" with whom? What are the most popular cliques? Who are "enemies"? Who are friends and/or allies?). After the smaller student groups have created their flowcharts, they present their ideas to the class. As their peers present, students look for similarities/differences. How close are the various charts? What are the students' reactions to the various versions?

Possible Transition

"Now that we have mapped how cliques interact at our school, I want us to delve into the idea of 'collective self-esteem.' 'Collective self-esteem' refers to how people who belong to a group have positive or negative self-esteem based on how they evaluate the group and its actions. Thus, Ponyboy feels like he belongs to the Greasers and gets his worth (his self-esteem) from what that identification means to him. So, what worth is created by an individual belonging to a particular group? How do the interactions of various groups affect one's self-esteem belonging to a different group? These are some of the questions that we are going to explore in the next activity."

Film/Literature Comparison Activity

Figure 27.1 provides a list of films to use as clips in class or as outside class viewing. This plan serves as a culminating lesson for the novel. Thus, students complete the novel portion with minimal difficulty and effort (Figure 27.2). To keep the discussion "safer" for students and still allow them to feel as if there are experts on cliques, using film can accomplish an excellent comparison tool.

Students begin the Film and Literature Analysis: Characterization guide (Figure 27.2) as a group, class, or individually by completing the first box for the novel by choosing either the Socs or the Greasers. Citing examples and quoting from the novel, students record their observations about the chosen groups' behavior throughout the novel. This activity could also serve as a modified jigsaw where partners or groups complete one box and then regroup with one another so that ultimately all of the boxes are answered sufficiently.

Clips from such films as *The Breakfast Club* (the final letter explaining who the individuals are) and/or *Mean Girls* (where the cafeteria is

Title	Year	Director	Rating
10 Things I Hate about You	1999	Gil Junger	PG-13
American Graffiti	1973	George Lucas	PG
American Teen	2008	Nanette Burstein	PG-13
The Breakfast Club	1985	John Hughes	R
Clueless	1995	Amy Heckerling	PG-13
Dangerous Minds	1995	John Smith	R
Dazed and Confused	1993	Richard Linklater	R
Dead Poets Society	1989	Peter Weir	PG
Fast Times at Ridgemont High	1982	Amy Heckerling	R
Heathers	1989	Michael Lehman	R
Mean Girls	2004	Mark S. Waters	PG-13
Not Another Teen Movie	2001	Joel Gallen	R
The Outsiders	1983	Francis Ford Coppola	PG
Rebel without a Cause	1955	Nicholas Ray	UR
Sixteen Candles	1984	John Hughes	PG
Varsity Blues	1999	Brian Robbins	R
West Side Story	1961	Robert Wise/Jerome Robbins	UR

Figure 27.1. Potential film bibliography.

explained to Lindsay Lohan's character) can highlight film portrayal of the various cliques of teenagers or assign entire films for comparisons with the novel via the guide sheet. Regardless, I recommend showing clips from the Francis Ford Coppola version of *The Outsiders* (particularly the opening drive-in extended scene and/or outside of the grocery store when Ponyboy and the Soc talk inside the car). This activity allows for a safer distance from the students' personal experience. While they will inevitably connect to particular groups or characters when analyzing the film's characters and the subsequent interactions and behaviors of the group to which they belong, this "stepping away" allows students to be more critical and analytical as the group is a safe distance from their own perceived reality. Students then complete the Film and Literature Analysis: Characterization sheet based on a film and the novel (I have done "analysis parties" in the past where a group watches an entire film as an out-of-class assignment with success). The class then reconvenes and discusses the groups and the group interactions by responding to the following questions: How did different groups act/react to one another? How did individual members of the groups act/react to each other? Who talked to whom? Who was mean to whom? Who played well with others? Who didn't?

Considerations	Film: Group/Characters:	Novel: Group/Characters:
Behavior		
Appearance		
Dialogue		
Feelings		
Interactions		

1. Write a thesis statement about each of the groups/characters:

2. Write a thesis statement of comparison between the groups/characters:

Figure 27.2. Film and Literature Analysis: Characterization guide.

Possible Transition

"We've read about and watched cliques interacting with other cliques. We started out this particular lesson mapping out our school's different cliques. I would like to return to that flowchart and introduce you to a website for an organization that is working to bring together the different groups in a school in a meaningful way."

Closure: Mix It Up (Southern Poverty Law Center's Teaching Tolerance Initiative)

This lesson has moved from the personal experience of the students (e.g., brainstorming lists of cliques) to the media representations of the groups (e.g., film and novel comparison). In the end, *The Outsiders* allows students the opportunity to appreciate, understand, and cooperate with a variety of different groups.

As explained on the *Mix It Up* website (http://www.tolerance. org/mix_it_up/), "*Mix It Up* seeks to break down the barriers between students, improve intergroup relations and help schools create inclusive communities where there are fewer misunderstandings that can lead to conflicts, bullying or violence." Sound familiar? If used as a culminating activity, students can easily see the connection to the "moral" of *The Outsiders* with its multiple acts of violence leading to greater tragedy. I end this lesson introducing students to the Southern Poverty Law Center/*Teaching Tolerance* website and related activities through a final activity/call for social justice within the school—the organization and implementation of a Mix It Up Day in the school cafeteria.

Mix It Up Day encourages students to sit somewhere else for lunch for one day. Through a variety of materials and suggested activities from the website, students and teachers organize, advertise, and implement a schoolwide Mix It Up Day as the culminating activity for this lesson.

Assessment

Assessments and activities are connected directly to the three stated lesson purposes. Informal assessment includes introductory brainstorming activity, discussions, and question and answer with students. Formal assessments include completion of the Film and Literature Analysis Guide sheet, as well as initiative and completion of the Mix It Up Day activities (depending on the activities selected and incorporated).

Considerations

This lesson series is created with an eye toward social justice issues—issues I believe are relevant not only to current students but also to the text and interpretations of *The Outsiders*. Therefore, the lesson includes a hands-on culminating activity that takes the novel into the "real world" of our students, asking them to analyze, engage, and include others in their educational and social environments. In effect, the activity takes students from a text that shows factionalism ending in violence to a reality in which students become the protagonists of their own lives, empowered to make small changes and affect the status quo.

28 *The Outsiders* Custom Poem Web: Character Analysis through Poetry

Christen E. Tulli
Pocahontas Middle School, Henrico, Virginia

Purpose

This lesson series challenges students to analyze key characters in *The Outsiders* by applying themes from various Robert Frost poems and one Stevie Wonder song. They use critical thinking skills to read and analyze the provided poems, make connections between lines of the poems to the characters from the novel, and synthesize these connections into a final product. It works especially well in academically advanced classes or any classes with students who can multitask easily because it gives students a chance to exercise several English language arts skills at once. It also allows students to analyze complex poetry and engage in lively group discussions.

Materials

- A copy of the following Robert Frost poems: "Acquainted with the Night," "Fire and Ice," "Nothing Gold Can Stay," "The Road Not Taken," "On Going Unnoticed," "Ghost House," available at http://www.ketzle.com/frost/.
- A copy of the lyrics of Stevie Wonder's song "Stay Gold," which you can find on numerous sites with a simple Web search
- A copy of the post-reading questions (Figure 28.1)
- Large sheet of bulletin board paper (or poster board) and markers
- Copies of Rubric and Rules of Custom Poem Web (Figure 28.2)

Introduction

These activities engage students because they can play with poetry while examining the personality of a character from *The Outsiders*, rather than forcing them immediately to create their own poem or asking them to dissect and analyze individual lines. Students can be creative, but they also find evidence from the text to justify their choices. This activity leads students to see that the tone and emotion in poetry are what make it fascinating, and they do not have to read, analyze, and regurgitate meaning to reach that conclusion.

Connections

Through the series of activities, students recognize the interdependent nature of all major English language arts skills: reading, writing, speaking, listening, and viewing. For instance, instead of silently reading the Robert Frost poems, students make decisions about how the poems should be read and which lines are significant enough to be read aloud as a group. In this process they are "mining the texts for meaning," as Blau (Chapter 1) suggests, while also developing as "critical readers" (Jago, Chapter 2). The reading portion of this activity mutually reinforces listening and discussion skills, evident when students are asked to listen to each poem while thinking of how it applies to their designated character's personality and experiences. After discussing their character using the post-reading questions, students synthesize their perceptions of the character to create a poem. They are, in essence, taking responsibility for their own interpretations and creations (Probst, Chapter 4) as they perform these poems, explain the decisions they made, create symbols, and view and respond to other groups' poem webs.

Activities

Setting Up the Lesson

After I divide students into groups of three or four, each group selects one of the following characters from *The Outsiders*: Ponyboy, Johnny, Dally, Darry, Cherry, Bob, or Soda. Depending on the number of groups in the class, more than one group may work on the same character. Each group receives a packet containing all the Robert Frost poems as well as the lyrics to Stevie Wonder's "Stay Gold." Each group selects a leader. *Note:* To make this assignment more interdisciplinary, I incorporate music by softly playing Stevie Wonder's "Stay Gold" in the background. I have found that this extra touch engages my students and creates a greater appreciation for the lyrics.

Reading and Listening

The groups read each of the poems aloud as a choral reading. In my class, this means that the students can take turns reading lines, but they are also read some of the poems or individual lines from the poems as a group. Ask students to read each poem silently first, decide on which lines resonate with them the most, and assign these lines to be read aloud as a group. For instance, students often choose to read the last line of each stanza in the song "Stay Gold" together as a group because these lines reinforce the theme of maintaining a sense of innocence. For the other lines, the group leader can designate individual readers.

Because reading aloud is such a significant part of this assignment, I often model choral readings with my class using the poem "Nothing Gold Can Stay" prior to this lesson. The students help me decide which line we should read together as a class, and I assign pairs of readers for the other lines. This practice helps students become comfortable with deciding how a poem should be read. Students do not have to overanalyze the poem or dissect every line to be successful because the focus is on enjoying the tone of the poem and considering how it can apply to their designated character.

When students take the time to plan how poems will be read aloud, they become active participants. My students have often become animated when they passionately read a powerful line together. This reading exercise reiterates that both speaking and listening should be *purposeful*. Students listen to the orally performed poems through the ears of their designated character. After each poem, students briefly answer the post-reading question (Figure 28.1). For more accountability, the group leaders can record the group's brief response to each post-reading question.

Directions for Assignment

Each group collaboratively analyzes its designated character and, using the provided packet of poems, creates a custom poem web to represent that character's personality. The directions and rubric prove helpful (Figure 28.2).

Selected Robert Frost Post-Reading Questions

"Acquainted with the Night"

Post-reading question: Has your character ever felt utterly alone at some point in the story? Discuss as a group by citing at least one example from the novel.

"Fire and Ice"

Post-reading question: Has your character ever felt hateful or cruel at some point in the story? Discuss as a group by citing at least one example from the story.

"Nothing Gold Can Stay"

Post-reading question: Has your character shown any examples of having lost his or her innocence? Discuss as a group by citing at least two examples from the story.

"The Road Not Taken"

Post-reading question: What is one life-altering choice your character has made? Discuss briefly as a group and assess this decision. Discuss whether you agreed with this choice or not.

"On Going Unnoticed"

Post-reading question: In the poem "On Going Unnoticed," Robert Frost notes how insignificant we all are in the grand scheme of nature. Do you think your character has ever felt insignificant or small? Cite an example from the story to prove your point. If you don't think that he or she has ever felt this way, what experience would cause the character to feel this way?

"Ghost House"

Post-reading question: Compare your character to another one in the story. Who of these two characters is more in touch with nature and the idea of enjoying solitude? Please discuss as a group and cite one example from the book to support your answer.

Stevie Wonder, "Stay Gold"

Post-reading question: Did your character have any small part of him or her that was still pure, innocent, kind, or happy? Briefly discuss as a group citing at least one example from the book. If you feel that your character was *not* able to "stay gold," cite one example from the book that supports this idea.

Figure 28.1. Post-reading questions.

Rubric and Rules for Custom Poem Web

Directions: You may have brainstormed for an essay before using a "bubble web" format. Today, you will be using a similar format when you analyze and create a custom poem for your designated character. You will use *only* the lines from the provided poems to create your custom poem. After writing the custom poem in the middle of your sheet of paper, create stems to three different examples from the book with corresponding page numbers that support why you feel the lines you selected fit with your character and his experiences. For example, if you choose to use the lines "I have been acquainted with the night" for Johnny, you may want to have the example of how he fell asleep in the vacant lot stemming off this line in your custom poem.

Rules and Rubric for Custom Poem Web

1. You may use as many poems as you want. You *must* use at least two.

_____ *out of 10 points for following this direction.*

2. You *have* to use the entire line from a poem. You *cannot* add any words *or* take any words away from the line.

_____ *out of 10 points for following this direction.*

3. You may use as little or as many lines as you want from each poem, and you may put the lines in *any* order you choose.

4. Your poem does *not* have to make perfect sense. You should, however, try to think of lines that correspond with your character's personality or experiences. Also, your poem should have a tone (angry, lonely, devastated, peaceful) that fits with your character's personality.

5. After writing your poem, create stems to three different examples from the book *with corresponding page numbers* that support why you feel the lines you selected fit with your character and his or her experiences. Each should be in a different color.

_____ *out of 45 points (15 points for each relevant example that includes page number and corresponds with appropriate line in custom poem)*

6. Create three small symbols to represent the three different personality traits each example depicts. *For example:* A small drawing of a ram could represent Dally's stubbornness, which correlates with an example about how Dally was determined to commit suicide.

_____ *out of 15 points (five points per symbol)*

7. Please employ repetition in your poem by selecting at least one significant line to be read more than once.

_____ *out of 10 points*

8. You will read this poem as a group. Each person will need to read at least one line on his or her own. Any lines that are repeated should be read as a group. I expect you to read loudly, facing the class, maintaining eye contact, professional demeanor, and confident body language. I will expect your group to be able to rationalize the choices you made as well as explain the tone you were trying to portray.

_____ *out of 10 points*

Total points: Comments:

Figure 28.2. Assessment rubric.

Writing "Custom Poem"

Students work together to write the custom poem. The group leader selects one person to write this poem on the provided large sheets of bulletin board paper or poster board.

Creating Web of Character Traits and Examples

Students then pull out their copies of *The Outsiders* and work together to find three specific examples that support why three separate lines from their custom poem fit their designated character's personality (Figure 28.2). They write these examples in the margins of the paper with "threads" or "stems" connecting to the lines of the custom poem (i.e., in the style of a bubble map). Each group draws a small symbol to represent the personality trait that corresponds with each of the three examples from the book; for instance, a ram could represent an example that depicts a character's stubbornness.

Sharing

The groups share their poems and explain why they chose three specific lines by citing their examples to the class. After each group presents, we debrief as a class by exploring the questions below.

1. How did this group's custom poem represent its designated character?
2. Which specific words in the custom poem contributed to the tone the group was trying to create?
3. Explain which line you found represented this group's character the best.
4. Were there any lines that did *not* accurately represent this group's character and his or her personality? Explain.

Assessment

This assignment is successful with secondary students because they have the opportunity to work with poetry in an unconventional way while still focusing on character analysis. Students are assessed on their analytical, speaking, and reading skills with the provided rubric (Figure 28.2). I sometimes assign a participation grade for answering one of the debrief questions that follow each group's presentation, which helps to encourage quieter students to contribute.

Considerations

This lesson is designed as a higher-level thinking activity for focused students who can engage in respectful, engaged discussion. It can be modified for classes who struggle with staying focused or engaging in classroom discussion in several ways. First, the group leaders can record their group members' collective responses to the post-reading questions. A participation grade during the debrief portion of the class discussion may also serve as an accountability measure. Third, the group leaders may assign each person a role so that everyone has a purpose (i.e., a "recorder" to write out a custom poem, a few "passage pointers" to find three specific examples from the book, an "artist" to draw symbols, etc.). With a few modifications, this lesson can fit into any classroom environment and is an engaging way for students to delve into characters' personalities from *The Outsiders*.

29 Social Class and *The Outsiders*

Corbin Wright
Glen Allen High School, Virginia

Purpose

Students often read a novel assigned in English class, study for the test, put it away, and forget about it. It is my job to help them create a connection to the writing, to see how it pertains to their lives, and to learn something from the characters' actions. With this goal in mind, I try my best to broaden the novel study by incorporating cross-curricular connections, critical thinking skills, and lively discussion.

While examining S. E. Hinton's portrayal of social class and how it guides the characters' fate, we look carefully at aspects of social studies, current events, and even math as we interpret graphs, pictograms, and trends. I have the students read articles about social class in modern society and how it is portrayed in the media. I require them to think deeply about these issues, probing them to think about how they view one another and the effects these views can have on others as well as themselves. In addition to these supplemental activities, however, my students continue to practice their writing skills through creative assessment, and they practice asserting themselves in class discussion, always encouraged to use support from their life experiences and the novel.

In essence, incorporating other sources and curricular materials helps to broaden students' literary experiences; it further deepens their knowledge of character motivations and themes and, in the words of Brazilian educator Paulo Freire, leads them toward a deeper literacy of "reading the word and the world."

Materials

- *The Outsiders*
- One or two supplemental readings on social class: I have used various sections of Barbara Ehrenreich's book *Nickel and Dimed: On (Not) Getting By in America* (2001) with great success. Specifically the chapter titled "Cash Poor" becomes relevant when

discussing our society's economic stratification and how it relates to social hierarchies. This may be too advanced, too easy, or not appropriate for some students; other texts may prove useful as well. A quick search of the *New York Times* website reveals several articles written about social class in modern society, some of them written for younger audiences, and others viewing the differences through various lenses.

- Access to a computer: It is helpful for students to have access to a computer. I like for students to check out Wikipedia's "Social Class in the United States" page: http://en.wikipedia.org/wiki/Social_class_in_the_United_States. While I do not use Wikipedia in class exclusively, this particular entry provides a strong overview and several thought-provoking graphs that spark discussion, encourage critical thinking, and maintain a cross-curricular component.

- Loose-leaf paper for student notes

Introduction

I introduce students to the concepts of social class and ambiguous hierarchical systems by beginning discussion at a localized, eighth-grade level. First, I openly discuss the intent and purpose of the lessons with students so that they can envision the lesson itself: that we will discuss social class, how it relates to Hinton's novel, and how we see its effects on a daily basis. Then, I relate it to the students' experience of how a microcosm of social class is in their school on a daily basis through peer groupings and cliques. Having students critically analyze the lines they draw in the sand of inclusion and exclusion, and the distinctive characteristics of each student grouping, helps them to understand that our larger society is divided in much the same way. While society's divisions are not typically based on individual interests such as gaming, sports, or other activities, some of the same outward choices that dictate group membership in school also hint at social class distinctions in the real world such as clothes, cars, and vacations. In essence, what students experience as cliques is the beginning of their experiencing larger social classifications. Finally, students discuss in a fishbowl setting the relationship of these larger themes of social and economic stratification, stereotyping, and mobility to the novel itself, and how what they see in school and society is reflected in the characters' lives, decisions, and attitudes. The lesson concludes with a creative, independent writing assignment that allows students freedom of expression while, at the same time, guiding them toward artistically expressing how social class plays a pivotal role in Hinton's novel and her characters' life experiences.

Connections

This lesson series closely connects to the literature approaches as discussed in this text by Blau, Jago, Wilhelm, and Probst (Chapters 1–4). As the pedagogical approaches of these educators suggest, it is essential that students create meaning for themselves and direct their own discussion and journey through the novel. As Wilhelm explores in depth, true teaching begins with lessons that allow students to form connections between the story and themselves. Discussion within the context of an important theme, one that encourages not only dissection of the novel but also of the world around them, leads to internalization, true knowledge of the subject matter.

To begin, this lesson requires students to analyze both a theme of the text and a real-world issue: social class. Through discussion, students work together to create their own definition, words that reflect their experiences with class groupings that can be applied to the larger context of society and Hinton's characters. They not only grapple with the plight of the characters' social standing and the reason(s) Hinton would choose to make this a focus of her plot, but they work toward a larger understanding of what social classification looks like in the real world, in their lives, why it exists, and how it is created. Seeing that they, too, are like the Greasers and Socs in that they participate, albeit possibly unknowingly and naively, in social stratification makes the text's theme more believable, more authentic, and, as a result, more captivating to read and discuss.

There is room here for varying opinions, and there is much discussion and response to these different ways of viewing the rich theme of human groupings. Furthermore, the lesson values independence of thought, probing students to find other situations in which the novel's themes present themselves, as well as think about how the novel would be different if even one character became "upwardly mobile." Jago's discussion of how she integrates question papers into the curriculum works in much the same way. Allowing students to form their own questions, "handing the reins over," so to speak, allows for more authentic, personal interpretation with the text. As Jago notes, this can be uncomfortable for both teachers and students at first because it goes against the grain of how we have come to envision what the classroom looks like. It means that each of our classes will take different themes from the literature, and the discussion may branch into different topics. But as Probst and Blau recount, it is this individualization that teaches students how to apply theme to real situations, engage and question the world around them, and refine their ways of knowing, being, and learning.

Activities

1. I first discuss goals of the upcoming activities with students.

   a. I define and discuss social class, how it is portrayed in the novel, how the students see it on a more localized level every day, and how it is portrayed in society as a whole.

2. Brainstorm with students the different groupings they see within the school. This will initiate responses such as jocks, drama kids, academic kids, "Goths," gamers, etc.

   a. I sometimes remind students that respect for diverse opinions, styles, and social groupings is essential for a worthwhile, meaningful group discussion. While talking about peer groupings is important and relevant, it also lends itself to both flattering and hurtful vocabulary. As such, I encourage students to be specific in their discussion of classifications and characteristics, but specific names should not be included in our discussion.

   b. We record the groups that are brainstormed on the board.

3. I discuss these groupings with students, exploring the following questions: How easy is it to move from one group to another? If one moves groups, what might his or her motivation(s) be? What are the characteristics of each group? What stereotypes exist? What is positive about being associated with a group? Negative?

4. Next I ask students to think about the following statement: "What you experience in school is a microcosm of society as a whole." I give students a few moments to brainstorm or write their thoughts about this hypothesis, considering the following questions: Do you agree or disagree with the statement? What support can you use from class discussion, the characters' actions and motivations, or personal experiences to help make your argument convincing?

5. Our next step is to brainstorm a definition of *social class* on the board.

   a. *Social Class:* A broad group in society having the same social, economic, and/or educational status.

6. We discuss the various social class groups, while reflecting on the definition. Occasionally I provide one group (upper class) and have them determine the others (lower, middle, upper middle).

7. Students work within smaller groups to make a list of characteristics of each social class classification, referencing the definition on the board (education, income, occupation).

8. We return to class and conduct a fishbowl discussion. EdChange's Multicultural Pavilion on the Web (http://www. edchange.org/multicultural/) provides a great overview of instructions for this strategy. I then pose the following questions to students:

   a. How easy is it to move from one group to another (i.e., Can we climb the social ladder)?

   b. If you are able to move up the ladder of social class, how difficult do you think it would be?

   c. What stereotypes exist in each group?

   Depending on how advanced the class is and how the discussion is going, it may be worthwhile to lead students in thinking about larger issues such as, Are we really the land of opportunity or is that reserved for the upper class?

9. Our next step is to connect class discussion with other texts. Students read and discuss the implications and themes suggested by the following resources.

   a. Wikipedia—Students log onto the Wikipedia URL listed under the "Materials" section. With partners, they analyze the various graphs, predict trends, and evaluate the implications. Using Figure 29.1, partner groups grasp the connections between education level, income level, and social classification.

   b. Barbara Ehrenreich's *Nickel and Dimed* excerpt—I like to have students read an excerpt from this novel. Primarily, I use this selection to connect Hinton's work to other modes of literature because it raises significant questions about our culture, social class, and group perceptions. We always follow it with large-group discussion or a brief journal writing assignment.

There are many useful pieces of this nonfiction, personal account that can be used, but I find the section entitled "Cash Poor" to be the richest in terms of discussion and relation to the novel. Not only does it highlight simple, inherent differences between social classes, but it also provides a "slice of life" of our country's modern, economically disadvantaged. I find it useful to also give students a summary of the rest of the novel, Ehrenreich's "experiment," and that while she had difficulty making ends meet and surviving on minimum wage, these workers with whom she developed friendships most often do not qualify for government assistance of any sort. Connections to the text and the real world emerge when students write and discuss with each other the implications of these discouragements, inequalities, and misfortune.

Directions: Using the website below, look at the graphs provided on the page and answer the questions that follow. Continue your writing on the back of this page, if necessary.

http://en.wikipedia.org/wiki/Social_class_in_the_United_States

1.

Name of social class	Example of type(s) of job held by group	Average income (add the figures given and divide by total number of figures)	Education level
Upper Middle Class			
	sales		
		25K+20K+15K = 60K 60K / 3 = 20K	
			High school or GED

2. What is the average salary for a female high school graduate?
3. What is the average salary for a male high school graduate?
4. Why do you think there is a difference between these two salaries? What might this say about our society?
5. What reasons might explain why there seem to be more full-time jobs available at higher income levels?
6. An ability to seek higher education (college) is related to what two factors? Hint: See red, green, and blue graph on the right of the page.
7. Why do you think this might be?
8. What conclusions can you draw by looking at the correlation between income level and political party affiliation?

Figure 29.1. Understanding social class.

10. Bringing it back to the novel:

    a. As an extension of the former activity, we now list the social class groups we see in *The Outsiders* and include the elements under the social class to which they belong.

　　　　b. We provide examples from the text, descriptions, and
　　　　　 why (using the definition of social class) each character
　　　　　 is categorized as such.

　　　　c. We then discuss, How easy would it be for Johnny or
　　　　　 PonyBoy to become a Soc?

Assessment

The first word that comes to mind when I think about how my students
react to Hinton's *The Outsiders* is *engaged*. The classroom discussion is
lively, and their writing is descriptive, supportive, and often loaded
with personal connections. In fact, their positive reception of the novel
is so intense that I have often heard discussions about Tex, Ponyboy,
Johnny, and Dallas in the hallway and at lunch. They like the tough grit
of the characters, the seriousness of their plight, and are activated to
read ahead by Hinton's ability to create a page-turning conflict. I look
forward to teaching this novel because it brings out some of the best
work I receive all year.

　　　I have taught this novel only to eighth-grade students, but it was
successful among that age group because of its rich themes. Hinton
creates realistic characters, realistic problems, and a world that mimics
their own. Part of what I try to do while teaching *The Outsiders* is help
the students see themselves in the characters. In addition to social class,
we talk about identity, growing up and finding a place among family
and peers and in modern society. They not only come away from the
unit with a better understanding of many literary elements, they come
away with a new appreciation—sometimes with themselves, sometimes
with a new book, and always with a variety of real-world, twenty-first-
century skills.

　　　One of my favorite forms of assessment is a creative writing assignment. Not only does it give them further practice with organization
of ideas, usage, mechanics, and supporting evidence, but it also asks
them to think outside the box, draw on their creativity, and contribute
to the story itself. For this particular lesson, I pose the following prompt:

> Choose a "Greaser" from *The Outsiders* and have the character
> move up the social ladder. It is ten years from when the story
> took place, and the character you chose is now in the same social
> class as the Socs. Write a scene in which the character comes into
> contact with his old friends. What is the conversation like? How
> has his appearance changed? What does he sound like? What
> repercussions has this change had on the other characters? The
> old neighborhood?

OR

> We know that Ponyboy connects with Robert Frost's poem "Nothing Gold Can Stay." Its themes speak of a loss of innocence, the cycle of life, and the notion of carpe diem. What other poem have you read that may be associated with the changed individual from the scenario given above? Specifically, what lines from the poem connect to the character's plight? What images symbolize this conflict?

The possibilities for these written assignments are nearly limitless. For the first prompt, I have had students turn in work that reflects changes in Hinton's original character dialect, ranging from the new character's use of Standard English and an obvious display of a larger vocabulary, from the "Greaser" dialect of colloquialisms and setting influences. Having students create these differences in speech requires them to reflect on the language and syntax itself, as well as better understand why writers make specific choices. In addition, our discussion of social hierarchies comes into play with this assignment. As the new character gains status, the lines between old friendships become more forced. The new conversations between the character who has become upwardly mobile and his old friends are often awkward, disengaged, and littered with a sense of pity from both sides. It is remarkable to see students internalize class discussion and careful reading in this way. They have moved from reading "on the line," to "between the lines," and finally in this assignment, "beyond the lines" and into the world of writing itself.

For the second prompt, students often complete their own research of poems from our library database. Robert Frost is a popular example, as are Emily Dickinson, Langston Hughes, and Dylan Thomas. I welcome students to bring their examples of poetry from popular culture and music. I have received lyrics of bands ranging from punk, to heavy metal, to "oldies" that were written during the time period of the novel. Seeing how students connect the lyrics and also the sound devices of the songs, themes, and tone to the novel is an enlightening experience. They often introduce such great ideas that their connections can be used the following year within the unit to help students relate to the novel in a more universal manner.

Considerations

This lesson is intended to guide students to analyze the text and the world around them. Whenever I am able to bring in other subject areas and genres of writing, I feel that it makes the learning within the classroom more personal and relevant. I enjoy guiding them beyond analysis of mere characters and themes, while helping them place literature study in the broader perspective of examining themselves, their peers, and their community. Making literature study more personal not only requires students to grapple with the broader implications that instigated the writing of such themes, it is the beginning of creating lifelong learners.

One of the many reasons this lesson is so interactive, allowing peer groupings, large-group discussions, and independent work, is that I want the students themselves to guide the points of discussion. This flexibility makes the lesson easily adaptable to many learning styles. The nature and topic of the lesson immediately encourage participation from students, and with probing questions, I notice a difference in the depth of discussion. While some classes may need guiding questions written on the board to help them with the peer or fishbowl discussion, more advanced classes will internalize the lesson, guiding the discussion to how it most relates to their lives. I adore the nature of this because it easily differentiates for ability levels while still allowing for personal connections to be made.

From previous experience, I caution teachers to exercise a conversation with students about stereotyping before beginning the lesson. The classroom environment needs to be a safe place for students, a room where they know that each opinion is respected and given in an appropriate manner. I think it is valuable to preface this lesson by reminding students that while stereotypes exist, they are not always true. In addition, it is a good idea to share with students that while we will be discussing such stereotypes, the lesson needs to remain positive, and it is not a time to negate groupings within the school, spread rumors, or mention specific names and circumstances. I have found that students are surprisingly receptive to this guidance and are able to maintain a positive, critical discussion.

There are also several extension activities that can be added to this lesson series. In the past, I have provided students with a collection of newspaper websites from around the country to visit on my delicious website (a social bookmarking site at http://www.delicious.com/). Students surfed these sites and saved headlines pertaining to social class issues. We then printed and cut out the headlines, placing them on a wall in my classroom, which came to be a visual representation of the pervasiveness of social classification and its effects in modern society. I have also had students blog with one another following our class discussion or as an opening activity. I find this particular activity a worthwhile one, as students respond to one another's perceptions and reactions and continue to discuss among themselves. There are also some wonderful lessons that incorporate music, poetry, and social class that can be found on the PBS (http://www.pbs.org/) and ReadWriteThink (http://www.readwritethink.org/) websites. Truly, the possibilities are endless with a little creativity and adaptation.

IX *The Chocolate War*: So Bad, It's Good—And That's Why We Need to Teach It

Lisa Scherff
University of Alabama

"Some people can't stand cruelty, Jerry. And that was a cruel thing to do to a guy like Eugene"

—Goober, *The Chocolate War*, p. 158

The Chocolate War, which I first read in 2005 (shocking, I know!), changed my life. Never before had a book been so disturbing that I had to put it down, take a break, and then come back to try to finish; I liken it to going to the bathroom during a scary movie. I had so many questions about the plot and characters: Could Archie really be that evil? What happened to make him that way? What could drive a priest like Brother Leon to become so manipulative and sadistic? But, I had many questions that went beyond the story itself.

In Chapter 4 of this book, Probst writes, "the heavy burden is the reader's responsibility to question what he is not inclined to question, to question what he firmly and absolutely believes." I would argue that *The Chocolate War* is a book that lends itself to this type of beyond-the-book questioning: Who and what is good and evil? Are "saints" really saints? What does it mean to stand up for what you believe? Is it okay to disturb the universe?

Why *The Chocolate War* Belongs in English Classes

As a middle school and high school student, I was not exposed to young adult literature in my English classes. I can remember a steady stream of classics, some better than others, that we trudged through. We most often read chapters at home, completed study questions, took quizzes, went over the answers to the study questions, and then had a 100-question test at the end. Perhaps if I had been allowed to read and analyze *The Chocolate War* instead of Camus' *The Stranger* or Hardy's *Tess of the d'Urbervilles*, I would have gotten more than a C on all of my papers in AP English. I might also have been more likely to read outside of class. I am not knocking the canon; I believe all students should be exposed to classic texts. However, I am arguing against reading them just because they are classics. That is one reason why I am so excited to see quality young adult titles included in this volume.

In *Classics in the Classroom* (2004) Carol Jago writes, "There is an art to choosing books for students. First I look for literary merit. Without such merit, the novel will not stand up to close scrutiny or be worth the investment of classroom time" (p. 47). I think *The Chocolate War* meets Jago's criteria and am sure that the lessons in this chapter will help students explore them because of the variety of activities they offer. Through Alan Brown's unit (Chapter 30), students can counter the bad in the novel by doing good. Whether through exploring their own emotions or being good Samaritans, students can see and understand their own limitless possibilities. Joan Mitchell's unit (Chapter 31) pairs the novel with *Lord of the Flies*, *Heart of Darkness*, and *Civil Disobedience* for students to study man's relationship to society. In my lesson (Chapter 32), students become the critics and curriculum experts; using Jago's criteria, they determine whether the novel is worthy of whole-class teaching. Megan Hastings's lesson (Chapter 33) focuses on the value of *The Chocolate War* and other young adult novels as companion pieces for teaching *The Scarlet Letter*—a fascinating way for students to explore the connection of young adult novels' themes and those of a classic high school novel.

Reference

Jago, C. (2004). *Classics in the classroom*. Portsmouth, NH: Heinemann.

30 Investigating the Outcomes and Consequences of Decision Making: A Unit Plan for Teaching *The Chocolate War*

Alan Brown
University of Alabama

Purpose

I have created a unit plan for Robert Cormier's *The Chocolate War* that I would use for any other work of fiction; it will serve as a guide on the journey through a new fictive world and as a way to spark each student's imagination. In fact, it is my intention to do exactly what Jerry, the protagonist of this novel, struggled so mightily to do himself: to shake up the universe. I think it is safe to say that high school students live in their own universe. Yet, the most satisfying moments of my teaching life have come when students escape that bubble and find new directions, create new opportunities, and imagine new ways of living that were completely unimaginable only moments before.

The merits of choosing a text such as *The Chocolate War* are relatively straightforward and simple. This book appeals to a group of students who are typically difficult to reach: high school males. I know this difficulty first-hand because I was once the student who sat in the back of the room and did just enough so that teachers would leave me alone. I was also the student who never caused any trouble but who cared little about reading and spent most of the class bored. Yet somehow, strangely enough, I find myself as a high school English teacher many years later. Actually, it was young adult novels that helped me transition from a reluctant reader to an enthusiastic one, although I realize that the texts themselves are not enough; they must be coupled with reality, interest, and activity. This combination was my aim in creating what follows, a unit for teaching *The Chocolate War*.

Materials

All of the supplemental readings in my unit can be found by using a basic online search engine. The Interaction Outline (Figure 30.1), the Fifty Good Deeds Project (Figure 30.2), and the Samaritan Checklist (Figure 30.3) are all included here. Materials are listed in the order they are used in the unit plan.

- "A & P" by John Updike
- Reader Response Journal
- Interaction Outline (see Figure 30.1)
- The Parable of the Good Samaritan
- "Thirty-Eight Who Saw Murder Didn't Call the Police" by Martin Gansberg
- Good Samaritan Statutes
- "Thank You, Ma'm" by Langston Hughes
- Fifty Good Deeds Project (see Figure 30.2)
- Samaritan Checklist (see Figure 30.3)

Introduction

I have always heard that to be a great person, you must do great things. I often ask my ninth graders about the great things they hope to accomplish. Some see themselves on the big stage, whether it be singing for thousands of screaming fans or hitting the game-winning shot at the buzzer. Others plan to save lives, protect the innocent, or open their own businesses. So I nod in approval at the greatness of these dreams, and I ask a question that routinely produces blank stares and raised eyebrows. "What about visiting someone in the nursing home or picking up trash in the school parking lot?" I must be the first to admit that, as a high school student, toting a trash bag around the school parking lot was not my idea of a great time, nor is it now. However, I suppose age and experience have changed my worldview ever so slightly because I realize that doing something great actually serves a greater purpose than my own entertainment. Every year I try to convey to my students that greatness comes in all shapes and sizes, and that it only takes a moment to achieve.

Achieving greatness involves decision making above all else. We make decisions daily that affect not only how we live our lives but also affect anyone with whom we come into contact. In reading *The Chocolate War*, I was struck by the many difficult decisions Jerry and his peers routinely had to face. At first glance, as adults we may see The Vigils and their "assignments" as mere exaggerations of what is happening in our schools; but, on further review, these assignments symbolize the negative pressures that our students face on a regular basis. For this reason, *The Chocolate War* is a wonderful tool for introducing students—particularly ninth graders just entering high school—to the realities that lie ahead. After all, each of them has a bit of Jerry, or Goober, or even Archie inside them. Over the course of this unit, students engage in readings, discussions, and activities that help them come to grips with the pressures of high school, better understand their own identities and the social characteristics of their peers, examine the processes by which their decisions have outcomes and consequences, and realize just how important the decision to achieve greatness truly is.

Connections

It is quite possible that talk of using literature to promote sound decision making is lost on our students unless we as teachers provide an appropriate model of behavior (i.e., demonstrating a passion for reading and making sound decisions ourselves) and unless we find a means to motivate our students to do the same. The five initial chapters in this text argue strongly that for students to become engaged, they must first be drawn to the literature itself. To make this happen, I turn to Archie, the antagonist from *The Chocolate War*, who developed a scheme for selling chocolate when things looked bleakest. His plan was simple: "We make selling chocolates popular. We make it cool to sell the things."

My goal in this unit is to spark an interest in all students but especially those who are reluctant by nature. I may never make reading cool, but by making my school a parallel universe to Trinity School, I am offering students a chance to become characters in their own real-life soap opera. As Jago (Chapter 2) points out, if I can entice them even momentarily, I have given them a chance. And if I can put together enough of these moments where my students see parts of themselves in the literature, then I have made it to the brink of what Blau (Chapter 1) and Probst (Chapter 4) call students' constructing meaning. From there, I can create what Wilhelm (Chapter 3) labels inquiry contexts for my students to establish their own questions and, in turn, promote what Moore (Chapter 5) calls pluralistic, or multiple, interpretations of a single reading. As teachers, we must believe all of this is possible. If Archie and The Vigils can sell close to 20,000 boxes of chocolate, surely we can sell a classroom of students on reading!

Activities

Prereading Activities

1. Ask students to jot down events from a normal day in their lives. Their schedule should begin when they wake in the morning and end when they go to sleep at night. Most importantly, it should be as detailed as possible (including brushing their teeth, petting their dog, going to their locker, watching specific television shows). Once they have completed the brainstorming, encourage students to pair with a classmate to share their schedules and note the similarities and differences. Afterwards, allow students to share parts of their schedules and to discuss the decisions they make every day, both consciously and unconsciously, and how these decisions affect their daily activities. Eventually, the discussion should move toward how their decisions, and thereby their actions, wind up affecting others around them.

2. Have students read "A & P" by John Updike. This short story, set in a local grocery store and narrated by Sammy, a teenage employee, serves as a useful introduction to character in *The Chocolate War*. In Sammy, we find many similarities to Jerry, such as his defiance, courage, and disappointing interactions with girls. Use the key terms from the reader response journal below to identify characteristics that apply to Sammy while making sure students have an understanding of each term. Afterwards, discuss as a class a few of Sammy's decisions, their outcomes, and the potential consequences he faces as a result.

During-Reading Activities

3. Reader response journal: Each of the key terms below plays a role in the actions of the characters as well as our students' decision-making processes. For each chapter, have students use the key terms to address the three reader response questions:

Key Term	Chapter	Key Term	Chapter
loneliness	1	triumph	12
toughness	2	guilt	13
love	3	desperation	14
expectation	4	opportunity	15
intimidation	5	trust	16
doubt	6	suffrage	17
humiliation	7	uncertainty	18
fear	8	disruption	19
boredom	9	control	20
power	10	defiance	21
fury	11	apathy	22

Key Term	Chapter	Key Term	Chapter
effort	23	weakness	32
trouble	24	reliability	33
patience	25	presence	34
courage	26	vengeance	35
popularity	27	luck	36
respect	28	helplessness	37
cooperation	29	knowledge	38
freedom	30	silence	39
violence	31		

   i. How has this key term been relevant to some aspect of your life or to the life of someone close to you?

  ii. How does this key term relate to specific characters from the chapter?

 iii. What decisions have been made as a result of this key term?

4. Collaborative Activity: After every fifth chapter (Chapter 5, Chapter 10, etc.), split students into small groups. In these groups, students compare their answers for each journal entry and then complete the Interaction Outline (see Figure 30.1). The purpose of this form is to provoke critical thought and analytical dialogue from students concerning at least one specific decision by a character and the outcomes and consequences of that decision. On the back of the Interaction Outline form, each group responds to the following prompts based on the previous five chapters.

   a. Describe at least one occasion when a character could have acted differently to help someone else.

   b. Of the five previous key terms, which one has most profoundly affected the plot thus far?

   c. What decisions will need to be made in the upcoming chapters? Make at least two predictions.

   d. Creative Writing Activity: Once students have completed the novel, many will be left wanting more. Cormier's text is certainly a cliffhanger, so take this opportunity to show students that where a writer leaves off is where creative possibilities begin. Have students write Chapter 40 to *The Chocolate War*, which will detail the last weeks of the semester at Trinity School. Although they have creative freedom in this endeavor, encourage them to focus at least in part on the following details.

     ■ Jerry and Goober's experiences at Trinity

     ■ The ninth-grade football team

     ■ Jerry's relationship with his father

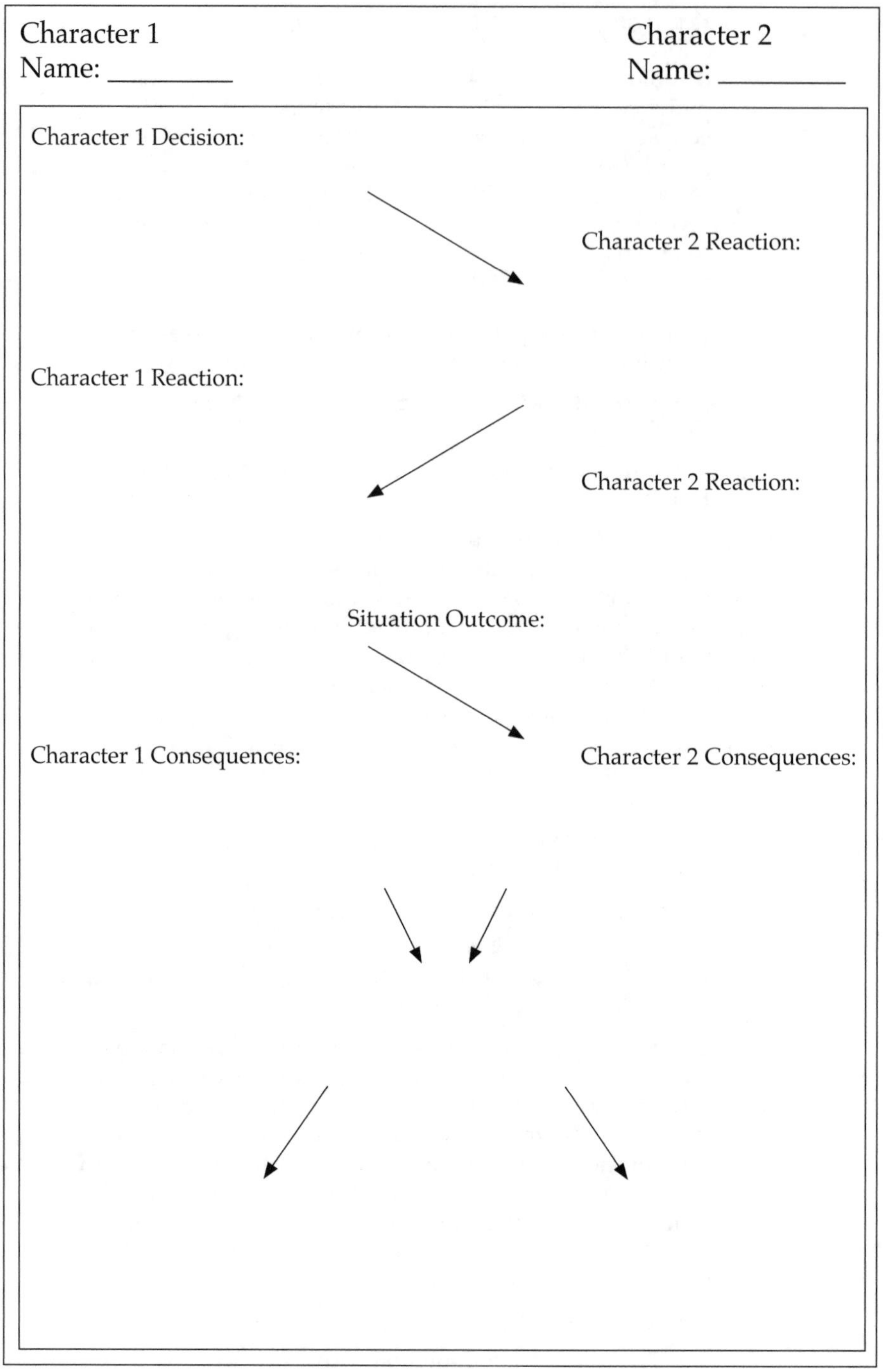

Character 1
Name: _____

Character 2
Name: _____

Character 1 Decision:

Character 2 Reaction:

Character 1 Reaction:

Character 2 Reaction:

Situation Outcome:

Character 1 Consequences:

Character 2 Consequences:

Figure 30.1. Interaction Outline handout.

- Jerry's relationship with Ellen Barrett
- Archie's relationship with The Vigils
- The tension between Archie and Emile Janza
- The tension between Brother Leon and Brother Jacques
- Proceeds from the fundraiser

e. Supplemental Resources: While reading *The Chocolate War* and focusing on the decision making of the characters, as well as those of your students, try incorporating these supplemental resources throughout the novel. These activities offer interesting perspectives when tied to aspects of the novel, including the final boxing match between Jerry and Janza. They are also important components of the final project.

  i. The Parable of the Good Samaritan: This parable, originally from Luke 10: 30–37 of the Bible, tells the story of a man in desperate need of aid after being robbed and beaten. While others passed him by, a Samaritan stopped to offer him assistance. After reading the parable, initiate dialogue with students regarding times when they have stopped to help another, or perhaps times when they have been unable or unwilling to help someone in need.

  ii. "Thirty-Eight Who Saw Murder Didn't Call The Police": This article, written by Martin Gansberg and published in the *New York Times* on March 27, 1964, describes an incident from Queens, New York, where thirty-eight citizens witnessed the murder of Ms. Kitty Genovese, yet not a single person called the police. Although the exact events of that evening have long been disputed, this article offers students an introduction into themes from *The Chocolate War*, such as cruelty and apathy, and will certainly produce a rousing conversation within the classroom. Although students may not be able to relate directly, they can make personal connections such as watching a fight at school or slowing down on the highway to see an automobile accident.

  iii. Good Samaritan Statutes: Most states now have laws protecting good Samaritans from being held liable after helping those who are injured or ill. Although legal ramifications hardly factor into the sequence of events in *The Chocolate War*, there are several cases where characters from the story could have helped one another, but didn't do so out of fear of possible repercussions. A prime example is when Brother Leon accuses Bailey of cheating, yet his peers are not willing to stand up for him because they are scared of Leon's wrath.

iv. "Thank You, Ma'm": This classic short story by Langston Hughes is a quick and entertaining selection that can be used for teaching students the power of good deeds even toward those who initially do them wrong. Such is the case of Mrs. Luella Bates Washington Jones who supported young Roger even after he tried to steal her purse. As students write the final chapter of *The Chocolate War*, Hughes's story will provide an opportunity for students to consider possibilities other than violence and revenge for characters such as Jerry and Janza.

Post-Reading Activity

5. Fifty Good Deeds Project: The final project for *The Chocolate War* takes place over the entire semester. Whereas each of the students at Trinity High School was asked to sell fifty boxes of candy, this project requires students to become (or hopefully remain) good Samaritans in their homes, their schools, and their communities by accomplishing *at least* fifty good deeds by the end of the semester. It is worth acknowledging that some students will try to take advantage of such a project. Regardless, it is my firm belief that the risk of some students not participating or not being truthful in their participation is certainly worth the reward of those who will participate. The project overview, the necessary instructions, a list of good deeds, and the evaluation criteria can be found in Figure 30.2. A Samaritan Checklist for students to record their good deeds can be found in Figure 30.3.

Assessment

The first three during-reading activities (the reader response journal, the collaborative activity, and the creative writing activity) serve as the primary assessment instruments for this unit. Although each activity intends to promote student involvement with the text, each one also offers a little something different. The reader response journal allows students to work individually, relate the events of each chapter to a theme, and connect those themes to their own lives. The collaborative activity permits students to work together to witness how one simple decision can turn into a complex web of interactions. This activity also focuses on outcomes and consequences similar to ones students may ultimately face during their high school experience. Finally, the creative writing activity offers students an opportunity to showcase their overall knowledge of the storyline by using their imaginations to write an appropriate ending to the novel.

Fifty Good Deeds Project

Project Overview

The final project for *The Chocolate War* will take place over the course of the semester. This project will require you to become an active Samaritan within your home, your school, and your community. Whereas each of the students at Trinity School was asked to sell fifty boxes of candy, your task is to accomplish *at least* fifty good deeds between now and the end of the semester.

Voluntary Status

Although the students of Trinity School, such as Jerry, had the option to decline selling candy, you should understand that this project not only serves as a grade, but the culmination of your good deeds will also serve a much greater purpose. Therefore, you do not have the option to decline as Jerry did, but this shouldn't be a concern since you are already good Samaritans anyway!

Parts of the Project

1. Completion of fifty good deeds
2. Samaritan checklist
3. Final reflection and presentation

Good Deeds

A list of ideas for possible good deeds is offered below. This is merely a starting point, however, as we will add to this list regularly as the semester moves forward. Please note that a major part of the evaluation criteria is the quality of your accomplishments. Therefore, holding a door for someone fifty times is certainly not appropriate. Instead, push yourselves to truly make a difference in the lives of others!

- Hold a door for someone
- Assist someone who has his or her hands full
- Visit someone in the hospital or nursing home
- Send someone a birthday card or a kind note
- Volunteer for extra chores or activities around your house, school, or church
- Volunteer to be a dog walker at the animal shelter
- Shovel a neighbor's driveway when it snows
- Pick up trash in your school's parking lot
- Support your friends by going to their games or performances
- Recycle bottles, cans, paper, etc.
- Give blood

Samaritan Checklist Instructions

1. Do a good deed.
2. Once you have finished, write it under Accomplishments.
3. Include the date, the place, and the beneficiary of your good deed.

continued on next page

Figure 30.2. Fifty Good Deeds Project assignment.

Figure 30.2 continued

Final Reflection Instructions

Your final reflection should be 2–3 pages typed (1" margins, 12-point font, double-spaced) or 3–4 pages written. Please include the following components:

1. Description of your favorite good deeds throughout the semester
2. Discussion on what you have learned about yourself and others during this project
3. Discussion on what *your universe* would be like if more people were good Samaritans

Final Presentation Instructions

Presentations should focus on at least two of the final reflection questions listed above. All presentations should be approximately five minutes in length and include a visual aid. Presentations will take place toward the end of the semester.

Evaluation Criteria

The fifty good deeds project will be worth a major test grade and will be scored based on the following criteria:

1. Completion of good deeds (20 points)
2. Quality of accomplishments (20 points)
3. Final reflection (20 points)
4. Final presentation (20 points)
5. Visual aid (20 points)

Samaritan Checklist

For each good deed, list the accomplishment, the date, the place, and the beneficiary of the good deed.

Accomplishment   *Date*   *Place*   *Beneficiary*

Figure 30.3. Samaritan Checklist handout.

The Fifty Good Deeds Project can also be used as a primary assessment tool throughout the semester. Since teaching English is more than mastering mere content, and because *The Chocolate War* is a tremendous entry point into connecting the classroom with the cultures of our students, we can use the novel to help students grow into responsible and compassionate young men and women. This project is an attempt to do just that.

Considerations

As I reflect on this unit, I am pleased with the flexibility it offers teachers and the freedom it allows students. I find that students have a better chance of becoming invested in literature if given choice and an opportunity to think for themselves. Yet, one of the challenges of teaching any novel can be the need to move along at a fast enough pace, but still offer time for ensuring understanding, analyzing meanings, reflecting on past events, and predicting what lies ahead. Fortunately, this is an obstacle that can be overcome by colleagues who add and subtract as they see fit, and open themselves up to possibilities that lie well beyond the reach of what you find here.

31 Do I Dare Disturb the Universe? Teaching *The Chocolate War*: Using Character Analysis and Dramatization to Engage in Thematic Discussion

Joan F. Mitchell
University of Alabama

Purpose

This unit plan is designed to engage students in reading *The Chocolate War* as part of a study on humanity's relationship to society that includes works such as *Lord of the Flies* by William Golding, *Heart of Darkness* by Joseph Conrad, and *Civil Disobedience* by Henry David Thoreau. As a result of this unit, students will be able to

- engage in the context of the novel through an exploration of both personal and societal connections;
- analyze characters effectively through close observation and dramatization;
- support conclusions about characters and thematic ideas using textual evidence;
- explain how an author's characterization is inextricably linked to thematic ideas; and
- connect the thematic ideas of this novel to the other works in the overall study of humanity's relationship to society.

Materials

- TV/VCR or TV/DVD player
- VHS or DVD copies of the following films: *Mean Girls, High School Musical, Pleasantville, The Breakfast Club*
- Reader response journal—This could be a section in a daily journal or a separate notebook.
- Character chart ("Student ID"; see Figure 31.1)

- Character interview sheet (see Figure 31.2)
- Character/theme continuum handout (see Figure 31.3)

Introduction

The Chocolate War serves as an effective entry point to a study of man's relationship to society because it speaks directly to students' experiences in high school. While issues of conformity or human savagery might appear to be "just another set of literary themes" to find, these concepts are removed from the literary world and brought into sharp focus in the lives of students through this novel. To engage students prior to reading the novel, I present brief clips of several current, popular movies (e.g., *Mean Girls, High School Musical, Pleasantville*) and one classic teen drama, *The Breakfast Club,* that depict issues of conformity and nonconformity in high schools. The majority of students are familiar with these films, but usually only because of their entertainment value. While students are watching, I ask them to record details about the attitudes of the students and the mood of the school environment. Then they denote similarities and differences to their school experiences.

After they have made these observations and critiques, we discuss the portrayals in each of the movies and whether or not the students perceive them as accurate or exaggerated. This leads to a discussion of students' perception of their own school, a microcosm of "society" at this point in their lives. Students then respond to the first reader response journal prompt: "In high school, is it better to conform to the expectations of a dominant group of students (i.e., older students, 'popular' students, etc.) to protect yourself or risk being ostracized by refusing to conform? Explain your response." Because discussing one's insecurities about fitting in or not fitting in can be intimidating, this journal topic encourages students to respond on an individual level concerning their own struggle between conformity and nonconformity. If any students feel comfortable discussing what they wrote, it provides a unique opportunity for others to hear about similar experiences and emotions toward the school environment that are often squelched by a desire to appear confident and in control.

Once the students are prepared for the thematic context of the novel, we engage in a discussion about the language used in the title of the novel as well as the first line of the book. I ask students to brainstorm adjectives and feelings usually associated with *chocolate* and then those associated with the word *war*. We then discuss why Cormier would pair these words together so abruptly. Then the students read the first line of the novel: "They murdered him." I ask them to write in their response journals their first reactions to this line and what it might represent in the novel. What is Cormier talking about? Why would he begin the novel this way? What predictions could we make from this first line? We discuss these ideas so that students are excited to continue reading because the ominous tone has already been set from the beginning.

After these introductory activities, students read the majority of the novel individually while keeping a reader response journal and tracing character traits throughout the novel. These introductory activities will connect the novel to their own experience from the beginning and challenge them to consider the author's purpose throughout in relation to the tone of both the title and first line.

Connections

Several of the introductory essayists in this text share a desire to empower students' personal discoveries and engagement in literature and diminish the role of the teacher as the literary "expert" in the classroom. Blau (Chapter 1) contends that students lack authentic knowledge because teachers too often *tell* them the "correct" interpretations without guiding their personal discovery. Similarly, Jago (Chapter 2) suggests that too many of the questions that teachers ask in an English class are teacher-directed and ultimately answered by the teacher. This unit plan empowers students to ask questions of the text through their reader response journal. While they are gathering evidence about each character, they are recognizing patterns of behavior or central conflicts without being directed toward a particular response by overly leading study guide questions. Because they have the freedom to pose questions or express reactions to the novel as well as observing character development, students come to class armed with ideas and details from the text, and they begin to co-construct knowledge with their peers and teacher guidance.

According to Wilhelm (Chapter 3), teachers must encourage *real* reading through posing essential questions that make the text relevant and personal. For this unit, the essential question is summarized in the protagonist's driving question: "Do I dare disturb the universe?" Students are invited to examine their own school environment and question the power of conformity in their lives. By studying the thoughts, words, and actions of each of the boys in the novel, the students are constantly reflecting on how *they* would respond in the same situation and learn to look critically at themselves and the actions of their peers. As Probst (Chapter 4) suggests, they need to question and challenge their beliefs and perspectives about the world. Through *The Chocolate War*, students must come to terms with a protagonist who seemingly fails when he resists conformity. The "good guy" seems to lose, and they must determine why the author allows this. Through the character continuum activity, students rank characters in terms of their level of conformity and their relative "goodness." Once they have made these decisions, they are asked to decide where the author stands on the issues of conformity. Would he "dare disturb the universe" or is he advocating for the safety of conformity? These are difficult questions for students in the throes of high school, but they inevitably challenge them to examine their familiar environment with a fresh perspective.

Wilhelm (Chapter 3) also advocates for interactive strategies that engage students and develop their imaginations. The character interviews in this unit plan are similar to his suggestion of the hotseat in which a literary character is questioned by the class to determine his or her perspective. Aside from engaging the students in the lives of the characters, this process also enhances their imaginations as they have to extrapolate responses from the characters that are beyond the scope of the text. By taking on a character's persona or serving as an interviewer, students effectively extend the text into their own worlds and engage it in a dialogue. This strategy makes them feel like character experts and thus prepares them for a formal character analysis. As Jago suggests, student engagement is not a substitute for formal analysis, and students must not be asked to analyze a work before they understand it. The reader response journals, character identification sheets, character interviews, and character continuum discussions combine to provide students with a deep understanding of the text so that they are prepared to analyze it effectively in a character analysis and demonstrate their ability to draw conclusions about thematic ideas from their character studies.

Activities

1. *Introduction to novel through movie clips related to issues of conformity.*

   a. Show brief clips of the following popular movies related to issues of conformity in high school: *Mean Girls, High School Musical* (song: "Stick to the Status Quo"), *Pleasantville,* and/or *The Breakfast Club.*

   b. Ask students to note observations about the attitudes of the students and the mood of the school environment. Then they should explain how each portrayal is similar to or different from their own high school experience.

    c. Discuss these portrayals as a class to determine whether or not the portrayals are exaggerated or accurate. This discussion leads into the first reader response topic below.

2. *Reader Response Journal:* This journal will serve as the students' "conversations" with the novel as they read. In class I will prompt them to respond to questions or ideas throughout the novel such as the sample prompts suggested below. Outside of class students will use the journal to pose questions, express reactions, or record interesting ideas as they read.

    a. Prior to reading:

- In high school, is it better to conform to the expectations of a dominant group of students (i.e., older students, "popular" students, etc.) to protect yourself or risk being ostracized by refusing to conform? Explain your response.

- Examine the title and the first line of the novel. Why do you think Cormier chooses this language? Based on your conclusions, write a brief synopsis of what you think will happen in the novel.

    b. During reading:

- Imagine that you are Jerry at this point in the story and write a letter to your mother (who has passed away) explaining what is happening and how you are feeling.

- Choose one character in the story with whom you most relate and explain why. Would you have handled this situation in the same way as this character did?

    c. After reading:

- Cormier fills the final scenes of the novel with suspense leading toward a surprising conclusion. Rewrite the ending of the novel to suggest a different outcome. You may either imply how this ending changes the message of the novel in your fictional piece or explain it separately.

- This entire novel happens within the context of a small preparatory school for boys. Predict how you think these boys will behave as adults. What does this suggest about the world outside of this small school? Explain.

3. *Character Chart ("Student ID"; Figure 31.1):* In keeping with the theme of conformity, these character analysis sheets are designed to look like student IDs from Trinity School. Because Cormier organizes his text according to different characters'

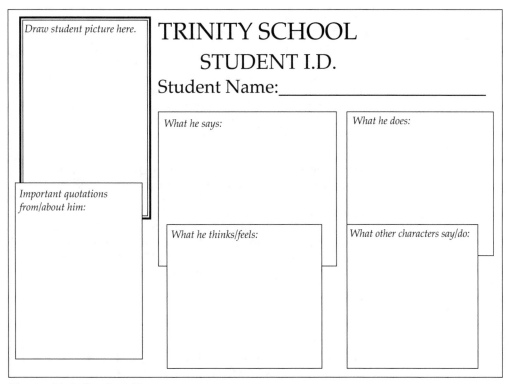

Figure 31.1. Student ID.

points of view, it is fitting to focus on the characterization of different individuals throughout.

a. For each of the major characters in the novel, students record details about what they say, do, feel, and think as well as what others think of them on their "student ID card." They should note any changes that the character seems to undergo throughout the novel with an asterisk (*). Include some particular quotations that seem to reflect something significant about that character's personality. Students should continue to record these details while reading, and then begin writing questions that they would like to ask this character if they had a chance to talk to him.

b. Prior to reading the final chapters, students will choose a character that they find most interesting to focus on in the final scenes. The students will be grouped according to these characters to serve as "experts" on the particular character they chose.

4. *Character Interviews (Figure 31.2):* This dramatization of the characters brings them to life in a way that allows the students to engage with them. Because the students representing each character have so much textual evidence about them, their responses should always be in keeping with what the character would have said based on what Cormier reveals about them. However, the questions should push students to extrapolate beyond the confines of the text to guess at a character's motives or desires even when they are not directly uncovered in the text.

   a. After reading the final chapters together as a class, students will meet in their character groups to discuss that character's role in the final scenes. Then they will nominate one student in the group to take on the persona of that character to be interviewed by the class. They will work together to prepare that student to be interviewed by reviewing details collected throughout the novel and posing sample questions to him or her.

As you read, record questions that you would like to ask this character if you had a chance to talk to him. Leave space for the responses to these questions.

Q.

A.

_____

Q.

A.

_____

Q.

A.

_____

Q.

A.

_____

Figure 31.2. Character interview.

  b. Each group will add final questions for all characters to their character interview sheets in preparation for the interviews.

  c. Then each "character" will be interviewed by the class about motives, decisions, beliefs, and actions. The character's responses should be based on evidence gathered in the text throughout the novel as well as in the final scenes.

  d. Sample questions may include the following: (1) Goober: Why didn't you stand up for Jerry when he needed you? (2) Jerry: Why didn't you just sell the chocolates? (3) Archie: Do you think of yourself as a "good" person? (4) Brother Leon: What do you perceive as your role in the school?

5. *Character Continuum (Figure 31.3):* After students have interviewed each character, they should feel comfortable making final decisions about where to position those characters in relation to some of the major issues of the novel. This activity is especially effective because it causes students to think critically about character and theme and to defend their choices with textual evidence. When students must make a decision about the author, they are unknowingly identifying both the author's purpose and critical thematic ideas.

  a. After the character interviews, students individually rank each of the characters on two separate continuums. The first continuum is between good and evil, and the second between conformity and nonconformity. (If students feel that a character has changed on the continuum, then they can denote that by placing a subscript of 1, 2, 3, etc. beneath the character's initial.)

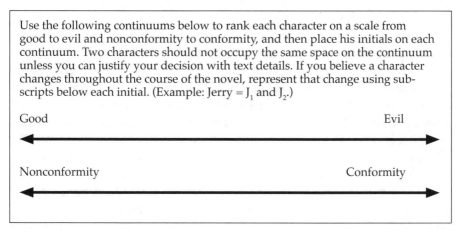

Use the following continuums below to rank each character on a scale from good to evil and nonconformity to conformity, and then place his initials on each continuum. Two characters should not occupy the same space on the continuum unless you can justify your decision with text details. If you believe a character changes throughout the course of the novel, represent that change using subscripts below each initial. (Example: Jerry = J_1 and J_2.)

Good   Evil

Nonconformity   Conformity

Figure 31.3. Character continuum.

   b. Students then briefly discuss their decisions in their char-
      acter groups so that they have a chance to justify their
      choices before discussing them with the whole class.

   c. As a whole class, the students debate the placement of
      each character on each continuum using details from the
      text to justify their choices. The class tries to come to a
      consensus for each character's placement.

   d. Finally, the students will use the two continuums to de-
      termine Cormier's position on issues of conformity and
      nonconformity and the nature of humanity (e.g., Would
      Cormier "dare to disturb the universe?").

6. *Character Analysis Paper*: At this point students have traced
   the characters throughout the novel, interviewed them, and
   placed them on a continuum to determine their values. Each
   student will write a character analysis about the character the
   group studied. This analysis should ultimately explain how
   that character functions in the novel and how he contributes
   to some of the major thematic ideas previously discussed.

Assessment

Discussions of the reader response journals and character observations
throughout the novel provide opportunities for informal assessment of
student engagement in the novel as well as their developing understanding. As a tool for reflection, students submit their "best" journal entry
and their "best" character ID and write an explanation for why those
pieces are significant. The character interviews also allow for informal
assessment because both the questions and the responses indicate
students' critical thinking and engagement with the text. Their ability
to extrapolate characters' responses beyond the scope of the text itself
demonstrates a deeper understanding of the characters and the issues
that they face. One of the most effective assessment opportunities is the
debate concerning the character continuum. Students typically become
passionate about defending their choices, and to prove that they are
correct, they inevitably return to the text to find proper "evidence."
They are essentially writing an argumentative essay aloud without even
realizing it.

Because the character interviews and continuum exercises involve
group and whole-class interaction, the character analysis paper is a
necessary component for formally assessing individual understanding of a character's development and how he functions in the novel or
how he contributes to a thematic idea. This paper asks students to form
connections between the characters they have gotten to know so well
and the deeper issues that drive the novel to its shocking conclusion. It

moves the students from a personal interaction with the character to an understanding of *why* the author included him and what he represents in the novel as a whole.

Considerations

The beauty of *The Chocolate War* from an educator's perspective is its accessibility to students and its relevance to their daily lives. Although the events at Trinity School may seem extreme, the undercurrent of peer pressure and cruelty is an unfortunate pattern in high school and ultimately in society at large. Thus, the primary challenge is not helping students relate to the events of the text, but taking advantage of the accessibility of characters and issues in the novel to empower students to think critically and develop original ideas about the author's craft and purpose.

This unit plan is successful with students because it both engages them personally and challenges them to critically approach the text. The introductory activity as well as the reader response journals draw students into the world of the text and constantly ask them to place themselves in that context. The journals and the character identification sheet create an arsenal of questions that they are posing and details about characters without students' wondering if their interpretations and questions are "right" or "accurate." They are building material for their analysis throughout so that by the time they get to the character interviews and character continuum, students naturally draw on their own knowledge about the text. Because I am acting as a guide and not an expert in both of these major activities, the students are empowered to use all of the details they have gathered to construct meaning with one another. Finally, the character analysis paper serves as both an assessment and proof to the students that they are capable of drawing important conclusions about the major issues in the text through the lens of one character. They can do this with confidence because they have gathered evidence individually, used their classmates as a sounding board, and drawn conclusions about the author's purpose as a class. Ultimately, they remain invested in the process because they understand that the book speaks to their own experiences as high school students and as individuals in a world that they are still trying to figure out. While most of the movies concerning nonconformist teenagers ultimately end with the protagonist succeeding in challenging the status quo, this novel's nonconformist hero fails. Cormier forces students to decide if it is worth it to "disturb the universe," for that single decision could impact their choices and actions for life.

32 Is It Worthy? Determining Whether *The Chocolate War* Should Be Taught in English Class

Lisa Scherff
University of Alabama

Purpose

This lesson is designed to involve students in a discussion concerning what texts should be taught in English class and why. After students finish reading Cormier's *The Chocolate War* they apply criteria for text selection (as described by Carol Jago in *Classics in the Classroom*, 2004) to determine whether or not the novel is worthy of whole-class study.

- Students apply a wide range of strategies to comprehend, interpret, evaluate, and appreciate texts. They draw on their prior experience, their interactions with other readers and writers, their knowledge of word meaning and of other texts, their word identification strategies, and their understanding of textual features (e.g., sound-letter correspondence, sentence structure, context, graphics).

- Students apply knowledge of language structure, language conventions (e.g., spelling and punctuation), media techniques, figurative language, and genre to create, critique, and discuss print and nonprint texts.

- Students participate as knowledgeable, reflective, creative, and critical members of a variety of literacy communities.

- Students use spoken, written, and visual language to accomplish their own purposes (e.g., for learning, enjoyment, persuasion, and the exchange of information).

Materials

- Copies of *The Chocolate War*
- Handout (Figure 32.1), enough for two per student

- Poster paper, large sticky notes, whiteboard, etc.
- Markers (two colors per group)

Introduction

Mandated reading lists; No budget for class sets of novels; That's what we've always taught; It's in the anthology. Sound familiar? These four statements sum up why teachers sometimes teach the novels they do. Yet, there are other forces that drive literature choices, such as students' reading levels, censorship, student interest, and literary merit. This last reason is the impetus for this lesson.

By inviting students to critique and analyze *The Chocolate War*, and thus determine whether it is worthy of whole-class instruction, they become curriculum experts. Moreover, Jago's criteria (see Figure 32.1) for choosing whole-class texts become the starting point for critical discussions concerning language and style, plot, characterization, themes, symbols, and literary theory. In short, students not only critique the novel but assess it on the literary merits of its elements.

The lesson can be adapted and differentiated so that students at all levels can be text critics and analysts. Students can work alone and/or in pairs to compare and contrast their evaluation of the novel (or alone, in pairs, then as a whole class). Another way to complete this lesson is through small groups with each focusing on one criterion and reporting their findings to the class for a larger discussion.

Connections

In Chapter 1, Blau describes the typical English class: students come to class expecting the teacher to have all the answers, copy that information down (or read commercial summaries), and answer the teacher's questions. Blau believes that what students learn is "false knowledge. It is not the product of their own experience of the texts." I would extend Blau's argument one step further, asserting that teachers choose and evaluate texts in much the same way. What about students' evaluator experiences? To what extent do teachers query students regarding their appraisal of a text? And, if students deem a text to be subpar, is that taken into consideration? As readers and literary critics, students have valuable input regarding the books they read in English class.

Criterion 1: Written in language perfectly suited to the author's purpose
Criterion 2: Exposes readers to complex human dilemmas
Criterion 3: Includes compelling, disconcerting characters
Criterion 4: Explores universal themes that combine different periods and cultures
Criterion 5: Challenges readers to reexamine their beliefs
Criterion 6: Tells a good story with places for laughing and crying

Figure 32.1. Jago's criteria for text selection.

Activities

The sequence of activities below offers just one possible way this lesson can be taught.

1. Introduction to the Jago Criteria

    a. After reading *The Chocolate War*, the teacher tells students that they are going to be curriculum experts. Their job is to use six criteria to determine whether the novel should be taught as a whole-class novel.

    b. Using an overhead or Elmo, the teacher displays the six criteria (Figure 32.1) for the class to see.

    c. The teacher goes through each criterion, asking students what they think each means and clarifying confusion when necessary.

2. Modeling and Practice

    a. Using a short story or novel that the class is already familiar with, the teacher and students go through each criterion, coming up with reasons why it does or doesn't apply to the text.

    b. After going through the criteria, the teacher follows up to make sure that students understand the procedure.

3. Application

    a. The teacher puts students into small groups (three to five students) and assigns each one a criterion to be responsible for discussing. Each group will be responsible for sharing their analysis with the rest of the class. Groups will be directed to have a note taker, a speaker, and a follow-up note taker. (This point is where the lesson could be differentiated by ability level. Students who have difficulty with higher levels of questioning or literary analysis could be assigned to work on criterion #6, which is more plot based.)

    b. Students are directed to use their novels to find textual evidence for their responses.

    c. Students can use chart paper or large sticky note paper to record their responses. One student should be the note taker (using one marker only), while the others collaborate using their novels.

    d. Teacher hands each student a copy of Figure 32.1 for note taking.

    e. When their discussion is finished, each group presents its findings. One person speaks for the group. While one group presents, the others fill in their Figure 32.1 sheets.

  f. After each group shares, other groups offer feedback, discussion, and/or dissension through comments, questions, and textual evidence. These points are noted by the second note taker.

  g. Each group adds the new ideas to their chart/sticky note paper. The group utilizes the second marker to show evidence that contradicts its findings/responses.

4. Reinforcement

  a. After all groups have presented and follow-up notes are added to their charts, each group creates a second version of their chart. They use one marker color for ideas that support their claim and another color for those they do not believe support their claim.

  b. The charts are posted and the students do a modified Gallery Walk to revise or redo their Figure 32.1 sheets.

5. Extension Activity

  a. Students write an essay in response to the prompt "Should *The Chocolate War* be taught next year?" They can use the Figure 32.1 handout to support their writing. For students who have difficulties doing more formal literary analysis papers, this lesson provides an excellent framework.

  b. Students can use the Figure 32.1 handout to make the case for including one of their favorite books as a whole-class text.

Assessment

Students always like to provide input about what they read in class, but I have found that just asking why a book is good yields superficial responses. This lesson asks them to dig deeper, to use their interaction with the novel and textual evidence to support their opinions. They become experts of sorts because of the scaffolding of the criteria.

  Although this lesson is summative in nature, it is formative, too, so I would primarily assess it in terms of participation. Because this lesson is based on a cycle—introduction, modeling, practice, application, and reinforcement—students have multiple opportunities to build on and clarify what they know. Teachers can informally observe and evaluate students' engagement and participation in Steps 1–3. More formative evaluation could result from the charts completed in Step 4. Teachers could also provide groups with self-feedback and peer response forms. An essay such as the one described above could be used as an individual graded assignment.

Considerations

This lesson could work as part of any unit that includes *The Chocolate War*. For example, John Updike's short story "A&P" (included in Alan Brown's unit in Chapter 30) could be the model that teachers and students complete together to "try out" Jago's criteria before using it to examine the novel. The lesson could potentially be included in Joan Mitchell's unit (Chapter 31), especially given both lessons' focus on characterization and theme. This lesson also works because it can be differentiated. All students can take part, even those who might have difficulties with picking out symbols or identifying theme(s).

However, the primary reason this lesson works is that it asks for student input. It requires students to go beyond answering the question of whether they "liked the book" or thought it was "good." Without realizing it, students become literary analysts and are provided with a scaffold and confidence to write an analysis paper.

33 A Better Scarlet Letter: Teaching *The Scarlet Letter* Using Young Adult Novels, Including *The Chocolate War,* through Literature Circles

Megan Hastings
Auburn High School, Auburn, Alabama

Purpose

This lesson plan is a small component of a larger unit in which students compare a whole-class reading of Nathaniel Hawthorne's *The Scarlet Letter* with various young adult novels, one being *The Chocolate War*, that are read and discussed by students in literature circles. The themes of isolation, branding, nonconformity, and overcoming one's past/actions abound in all texts that students will read and discuss. Each literature circle group reads a different young adult novel, each of which connects, in some way, to *The Scarlet Letter*. The purpose of this unit is to build students' understanding of classic literature through the thematic and/ or character comparison(s) with a young adult novel of choice.

Materials

- Computer and Internet access
- Reader response journal (students create these in class using five sheets of loose-leaf paper folded in half and stapled like a small book; students complete literature circle assignments and other responses in these journals)
- Index cards for students to assess their young adult novel of preference
- Poster board, markers, glue, scissors for final project poster presentations
- Young adult novels for literature circles:
  - Laurie Halse Anderson, *Speak*

- Sherman Alexie, *The Absolutely True Diary of a Part-Time Indian*
- Anne Cassidy, *Looking for JJ*
- Walter Dean Myers, *Monster*
- Jerry Spinelli, *Stargirl*
- Barry Lyga, *Hero Type*
- Robin Brande, *Evolution, Me, and Other Freaks of Nature*
- Robert Cormier, *The Chocolate War*
- Copy of Robert Frost's "Mending Wall"
- Final project handout (Figure 33.1)
- Character journal instruction slip (Figure 33.2)
- Literature circle role guide (Figure 33.3)
- Character Facebook page (Figure 33.4)

Introduction

In this unit, it is important to remember that each student is reading two books. The entire class is reading *The Scarlet Letter* while student groups are reading various young adult novels, one of which is *The Chocolate War*. Therefore, the introduction for this unit is more geared toward *The Scarlet Letter* and the themes that are common between the classic text and all the young adult novels. The introduction for the unit occurs in two parts. First, a quickwrite question guides students toward thinking about the theme of overcoming one's past and forgiveness/guilt: How are you influenced by the past? Have you ever had to overcome your past and how did you do so? After discussing student responses, I hook students into the theme of alienation and isolation that is found throughout all novels by reading and discussing Robert Frost's "Mending Wall."

Connections

All of the writers in the first five chapters of this book encourage teachers to bring relevance and authenticity to the literature. The notion of nonconformity is and has always been a major topic in the lives of adolescents, and *The Chocolate War* presents an ideal array of questions for discussion that students find relevant to their own lives. The literature circles that are the core of this lesson help to personalize the text for students, as Blau (Chapter 1) advocates, since students bring in the passages they find most puzzling and intriguing to them. Also, according to Jago's (Chapter 2) idea that classics can be relevant and teachable in the classroom today, this lesson intertwines the literary greatness of *The Scarlet Letter* with the relatable nature of young adult novels such as *The Chocolate War*. Students need guidance reading most canonical works, and *The Scarlet Letter* is no exception. However, students usually do not need guidance with young adult literature that was written primarily for a teen audience, with teen characters and relevant issues for adolescents, which is why the young adult novels are discussed and led by student groups, not the teacher. Finally, Wilhelm (Chapter 3) supports the notion of readers "becoming one" with the book. To successfully teach this unit/lesson, teachers should read and become familiar with not only the novel but also how to blend it into the students' everyday lives.

Activities

These activities are completed in a series of days/weeks in which the students read *The Scarlet Letter* as a whole class and their group young adult novel. I read and discuss *The Scarlet Letter* three to four days a week and students meet in their literature circle groups one to two times a week for a total of seven meeting times over a five-week period. The activities below are those that focus specifically on *The Chocolate War* literature circle group.

Day 1: Introduction

1. After completing the quickwrite, poetry analysis, and discussing the notions of overcoming the past, alienation, and isolation, students create their reader response journals. Students will create these in class using five sheets of loose-leaf paper folded in half and stapled like a small book; students will complete literature circle assignments and other responses in these journals.

2. Next, I give an overview of the unit for the students by showing them a copy of *The Scarlet Letter* and each of the young adult novels to give them a sense of the books.

3. Students then participate in Speed Book Dating in which all the young adult novels are passed around the room every two minutes. In the two minutes, students read and skim over the book, writing down on an index card the books they are most interested in reading for their literature circles.

4. I then assign students to their literature circle group and give them reading assignments.

5. I explain the process of literature circles to the students focusing on the roles students take.

6. Next students determine their circle's reading schedule for completing their young adult novel on the dates I set for the class to meet. Students also decide which role each will complete for the first meeting. Every student will eventually complete all roles in literature circles by the end.

7. I hand out the Final Project Instruction sheet (Figure 33.1) for students and review it so that students will know what they are expected to accomplish by the end of this unit. Have students keep this in their notebook.

First Literature Circle Meeting for *The Chocolate War*

1. Share literature circle findings and insights.

2. Character journals (to be completed in reader response journal) (see Figure 33.2)

3. Decide on literature circle roles and reading stopping points for the next meeting (see Figure 33.3).

Second Literature Circle Meeting for *The Chocolate War*

1. Share literature circle findings and insights.

2. Complete character Facebook page for a character from *The Chocolate War* (see Figure 33.4).

3. Decide on literature circle roles and reading stopping points for the next meeting.

Third Literature Circle Meeting for *The Chocolate War*

1. Share literature circle findings and insights.

2. Venn diagram (create on a separate piece of paper) comparing *The Chocolate War* and *The Scarlet Letter* using comparison questions.

3. Decide on literature circle roles and reading stopping points for the next meeting.

Fourth Literature Circle Meeting for *The Chocolate War* (book should be completed)

1. Share literature circle findings and insights.

2. Discuss final project roles and how to prepare for completing both individual and group segments of the final project.

3. Begin working on the individual portion of the final project.

***The Scarlet Letter* and YA Unit**

YA Novel: *The Chocolate War*

Robert Cormier

Final Project (a total of 300 points) includes:

- Universe Disturbers Research and presentation (group work—200 points)
- Comparison Paper that explains the differences and similarities between *The Scarlet Letter* and *The Chocolate War*; use specific details from the text to support your opinions (individual work—100 points)

Universe Disturbers Research

Research one of the following men/women that are considered universe disturbers. From your research, determine why these men/women are considered universe disturbers. What did they do/not do? What time period did they live in? How do they still influence the world today? Write a one-page summary of their life and their universe disturbing-actions/qualities.

Universe Disturbers (choose one):
Martin Luther King Jr.
Mahatma Ghandi
William Wilburforce
Elizabeth Katie Stanton
Rosa Parks
Martin Luther
Frederick Douglass
Olaudah Equiano
Abraham Lincoln
Joan of Arc

Class Presentations: Do I Dare?

Create a poster that artistically expresses the biographies of five universe disturbers and the qualifications on which considers them to be a "universe disturber." Also include somewhere on your presentation how the universe disturbers relates to characters in *The Chocolate War* and *The Scarlet Letter*. (Only four universe disturbers may be used from the list provided above. Search for one other universe disturber who is not in the universe disturbers list above and be sure to provide evidence as to why you consider this person to be a universe disturber.)

Figure 33.1. Final project handout.

Character Journals: Choose a character to follow while you read your young adult novel. Your task is to write a journal entry from the point of view of this character that presents the character's thoughts, motivations, feelings, and/or responses to what is happening in his or her life. Your character journal will be shared with your group (a minimum of two paragraphs in your reader response journal).

Figure 33.2. Character journal instruction slip.

Summarizer
Do one of the following:
1. Write a fifty-word, twenty-five-word, and a one-sentence précis that summarizes today's reading. Then choose one word and finally a symbol that represents the key point of today's selection.
2. Prepare a fifty-word and twenty-five-word précis on today's reading selection.
3. Construct an outline that depicts the plot events of today's reading selection.
4. Complete a sequence chain of the plot events in today's reading selection.

Illustrator
Do one of the following:
1. Select a piece of published artwork that embodies the same feelings and emotions evoked from the setting and mood of today's selection. Prepare a rationale for your choice of artwork.
2. Create an original piece of artwork that depicts the feelings and/or emotions evoked from today's selection.
3. Create a storyboard or illustrated sequence outlining the events that occur in today's selection.

Literary Luminary
Do one of the following:
1. Select a passage that supports one of the underlying themes in the novel that we've been discussing in class. In addition, choose one passage that is a negative or opposite representation of the underlying theme. Explain your passage choices and support with textual references.
2. Select two passages that *most* help us understand the theme of the selection. Defend why you chose these two passages.
3. Locate five controversial and/or thought-provoking passages from the text. Discuss how the passages support the theme of the story.
a. Locate five surprising and/or humorous passages from the text that help develop the main idea. Explain why you chose these passages.

Character Creator
Do one of the following:
1. Pick a character in the novel and explain how a contemporary/popular-culture figure embodies the same characteristics of this character.
2. Develop and illustrate an extended metaphor that represents attributes, values, beliefs, etc. of a central character.
3. Step inside the mind of a character and create a sensory study by describing his or her thoughts/dreams, values, relationships, perceptions, feelings, and journeys, based on today's reading selection. Consider the following questions: What does the character think and dream about? What are his or her perceptions? How is he or she perceived by others? How does the character feel about certain people/issues? What special relationships has the character established? What journeys do you foresee for your character? What journeys has he or she already taken?

Figure 33.3. Literature circle role guide.

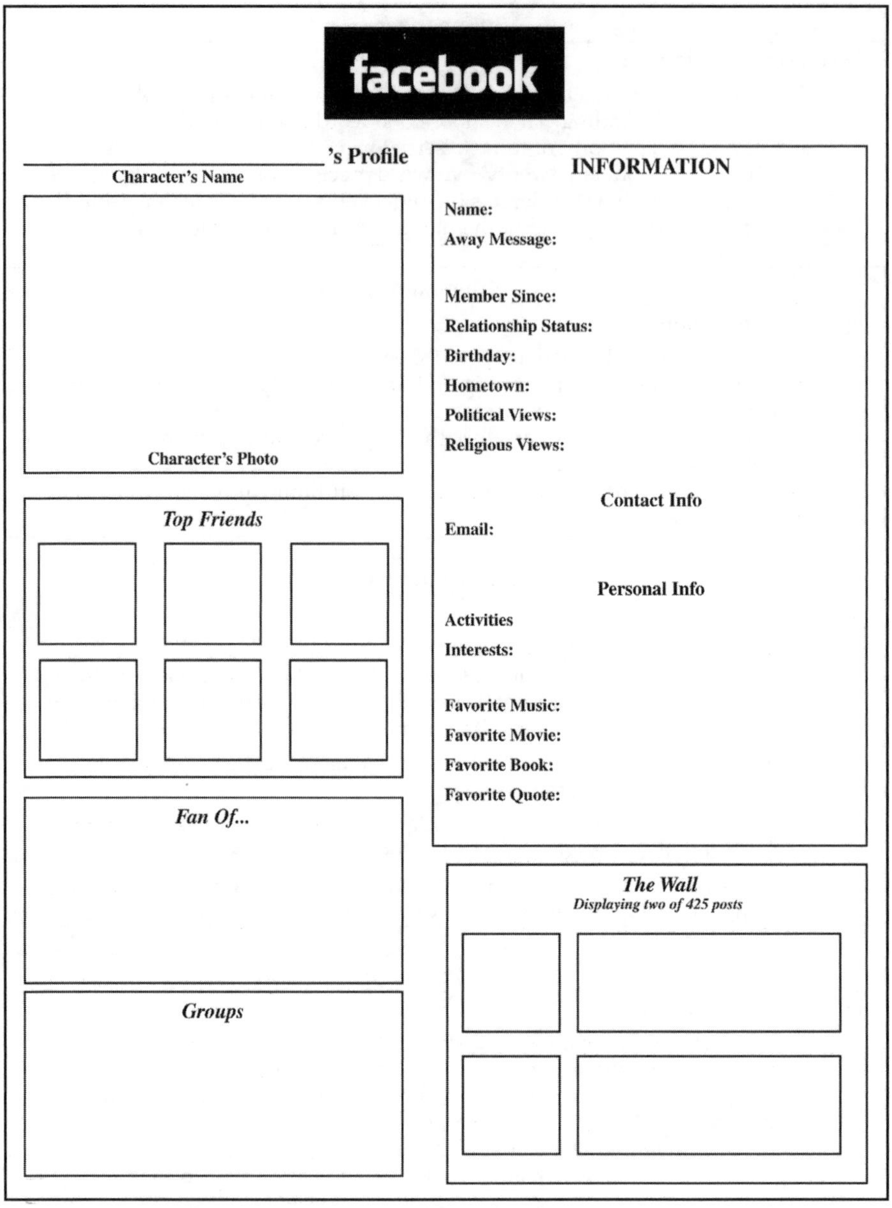

facebook

_____ 's Profile
Character's Name

Character's Photo

Top Friends

Fan Of...

Groups

INFORMATION

Name:
Away Message:

Member Since:
Relationship Status:
Birthday:
Hometown:
Political Views:
Religious Views:

Contact Info
Email:

Personal Info
Activities
Interests:

Favorite Music:
Favorite Movie:
Favorite Book:
Favorite Quote:

The Wall
Displaying two of 425 posts

Figure 33.4. Character Facebook page.

Fifth and Sixth Meetings for *The Chocolate War*

1. Work on Final Projects

Seventh Meeting for *The Chocolate War*

1. Present Final Projects to class as a group

Assessment

Students are assessed both formally and informally throughout this unit. Specifically regarding *The Chocolate War* literature circle groups, students are assessed both formally and informally on an individual and on a group basis. On an informal individual basis, student literature circle participation and activity completion are evaluated. The student comparison paper that is included in the final project is assessed on a formal individual basis. As a group, students are assessed informally on the level at which they work together both during literature circle discussions and final project work times. Students are formally assessed as a group from a part of their final project, which includes a class presentation. At the closing of the unit, students anonymously evaluate each group member's work and contribution to the group.

Considerations

Overall, I find that students enjoy working with *The Chocolate War* and all the young adult texts in this unit. Because students generally have a difficult time interpreting and reading *The Scarlet Letter*, I wanted to incorporate a variety of young adult novels to read alongside a class reading of *The Scarlet Letter*. In the end, students understood *The Scarlet Letter* more completely due to the comparison of the young adult novel and the classic. I could clearly see a deeper understanding of *The Scarlet Letter* when I added the study of the young adult texts. Students often do not need as much guidance reading a young adult book; it was written for a teen audience and usually easily engages them. However, students do need guidance reading classic texts, such as *The Scarlet Letter*, so I found that by incorporating the young adult novels with similar themes it truly helped my students understand and appreciate all texts. Therefore, this unit gave them a better *Scarlet Letter* experience.

If you adopt a unit like mine, you will need to stay organized and very clear. Scheduling and organizing all the books and plans for each young adult text as well as the entire unit on *The Scarlet Letter* is a monumental task. Yet it is a task that, if done properly, can be rewarding in the end when students make insightful connections and understand the relationships between the novels. Often, students come to my class with little to no exposure to young adult literature, so this unit usually does a terrific job of not only exposing young readers to texts that are written with them in mind but also getting teenagers "hooked" on reading and actually wanting to read more. When I first taught this unit, a former reluctant male reader came to me asking advice on future young adult books to read; I knew then that I will always teach *The Scarlet Letter* in conjunction with young adult novel literature circles.

X Teaching Zora Neale Hurston's Classic, *Their Eyes Were Watching God*

Joan F. Kaywell
University of South Florida

It is not surprising that the roundtable discussion I led at the NCTE Annual Convention in Nashville in 2006 was filled beyond capacity, speaking to the popularity of Zora Neale Hurston and her critically acclaimed masterpiece, *Their Eyes Were Watching God*. The conversations were rich, so I have chosen the best ideas of the participants as the lesson plans for Hurston's novel.

The activities offered in this chapter assume a teaching stance based on a transactive model of reader response theory. This model assigns equal significance and responsibility to the reader and the written text for constructing meaning (Probst, 2004; Rosenblatt, 1985). All of us assume that student readers base their interpretations of literary works such as Hurston's on both their personal experience and their knowledge of the historical condition of African Americans. The teachers' lessons are full of activities that integrate all of the language arts—reading, writing, speaking, listening, and viewing—as they explore her novel. A crucial dimension of language that is featured in the lessons is metacognition, the ability to reflect on what one knows and to recognize gaps in understanding when gaps exist. Self-monitoring comprehension checklists, predict-the-plot exercises, double-entry journals, and other activities prompt these metacognitive abilities.

We offer four lessons on *Their Eyes Were Watching God* that should provide a range of ideas to high school English teachers without insisting on a single rigid approach. The teacher's individual instructional style and students' learning strengths, needs, and interests will ultimately have a profound influence on the lessons' outcomes.

References

Probst, R. (2004). *Response and analysis: Teaching literature in secondary school* (2nd ed.). Portsmouth, NH: Heinemann.

Rosenblatt, L. M. (1985). The transactional theory of the literary: Implications for research. In C. R. Cooper (Ed.), *Researching response to literature and the teaching of literature: Points of departure*. Norwood, NJ: Ablex.

34 Building Understanding of Character in *Their Eyes Were Watching God*

Pamela Sissi Carroll
Florida State University

Purpose

The purpose of this lesson is to help students understand Janie Crawford's life and the ways she makes meaning of it. A rich array of instructional constructs is used to promote students' deep understanding of Hurston's amazing characters.

Materials

Students need to have a copy of Hurston's novel and access to television. A Learning Journal needs to be kept throughout the reading of the novel.

Introduction

Hurston's novel presents the intriguing story of Janie Crawford's path toward self-realization and fulfillment. Janie lives for years unaware that she is black and, therefore, socially disadvantaged in the Depression-era South. Through love for her granddaughter, Janie's grandmother arranges for her teenaged granddaughter to marry an old man, Logan Killicks, because he can provide Janie with property and security. What he does not provide is love. Janie despairs in his lonely house and is easily tempted to stray by flashy, generous Joe Starks. Joe marries her and then takes Janie to Eatonville, an exclusively black town in Florida, where he quickly establishes himself as a leader. Soon Janie realizes that she is, again, nothing more than a man's property. She hides her feelings beneath docile acquiescence until Joe dies. On his death, she performs the proper grief rituals, then releases her long hair and revels in her freedom, explaining that "Mourning oughtn't to last no longer'n grief" (89). Soon Janie takes up with Tea Cake, a roustabout who is her prince, a man who "could be a bee to a blossom" (101), and to whom she becomes totally committed. When Tea Cake is bitten by a rabid dog and Janie must save her life by ending his, Janie's response is genuine sadness. But she attends his funeral in overalls, "too busy feeling grief to dress like grief" (180). Despite the murmurings and accusations of folks when she returns, alone, to Eatonville, Janie lives her remaining days in peace, with dreams of "goin on de muck" (122) and the memory of Tea Cake himself etching "pictures of love and light against the wall" (184). Our work as a class focuses on Janie's story and our attempt to develop insights about her life struggles and those of other characters in Hurston's novel.

Connections

This book's first five chapters are wholly compatible with the attempt to illuminate the characters in Hurston's novel. Wilhelm's push (Chapter 3) for radical departure from a focus on the formal dimensions of texts is particularly consonant with the pathways suggested in this lesson plan. A list of powerful books that amplify the experiences found in the Hurston novel includes the following:

- *I Know Why the Caged Bird Sings* by Maya Angelou: Angelou's autobiography of her love- and trouble-filled childhood.
- *Invisible Man* by Ralph Ellison: The disturbing account of a Southern black man who goes underground in the North.
- *To Be Young, Gifted, and Black: Lorraine Hansberry in Her Own Words* by Lorraine Hansberry: Hansberry's autobiography of her growth as an artist.
- *Dust Tracks on a Road* by Zora Neale Hurston: Hurston relates how she came to look at the world as an artist and traveler.
- *The Color Purple* by Alice Walker: A novel about black women—and men—as they face life in the Deep South.
- *Jubilee* by Margaret Walker: A historical novel about life in the South.
- *Black Boy* by Richard Wright: Wright's autobiography of his childhood in the South.
- *Witness* by Karen Hesse: *Witness* chronicles in verse the lives of eleven members of a small Vermont town after the Ku Klux Klan arrives.
- *The Legend of Buddy Bush* by Shelia P. Moses: As told through the point of view of his twelve-year-old niece, Buddy Bush,

an African American man living in North Carolina during the 1940s, is accused of raping a white woman and has to face the injustices of the times.

Activities

Divide the class into cooperative learning groups of four or five students. Each student is required to maintain a Learning Journal that is collected by the teacher for part of the unit evaluation. When group projects are assigned, appoint a group clerk to keep track of the group's division of labor. When individual projects are assigned and completed, they should be shared within the group. It is the clerk's responsibility to manage time so all activities can be fully discussed. While students need to be responsible for the direction of discussions about the novel, the teacher will need to establish some guidelines that will help students focus their attention and energy during group discussions. Have students use their response journals as a place to record their pre-discussion ideas about the texts. Discussion can proceed based on group members' individual readings of the book that range from literal to abstract levels.

Groups may designate a member leader, who then decides on a particular focal point for the group's discussion. Examples could be the literary elements of character, plot, point of view, or the growth of Janie or another character over the course of the novel. The discussion is followed by students' written responses that are informed by the group's interaction. In addition, students should complete a self-monitoring checklist. This activity should be introduced during a minilesson in the first few days of the instructional unit. In this reflection students periodically stop their reading to ask themselves comprehension questions such as the following:

- What did I just read?
- Does it connect with what I read before?
- What might happen next?
- Am I confused about any details?

Instructional Activities

Following these introductory activities, you can present numerous individual suggestions divided into three separate groupings—Speaking/ Listening/Viewing, Reading/Thinking/Metacognition, and Writing—to indicate which language arts skills are of predominant concern in the activities of the sections. Overlaps occur, reinforcing the idea that language skills are interrelated.

The Special Voice

Following Blau's suggestion (Chapter 1), students are brought together for a whole-class session during which they view and listen to excerpts from popular television shows and movies that feature southern characters and settings. The class uses these excerpts to discuss characteristics of pronunciation, inflection, and rate of speaking, to create a list of descriptions of the southern voice. Possible television shows and movies include the following:

- *Blue Collar TV*
- *Paula's Home Cooking*
- *Two-a-Days*
- *Designing Women*
- *The Color Purple*
- *Divine Secrets of the Ya-Ya Sisterhood*
- *Fried Green Tomatoes*
- *The Green Mile*
- *Sweet Home Alabama*

In addition to television and film, many of Zora Neale Hurston's books have been recorded onto tape and/or CD. Playing excerpts will train the students' ear to understand the vernacular used in *Their Eyes Were Watching God*. There is also a *Their Eyes Were Watching God* miniseries produced by Oprah Winfrey that starred Halle Berry that is useful for this purpose.

Following this activity, students return to their groups and select one excerpt from Hurston's novel that is particularly rich in dialogue. Group members then write a script that imitates the novel's language and distribute it to other participating group members. After independent practice, groups rehearse and then perform the creative interpretation and extension of the text. If possible, videotape the performance and show it to the whole class during the culmination of the unit.

Oral Histories

Students can also interview a member of the community or their family to gain depth of information about the community's move toward racial desegregation or the impact of the Great Depression on the community. Interviews with the community or family members should be audiotaped so students can transcribe the taped conversation and turn in the tape and written transcription for presentation to the group. Students should prepare a list of interview questions and practice using the questions (with a recording device) with a classmate. All class members who choose to complete an oral history will be required to meet with the teacher for a brief minilesson on interviewing guidelines during the second day of activities work. Teachers may find Sam Totten's (1980) practical description "Person to Person: An Oral History Project" helpful.

Point of View

By examining Hurston's use of point of view, students can experiment by rewriting passages from another perspective. It is important that students choose an appropriate excerpt for this purpose, a passage in which the reader discovers something new and significant about a character. Select a critical passage and rewrite it from another character's point of view.

Graphic Organizer

This activity asks students to construct and continually upgrade a graphic overview of the novel. The overview may simply reflect Hurston's plot structure, highlight Janie's development, or connect places or settings with actions associated with them. You should encourage students to develop graphic overviews based on their understanding of the novel. One student might create a cluster diagram related to themes while another fills in a timeline. A group member who chooses this activity might review the entries daily and offer reports to the group, thus allowing other group members to benefit from his or her insights.

Life Map

Using a T-chart, plot the emotional ups and downs of one of the characters. The horizontal line designates a timeline or sequence of events, and the vertical line represents degrees of pain and joy, or goodness and evil. The character's events are plotted on the T-chart and connected by dashed lines. Students should be encouraged to use images to represent each of the life events. A chart of Janie's search for love might look like Figure 34.1.

Assessment

The instructional objectives below offer simple ways to assess students' progress in understanding the novel.

- Name important actions and consequences of Janie's actions in the novel. (comprehension)

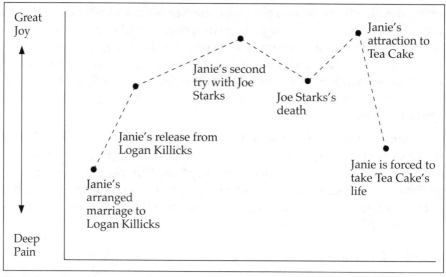

Figure 34.1. Life map.

- Recognize two themes that are central to the novel. (comprehension)

- Point out regional characteristics that are present in the novel, television shows, and movies that have southern settings. (application)

- Compare and contrast elements such as setting, plot, characterization, and theme in Hurston's novel with those of current television shows and movies. (analysis)

- Describe Hurston's treatment of social and racial circumstances in her novel. (analysis)

- Make predictions about future events in the novel based on information given by the writer and inferred by the reader. (synthesis)

- Make note of Hurston's use of voice and determine if it seems authentic, moving, compelling, and readable. (evaluative)

- Evaluate the novel in terms of its artistic quality and its social significance for both African American and white readers. (evaluative)

- Note some of the most intriguing artistic qualities of Hurston's insights. (affective)

- List some of the most enjoyable vignettes of Hurston's novel. (affective)

More broadly, if students can make connections between the novel's characters and less-well-drawn ones in movies and television shows, you know they are deepening their understanding of the novel. Assessment can as well be based on the quality of products included in the student's journal; on their oral, listening, and dramatic activities; on their group contributions and products; and on their performances and reading quizzes and/or novel tests. Self-evaluation of learning and attitudes toward the subjects and themes studied during the unit may also be used as important evaluative tools. You know, through daily authentic, less-clearly specified markers, how to asses the progress of your students.

Considerations

Their Eyes Were Watching God is a most unusual novel because of Hurston's exclusive focus on the lives of African American characters in a special setting apart from white society. It allows students to carefully follow her characters' interactions without the horrific distraction of white racism and the primacy of black-white relationships. Janie's world and her interactions with other African Americans occupy the readers' attention and allow for a deep understanding of Janie to emerge.

Reference

Totten, S. (1980). Person to person: An oral history project. In C. Carter & Z. Rashkis (Eds.), *Ideas for teaching English in the junior high and middle school*. Urbana, IL: National Council of Teachers of English.

35 Using Students' Intuition to Explore Characters in *Their Eyes Were Watching God*

Shayna Philipson
Fletcher Intermediate School of Science and Technology
Aurora, Colorado

Purpose

The purpose of this lesson is to develop a strong understanding of the characters in *Their Eyes Were Watching God* through a series of writing responses to their growth, their relationships with each other, and suppositions about their interior lives.

Materials

Students need to have a copy of Hurston's novel and a readiness to use their imaginations to better understand the characters she creates.

Introduction

Because the ideas for teaching Hurston's novel first emerged from a set of conversations at an NCTE Annual Convention and later solidified in continued conversations between three of us, it is hard to draw strict boundaries between the ideas of a thoughtful conversant at the Convention in Nashville or one of the three of us who continued the inquiry in Florida. The ideas are more important than the credits or citations if they can be helpful to those teachers who read the book and become better at coaxing stronger understanding of Hurston's characters. Pamela "Sissi" Carroll's introduction, which presents a narrative that includes the central events of the book, squarely coheres with my own and serves as an opening to this lesson plan, as well.

Connections

The use of intuition and non-discursive writing to elicit students' under-standing of the novel connects solidly with Wilhelm's quest (Chapter 3) for a different kind of reading and deeper response to novels. It is close kin to the ideas of Blau (Chapter 1), Jago (Chapter 2), and Probst (Chapter 4) in that it banks on students taking responsibility for truly engaging the text. It depends, as well, on what Moore (Chapter 5) calls culturally based reading of the text, looking at history, social settings, and cultural shifts.

Activities

We present nine activities designed to build students' understanding of Hurston's novel through a variety of unusual writing assignments that focus on character. They can be used in any sequence you choose.

1. *Character Circles*

   a. In the center of a sheet of unlined paper draw a small circle that is approximately 1 □ inches in diameter.

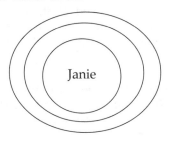

   b. Write the name of the protagonist in the center of the circle.

Add concentric circles, one for each character who is somehow connected to Janie. Be sure to write the name of the secondary character who has the closest relationship to the protagonist on the circle closest to the center circle.

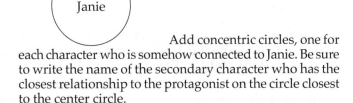

    c. If two characters share an equal relationship with the protagonist, put their names in the same concentric circle.

    d. Continue adding characters' names, moving farther from the center to indicate relationships that are increasingly distant from the protagonist or focal character.

These character circles can be reviewed and revised periodically so that students can reflect on the relationships between Janie and the other characters and write brief paragraphs that comment on these relationships.

2. *Daily Reactions*
During the last ten minutes of an in-class reading period, students should write a response to what has transpired in the novel using the four-part guideline below:

    a. Write a summary statement of what the text was about. This task draws on your transaction with the text to construct meanings that are based both on your sense of what happens in the text and personal experiences that relate to it.

    b. Write a personal statement of what the text means to you. This writing requires you to reflect on the personal significance of your reading. It may also include an evaluative statement that explains your attitude about the novel and your progress in the reading experience.

    c. Make a list of any unfamiliar vocabulary words, noting the sentences and page numbers where such words occur.

    d. Write a double entry journal where you choose one particularly memorable, provocative, alarming, or confusing vignette, which you transcribe on the left side of a page. On the right side, you should comment on the quotation in any way that seems appropriate.

3. *Newspaper Article*
Students read several news articles to gain a sense of such special writing and compose an article for a local newspaper. A possible topic might be an article on Janie's tragic decision about Tea Cake and the rabid dog.

4. *Poem/Song*
On the night after Tea Cake's death, Janie is accused of not properly mourning for her beloved. Write a poem using her words to express her true grief. A poem focused on another poignant moment would work just as well to elicit students' intuitive response.

5. *Skit/Role-Play*
A group might want to work together to write a brief script that captures a specific scene described by Hurston. Another possibility is to extend or rewrite a scene to role-play it.

6. *Letters*
   Students take on the perspective of a character and write a letter to another character in the novel. Possible subjects include Tea Cake writing a critical letter to one of his friends or Logan Killicks's letter from Janie's grandmother encouraging their marriage.

7. *Postcard*
   Students illustrate a postcard with a scene from the novel focused on Janie; on the reverse side write a note from her to another character. Students might also imagine a postcard Joe Starks sent to his friend about Janie.

8. *Autobiography/Diary*
   Students step into a character's role and write a day's entry in their autobiography that includes the character's disappointments and aspirations. A major or less central character will work for this activity.

9. *Obituary*
   Students write an obituary for a character who dies or for one they imagine dies. Tea Cake or another character would work well for this assignment.

Many of these nine writing activities echo and respect students' intuitive understanding of characters and texts. They enlist deep understanding and solid student engagement.

Assessment

We can assess students' more intuitive responses by judging the quality and authenticity of their language and the adroitness of their insights on character, particularly Janie's character shifts. We can see the rigor and inventiveness of their written constructions and their engagement as they discuss their understanding with their fellow students.

Considerations

There are many fine reasons for teaching Hurston's novel, but its unique place in the canon is a powerful, compelling reason to teach her masterpiece. Her book is famously southern yet in spite of its Deep South setting, tantalizing flashbacks, and gothic features, it does not seem to fit the southern mold well. It also supremely partakes of the world of black women authors with its masterful language and its devastating social insights, but it sets itself apart by its delicate rendering of African American experience and the fact that it so clearly predates later writers' contributions. It is a jewel that we can praise unceasingly and lovingly embrace.

36 The Place for Self-Discovery: The Psychological and Physical Landscape for Love in *Their Eyes Were Watching God*

Kendra Hege Gallos
Mount Tabor High School, Winston-Salem, North Carolina

Purpose

In 1975 Alice Walker authored the pivotal article, "In Search of Zora Neale Hurston"; it was a landmark piece, both for its scholarship and Walker's reintroduction of Hurston into literary study. One of Hurston's most celebrated works, *Their Eyes Were Watching God*, is now read in almost every high school classroom in America and frequently appears on College Board's AP Literature and Composition exam. While her novel was hungrily consumed by Walker's contemporaries at the MLA convention in the 1970s, we need to know how to make this a novel of self-discovery relevant to the modern teenager.

Alice Walker says of *Their Eyes Were Watching God* that "it speaks to me as no novel, past or present, has ever done" (qtd. in Bush, 1988, p. 1027). My hope is that this novel of struggle and ultimate self-discovery will speak to the students too and that they will find that the answers are within themselves.

Materials

Throughout this unit I keep the projector connected to my computer. The websites provided in this lesson are the main external resource and I like to refer to them daily during my teaching and their discovery.

Introduction

I begin the study of *Their Eyes Were Watching God* with the real heroine of the story, the author Zora Neale Hurston. Before students read the first word in her novel, we look at the author and the Harlem Renaissance to pique their interest. I like to display the art and sculpture on my computer projector and play the music of Duke Ellington in the background.

The following are the websites I use for the art:

1. Rhapsodies in Black: The Art of the Harlem Renaissance: http://www.iniva.org/harlem/

2. Eyecon Art. Art History Pages. The Harlem Renaissance: http://www.eyeconart.net/history/Harlem.htm

Some of the guided questions I use for this prereading study include the following:

Group Questions for the period 1919–39—The Jazz Age and the Harlem Renaissance

Discuss the following questions with group members before you write down your answers:

1. What is significant about the history of the period?

2. Describe the dress styles of men and women in this period. How are they different from previous eras in fashion?

3. Who were the significant literary figures of the period? What did they contribute to the literary canon?

4. What do you notice about the art when you look at it? What types of art were popular before this period?

5. Describe the music of this period. Is the music of Harlem different from the music of mainstream America? Do you think you would have liked it? What made Jazz unique?

Connections

Wilhelm's (Chapter 3) wide-open stance on texts and his sense of how students can respond to them is close kin to how I like to teach Hurston's novel. The story quilt finale, amazingly rich websites, Ruby Dee's deft rendering of Janie's narration, the outreach of Google Earth to understand the enormity of the Everglades, the pulse of Harlem's blues all partake of the new ways Wilhelm wants us to open up reading for our students. Blau's (Chapter 1) and Jago's (Chapter 2) ideas, via Rosenblatt, of students "eating their own dinner" and avoiding "the anxiety of right reading" coincide with all that I want my students to accomplish for themselves. These connections are not a reach for me; they resonate with the core of my teaching.

Activities

1. Setting

After the introduction to the author and the Harlem Renaissance, I guide students to "see" the setting. What did South Florida look like in 1900? Use Mapquest to help students find Eatonville (http://www.mapquest. com/maps/map.adp?address=&city=Eatonville&state=FL&zipcode= &country=US&cid=lfmaplink). This website offers historical information on Zora Neale Hurston and Eatonville: Exploring Florida. Famous Floridians: Zora Neale Hurston: http://fcit.usf.edu/Florida/lessons/ hurston/hurston.htm.

2. Language and Listening

The language can be difficult for some students and I find that books on tape help students hear the intonation and pace of the language. On the first day I play Chapter 1 so they can "listen" to the "porch talkers" as Janie returns to town. My favorite version of this novel is read by Ruby Dee. I ask students to read at least two chapters each night. I generally begin each lesson with a guided question and conclude with thoughts for the next day. Listed here is a brief summary of the day-to-day study. Included are more websites to aid in following Janie's journey:

Day 1, Chapter 1

Have students make a list of all the people Janie sees on her way back into Eatonville. It is essentially the beginning of the end of the novel (a "framework" story); the relationship between Janie and her best friend Phoeby is established and the story is a mixture of first-person narration and an omniscient narrator. We conclude the day by exploring what Janie means when she says, "So 'tain't no use in me telling you somethin' unless Ah give you de understandin' to go 'long wid it" and our predictions about what we will learn about Janie in the upcoming chapters.

Day 2, Chapters 2 and 3

Here we consider the significance of the first two things Janie tells us about herself, the time frame of the novel, the image of the pear tree episode and its significance to the story as a whole, and how Janie's first dream was dead and its meaning for her as a woman.

Day 3, Chapters 4 and 5

These chapters concern Janie's marriage to Logan and her subsequent marriage to Joe; what makes these men so different, what makes it so easy for Janie to leave Logan?

Day 4, Chapter 6

Because this is the longest chapter in the book, we explore its place in the novel, how the length relates to Janie's feelings about the town and the "porchtalkers," Jody's hitting her, and the importance of the funeral of the mule.

Day 5, Chapters 7 and 8

Students make a list of their reactions to the incident in the store between Janie and Joe and how it marks the end of their marriage. To wrap up these chapters, we examine Janie's response to Joe's death and its importance to her growth.

Day 6, Chapters 9 and 10

In these chapters we examine Janie's new life without Joe, paying particular attention to the funeral, Janie's harsh feelings for her grandmother, Hezekiah taking the place of Joe, the appearance of the mysterious stranger, Janie learning to play checkers, and more.

Day 7, Chapters 11 and 12

In these chapters, we discuss Janie's courtship with Tea Cake, their age difference and what about that concerns Janie, Phoeby's reaction when Janie tells her they are going to get married, and how Tea Cake assures Janie of his affections for her.

Day 8, Chapters 13 and 14

We consider why Tea Cake has stolen Janie's money, their move to the Everglades and the host of characters they encounter, and the effects on Janie of the immensity of the Everglades and the lake's flood (http://www.florida-everglades.com/map.htm, http://encarta.msn.com/map_701517038/everglades.html).

Day 9, Chapters 15, 16, and 17

In Chapter 15, we examine the sensitive issue Janie and Tea Cake experience of jealousy in their marriage and who is responsible for it. In

Chapter 16 we discuss Janie's reaction to Mrs. Turner and the shift in narrative voice. Chapter 17 continues the exploration of Tea Cake's reaction to Mrs. Turner's racism and the moral responsibility for destruction of her restaurant.

Day 10, Chapter 18

Chapter 18 allows us to explore Tea Cake's and Janie's many tender moments and the depth of their love. We explore the environment of Palm Beach and what students predict will happen to them there.

Day 11, Chapters 19 and 20

Students discuss what they think of the way the story ends, how Tea Cake dies, what Janie means when she says "I was too busy feeling grief to dress like grief," the return of the story-frame with Janie and Phoeby discussing how the death of a loved one can be uplifting.

3. Culminating Activity: The Story Quilt

This activity has been passed from one generation of teachers to another so it is appropriate that it is called a Story Quilt. It is a collaborative activity that allows the class to work together and connect with the storytelling of Janie to Phoeby. I ask students to plot her journey—physically in the creation of the illustrations and through the use of language as they find and transcribe her words during the journey.

Guided Study for the Quilt

In our study of Janie's journey to self-discovery, we have examined some crucial moments in her journey. Your assignment today is to examine each chapter and build a quilt of poignant scenes that contribute to the development of the theme of the novel.

Part 1: Your group chooses which two chapters to work on.

Part 2: Discuss the statements below extensively and reach a group consensus before you begin to write.

- Choose a short scene from your chapter that illustrates the core ideas in it.
- Choose a quotation that supports your choice.
- Explain how these scenes/quotations are significant to the novel's overall theme. Why are they important? (When you present your piece of the quilt to the class, you will need to be able to successfully argue your point.)

Part 3: Once you have completed Parts 1 and 2, your group should illustrate your scenes on the paper provided. Write your quotation underneath each illustration.

Part 4: Once all of the groups have completed these three steps, your group will present your part of the quilt, make your argument for your choice of scenes and quotations, and add your pieces to that of your class members.

Assessment

There are various assessments I use throughout the study of this novel. I give reading quizzes and a final test that includes objective questions and an essay. The final assessment of this book comes in a comparison-contrast essay my students write connecting it to *The Awakening* by Kate Chopin. The Jazz Age and Harlem Renaissance questions are graded for historical accuracy and the Story Quilt is assessed in terms of students' effort and accuracy. Not all of them can draw, but they can choose representative quotations.

Considerations

Hurston's novel is important because of its presentation of Janie's life changes and her struggle for more agency than that of a mule. This is a powerful human dimension of the novel. It is also crucial to help students see the story structure she builds through her extended flashback and to help them understand how and why Hurston made the unusual decision to shift her novel's point of view and that they connect these formal matters with the core ideas of independence and agency she explores in the novel.

References

Bush, T. (1988, November 16). Transforming vision: Alice Walker and Zora Neale Hurston. *Christian Century*. Retrieved from http://www.religion-online.org/showarticle.asp?title=965

Walker, A. (1975, March), In search of Zora Neale Hurston. *Ms. Magazine*, 74–79, 85–89.

37 Perception of Gender and Gender Relationships in *Their Eyes Were Watching God*

Laura B. Frazier
Eastside High School, Alachua County, Florida

Purpose

In this unit, students explore Zora Neale Hurston's *Their Eyes Were Watching God*. Set in an all–African American town and told from a female's perspective, this novel presents a unique view of American life; it is a product of the historical and cultural burst of creativity in America during the Harlem Renaissance.

In planning the unit, I considered the question, "In what ways are all narratives influenced by bias and perspective?" In *Their Eyes Were Watching God*, Hurston's perspectives are threaded throughout the story, most notably, her ideas about gender. During this week of study, students explore the author's gender concerns as they relate to character development. Students analyze the influence of gender on the main character's development to answer two guiding questions: "How do we form and shape our identities?" and "How are people transformed through their relationships with others?"

Because reading is an interactive process between the reader and the text to build understandings, my main purpose during this unit on *Their Eyes Were Watching God* is to help each student exercise critical thinking and good reading skills to discover and evaluate different perspectives. By modeling skillful reading strategies, I hope to present a solid foundation in reading literacy and assist students in becoming careful thinkers.

Materials

For the activities in this unit, I use a wide variety of materials to appeal to students with various learning styles. Every student will need a copy of *Their Eyes Were Watching God* by Zora Neale Hurston and a planning calendar (Figure 37.1). For Lesson 1, students are provided with a group discussion handout (Figure 37.2), a found poetry handout (Figure 37.3), and markers or colored pencils, magazines, glue, scissors, and colored paper. For Lesson 2, students will be provided with a literary analysis handout (Figure 37.4). For Lesson 3, students will need to use the literary analysis graphic organizer from the previous lesson. They will also be provided with a fishbowl discussion handout (Figure 37.5) and a perspective taking handout (Figure 37.6). For assessment I use a discussion evaluation sheet (Figure 37.7).

Introduction

Before we begin these activities, my students have read through Chapter 15 of the novel. During this unit, the class will take a break from reading to reexamine and reread pertinent sections of the text. I believe it is important to pause the reading process to encourage students to step back and reflect on or reconsider the text itself. By pausing the text, I hope to model good reading skills and illustrate ways to deepen understandings of reading material.

Before we begin the novel, I explain that they need to think about the text in relation to the larger unit question: In what ways are all narratives influenced by perspective? I also ask students to take note of moments or quotes in the text that illustrate Hurston's perspectives on gender. While students are reading the text, I will consistently remind them of this task and let them know they will be using these quotes for a later activity.

Connections

Through reading, writing, thinking, listening, and speaking about the novel, students are able to explore the human experience, taking on different perspectives and dealing with various themes. I believe, like Wilhelm (Chapter 3), that it is important for students to relate literature to their personal lives. Our nation is a culturally rich community of individuals from different backgrounds with distinct life experiences and multiple perspectives. It is imperative that our nation's youth are capable of working and thriving in a world full of differing opinions.

I believe, too, that it is crucial for students to view literature through various critical lenses, as Moore (Chapter 5) suggests, because it helps them to develop an understanding of opinions and ideologies aside from their own. Attempting to view literature through a different perspective helps students become more sympathetic to the different points of view they encounter in their daily lives. This activity makes this particular instruction relevant to my students' lives by encouraging each of them to be actively involved in their learning; they learn skills and content through personal interaction, practice, and experience.

Activities

Lesson 1: Gender Perspective in *Their Eyes Were Watching God*

Throughout their time reading this novel, students are asked to make note of specific quotes in the text that relate to gender. Encouraging students to look for thematic patterns in the text helps give direction and purpose to reading (see Figure 37.1). First, students draw on these gender quotes to explore the author's perspectives and their influences on the novel. This activity may take one or two class periods. Students will spend time in small groups discussing and comparing their quotes (see Figure 37.2). Each group will attempt to discern what Hurston is trying to convey about gender conventions, noting her opinions toward the subject. Students will then work individually to create a found poem using the gender quotes pulled from the novel (see Figure 37.3). Students will also illustrate the core idea of their poem by creating an artistic border to frame their words. I try to make time for the students to share their poems because they allow students' diverse learning styles and preferences to flourish.

Lesson 2: Literary Analysis—Gender and Character Development

Students reexamine specific chapters in the text to trace the development of the main character in the novel. I select seven chapters from the novel; students choose to reread two of them. Rereading to retrace Janie's relationship with each husband will help my students better understand how Hurston shapes Janie's development through interactions with other characters. I believe that revisiting earlier parts of the text strengthens reading comprehension and allows the reader to better grasp the text (see Figure 37.4). After rereading, students create a graphic representation of Janie's character development as it is influenced by her relationships with others. Students have some freedom in constructing a timeline, chart, or diagram to complement their rereading activity.

Monday	Tuesday	Wednesday	Thursday	Friday
Introduction to *Their Eyes Were Watching God*—Essential questions (what influences a text/ author bias & perspective)	Chapter 1 (pp. 1–7) *Begin noting gender quotes in novel*	Chapter 2 (pp. 8–20)	Mini-fishbowl discussion— "Who is Janie?" Homework— Chapter 3 (pp. 21–25)	Chapters 4–5 (pp. 26–50) (finish for homework over weekend)
Short reading quiz (1–5) Group activity—identify-ing themes Homework— Chapter 6 (pp. 51–75)	Group activity (cont.) & presentations Homework— Chapters 7–8 (pp. 76–87)	Chapters 9–10 (pp. 88–99)	Discussion (6–10)— themes & essential questions Homework— Chapters 11–12 (pp. 100–115)	Short reading quiz (6–10) Chapters 13–15 (pp. 116–138) (finish for homework over weekend)
Pause in reading **Gender perspectives activity (Chapters 1–15)**	**Gender perspectives in found poetry**	**Literary analy-sis/close read-ing activity (reexamining Chapters 3, 4, 7, 8, 10, 11, & 15)**	**Perspective taking— Preparing for fishbowl discussion**	**Analyzing novel through critical lenses (feminist & Marxist)— Fishbowl discussions Homework— Chapters 16–17 (pp. 139–153)**
Chapter 18 (pp. 154–167)	Chapter 19 (pp. 168–189)	Chapter 20 (end—pp. 190–193) Small-group discussion ques-tions (reactions to novel)	Discussion (Chapters 1–20)—the individual vs. the communi-ty & author's influence on text	Review/prepare for text on novel & essay response (on Monday)

Figure 37.1. Planning calendar.

Group Discussion Handout (Front)	
Their Eyes Were Watching God Gender Perspectives—Small-Group Discussion	
Beginning of quote & page #:	Hurston's perspective on gender & its influence on the novel:

Figure 37.2. Lesson 1: Group discussion handout.

Figure 37.2 continued

Group Discussion Handout (Back)

*Please fill out one chart per group member:

Group Member's Name:

For the statements below, rate this person's involvement in the group activity from 1 (weak) to 5 (strong). Please be fair and honest in your evaluation.
   1. This group member actively participated in the activity: ____
   2. This group member added to group discussion: ____
   3. This group member worked well with everyone in the group: ____
   4. Additional comments:

Group Member's Name:

For the statements below, rate this person's involvement in the group activity from 1 (weak) to 5 (strong). Please be fair and honest in your evaluation.
   1. This group member actively participated in the activity: ____
   2. This group member added to group discussion: ____
   3. This group member worked well with everyone in the group: ____
   4. Additional comments:

Group Member's Name:

For the statements below, rate this person's involvement in the group activity from 1 (weak) to 5 (strong). Please be fair and honest in your evaluation.
   1. This group member actively participated in the activity: ____
   2. This group member added to group discussion: ____
   3. This group member worked well with everyone in the group: ____
   4. Additional comments:

Their Eyes Were Watching God
Found Poetry

What is a found poem?
"Found poems take existing texts and refashion them, reorder them, and present them as poems. The literary equivalent of a collage, found poetry is often made from newspaper articles, street signs, graffiti, speeches, letters, or even other poems. A pure found poem consists exclusively of outside texts: the words of the poem remain as they were found, with few additions or omissions. Decisions of form, such as where to break a line, are left to the poet."
(Information from Poets.org—"Poetic Form: Found Poems,"
http://www.poets.org/viewmedia.php/prmMID/5780)

Found Poetry Assignment:

Write a poem that presents your idea of Zora Neale Hurston's perspective on gender. Use the quotes from the novel that helped you form your opinion. The purpose of this assignment is to illustrate your understanding of the author's biases and their influence on the novel in a creative way. Your final poem must be typed.

In addition to forging the quotes into a poem, include a border around your poem that serves as a visual representation of Hurston's perspective on gender. You may draw, cut the paper, use computer graphics, or create a mini-collage, etc. for your visual. It may be simple, as long as it portrays the message of your poem.

Rubric Guidelines:

The poem will be assessed on a 50-point scale based on the following categories:

- The poem creatively combines the chosen quotes to clearly convey Hurston's perspective (10 pts.)
- The poem draws from at least five different quotes and the page numbers are referenced (10 pts.)
- The poem is presented in a logical sequence (5 pts.)
- The poem is at least ten lines in length (5 pts.)
- The forged poem is typed (5 pts.)
- The poem has an original, captivating title (5 pts.)
- Includes a perceptive, creative visual that mirrors the meaning conveyed in the poem (10 pts.)

*Assignment is due on Wednesday (Day 3 of Focus Week)
*Failure to complete this assignment will result in a failing grade.

Questions or confusions?
Just ask me! I have several examples of Found Poems to show you, if necessary.

Figure 37.3. Lesson 1: Found poetry handout.

Their Eyes Were Watching God

Literary Analysis Activity

A key to developing strong reading and analytical thinking skills is the practice of stepping back and reexamining what you have previously read. By closely rereading sections of a text, readers develop a deeper understanding of the text as a whole.

You are going to trace Janie's character development throughout the novel by reexamining her relationships with others. When considering Janie's characterization, keep these essential questions in mind:

1. How do we form and shape our identities?
2. How are people transformed through their relationships with others?
3. How do other people's biases and perspectives influence a person's identity?

Instructions:

Reading strategy activity:

- **Choose** two of the chapters listed below (each chapter must focus on Janie's relationship with a different character—i.e., you cannot choose two chapters about the same character).

      Chapter 3 (pp. 21–25)—Logan Killicks
      Chapter 4 (pp. 26–33)—Logan Killicks & Joe Starks
      Chapter 7 (pp. 76–80)—Joe Starks
      Chapter 8 (pp. 81–87)—Joe Starks
      Chapter 10 (pp. 94–99)—Tea Cake
      Chapter 11 (pp. 100–109)—Tea Cake
      Chapter 15 (pp. 136–138)—Tea Cake

- **Reread** the first chosen chapter.
- **Reread** this chapter a second time.
    o **Highlight** or **underline** moments in the text that might answer the essential questions pertaining to Janie's identity and character development (noted above).
- **Reread** the second chosen chapter.
- **Reread** this chapter a second time.
    o **Highlight** or **underline** moments in the text that might answer the essential questions pertaining to Janie's identity and character development (noted above).

Synthesis activity:

- On a separate sheet of paper synthesize your findings by creating a timeline, chart, or diagram that illustrates your conclusions about Janie's character development and the influences on her development in your chosen chapters.
- Be sure your timeline, chart, or diagram:
    o References both chosen chapters
    o Includes page numbers to support your findings
    o Answers the posed essential questions in relation to Janie's characterization

Figure 37.4. Lesson 2: Literary analysis handout.

This approach is used to help them demonstrate their understanding of the links between character development and the influences on the development. It helps the students think about influences on character development in *Their Eyes Were Watching God* that will prepare them for the third lesson.

Lesson 3: Exploring Literature through a Critical Perspective

Students will prepare for and participate in a fishbowl discussion (see Figure 37.5), which may take two class periods. I explain "perspective taking" to the class, indicating that they will be using a perspective as a filter for participating in a fishbowl discussion the following day (see Figure 37.6). I emphasize the importance of applying critical lenses to literature, explaining that it allows students to think in new and different ways. To promote meaningful and successful student-led discussion, students spend time in pairs discussing their assigned critical lenses and developing questions and comments for the seminar. The students use their timelines, charts, or diagrams from the previous lesson to help them prepare for the fishbowl discussion. Students participate in one of two discussions, using different critical lenses to approach the text. The Marxist and feminist critical perspectives allow students to deeply explore the conventions of gender in the novel, specifically in relation to power and individuality. This student-led discussion provides an opportunity for students to learn skills and content through personal interaction, practice, and experience. Each student is expected to participate, especially since they have been given ample time to prepare for the conversation. Students can participate by asking a question or responding to a question or previous idea and I help facilitate the conversation by signaling when the discussion groups should begin, end, and switch.

Assessment

This unit provides opportunities for students to demonstrate their knowledge of the literary work in several ways: class discussion, writing, and creative projects. Student understanding is based on their performance on each activity. Every lesson requires the students to hand in a piece of work and grades are related to tangible evidence of student effort. Every assignment is meant to prepare students for the culminating fishbowl discussion. Throughout the week, I will assess whether the students link the theme of gender to Hurston's personal perspectives and demonstrate an understanding of the influences on Janie's development as a character (see Figure 37.7). Students synthesize these understandings

Fishbowl Discussion Handout (Front)

"How to"—Fishbowl Discussion

What is a "Fishbowl" Discussion?

A fishbowl discussion is a student lead, academic conversation. In a fishbowl discussion, students are arranged in two circles (as illustrated in the diagram). The students in the inner circle are inside the fishbowl. The inner circle will discuss the topic at hand—each student is expected to participate in the discussion. The students in the outer circle are observers. The outer circle listens to the conversation taking place—students are often given a task to guide their listening.

Facilitating a discussion:
1. Ask open-ended questions.
2. Wait for replies (remember: good open-ended questions require time to think).
3. Whenever possible, respond to or build on the idea(s) of the previous speaker.
4. If there is confusion, ask the speaker to clarify or explain his or her idea.
5. Support ideas with specific examples from the text.
6. Change the topic by asking new open-ended questions.
7. Deepen the discussion by considering:
    o Cause & effect
    o Compare & contrast
    o Counter an idea
    o Apply thinking to a different example
    o Relate to personal experience

Open-ended questions:
    o Arise from genuine curiosities
    o Have no single "right" answer
    o Can best be answered by references to the text

*Use this space to brainstorm some possible open-ended questions:

Things to avoid:
1. Asking yes or no questions.
2. Impatience.
3. Rephrasing what another person has said.
4. Relying on the teacher—this is a STUDENT-LED discussion!! You can do it!

Source: Greece Central School District. (2004). *Socratic Seminars*. http://www.greece.k12.ny.us/academics.cfm?subpage=487

Figure 37.5. Lesson 3: Fishbowl discussion.

Figure 37.5 continued

Fishbowl Discussion Handout (Back)

Fishbowl Leader

Rather than following a predetermined plan, the conversation flows in response to comments made by participants. Here are some tips to keep the discussion running smoothly:

- At the start of the discussion, your role is to get the discussion moving by setting the stage. You may want to open with a few brief comments about how the conversation should flow and to remind everyone that they should actively participate.
- Choose an introductory question in advance that is broad and open-ended.
- Allow time for the group to process the dialogue.
- Listen carefully so that you can follow every response with a clarifying or sustaining question if need be.
- Stick with the subject at hand, and encourage the group to turn to the assigned texts frequently to support their ideas. Do not let the discussion wander or the participants go off on tangents.
- Neither praise nor put down comments—remember that your role is to be a co-learner and discussion facilitator, not an authority on "correct" thinking.
- At the end of the discussion, you may want to end the seminar with, "That's a good place to stop," and briefly sum up the discussion.

Fishbowl Participant

1. Refer to the text when needed during the discussion.
2. It's okay to "pass" when asked to contribute.
3. Do not stay confused; ask for clarification.
4. Talk to the participants, not just the leader.
5. Stick to the point currently under discussion; make notes about ideas you want to come back to.
6. Don't raise hands; take turns speaking.
7. Listen carefully and respectfully.
8. Speak up so that everyone can hear you.
9. Discuss the ideas rather than each other's opinions.
10. You are responsible for your participation.

Source: Greece Central School District. (2004). *Socratic Seminars.*
http://www.greece.k12.ny.us/academics.cfm?subpage=487

Perspective Taking Handout (Front)

Their Eyes Were Watching God
Perspective Taking—Fishbowl Discussion Preparation

We have taken a break from reading to further explore the issue of gender and Janie's character development in the novel. Tomorrow we will be having a whole-class discussion about these aspects of the novel. Think about and be prepared to discuss these essential questions in relation to the novel:

1. In what ways are all narratives influenced by bias and perspective?
2. How do we form and shape our identities?
3. How are people transformed through their relationships with others?

Using the critical lens described below, you will analyze the novel through a specified perspective to note the ways in which bias and perspective influence literature.

Feminist Criticism

Assumptions

1. The work doesn't have an objective status, an autonomy; instead, any reading of it is influenced by the reader's own status, which includes gender or attitudes toward gender.
2. Historically the production and reception of literature has been controlled largely by men; it is important now to insert a feminist viewpoint to bring to our attention neglected works as well as new approaches to old works.
3. Men and women are different: they write differently, read differently, and write about their reading differently. These differences should be valued.

Strategies

1. Consider the gender of the author, the characters: What role does gender or sexuality play in this work?
2. Specifically, observe how sexual stereotypes might be reinforced or undermined. Try to see how the work reflects, or distorts, or recuperates the place of women (and men) in society.
3. Imagine yourself as a woman reading the work.

Source: Beach, R., Appleman, D., Hynds, S., & Wilhelm, J. (2006). *Teaching Literature to Adolescents*. Mahwah, NJ: Erlbaum (pp. 186–189).

Figure 37.6. Lesson 3: Perspective taking.

Figure 37.6 continued

Perspective Taking Handout (Back)

Their Eyes Were Watching God
Perspective Taking—Fishbowl Discussion Preparation

We have taken a break from reading to further explore the issue of gender and Janie's character development in the novel. Tomorrow we will be having a whole-class discussion about these aspects of the novel. Think about and be prepared to discuss these essential questions in relation to the novel:

1. In what ways are all narratives influenced by bias and perspective?
2. How do we form and shape our identities?
3. How are people transformed through their relationships with others?

Using the critical lens described below, you will analyze the novel through a specified perspective to note the ways in which bias and perspective influence literature.

Marxist Literary Theory

Assumptions

1. The German philosopher Karl Marx argued that the way people think and behave in any society is determined by basic economic factors.
2. In his view, those groups of people who owned and controlled the major industries could exploit the rest of the population, through conditions of employment and by forcing their own values and beliefs onto other social groups.
3. Marxist criticism applies these arguments to the study of literary texts.

Strategies

1. Explore the way different groups of people are represented in texts. Evaluate the level of social realism in the text—How is society portrayed?
2. Determine the ideological stance of the text—What worldview does the text represent?
3. Consider how the text itself is a commodity that reproduces certain social beliefs and practices. Analyze the social effect of the literary work.

Source: Beach, R., Appleman, D., Hynds, S., & Wilhelm, J. (2006). *Teaching Literature to Adolescents.* Mahwah, NJ: Erlbaum (pp. 186–189).

Student	Did this student participate actively in the discussion?	Did this student demonstrate organized thinking and insightful analysis?	Did this student cite reasons and evidence to support his or her statements?	Did this student utilize appropriate discussion skills and demonstrate civility?

Fishbowl Discussion—Teacher Evaluation

Grading Scale: 1 to 5

Figure 37.7. Lesson 3: Discussion evaluation sheet.

in the fishbowl discussion, providing evidence from the text to support their analytical thinking through their assigned critical lens.

Considerations

In designing and implementing these lessons, I am aware of students who are learning English as a second language. For example, I purposefully provide time for students to work in pairs or groups so all English Language Learners (ELLs) can interact with native speakers as a way to develop their second language oral communication. The found poem activity also allows ELLs to use concrete language from the text itself to create a poem. And, the graphic representation of Janie's character development prompts ELLs to use pictures and simpler language to illustrate their understandings of the text. Finally, by having students discuss their critical lenses and prepare comments and questions prior to the fishbowl discussion, ELLs are given the time to prepare and feel more comfortable before discussing these ideas with a group. ELLs are given the opportunity to freely ask questions or respond to student comments in the fishbowl discussion. Though this can be an intimidating and challenging task, open discussion provides concrete practice of second language oral communication.

XI Engaging Students on the Journey of *Bless Me, Ultima*

MaryCarmen Cruz
Tucson Unified School District, Arizona

Rudolfo Anaya's *Bless Me, Ultima*, often cited as required reading, has won a variety of awards and is acclaimed as an American classic. Told in the first person, *Bless Me, Ultima* is the story of a young boy growing up in a small village in New Mexico during the 1940s. Students relate to the young protagonist Antonio. While he is still far from adolescence, he asks many of the same kinds of questions, searching for meaning, that teenagers do. Through Anaya's craft, Antonio's ontological journey is one that readers experience culturally, socially, spiritually, and psychologically with him.

Antonio Juan Márez y Luna is nearly seven when the story opens and Ultima, a *curandera* and wise woman, comes to live with his family. She becomes a guide for him as he matures from innocence to understanding. Antonio's parents raise him with love but have differing views on his destiny. His father Gabriel wants him to follow the ways of the Márez family, free-spirited and independent, able to pursue his future wherever the wind takes him. His mother María, coming from a deeply established history with the land, wants him to follow the tradition of the Luna family and become either a farmer or, even better, a priest. While these two influences seem at odds to young Antonio, Ultima acts as a mediator to help him understand that he is the one to accept and shape those influences into his own reality. Themes that emerge in the novel include the search for identity, finding one's role in the universe, and coming of age.

Bless Me, Ultima is a stylistically sophisticated yet accessible text. It is often considered a bilingual novel because Anaya adeptly weaves English and Spanish together offering translation of neither. Meaning, audience, and purpose of the utterance are always key in the choice of language. Another related component of the novel is Anaya's skillful interlacing of Christian, native, and indigenous symbols and mythology to illustrate the various perspectives that intersect Antonio's world. From the names of his parents María Luna and Gabriel Márez—alluding to Christian ties and connections to the earth—to the white sun and juniper significant in much Native wisdom to the golden carp, symbols become part of Antonio's journey to make sense of his world and shape his identity.

Through its rich lyrical prose, imagery, themes, and symbolism, *Bless Me, Ultima* allows us to reflect on relationships, beginnings and endings, innocence, and conflicts and healing. Antonio's story is a poignant tale of hope; it is about finding harmony and making meaning of life. Ironically, *Bless Me, Ultima*, like many other classics, has been banned by critics who object to the content or language. Still readers relate to Antonio's journey from innocence to mature awareness. It is real on many levels and the story appeals because the themes are relevant and timeless. Students care about Antonio as he finds his way toward the adult world. They find that *Bless Me, Ultima* is one of those novels that leaves them reading the last page ever so slowly because they do not want the story to end.

The four lesson narratives that follow show us not just how to engage students in Anaya's novel; they offer us avenues for helping our students travel their own journeys to discover their own meanings. By exploring their own truths, students make personal connections and build a relationship with the novel. They also consider the power of language, symbols, and myths both to enhance story and to engage readers.

38 Finding Ourselves in Antonio: Teaching *Bless Me, Ultima*

Bobbi Ciriza Houtchens
Education Consultant

Purpose

Rudolfo Anaya has blessed us with a novel that appeals to a wide audience, from kids to adults, living in a variety of environments. Although my students live in an urban, poor community, the lessons and perspectives in this classic Chicano novel serve to take them out of themselves, out of their surroundings, and expose them to the growing up experiences of a boy who has much in common with them, even though he lives in the country and my students live in the city. Much like six-year-old Antonio, my students are grappling with the same universal questions: What is truth? What is innocence? What is knowledge? Who am I? What do I believe in? What and who will I become? How much of my life is determined by my circumstances and how much by my own free will? What power do I have to make changes in myself and in my surroundings?

By exposing my students to the life questions posed in this novel and to Antonio's struggle to find answers, I help my students connect to Antonio's struggles and, as a result, reflect on their own lives and directions, see that they have the power to make decisions about their lives and, though their lives and communities help shape them, they are not helpless victims of their circumstances.

Materials

- Copies of *Bless Me, Ultima* for each student
- Bilingual dictionaries, Internet access to Spanish/English translation capabilities, or bilingual friends/family members
- Life influences chart, copies for each student and projectable chart (overhead or computer) (Figure 38.1)

- Sample think-aloud and coding (Figure 38.2)
- Discussion group protocols (Figure 38.3)
- Hot seat and frozen tableaux handout (Figure 38.4)
- Student journals

Introduction

Bless Me, Ultima is one of many works we explore during our year study-ing American literature as windows into ourselves and our worlds. My students begin the year reflecting in their journals about the questions posed above, and then using literature we read to expand their own knowledge and experiences. In addition to works covered in high school from their literature anthologies, they have read or been exposed to such longer works as *Adventures of Huckleberry Finn*, *I Know Why the Caged Bird Sings*, *Esperanza Rising*, *Romeo and Juliet*, *Catcher in the Rye*, and *The Odyssey*. My students are accustomed to working in literature discussion circles, sometimes when they are reading the same piece and sometimes when reading different works. Regardless, they are accustomed to work-ing in groups to focus on specific literary techniques, issues shared across works, or to focus on specific areas within the same novel. Their journals serve as tools for note taking, as well as to focus discussions and as a reference for citations in subsequent essays.

Connections

This lesson makes use of Blau's (Chapter 1) and Jago's (Chapter 2) student-centered approaches, relying on the students to bring questions, connections, and reflections to their discussion groups and then to the entire class to understand the novel and themselves. Because my stu-dents are in the same literature discussion groups throughout the novel, they develop trust among group members and an appreciation for the strengths and insights that each individual brings to the group, includ-ing cultural information and language skills important to this novel.

We have discussed that reading is a conversation between the author and the reader, that each reader brings her or his own voice, ex-periences, and perspectives to the reading, and that we might all have a slightly different interpretation of character motivations, author's intent, and metaphorical significances. My class is set up as Wilhelm (Chapter 3) describes, as a way to reframe English language arts studies to be a personal and social study and inquiry, as I work to provide my students with the skills described by Paolo Freire to read themselves, others, and their worlds. This lesson moves students through Wilhelm's evocative, connective, and reflective stages, as they lose themselves in the novel, discuss how their own experiences relate to those of Antonio, and then to reflect on what actions they might take as a result of their new knowledge, including visualizing their possible futures. This novel provides many opportunities for students to engage in what Probst (Chapter 4) describes as accepting the challenges to our beliefs, suffering the discomfort of facing these challenges, and discovering ways to reconcile these beliefs with new knowledge and perspectives gained from the reading.

Activities

Day 1

- Before distributing the novel, I model how to complete the Life Influences chart, demonstrating how four areas—Cultural Background, Family, Community, and My Self—have influenced my life (Figure 38.1). I think aloud about this chart while completing it in front of the class, modeling thought processes; students must make their own distinctions about whether a value or belief they hold was acquired from one or the other area. At the bottom of the chart, they write a statement about one of the following:
    1. "My future is built out of what I experience in my childhood."
    2. "My life's experiences can make me either weak or strong."

    Figure 38.1 is an example of how I filled the chart out for myself.
- Students complete their individual charts and share what they are comfortable sharing with their groups.
- Students volunteer to share parts of their charts with the class, and I write their comments on a large class compilation chart, which is posted on the wall.
- Students then take time to modify or expand on their individual charts.

Day 2

- While distributing the novels, I invite students to explore the cover of the book and the pages before the introduction, noting what they know, what questions they have, and their conjectures about the novel. We share these and note them on chart paper to post on the wall.
- To provide visual and cultural context for the novel, I show parts of three video clips from the New Mexico Tourism

CULTURE	FAMILY
• *Definition and importance of family* • *Spirituality* • *Love of Spanish* • *Food preferences*	• *Respect for elders* • *Concern for others, particularly the underdog* • *Generosity* • *Value of hard work* • *Sense of humor* • *Optimism*
COMMUNITY	SELF
• *Understanding of different types of people* • *Belief that anyone can rise above their circumstances* • *Belief that life is tough, but never hopeless*	• *Belief that I can rise above any adversity* • *Love of adventure* • *Power of love and forgiveness*
Response to quotations:	

Figure 38.1. Life influences chart.

Department at http://www.newmexico.org/video/index.php. I use the Mesalands Scenic Byway video to show what Las Pasturas might have looked like, noting that this area, a *llano*, was once an ocean (*mar* in Spanish), as well as Rte. 66, which passes through our city near the school. I also use the part of the Turquoise Trail video that shows Cerrillos and Madrid as possible examples of the town in the novel, and the Taos High Road video, focusing on Las Trampas and Chimayo for visuals of the town and church.

- Then I explain coding—a technique for noting our thoughts as we read for later journal possibilities. We code in pencil in the margins of the novels (easily erased when the novel is completed). I use an overhead of the introduction and mark in the margins as I read and think aloud about my reading. The codes we use for this novel are the following:
  - { to indicate a passage that needs clarification
  - = to indicate a connection we found to something we know or have experienced in another place

- ? to indicate a question we want to ask the group or class
- * to indicate a revelation about ourselves or the novel

See Figure 38.2 for a sample think-aloud and coding.

■ I model taking some of my codes and my thoughts as a journal entry.

Bless Me, Ultima was my first novel. In the 1960s I was a young man teaching in the public schools in Albuquerque, New Mexico, and writing at night. **[I can't believe he had the energy or time to write a novel after teaching all day. I wonder what he taught—it couldn't have been giant classes of English!]** In the mid-sixties I married Patricia and she became my encouragement. **[Nice— that's how a marriage is supposed to be.]** I wrote over seven drafts of the novel, **[Seven drafts!! I'm not sure I could have done that many!]** and she read each one and shared her suggestions. **[That had to be true love.]**

I was born in 1937 in the small village of Pastura, New Mexico, in the llano (open plain) of the eastern part of the state. Soon after my birth my family moved to Santa Rosa on the Pecos River **[Cool—Pecos River. I wonder if that's where Pecos Bill came from?]** where I grew up. *Bless Me, Ultima* has autobiographical elements in it, after all, a writer utilizes his experiences. But the novel is a work of fiction which follows two years of the rites of passage **[Rites of passage? Like a quinceañera, or getting his driver's license?]** of the main character, Antonio. I wrote the novel in the first person because I identify very closely with Antonio. **[I wonder why he identifies with Antonio.]**

I didn't take creative writing classes while attending the university, so my effort was self-taught. Pounding the keys of an old Smith Corona typewriter late at night, I wrote draft after draft of the novel. **[Wow—self-taught and seven drafts on a typewriter? He had perseverance!]** The truly magical moment in the creative process was when Ultima appeared to me and instructed me to make her a character in the novel. **[Sounds like a hallucination. Maybe he was just tired!]** Suddenly, a boy's adventure novel became an intense exploration of the unconscious.

For me Ultima, *la curandera*, is a healer in the tradition of our native New Mexican healers. **[Wow, a *curandera*. Maybe she was speaking to him from the spirit world. My grandma used to consult one of these.]** She is a repository of Spanish, Mexican, and Native American teachings. Her role is "to open Antonio's eyes" so he can see the beauty of the landscape and understand the spiritual roots of his culture. With her guidance he begins to understand that the river, the open plain, and all of nature is imbued with spirit. Everything is alive; God is everywhere. **[She sounds like a priest.]** Suddenly the ordinary conflicts of childhood take on a deeper meaning. Antonio must now begin his journey into dreams and experiences that are extraordinary. This leads him to question why there is good and evil in the world.

When Antonio accompanies Ultima to El Puerto to cure the uncle who has been cursed by witches, he experiences what few children experience. He participates in a cleansing ceremony in which Ultima expels the ball of hair which made the uncle sick. Antonio has entered the realm of the shaman. **[Ooh, magic spells, spiritual cleansings. Sounds like this novel will be interesting.]**

Figure 38.2. Sample think-aloud and coding.

- The students then practice in their groups of four, each one taking a turn reading and thinking aloud and indicating the codes they are using. They have five minutes at the end of class to turn their codes into journal entries. As they work, I circulate to answer questions and record participation on an observation checklist.

- At the end of class, students share some of their journal entries.

Days 3–21

- Students read, code, and journal at home. We spend class time in literature discussion groups, a format with which they are familiar, following some of the protocols in Harvey Daniels's *Literature Circles: Voice and Choice in Book Clubs and Reading Groups* (2002; Figure 38.3) Students complete a chapter or combinations of chapters each night for homework.

Days 6 (after Chapter 7), 10 (after Chapter 11), and 15 (after Chapter 19)

- No reading is assigned on these evenings because we have "Hot Seat" or "Frozen Tableaux" on the following days. These days off give students who have other responsibilities, such as jobs, childcare, or other duties that might interfere with their nightly reading, a chance to catch up.

- Hot Seat is a dramatic approach mentioned in Wilhelm's article (Chapter 3) that allows students to examine different character's motivations. Tableaux is a similar dramatic approach but allows group, rather than individual, participation. Both are explained in Figure 38.4.

---

1. Students in the group rotating assuming the roles of Discussion Leader (encouraging everyone to contribute), Time Keeper (ensuring that the assignment is discussed in the amount of time provided), and Recorder (noting preparation and level and depth of participation of group members).

2. Discussion is guided by coding done the night before in the novels, as well as by journal entries. The Discussion Leader encourages students to ask their questions. When all questions have been presented or addressed, then difficult passages are analyzed and discussed for understanding, following Jago's rereading approach. Finally, group members are asked to share their revelations.

3. At the end of class, groups are asked to share the most significant question and discussion, new understandings and revelations.

Figure 38.3. Discussion group protocols.

Hot Seat

Hot Seat is a dramatic strategy used to help students understand character motivation.

For homework, students create a list of five to ten questions they would like to ask Antonio, Ultima, Antonio's father, mother or brothers, Tenorio, Horse, or whoever plays an important role in the chapters being discussed. Questions might focus on a character's motivation for their actions or on their thoughts behind something they said. Questions can also ask about the character's beliefs, values, background, etc.

In class the following day, student volunteers take the "hot seat" at the front of the class and, in the persona of the character, answer questions prepared by the rest of the class. It is useful to have different students play the same character in order to broaden the perspectives offered. I often give extra credit for the volunteers to encourage participation and regular credit for the questioners.

Spend the last ten minutes of class asking students to use their journals to note any new insights about themselves or the novel that they might have gained from this exercise. Ask volunteers to share before dismissing class.

Frozen Tableaux

Frozen tableau is a dramatic strategy in which groups of students create a scene from a chapter and freeze the action, using their poses, facial expressions, physical relationships to each other, and gestures to convey the characters, actions, and significance of an important event.

At the beginning of class, each group meets to select a scene from the chapters they have read and to decide how to portray the scene using all the members of the group. Each group then presents its scene to the class. There is no problem when groups present the same scene, as each one will have its own interpretation of its presentation and significance.

After the scene is frozen, the teacher or a student can pass behind the characters and, when tapped on the head, the characters must explain themselves in the scene, what they are doing, thinking, feeling. If the character is having difficulty, he or she might be coached with questions such as "Who are you? What is happening here? What are you thinking/feeling? Why are you doing this? What are you hoping happens next? What are you going to do after this?"

Spend the last ten minutes of class asking students to use their journals to note any new insights about themselves or the novel that they might have gained from this exercise. Ask volunteers to share before dismissing class.

Figure 38.4. Hot seat and frozen tableaux.

- I selected these points to engage the students in dramatic activities because they are pivotal in the novel and for Antonio's life. These chapters present the religious dichotomies in Antonio's life, as well as his questioning about losing innocence and gaining knowledge. These breaks also provide a rich opportunity for other characters to present their motivations and dreams for themselves and for the brothers in the family, including Antonio.

Day 22 (after completing the novel and discussions)

- Students fill out a Life Influences chart for Antonio, similar to what they did for themselves. At the bottom of the chart, they predict Antonio's future and explain why they made this particular prediction. The prediction might be prompted with these quotations from the novel:

    "Sometime in the future I would have to build my own dream out of those things that were so much a part of my childhood." (276)

    "Ultima said to take life's experiences and build strength from them, not weakness." (277)

- Before the end of class, students share with their groups and then with the class, and we construct a large chart to post next to the earlier class chart. We discuss similarities and differences in the charts.

Assessment

I build accountability into every step of this process, and participation is easy to grade. I assess student engagement with the novel through eavesdropping on their group conversations, collecting and reviewing reporting sheets from the recorders during group discussions, and observing student participation in Hot Seat and Frozen Tableaux.

Whether or not we have achieved the stated purpose is evident in the reflective essay the students write. In this essay, students are asked to write about how much their futures are determined by their cultures, communities, families, and their own will, using examples from *Bless Me, Ultima* as a springboard and their journal entries to provide evidence or examples for their essays. We use a writing workshop format, working in groups to brainstorm, plan, revise, and edit our essays. Often my students use a form of these essays for their college applications.

My students have a particularly strong connection to this novel because we live in the Southwest, even though urban Southern California is not typically Southwestern. However, because the influence of Mexico and the effects of colonialism are so prevalent in the area where we live, many of the traditions, values, cultural beliefs, and Spanish expressions are familiar even to my students who are not Mexican or Mexican American. And, even though the setting of the novel is rural, the violence in the novel is real in my students' lives and is just as difficult for them as it is for Antonio. In addition, Antonio's questions mirror the questions that many adolescents ask themselves: "Can I determine my own future?"

Considerations

Certainly this novel, like most good novels, deals with controversial topics: organized religion vs. indigenous spirituality and *brujería* (which is not accurately translated as "witchcraft"), profanity, sexuality, bullying, violence, and murder. I discuss with my students that if we never examine and discuss these issues, then it is difficult to make informed decisions about what we believe and how we live our lives. If a parent insists that his or her child not read this book, even after we have discussed its merits, then I provide an alternate novel.

In spite of these considerations, *Bless Me, Ultima* is one of my favorite novels to teach and often is named favorite novel of the year by my students. Knowing that it has been banned in some communities adds to its allure for my students, but it is Anaya's skill at telling a good story with so many layers that makes it a joy to read. Anaya's writing is like poetry, so I usually start each class period by reading a phrase or passage that has touched my soul, making my heart sing or tasting like poetry in my mouth. It is a novel that I encourage other teachers to teach and is one that I enjoy returning to year after year.

Reference

Daniels, H. (2002). *Literature circles: Voice and choice in book clubs and reading.* Portland, ME: Stenhouse.

39 Drawing Out the Meaning in *Bless Me, Ultima*

Val-Jean Ofiesh
Rincon High School, Tucson, Arizona

Purpose

Bless Me, Ultima offers students an opportunity to explore the dominant culture and heritage of the Southwest. In the story, young Antonio is the battleground for conflicting family traditions and belief systems. Students relate to Antonio's struggle to make sense of the world and determine its ultimate truths. While reading, students question the power of religion and mystical beliefs along with Antonio. Through this exploration and classroom discussions, students truly "see and experience the complexity of literature" (Wilhelm, Chapter 3) and create valid and personally meaningful links between the text and their personal schemas.

It is vital to have a layered plan of action that encourages students to learn to "construct meaning for themselves," as Blau stated in his essay (Chapter 1), enabling students to read independently and with initiative. This lesson series creates appropriate opportunities for the students to identify areas for further inquiry through an essential question and Question-Answer-Relationship (QAR), negotiate the meaning of difficult sections of the text through the think-aloud strategy, and explore this novel through visualization activities.

Materials

- *Bless Me, Ultima*—sufficient copies for each student to sign one out
- CD or audiotape of the book
- Map of New Mexico (optional: use to create concrete geographical connections)
- Students' class notebooks
- Mind map handout (Figure 39.1)

- Q-A-R handout (Figure 39.2)
- Storyboard assignment and rubric (Figure 39.3)
- Storyboard sketch form (Figure 39.4)
- Sample student storyboard (Figure 39.5)

Introduction

I begin each semester with a big question that creates a framework for all of our reading and writing assignments. This framework fosters deeper, extended thinking and gives students the opportunity to compare a variety of perspectives on an issue that connects our experiences as human beings. The essential, overarching question for this semester is "How do we retain our sense of identity and culture in a rapidly changing world?" and we display it prominently on the board. Later, during reading, the students generate important, related questions that I post around the essential question. Students decide which questions to post through the process of creating and evaluating their questions. For example, students reading *Bless Me, Ultima* typically add a question about respecting parents' goals for their futures versus following their own desires.

Next, I ask the students, "Can you imagine writing a story that would tell the important truths about your life and the times in which you live? What must be included?" As their anticipatory set, students create a personal mind map that shows their connections to family, community, culture/ethnic group, and their own hopes, ambitions, or dreams. I encourage them to think in iconic images and weave in cultural elements (Figure 39.1). Students explore beyond the superficial and stereotypes by speculating on the significance of the images. Students then present and display their mind maps in the classroom throughout the unit. We then discuss how their personal knowledge of the Southwest, the Spanish language and Mexican American culture, school, and home-life may help them when reading *Bless Me, Ultima*.

Connections

The strategies used in this lesson directly illustrate the concepts laid out by Blau, Jago, and Wilhelm in Chapters 1 through 3 of this text, including the use of essential questions to guide students into a deeper appreciation of the value of literature. The use of an essential question is just a starting point. Blau argues that students gain an authentic, versus false, knowledge when they "construct meaning for themselves." When students

Mind Maps ask students to answer questions or explore related ideas through visual representation. Simplified Mind Map instructions are presented in the steps below:

1. The topic is written at the center.
2. There are five supporting ideas, each with three or more examples.
3. Use pictures, symbols, arrows, etc. to represent ideas and show their relationships.
4. Use color.
5. Limit the number of written words. These are prompts and reminders for the presentation. Be selective in the word choices.

Students verbally explain the contents of their Mind Map and identify how ideas relate to one another.

An Overview of Mind Maps

Description of mind maps, advantages for using them, key points to consider, and steps for creating them: http://www.americansforthearts.org/animatingdemocracy/pdf/resources/tools/mindmap_overview.pdf

When Is a Mind Map Not a Mind Map?

Clever mind map of principles for creating mind maps: http://www.mindmaptutor.com/2009/07/when-is-a-mind-map-not-a-mind-map/

Sample Mind Maps

Sir Richard Branson: http://blog.iqmatrix.com/wp-content/uploads/2009/03/richard-branson-the-virgin-king-mind-map.jpg

Guru Mind Map: http://en.wikipedia.org/wiki/File:Guru_Mindmap.jpg

Personal Growth: http://3.bp.blogspot.com/_gLXHStaJ1RI/ScfIJ2BClZI/AAAAAAAABrA/WZl-u01cfLQ/s400/Personal+Growth+Mind+Map600.jpg

Keys to Happiness: http://studymatrixart.files.wordpress.com/2008/04/smx-spotlight-mind-map-keys-to-happiness.jpg

Figure 39.1. Mind maps: General instructions and sample sites.

construct the meaning, they also own and retain the skills gained through reading and interpreting the text.

Since this transfer of responsibility (from the teacher to the student) is critical to ownership, I choose two strategies to lead students to become constructors of meaning: think-aloud and Q-A-R. These strategies activate independent thought. Think-aloud demonstrates the process of building connections and demonstrates to students that it is normal when connections differ among readers. As recommended by

Jago and Wilhelm, this lesson also uses a think-aloud to aid student understanding. Early in the novel study, I model, supported by the "I do, we do, you all do, you do" scaffold for the students. Similarly, after I model, students employ the Q-A-R during reading. Successful implementation of the Q-A-R strategy (Figure 39.2) depends on following Jago's emphatic instruction to *"Resist answering these questions yourself."* Regardless of the difficulty of the question, it is more important to guide the students in the process of searching than to meet the time constraints imposed by an instructional or pacing calendar. I do add pieces of historical and cultural context when necessary.

Activities

Before I distribute copies of the book, the class reviews the essential question. On the first few days, students read while listening to the story on CD, read to each other in small groups, and read silently as individuals. During reading, students create their own questions and answers based on the Q-A-R approach. Students learned Q-A-R in an earlier study of expository texts; however, we review the process (Figure 39.2) and consider what might be different about a literary text. After reading on the first day, we briefly discuss the characters Antonio, Ultima, and Antonio's parents. The students' focus is surface-level at this stage.

Over successive days, I introduce the three types of questions from Q-A-R:

(a) surface level—an answer can be found directly on the page, no ambiguity;

(b) analysis level—the information is mostly in the text but you will need to use some of your personal knowledge or brain-power to answer the question; and

(c) deeper-thought level—questions that require reflection, thought, evaluation, or synthesis of ideas from multiple viewpoints or multiple texts.

Students practice creating questions for each level of the Q-A-R segments. They must include the answer and the page where they found the information.

After reading, students count-off into groups of four and use their notes on questions and answers to quiz each other within the groups. For closure, each group selects one question to ask the other groups.

It is my responsibility to ensure equitable participation. All students are required to record their questions and answers in their class notebooks. I check notebooks once or twice a week for participation credit.

Figure 39.2. Implementing question-answer-relationship (Q-A-R).

On the second day, students begin by summarizing what they read. I ask if any passages were "fuzzy." Students usually express confusion over the dream sequence. I demonstrate a think-aloud to show them how I would reread and question or make connections to make sense of the passage. I tell students, "When rereading, start at the paragraph before you became confused."

Model: Think-Aloud from Bless Me, Ultima, Chapter "Uno"

It was warm in the attic, and as I lay quietly listening to the sounds of the house falling asleep and repeating a Hail Mary **[He's praying.]** over and over in my thoughts, I drifted into the time of dreams. Once I had told my mother about my dreams, and she said they were visions from God **[Does his mother think he is a prophet?]** and she was happy, because her own dream was that I should grow up and become a priest. **[Antonio is only six, and his mother has already told him to become a priest.]** After that I did not tell her about my dreams, **[I guess he doesn't want to be a priest or a prophet.]** and they remained in me forever and ever . . . **[that feels like a bit of a burden for a child.]**

In my dream I flew over the rolling hills of the llano. **[Now it changes to italics. This must be Antonio's dream.]** *My soul wandered over the dark plain until it came to a cluster of adobe huts.* **[It's interesting that he believes his soul is wandering, traveling . . .]** *I recognized the village of Las Pasturas and my heart grew happy.* **[He must have good memories of his father's village.]** *One mud hut had a lighted window, and the vision of my dream swept me towards it to be witness at the birth of a baby.* **[Who is the baby? Didn't Antonio mention he was born in Las Pasturas? No. I don't think he could see himself as a baby, could he? What did it say at the beginning?]**

We return to the first page and see how it connects to what Antonio had said about his birth. Together we conclude that Antonio may be dreaming about his own birth and that we must hold this idea as a possibility. Next, we practice together as a whole group on two more paragraphs where we identify Ultima's presence and speculate on what his uncles may desire. Students then practice the next eight paragraphs with a partner. After a brief whole-group discussion in which the students recognize the conflicting families' ambitions for Antonio, the students usually have had adequate scaffolding to finish the last three paragraphs of the dream independently. We discuss the students' ideas and questions considering which, if any, of their questions to add to the important questions that surround and support our essential question.

Students gain ownership in the reading process through these activities (the mind map to connect to one's own experience, rereading using a think-aloud, and the Q-A-R technique). As we close each day's session, students share their questions, and we routinely move from checking reading comprehension into deeper analytical questions. Once students begin creating their own questions, I give them time to explore those ideas. In all classes, students are curious about Ultima and Antonio's dreams. They want to know if Ultima is a witch, and they seek clarification about Antonio's relationship with his brothers. I never give the students direct answers; instead, I ask them, "What do you think? Can you find something in the text that would support that conclusion?" By asking students to find evidence in the text or elsewhere, they extend their thinking about the characters and the narrative.

When students identify a question that requires extensive thought or the synthesis of ideas between readings, we consider adding it to our list of important questions that is posted prominently near our objectives. Some examples of the questions developed through this dialogue include the following:

- What do we consider when choosing between our parents' wishes and our own desires?
- How does knowledge of a location (place) help us make sense of a story?
- How do people's beliefs in the supernatural shape/create their experiences?

At this stage, the students are successfully using their reading strategies to improve comprehension and are independently raising the level of our classroom discussion. We cruise along, but to avoid boring twenty-first-century learners, I introduce a variety (change activity to visualization) and create a new challenge to validate their skill at reading independently. The task relates to their essential question.

We read Chapter 8 together, which again highlights the conflicting lifestyles of the Márez and Luna families. I ask students to take on Antonio's viewpoint while reading and consider our essential question from his perspective. How does Antonio hold on to his sense of identity and culture in his rapidly changing world? We practice the visualization strategy as if we are seeing the world through Antonio's eyes. I model expectations with a demonstration from the opening passage. After reading, we review and select key phrases to inform our visual image (note the underlined text).

> The <u>lime-green spring</u> came one night and touched the <u>river trees</u>. <u>Dark buds</u> appeared on <u>branches</u>, and it seemed that the same <u>sleeping sap</u> that fed them began to <u>churn</u> through my <u>brothers</u>. I

sensed their restlessness, and I began to understand why the blood of spring is called *the <u>bad blood</u>*. It was bad not because it brought growth, that was good, but because it raised from dark interiors the <u>restless, wild</u> urges that lay sleeping all winter. It revealed hidden desires to the <u>light of the new warm sun.</u>

We discuss what the illustration might look like—spring greens, budding trees by a river, the sap flowing like blood into the brothers' veins, and then churning—and then I draw a rough representation of the scene and add some color and captions to enhance the imagery. While deciding what words should accompany this picture, we focus on the metaphor of sap churning in his brothers' blood and connect this to their untamed nature, literally part of the llano, true descendents of the Márez clan. We continue reading the passage and identifying imagery, then complete two or three more frames in guided and small-group practice to anchor the concept. One or two students likely preempt the next assignment by asking, "Why can't we do that?" I respond, "What a great idea!" and hand out copies of the assignment to create a storyboard on an upcoming chapter (Chapter 10 or 11). These are crucial parts of the story that address Antonio's role as a healer (Chapter 10) and his encounter with the golden carp (Chapter 11).

The storyboard assignment (Figure 39.3) is comparable to creating a section or chapter of a graphic novel. Students work with a partner to create sequential scenes that relate the significant events and character responses for their selected chapter. They begin by selecting one of the designated chapters and then determine what is essential from the chapter. Blank storyboard forms (Figure 39.4) are available to prompt any reluctant artists. The format, while basic, helps students think in terms of images and accompanying captions. As they sketch, the main ideas and supporting details emerge. Students are literally and figuratively drawing out the text's meaning. Students turn the sketches into finished, full-color storyboards to be displayed and viewed (Figure 39.5).

Students work on this project in class for three or four days so that I can observe and interact with each pair. During these desk-side visits, I listen as students discuss what to include, argue for and against details, and make choices about supporting dialogue or captions. Through these observations, I learn about how they interpret the text. Their visuals give evidence of their reading and the inferences that connect to their own mental schemas. The images are generally a reflection of the students' schema, thinking, and belief systems, and are not limited to the text. The dialogue and captions provide insight into their abilities to process the text versus simply repeat it. This allows me to evaluate the depth of their processing, along with the final product.

Students work with a partner to create a storyboard for either Chapter 10 or Chapter 11 of the text. It may help some students if they think of this as a chapter of a graphic novel. The final product must illustrate twelve to twenty important scenes from the chapter and include dialogue and captioning as needed. The storyboards may be in black and white; however, the use of color is encouraged. Grading is based on a performance rubric that the students and teacher create following a "gallery walk." A sample rubric is shown below:

AREA	4	3	2	1
Content	The storyboard has 20 images relating major events in the correct order.	The storyboard has 15–20 images in the correct sequence that relate to major events.	The storyboard has 12–15 images in the correct sequence that relate to major events.	The storyboard has fewer than 12 images, but all relate to major events from the chapter.
Imagery	Meets descriptors in category 3 and provides imaginative and symbolic images that enhance the story.	Clear imagery that enhances the story. Two or more characters represented.	Basic images—stick figures, with traits or objects that help distinguish characters.	Basic images—stick figures, cannot tell characters apart.
Conventions	All dialogue and captions demonstrate correct spelling and grammar conventions.	Dialogue and captions have few errors in spelling, grammar, or punctuation.	Errors make the storyboard difficult, but not impossible to understand.	Errors make the storyboard very difficult to understand.
Aesthetic Appeal	The storyboard invites viewing; images are consistent and colorful or use a range of black and white values.	Images are consistent and colorful or use a range of black and white values.	Shows some care in choices and attempts at consistency; use of color or b/w values not always helpful.	Does not interest the viewer; may demonstrate sloppy or poor execution.

Figure 39.3. Storyboard assignment and rubric.

Figure 39.4. Storyboard sketch form.

Figure 39.5. Student sample of a storyboard.

By the time we finish Chapters 10 and 11—the heart of the book—students are meeting the ownership goal. They are reading independently, reflecting and thinking more deeply about issues, and taking the initiative to question and, later, understand what they read. The students have gained strategies to negotiate meaning and deal with uncertainty. Although students will finish the novel, it is their intense decision making about illustrating a chapter that demonstrates their mastery of reading. These representational choices are what we discuss subsequent to viewing the body of work.

The storyboard project is due at the end of Chapter 11. To ensure that students have a sense of what constitutes high-quality work, we do a pseudo gallery walk to view other students' work in the school. I scout the hallways, library, display cases, and other classrooms in advance to ensure that they will view several types of projects. Students consistently identify the quality of the work correctly. The class then creates a grading rubric for the graphic novels (Figure 39.3). The culminating activity allows students to read and evaluate each other's storyboards.

Assessment

This lesson offers several strategies for authentic engagement while providing the variety of tasks, personal choice, relevance, and creative outlets that today's students demand. Student-initiated lines of inquiry enhance the teaching-learning environment for all of us. Three components help create success: (1) scaffolding combined with grouping strategies, (2) Q-A-R without teacher-certified answers, and (3) relevant hands-on activity. First, students benefit from clear modeling of expectations with two levels of practice that increase opportunities for them to discuss the story with each other and explore their thoughts. Second, students care about questions they generate; therefore, they reflect more deeply on those questions. Although the lack of direct, definitive teacher responses frustrates some test-oriented students, pushing responsibility back to the students increases their ownership of the reading process. I always stress that there is no test and that I am more interested in their examining how they think about what they read and to work it out for themselves. Third, the personal involvement of creating a mind map assists students in building background knowledge while the storyboard provides variety and an alternative outlet for visual thinkers.

Throughout the book, everyone participates, and all are accountable for sharing in small groups. Students often say they enjoy deciding what to ask and working with each other. There is also a genuine sense of intrinsic, as well as extrinsic, reward for a student when his or her question makes it to the essential question list. The Q-A-R activity increases students' awareness of the text and their metacognitive skills while reading the text.

Students are also highly engaged by the mind map and story-board activities. Both assignments allow a strong degree of personal expression and interpretation. Even students who are uncertain of their artistic abilities are excited about their results. The students are clearly proud of their work and eager to see each other's illustrations, further extending discussion about the book. After we discuss their work, we look at their projects together. Students are consistently able to evaluate the submissions accurately based on the performance rubric they created; but, more importantly, they evaluate the content for accuracy and creativity. Throughout the study of *Bless Me, Ultima*, I give students credit for participation and completion of all activities. I also evaluate the quality of their think-alouds, Q-A-R, and final storyboard projects.

Considerations

When I first taught *Bless Me, Ultima*, I did not give enough consideration to the potential for negative reactions to the depiction of *brujería*, translated as "witchcraft" but closer to shamanism. This language became problematic when one student claimed that he could not read the book at home because of the references to witchcraft. Furthermore, I did not fully understand the meaning of some of the curse words used in the text. While this lack of understanding led to humorous, bonding discussions, it could have resulted in misrepresentations of our class or complaints from the parents. I now remind students that the use of curse words and inappropriate language are not part of our school culture. Although we read these words in the text, we do not use them when speaking or creating our own projects.

In the end, my students enjoy *Bless Me, Ultima*. In fact, a few students who rarely finish a book are surprised to find themselves reading ahead and genuinely caring about the characters and questioning the outcomes. Even when students come from completely different cultural backgrounds than the protagonist's, they understand conflicts over parental expectations, mystical beliefs, and identity. My students find meaning from their experience with this novel.

40 Connecting Worlds and Works: Teaching *Bless Me, Ultima*

Cecelia A. Lewis
Cochise College

Purpose

Anaya's novel, *Bless Me, Ultima*, provides an opportunity for students to connect what they know from personal and academic experiences with what they might like to know to include cultural and historical events. This novel also serves as the perfect bridge to connect the ideas and characters from Homer's *The Odyssey*, which is usually read in either ninth-grade or tenth-grade English, with the Native American myths that introduce the "American Experience" of eleventh-grade English. Therefore, this lesson series works well in either the tenth-grade or eleventh-grade English classroom because it focuses on how the multi-dimensional characters in *Bless Me, Ultima* contain similar traits to those in *The Odyssey* and how these seemingly different cultural and historical texts actually compare.

Materials

Students are provided with a preliminary list of characters from *The Odyssey* that may correspond with characters in *Bless Me, Ultima*. As they read, they are asked to determine who might best fit the role for each character (see Figure 40.1). A copy of Homer's *The Odyssey*, Edith Hamilton's *Greek Mythology*, and/or Internet access are necessary for research on Greek characters.

Introduction

Everything I know about teaching literature, I learned from English teachers, specifically, my colleagues in the field with whom I have discussed texts and classroom experiences. *Bless Me, Ultima* is no exception. My knowledge of the book, the way I teach the text, and the learning opportunities my students experience come from thoughtful, intentional conversations about a text that is both beautiful and baffling to many modern teen readers. This confusion prompted me to seek help and advice from my New Mexico colleagues, Susan Miera and Arlene Mestas, members of the Bread Loaf Teacher Network. These talented teachers helped me open this novel to my students by giving me the innovative ideas described here. Susan's gift was to pair my students with hers electronically as we read and discuss the text online. This online discussion provides each student a safe space to take risks while discussing the novel.

The second gift, provided by Arlene, was the basis for the central lesson presented here. In an online discussion on Breadnet, a professional education electronic Web conference, Arlene introduced me to Anaya's connection to Greek mythology and *The Odyssey*. She also provided me with a list of Greek characters that might have significant counterparts in the Anaya text. Through this discussion and subsequent exploration, I realized that this connection was not only a viable one but also a fascinating way for students to examine characters in the story.

Since the approach to the text is scaffolded, all parts of the study are integrated. Through the pairing of students, our classes work together to explore the novel. We deliberately pair students to benefit each of them. For instance, we paired Susan's AP eleventh-grade students with my tenth graders. The eleventh graders, although also reading the text for the first time, serve as mentors to the tenth graders as they explore literary devices and vocabulary. We have also paired twelfth-grade students for a more equivalent learning experience. In this type of pairing, the students explore the text to enhance comprehension, explore literary devices, and discuss character development.

The close, thoughtful analysis of a text is best done communally. Once students begin to unpack a piece of literature, they discover text elements they may have overlooked or neglected. Often this unpacking can come long after the reading experience has ended. That is why I introduce *Bless Me, Ultima* by brainstorming *The Odyssey*. We simply begin by writing down everything we know about *The Odyssey*. At first, the class is rather subdued, as the members of the class try to remember what they may have read (or pretended to read) in ninth grade or tenth grade. No one wants to look silly, so sometimes I must feed the process with a simple: "Okay, who might be the main character of this Greek epic poem?" or "Whose odyssey was it?" Once one student responds, the answers flow; the whiteboard fills with characters (human, mythological, and spiritual), events, and themes.

After we have exhausted our collective information about Odysseus and *The Odyssey*, I shift the conversation to why this ancient story is still considered a great work and why students continue to read it. Invariably many students complain that they hate reading the epic poem because the language is difficult, the characters are not "real," and nothing in it relates to their lives. After they finish their complaint list, I ask them to look at the whiteboard one more time and consider why they "know" the story so well, if in fact it is so complicated. Is it because they had to know it to pass the class? What other motivating factors allow them access to this work? Usually even the avid readers admit that the experience was made easier through the intervention of their friends. At this point I explain that we will begin a book about another hero's odyssey, and this time they will consult with another student, in another classroom, in another state, about the text. More often than not, students respond to this information in a cautious, careful manner.

I often hear whispers of "What is she saying?" and "Is she going to allow us to cheat?" ripple through the class, and their interest is piqued. Now is the time when I bring out Anaya's *Bless Me, Ultima*.

Connections

I am constantly baffled, and sometimes a bit saddened, when I hear how skeptical the readers in my classroom have become. Perhaps it is the current state of the world or politics that have brought them to this point, or maybe it is the lack of curiosity that denies them the opportunity to engage with a book; either way, as Probst (Chpater 4) explains, reader response is an integral requirement for a student to "suspend disbelief" and willingly engage in a reading relationship with the text. Whatever the reasoning, the reality remains that for many of our youth, entering into an agreement with an author while reading a novel is not an option. For many, the reading remains at surface level for comprehension purposes only. As a result, students resist the narrative when they encounter Ultima and the events Antonio witnesses while he assists her. This resistance provides an opportunity to discuss the reader and author relationships by posing the question, "Is there an implicit agreement between a reader and a text? When can one put the text down and say: 'No, you have gone too far!'" In reading *Bless Me, Ultima*, the disconnect often occurs for my students because they live in the southwestern United States, and too many of the events are surreal or unimaginable. They have never seen a house rained on by rocks; they have never seen the golden carp; they have never met an Ultima. In their view, if they have never seen or done these things, they cannot possibly exist. Rarely, however, is there a problem with these same students' accepting that a young boy can witness a murder. Sadly, this is an accepted reality; even if they have not witnessed a murder themselves, the news channels are replete with evidence. This blending of reality and magical thought often confuses students, and they become suspicious of the text.

For these reasons, I like to start them out with characters from *The Odyssey* and Greek mythology so that they experience a feeling of familiarity and trust (Figure 40.1). As the students research the Greek characters, they connect with the characters they meet in *Bless Me, Ultima*. They recognize that Antonio's father, Mr. Márez, is similar to Poseidon because "it is the blood of the Márez to be wild, like the ocean from which they take their name, and the spaces of the llano that have become their home" (44). As they review the Greek characters, they simultaneously come to know the characters in *Bless Me, Ultima*. This thoughtful, deliberate view of character traits provides the students with an opportunity to become invested in the text and in their interpretation of the text. It also leads them to the text to find their proof as Jago (Chapter 2) explains. This then becomes the student's exploration, not the teacher's.

Activities

After the brainstorming session on *The Odyssey*, students receive the requirements for their character comparison assignment. As we begin reading the text, students also begin writing to their online partners about it. The structure of the online writing is fairly simple and direct. The letters, which are emailed directly to me for submission to the corresponding instructor, are made up of three parts. A friendly, informal beginning serves as a social ice-breaker. The second section is text-centered and is usually a response to a prompt provided either by the class or me. In the third section of the letter students ask questions about the text to their reading/writing partners. In this exchange they explore the text together, clarify confusing sections of the text, and continue their conversation.

Following is a sample of an initial letter between students.

> Dear Janell,
> So being at home is being with your family, that's a good way to think of home. But I think that it is good to see new places, that way you know what home really means to you. You should never be afraid to go where you have never been.
> My Grandfather was a farmer and would grow cotton. He did this for twenty years and said that it was the most fulfilling work and made him feel proud. This is my dad's side of the family.

While reading *Bless Me, Ultima* you will be required to write a character book in which you will be comparing characters from *The Odyssey* with characters from *Bless Me, Ultima*. There are eight *Odyssey* characters for which you must find corresponding *Ultima* characters. Good luck!

Requirements

Character books must contain a minimum of sixteen pages, one for each of the eight *Odyssey* characters and one for each of the corresponding *Ultima* characters. You have artistic license to present the pages as you like; just remember to include the following:

> For each page, you must include the name of the character and an artistic depiction of the character. This may come in the form of a picture you draw, print from the Internet (be sure to cite properly if the image is a copyrighted image), or a symbol that you feel adequately represents your character. The *Odyssey* character must also have a definition of "who" the character is; please properly cite the source for your definition, i.e., *Grolier's Encyclopedia* or Edith Hamilton's *Mythology*. For the Ultima character, you must use a quotation from the character or about the character and the page number must be cited appropriately. Be ready to explain your choice if necessary!

Odyssey characters:

Zeus	Poseidon
Scylla	Demeter
Sirens	Odysseus
Charybdis	Polyphemus

Note: Two of the Greek characters can also be described as places. Please realize that in literature oftentimes places can also be seen as characters and settings.

Assessment Rubric: 80% for content—Character name, definition and/or defining quotation

10% for illustrations and/or aesthetic appeal

10% for mechanics

Figure 40.1. Character comparison: *The Odyssey* and *Bless Me, Ultima*.

This reminds me of Antonio's uncles in "Bless Me, Ultima". They speak to the earth and respect it just as my Grandpa did. (I just thought I share that with you.)

My mother's family would bring me a pouch full of cornmeal and a crystal that is a symbol of my journey. My dad's family would bring me a cross to show my Catholic faith. (I am telling you this because it is part of my assignment for this week.)

If you have any questions about the southwest or on the tribes up just ask.

Richard

As evidenced in this letter, when students begin writing to each other, they not only develop a relationship with the text but also with each other. When Richard begins his letter, he addresses Janell's previous letter to him, thereby extending the discussion beyond the initial introduction and forming a writing community. The second section connects the novel with the student writer, and the prompt is usually teacher generated. This example is taken from Chapter Uno when Antonio dreams of his birthing scene. The students visualize what their family members would bring to their birth and why. Finally, the students utilize the last section of the letter to extend the conversation. In his letter, Richard offers himself as a resource.

It is important to note that we establish the book divisions and the writing prompts prior to the beginning of the unit. We agree on a reading schedule and what sections of the novel will be discussed online. The main discussion of the novel still takes place in the regular classroom; the online component serves to enhance this discussion and learning. Joint planning is essential to our collaboration.

After completing the novel and writing to their partners about it, my students produce a character book that places an Odyssey and/or Greek mythology character alongside an Ultima character. The character books allow students an opportunity to display what they think the characters represent. As demonstrated in the assignment sheet, as long as the students are able to support the choice with textual evidence, there is no "wrong" answer.

Assessment

This text is successful for several reasons. First, the online collaboration provides each student with a personal reading partner who can help the reader negotiate the novel, much like Ultima and the various characters help Antonio negotiate his world. Because the students have been studying the novel together, they often come to an understanding of the characters together. Second, the character book provides the students with an artistic venue where they can display what they know about the characters and the book. It is important to note that this lesson is not necessarily a collaborative assignment. The writing partners may not be required to create their own comparison book. Although my students may be working on their own books, it is not unusual for them to ask their online partners for suggestions when looking for either images or text that supports the character choice in their books. Finally, the combination of both the online collaboration and the character book demands that the student read the text closely to respond appropriately to a partner and to suitably connect the characters. Through the online collaboration, the students develop their own texts in the form of the letters. Their correspondence soon becomes a record of the individual's journey through the novel. Students can reread their letters to pinpoint areas of the novel where they remember an event occurring or a character acting in a specific manner. There is a subtle, evident shift as students move from sharing their ideas online and vocalizing their ideas in the larger, riskier classroom setting. The classroom dialogue begins to resemble that of a living literary analysis. By comparing, analyzing, and supporting their choices, students establish themselves solidly in the novel and collect the textual evidence they need when they write the literary analysis essay required as the culminating assignment.

Incidentally, the due date for the character books is one filled with excitement and energy. Although not a requirement for the assignment, students are eager to present their books to the rest of the class and to demonstrate their understanding of the characters.

Considerations

This approach to teaching *Bless Me, Ultima* has been successful in a variety of classrooms in which I have employed it. However, I make it clear from the beginning that while I present these Odyssey characters for comparison to Ultima characters, they are by no means the only characters that might have corresponding traits. By connecting these characters, my main intent is to show students that Anaya works from literary and oral classical traditions that are timeless and universal.

It is important to note that the weight of the grades for either the online discussion or the character book should be left up to the individual instructor. I prefer to use these as tools with which the student can safely access the text. Therefore, the total percentage of points earned through these assignments does not carry the onus of the unit; however, it does serve as a cushion for students who do not perform well on tests. Additionally, the formal writing assignment at the end of the unit is the ultimate assessment for the text and is scored as such. Close exploration of character lends itself neatly to a literary analysis of the text. Having completed these assignments, students are confident in discussing the text through themes, character development, and setting.

41 Beginning with Ultima

Alfredo Celedón Luján
Monte del Sol Charter School, Santa Fe, New Mexico

Purpose

Rudolfo Anaya's *Bless Me, Ultima* is narrated in a bilingual *Norteño/a* vernacular: the English-Spanish-Spanglish dialect of northern New Mexico. The narration, as such, becomes a labyrinth of code-switches. Linguistic anthropologist Shirley Brice Heath (1983) has, in conversation (Bread Loaf, Vermont, 1987), postulated that code-switches transmit "bundles of information," often in single words and short phrases. *Bless Me, Ultima* is rich with serious and playful rhetorical strategies that manifest the subtle bilingual rhythms of narration and dialogue through colloquialisms that include allusion to place and extended metaphor. Students better understand the novel by unpacking the bilingual/bicultural nuances that are sown and cultivated in the landscape of the novel.

Materials

- *Bless Me, Ultima*—copies for each student
- Rudolfo Anaya's "Autobiography"—copies for each student
- *A Dictionary of New Mexico and Southern Colorado Spanish*, compiled by Ruben Cobos—a classroom set
- Handout of "Santa Fe's Street Names" (www.sfaol.com/history/street.html) by historian Marc Simmons—copies for each student
- Handout of Rudolfo Anaya's foreword to *Growing Up Chicana/o*
- Four websites students can explore:
  - SpanishDict: www.spanishdict.com/
  - NovelGuide: www.novelguide.com/BlessMeUltima/
  - SparkNotes: www.sparknotes.com/lit/ultima/
  - "In Rural Newman, Profanity Gets a Book Banned": articles.latimes.com/2009/feb/04/local/me-book-ban4

Introduction

I launch *Bless Me, Ultima* by considering whether the use of Spanglish, the purposeful code-switching between English and Spanish, is a rhetorical device in the first chapter. As a class we speculate on whether this bilingual narration will consistently yield literary blooms throughout the novel. We do this the first minute, first hour of engaging with the text.

This following lesson series may read like a script because of the conversational nature of the presentation, but it is not. It serves more as a talking road map to help others discuss the language of the novel. Using this plan as a script would come off as contrived. And since not all teachers have the same demography that I have in my classroom, it may not work to follow a script. Therefore, classrooms with Spanish/ bilingual students in their classes may require adaptation. Ditto for those who do not have bilingual students. It takes two or three days of block periods (seventy-five minutes) to deliver this lesson, depending on the level of discussion and activity.

Connections

This lesson links theoretically to Blau's essay (Chapter 1) in the sense that he uses Louise Rosenblatt's dinner metaphor, "taking somebody else's reading as your own is like having somebody else eat your dinner for you," to address the importance of students' engaging intellectually with a novel. He writes, "students may sometimes read the assigned literature (which is to say roughly decode and grasp a rough sense of a plot or situation), but rarely engage in the more serious intellectual enterprise of thoughtfully unpacking a difficult text or constructing a meaningful interpretation of what they have read."

This focus on interpreting code-switches also relates to Jago's (Chapter 2) suggestion that, "If we want students to read and respond to American literature, we will need to persuade them that what can be found between the lines in the stories of Mark Twain, John Steinbeck, F. Scott Fitzgerald, Rudolfo Anaya, and Toni Morrison is important and enduring. We also need to help students learn how to read between those lines for themselves." Unpacking a bilingual text is one way, among many, to read between the lines.

Activities

Days 1–2

The students in my Mexican American Chicano/a literature class sit in a Socratic circle. After they have read Chapter Uno, we begin by discussing the point of view of the novel. "What point of view is the novel written in?" I ask my students.

They answer that it is in the first person, of course.

"How do you know?" I ask.

Duh. "Because of the *I*," one says.

Okay, then I become the devil's advocate. I ask my students what Anaya means in page 1, paragraph 2 of the novel: "Let me begin at the beginning . . . the beginning that came with Ultima."

They have several interpretations of the passage. Some say that it begins when Ultima delivers him. Others say that Anaya means the story begins when Ultima moves in with the *familia*. Still others might say it begins when she intervenes with his destiny.

Then I ask, "So that's where Anaya's story begins, *really*?"

They begin to figure I'm messing with their heads. Eventually one says, "It's not Anaya's story, it's Antonio's."

Aha. "Well then, Antonio is telling the story in the first person?" I ask.

"Yes."

"A little six-year-old boy, who barely knows English, is narrating this very complex passage?"

"Yes, but he's telling it in the past, in retrospect."

Hmmm. "And Ultima is also a character?"

"Yes. Of course. Obviously."

"Can the narrative language of a novel also be a character in some sense?" I ask.

"What do you mean?"

"We'll get back to that," I say.

I ask my students to tell me about Ultima.

They say she's a *curandera*, a healer; they call her *la grande*; she is an old woman; she lives alone; she is the midwife who delivers Antonio; she moves into the Márez/Luna home; some of the people in the village suspect she's a witch; she has a cool owl.

Good. Very good. I tell them I am impressed by how much insight they already have—how much information they have gathered.

"Let's connect this to the world we live in," I say. I ask how many of them speak Spanish. A few raise their hands. I then ask how many come from homes where Spanish is spoken. More raise their hands. "How many of you read Spanish?" Three or four raise their hands.

"Okay, let's take a spelling test," I say. "Take out a blank sheet of paper. How many of you crossed or drove on Cerrillos Road to get to school today?" Nearly all of them raise their hands. "Spell *Cerrillos Road* on your sheet of paper."

"How many of you know at least one of these streets: Camino de la Cruz Blanca, Paseo de Peralta, Avenida Vista Grande, or Calle Sin Nombre?" All of them raise their hands. "Spell those street names."

After a few minutes I ask, "How many of you think you spelled the names of those streets correctly or got pretty close?" Most of them raise their hands. "Well then," I say, "give yourselves an A; you all read and write Spanish."

They act a little surprised, and they may argue a bit about not *really* being able to read or write Spanish simply because they can spell street names, but they will not be able to argue that they cannot read or write the names on the street signs, and that is where we begin our discussion about the code-switching in the novel.

"Even if you don't *really* know how to speak Spanish, we can unpack a code-switch," I say. "Most of the street names we encounter have English names: Walking Rain Road, Dancing Ground, Governor Miles, Richards Avenue, Rodeo Road, Zia, St. Michael's Drive, Old Pecos Trail. And each name has a history. When the street name is Spanish, it not only has a history but it also carries a bundle of information akin to the bilingual switches in *Bless Me, Ultima*."

I distribute a copy of New Mexican historian Marc Simmons's "Santa Fe Street Names," and we read and discuss it on the spot. Then we unpack a street name on our own.

We do *Calle sin Nombre*. "It's a proper name—not much to it," I say. "But if we think about it, that street had no name at one time. It was a washboard dirt road that went between two houses and led to another house a quarter of a mile back. *La gente* used to give directions to that road and those houses through landmarks. In Spanish they would say something like, 'Go on the bumpy road until you see a big cottonwood on the left, and then a little bit later you see two mailboxes on the right and then soon after that you'll cross an *arroyo* and see a big moss rock by the *piñon* and *sabino* trees, and that's where our road is.' Then an ordinance that mandated that all streets had to be named was passed."

As we unpack the street name, we chuckle a bit because we realize that when it came time to name the road, some defiant *loco* (local) with a sense of humor named it "Calle Sin Nombre: Street with No Name."

Then I ask students to unpack the names of the streets where they live for practice and fun. We conduct this discussion orally as students volunteer their street names. After a while, we move back to the book.

"Can we unpack words and passages in bilingual literature similarly?" I ask. "Let's try. *Ultima* is obviously also a proper name. But what does it mean?" I ask. One of the students who speak Spanish says it means "last" or "the end."

"Thank you," I reply, and then I provoke additional discussion by asserting that the sentence in the second paragraph of the first page, "the beginning that came with Ultima," really means that Antonio begins his story at the beginning that comes with the end.

Their heads spin (not literally, of course). My contention leads to arguments. Some say my statement is a stretch; others agree; still others flatly say that is ridiculous. Some do not care. I ask whether Anaya, the writer—not Antonio the narrator—is consciously using Spanglish to create double meanings or whether it just happens by coincidence. I ask, "Are his code-switches clever metalingual passages? Are we over-analyzing?" Some students will accuse me, as they have before, of not only shaking the bushes for hidden meaning or symbolism or metaphor but also of breaking the branches in my search.

I defend myself by saying, "Hey, we live in the Southwest, the terrain where the novel takes place. Specifically, we live in northern New Mexico, where we use the same lingo. We are in the novel. Every day we hear and read Spanish without really thinking about it. Here is our opportunity to tune in. As we read *Bless Me, Ultima*, I ask you to think about Anaya's creation of Antonio, the bilingual narrator, and I want you to ask yourselves, is Anaya creating two texts: one for the monolingual reader and the other for the bilingual reader? Is Antonio a reliable narrator? I'd like for you to identify and follow the bundles of information that are being transferred in the code-switches. We will discuss your findings in class as we review your reading assignments."

"In addition to paying attention to the elements of narration," I tell my students, "I'd like you to study the bilingual aspect of the novel—the narrative language itself. Unpack it. You don't have to do every passage, but be aware; probe; put your antennae on, and don't be afraid to break some branches while searching for meaning."

What about the students who do not know Spanish? I ask them to ask their bilingual classmates for translations and interpretations. I tell them we will discuss some of the switches in class. I ask them to ask their parents or neighbors or me. I ask them to do some interpreting themselves. And if they do not have anyone who knows Spanish in their lives, they ask their Spanish teachers or find an online Spanish-English translator (www.spanishdict.com/).

"Let's not bog ourselves down with incessant interpretations," I explain, "but as intelligent consumers of information, we want to negotiate the meaning of the text in this bilingual genre. It would take all our lives to decode every code-switch, but I want you to be curious when you notice the switch. So let's explore."

I give them a copy of Anaya's foreword to *Growing Up Chicana/o* to read for the next class meeting, and I ask them to log a reader response entry in their portfolios. I tell them we will do a read around of their journal entries and discuss the text at the next class meeting. In the foreword, Anaya explains:

> Some writers use a technique called code-switching, a bilingual approach to the story. The story is largely written in English, but at appropriate times Spanish is used. This technique reminds the reader the world of the Chicano is bilingual. . . . I suggest that this technique is a creative use of language that enhances the stories. (p. 9)

Days 2/3

When they return to the next class meeting, I say, "*Buenos dias les de Dios.*"

"*Buenos dias,*" or "Good morning," some say.

I ask them why I said, "*les de Dios.*" One of the bilingual students, Cinthia, says it means, "May God give you a good day."

"Well . . . I'm a public educator," I tell them, "I'm not supposed to mention God. I never do, but I did today in the context of literature, not religion, and thanks to Cinthia's translation, you now know what I said. Let's unpack it. How many of you have heard that expression from your parents or grandparents?"

Some of them raise their hands.

"Do they use the word *Dios*?" I ask.

A couple of them say yes.

I tell them that when I was growing up in Nambe, which was very much like Guadalupe or El Llano or Las Pasturas, my grandmother would always tag, "*les de Dios*" to my greeting if ever I only said, "*Buenos dias.*" We always had to mention God. It was religious in our growing up world, and it was cultural. It was real northern New Mexican stuff—the language of our place.

I hope one of them will say that a similar exchange happens with Ultima in Uno, but if no one speaks up, I point them to paragraph 6, page 11:

> "*Buenos dias le de Dios,*" Antonio's mother says.
> "*Ay, Maria Luna,*" Ultima answers, "*buenos dias te de Dios, a ti y a tu familia.*"

I tell my students it is not just "hello . . . good day, good morning" or any other phatic greeting. The above exchange must show respect for the elder (*le*) and for God and the whole family. It is not better or worse than any other social interaction. It simply is the way it was and sometimes continues to be in northern New Mexico. Our narrator Antonio cannot report it any other way. If the passage were translated or written in English rather than Spanglish, the texture of the language would be lost; it would be flat and beige.

We then take a look at Anaya's foreword. We discuss anything that jumps out at them from the text. I ask for volunteers to share their reader response entries. I ask them if they agree with Anaya that code-switching "enhances the stories."

We then fast forward to the bilingual metaphors in Antonio's dream on pages 5 and 6. I tell them we are going to act out Antonio's birth, and they will have complete, unrestricted creative license in this skit, although good taste should be practiced. I ask someone to play Ultima. I ask another volunteer to be baby Antonio. Ultima and Antonio go into the courtyard to plan Antonio's birth.

Then I draw an imaginary line in the Socratic circle and tell them the left side is named the Lunas, and the right side is named the Márez. The Márez leave the room and discuss all the ways that a Márez is unpredictable and violent, and the Lunas discuss the ways their family is bound to the earth.

I ask the Lunas to create a contemporary cornucopian setting for the birth of Antonio. They can do cut outs, draw on the boards, do mood music—anything that will produce a Luna ambiance. The Márez gather words and sticks and stones to break the Luna bones. The clans will become living, breathing metaphors.

After ten minutes or so, I ask Ultima and Antonio to go back into the room and coordinate their plan with the Lunas. After fifteen to twenty minutes I instruct the Márez to enter the room and disrupt the tranquil birth of Antonio with raucous behavior, as is done in the novel. Antonio does his thing. Ultima intervenes.

We get a few laughs and some awkward acting, but the point is that they have become not only members of their respective clans but also extended metaphors; they are, thus, unpacking the traits of the family names, which happen to be code-switches in themselves.

    This scene becomes an example of Anaya planting bilingual metaphors and of tilling them in the landscape of the literary conflict. The Luna/Márez schism is cultivated in the plot of the novel. The dramatic interpretation has given us another vantage point from which to study the narrative language as a rhetorical device.

Assessment

The methods of assessing whether students have learned to unpack code-switches come from class discussions, from writing double entry journals (interpreting and paraphrasing Spanglish passages), from small-group work (they interpret cooperatively and report back to the larger class), and from writing multigenre bilingual texts themselves in the forms of reader response, autobiography, quiz, vignette, and memoir.

    It is clear from our discussions and written activities that the students gain experience in ruminating on and unpacking code-switches. Furthermore, after this lesson, they become more attuned to the code-switching that happens in their daily lives through conversation, street signs, terrain, building names, etc. This awareness affirms their bicultural selves, as they have now witnessed their lives in the realm of contemporary American literature.

Considerations

Bless Me, Ultima is accessible to both bilingual and monolingual students even when read or taught in a region other than Southwest. Whether northern New Mexican Spanglish is familiar to students or not, the code-switches in the novel can be unpacked.

    Now back to the question I asked my students at the beginning of this lesson plan: "Can the narrative language itself be a character in the story?"

    They reply "yes," "no," or "maybe so." I tell them they are each correct in their analysis. I reiterate Blau's reference to Rosenblatt's metaphor—that is one reading is as valid as another, that an enchilada dinner cannot be savored by a surrogate, that unpacking text is an intellectual enterprise. And I remind them that reading between the lines, as Jago suggests, helps us better understand the intricacies of American literature.

Furthermore, I share with them the wisdom of Cheryl Glenn (2004), who in conversation (Bread Loaf Santa Fe, 2009) said, "Yes, the language of the first person narrator is the language of the story. In that sense, it is a character itself, often with all the complications of any other character." I argue, then, that unpacking the code-switches of Antonio not only helps us study the essential narrative elements of the novel, but it also yields a deeper understanding of the text through the exploration of Spanglish as a rhetorical device; this process, for me, is *la ultima palabra*.

References

Anaya, R. (1991). *Rudolfo Anaya: Autobiography as written in 1985*. Berkeley: TQS Publications.

Glenn, C. (2004). *Unspoken: A rhetoric of silence*. Carbondale: Southern Illinois University Press.

Heath, S. B. (1983). *Ways with words: Language, life, and work in communities and classrooms*. New York: Cambridge University Press.

Index

Editors

Joseph O. Milner serves as coordinator of the English Education Program, director of the Advanced Placement Institute at Wake Forest, and is the director of Visiting International Fellows Graduate Program. He is the author of an English methods text, *Bridging English* (Prentice Hall, 2007), and he has written numerous books and essays on English education, children's literature, aesthetics, linguistics, and American literature.

Carol A. Pope is a professor of English language arts at North Carolina State University where she teaches courses in young adult literature, teaching writing, teachers as leaders, and Trends in ELA Education. She has held numerous leadership roles in NCTE and CEE, has published in various NCTE venues, and is a former James Britton Award winner. She represented CEE in the creation of the online CITE journal and served as the first editor in the ELA section. Her research interests include the power of K–12 students as teacher educators; young adult literature, poetry performance, and digital video. She and Joseph Milner were editors of NCTE's *Global Voices: Culture and Identity in the Teaching of English* (1994).

Contributors

Mary Adler, a former middle school teacher, joined the California State University, Channel Islands, faculty in 2003, where she teaches undergraduate and credential courses in English education. She recently published *Writers at Play* (2009), which explores ways to teach creative writing with adolescents.

Roger S. Baskin Sr. has been employed for ten years as an educator in Fairfax County Public Schools. He has worked as a high school English teacher, an educational specialist, and currently as a middle school English teacher at Lake Braddock Secondary School. A doctoral candidate at George Mason University, Baskin is currently pursuing a Ph.D. in education leadership with a secondary concentration in education policy.

Sheridan Blau, professor emeritus of English and education at the University of California, Santa Barbara, is now teaching at Teachers College, Columbia University, where he heads the graduate program in English Education and the Teaching of English. He has published widely in the areas of seventeenth-century literature, composition theory, professional development for teachers, the politics of English teaching and learning, and the teaching of composition and literature. His book, *The Literature Workshop: Teaching Texts and Their Readers*, won the 2004 Richard Meade award for outstanding research in English education. He is a former president of NCTE.

Kimberly C. Bowen currently works as a research associate at Metametrics, an educational measurement company in Durham, North Carolina. She taught high school English many years before becoming a state and district-level literacy leader. She completed her doctorate in curriculum and instruction at North Carolina State University.

Jane C. Brocious is currently a part-time adjunct lecturer and academic advisor at North Carolina State University. She teaches an introductory education course for middle grades education majors and a junior-level field experience course in the College of Education. As academic advisor, she advises first- and second-year students in the Middle Grades Language Arts and Social Studies program in NC State's Student Success and Advising Center. She is retired with thirty-one years of service as a high school English teacher in Wake County Public Schools, where American literature was always her passion.

Alan Brown is a former high school English teacher from Summerfield, North Carolina, and currently a doctoral student in English education at the University of Alabama. He has a devoted interest in bringing young adult literature alive for high school students.

Elizabeth A. Callahan is in her third year of teaching English at Chapel Hill High School in Chapel Hill, North Carolina. Before her high school endeavors, Callahan worked in Head Start classrooms through the TEACH Americorps program based in Durham, North Carolina. Her studies began with a B.A. in English and folklore from the University of North Carolina at Chapel Hill and her master's in education from Wake Forest University.

Pamela Sissi Carroll, associate dean for Academic Affairs, College of Education, Florida State University, is the Mack & Effie Campbell Tyner Distinguished Professor of Education and Dwight L. Burton Professor of English Education. She considers time spent working with classroom teachers and their adolescent students, bringing young adult literature into the hands and minds of middle school and high school readers, among her greatest professional opportunities and joys. At FSU, she teaches courses on literature instruction and research, conducts research on adolescent literacy, and publishes work on adolescent literature and literacy. She is an active member of the Assembly on Literature for Adolescents of NCTE (ALAN), having formerly served as its president.

Jessica Conley has recently transitioned to New York after receiving her master's degree in education in 2009 from Wake Forest University and teaching in Winston-Salem Forsyth County Schools. She is currently supporting Columbia University and Barnard College students in providing educational enrichment programming to youth from low-income backgrounds in the Harlem and Morningside Heights communities. She currently lives in Harlem.

MaryCarmen Cruz is a teacher mentor in the Tucson Unified School District. For seventeen years she was coordinator of the English Language Acquisition Program and curriculum coordinator at Cholla Magnet High School, where she taught English language development courses, ninth-grade English, and Latino literature. She is a strong advocate for developing a curriculum that fosters cultural and linguistic diversity and is committed to helping her colleagues establish learning environments that promote quality learning for all students.

Bonnie Ericson is chairperson of the Department of Secondary Education at California State University, Northridge, and enjoys immensely her role as the university's liaison to a 1,000-student Los Angeles Unified School District high school located on the CSUN campus. She has taught English and content literacy methods credential courses, student teaching seminars, and English education M.A. classes. She has also served on numbers of NCTE committees, including the Secondary Section Committee, and edited *Teaching Reading in High School English Classes* (2001).

Amy Fitzgerald received a B.A. in English and a minor in creative writing from the University of North Carolina at Chapel Hill and an M.A. in education from Wake Forest University. She currently teaches ninth and tenth grades at R. J. Reynolds High School in Winston-Salem, North Carolina.

Laura B. Frazier is currently teaching ninth-grade English and sponsoring the National Honor Society club at Eastside High School in Alachua County, Florida. She graduated from Wake Forest University in 2008, where she studied English and secondary education. After earning a bachelor's degree, she earned a master's degree in English education from the University of Florida in 2009.

John Gabriel, a member of the DePaul University (Chicago, Illinois) faculty since 1997, teaches undergraduate and graduate credential courses in English education. He is a former Los Angeles area middle and high school English teacher.

Kendra Hege Gallos, a teacher for eighteen years, teaches American literature at Mount Tabor High School, Winston-Salem, North Carolina. In 2009, she worked on the state writing committee for eleventh- and twelfth-grade English curriculum. She also teaches for North Carolina Virtual Public School, where she serves as the course leader and coauthor of the AP Language and Composition course, as well as SAT Prep and English 3. Gallos is a National Board Certified Teacher but considers her greatest accomplishment her two boys, Danny and Christian.

Shayne G. Goodrum currently serves as team leader for Comprehensive Needs Assessment for the North Carolina Department of Public Instruction. She is a fellow of the Capital Area Writing Project at North Carolina State University, where she also completed her doctorate. Goodrum taught middle school and high school English and served as central office curriculum supervisor for most of her career.

Chad E. Harris received a B.A. in English from the University of North Carolina at Chapel Hill and an M.A. in education from Wake Forest University. He currently teaches eleventh and twelfth grades at West Forsyth High School in Clemmons, North Carolina.

Megan Hastings has a B.S. in secondary English education from Auburn University and an M.A. from the University of Alabama in secondary education–computers and applied technology. She is currently teaching English at Auburn High School in Auburn, Alabama.

KaaVonia Hinton is an assistant professor in the Darden College of Education at Old Dominion University in Norfolk, Virginia. She is the author of *Angela Johnson: Poetic Prose* (2006) and *Sharon M. Draper: Embracing Literacy* (2009), and coauthor (with Gail K. Dickinson) of *Integrating Multicultural Literature in Libraries and Classrooms in Secondary Schools* (2007) and (with Katherine T. Bucher) of *Young Adult Literature: Exploration, Evaluation, and Appreciation* (2009). Her reviews of young adult and children's literature are published regularly in *VOYA* and *ForeWord Magazine*.

Emily Houlditch received a B.A. in English from the University of North Carolina in Chapel Hill and an M.A. in education from Wake Forest University. She currently teaches tenth grade at Reagan High School in Pfafftown, North Carolina.

Bobbi Ciriza Houtchens has taught English learners and mainstream students in urban high schools for forty years. She has also taught in the School of Education at California State University–San Bernardino. Most recently she was selected to serve as a Teaching Ambassador Fellow at the U.S. Department of Education in Washington, DC. She has a B.A. and Licenciatura from Elbert Covell College, University of the Pacific, in Latin American studies, Spanish, and Teaching English as a Second Language, and an M.A. in biliteracy/biculturalism. Currently she enjoys being a consultant to school districts and education organizations across the nation.

Carol Jago has taught middle and high school for thirty-two years in Santa Monica, California, and directs the California Reading and Literature Project at UCLA. She was president of the National Council of Teachers of English (2009–10) and has written four books in the NCTE High School Literature series.

Tiffany A. Jones received a B.A. in English and a minor in creative writing from the University of North Carolina in Chapel Hill and an M.A. in education at Wake Forest University. She currently teaches tenth grade at Creekside High School in Fairburn, Georgia.

Elizabeth A. Kahn has taught English language arts for thirty-one years, currently at James B. Conant High School in Hoffman Estates, Illinois, where she serves as chair of the English department. She is coauthor of *Writing about Literature* (2009) and *Talking in Class: Using Discussion to Enhance Teaching and Learning* (2006). She is a National Board Certified Teacher.

JoAnne Katzmarek, a former middle and high school English language arts teacher for more than twenty years, currently is an associate professor in reading/language arts at the University of Wisconsin–Stevens Point. She earned her doctorate in literacy education from the University of Wisconsin–Madison.

Joan F. Kaywell, professor of English education at the University of South Florida, is passionate about assisting preservice and practicing teachers in discovering ways to improve literacy. She donates her time extensively to the National Council of Teachers of English (NCTE) and its Florida affiliate (FCTE). She is past president of NCTE's Assembly on Literature for Adolescents (ALAN) and is currently serving as its membership secretary. Kaywell has edited two series of textbooks: four volumes of *Adolescent Literature as a Complement to the Classics* and six volumes of *Using Literature to Help Troubled Teenagers Cope with*

[Various] Issues, and has written *Adolescents at Risk: A Guide to Fiction and Nonfiction for Young Adults, Parents, and Professionals* (1993). Her latest work, *Dear Author: Letters of Hope,* is her first trade book (2007).

M. Elizabeth Kenney has spent the last twenty years at Stevenson High School in Lincolnshire, Illinois, teaching courses in literature, composition, film, and media. She has contributed chapters to *Lesson Plans for Creating Media-Rich Classrooms* and *Lesson Plans for Developing Digital Literacies,* both from NCTE.

Leigh Ann Lane currently teaches ninth-grade English at East Wake High School of Arts, Education, and Global Studies in the Wake County Public School system of North Carolina. She obtained her National Board certification in 2004 and is currently working toward her master's degree at North Carolina State University. She lives in Wendell with her husband and two children.

Cecelia A. Lewis, a native of southern Arizona, has spent thirteen years teaching in local high schools in Cochise County. Currently, she teaches first-year composition at Cochise College in Sierra Vista, Arizona. Lewis is passionate about developing writing communities in her classrooms that provide her students an opportunity to explore the spaces in which they live.

Sheryl Long is an assistant professor of education at Chowan University where she teaches courses in literacy and technology as well as research methods. She has taught middle grades English language arts in several schools in North Carolina, courses in higher education, and presents regularly at the SITE Conference as well as at the NCTE Annual Convention. As a doctoral student, she was a recipient of the NC State Preparing for the Professoriate award. Her research interests and publications focus on young adult literature, film as text, teaching writing, and teacher preparation.

Alfredo Celedón Luján is a Norteño, raised in Nambe, New Mexico. He is a career educator, now a teacher of English at Monte del Sol Charter School, where he teaches middle level language arts and high school Mexican American literature. He has also been a teacher for the Pojoaque Valley Schools, where his middle school students received a First Place Award for their writing portfolio. Luján has worked closely with the Rainbow Strand Committee of NCTE and was a teacher participant in an Annenberg/CPB documentary. He has also been published in numerous journals.

Sherry Medwin taught English for thirty-two years at New Trier High School in Winnetka, Illinois. She has also taught reading methods courses at Northwestern University and Loyola University and currently teaches English at Truman College in Chicago.

Joan F. Mitchell, after receiving her bachelor's degree in English and M.A.Ed. in secondary English education at Wake Forest University, taught English for five years in North Carolina and Colorado. She is currently completing her doctorate in English education at the University of Alabama, with a research focus in improving writing pedagogy.

John Noell Moore is an associate professor of English education at the College of William & Mary, where he teaches preservice teachers in English methods, planning instruction in English, and literature for adolescents. He also supervises student teaching internships and conducts the internship seminar. A Virginia secondary school teacher for almost two decades, he is the author of *Interpreting Young Adult Literature: Literary Theory in the Secondary Classroom* (1997) as well as articles on English studies and English teaching in *English Journal, Callalloo, The ALAN Review, Theory into Practice,* and *The Virginia English Bulletin.* He is active in the National Council of Teachers of English and the Adolescent Literature Assembly of NCTE (ALAN).

Val-Jean Ofiesh currently teaches Sophomore English and AP Literature and Composition at Rincon High School in Tucson, Arizona. Her undergraduate studies at the University of Pennsylvania included extensive course work in world literature. She earned an M.A. in secondary education from the University of Phoenix and studied art at the University of New Mexico. Ofiesh uses her training as an artist to help students explore literature's visual elements.

Shayna Philipson teaches sixth and seventh grade in Aurora, Colorado. Her creative approach to literacy combines scaffolding the classics so struggling readers can approach the novels, along with implementing writers workshops. In her teaching career, Philipson is dedicated to the philosophy that all students can and should find a passion for learning.

Robert Prickett currently serves as an assistant professor of English education in the English department at Winthrop University in Rock Hill, South Carolina. He formerly taught English at the secondary level, taught education courses, and served as chair for the Education department at Centenary College of Louisiana in Shreveport, Louisiana.

Robert E. Probst, author of *Response and Analysis* (2004), is interested in the teaching of literature and reading instruction. Professor emeritus of English education at Georgia State University, Probst has published in many journals, including *English Journal* and *Voices from the Middle.* He presents at national conventions, including IRA and NCTE, and has served NCTE in various roles, including the Conference on English Leadership Board of Directors, the Commission on Reading, and column editor for *Voices from the Middle.* Coeditor of *Adolescent Literacy: Turning Promise into Practice* (2007), he is coauthoring, with Kylene Beers, *Book by Book: Strategies and Minilessons That Help Struggling Readers with Literary Texts* (forthcoming).

Sarah Rosas has been teaching fifteen years, currently at Oak Park and River Forest High School, Illinois, where she teaches ninth-grade English, American literature, and Advanced Placement language and composition.

Anna J. Small Roseboro (Calvin College, Grand Rapids, Michigan) has taught middle school and high school English and public speaking courses since 1967, earned National Board Certification in 1998, is past chair of the California Association of Teachers of English (2002–04), and authored *Teaching Middle School Language Arts: Incorporating Twenty-First Century Literacies* (2010).

Darlene Russell is an associate professor in the Department of Secondary Education at William Paterson University. She teaches English methods, educational foundations, and reading courses. She is the founder of the Nurturing Culturally Responsive English Equity Teachers (NCREET) Research Project.

Chelsey Saunders is in her third year of teaching English at Needham Broughton High School, an International Baccalaureate school in Raleigh, North Carolina. As a North Carolina Teaching Fellow, she received a bachelor of arts in English and Spanish from UNC–Chapel Hill and earned a master's degree in education with a concentration in English from Wake Forest University. In addition, she was asked to present "The Identity Crisis of Race" at the 2007 ACC Meeting of the Minds conference at the University of Virginia.

Lisa Scherff, a former high school teacher, is an associate professor of English/literacy at the University of Alabama. Her research focuses on opportunity to learn, teacher preparation and induction, and teaching young adult literature; she devotes her summers to leading an enrichment/service learning program for rising ninth-grade students. She and Leslie Rush (University of Wyoming) are the editors of *English Education*.

Lois T. Stover, former middle school and high school English teacher, is department chair and professor of educational studies at St. Mary's College of Maryland. She teaches a variety of courses, including classes in children's and young adult literature and secondary curriculum and instruction. A past president of ALAN, she edited the Young Adult Literature column for the *English Journal* for two years, and she has written numerous articles for journals, many book chapters, and several books on topics related to literacy and young adult literature.

Asra Syed is in her eleventh year of teaching at James B. Conant High School in Hoffman Estates, Illinois. She teaches ninth-grade English, eleventh-grade American literature, and AP language and composition.

Christen E. Tulli is in her seventh year of teaching English at Pocahontas Middle School in Henrico, Virginia. She received her bachelor of arts in English education from Longwood University in 2003, and she later earned National Board Certification in 2008. She has taught seventh-grade and high school English, and she currently teaches eighth-grade English language arts. Tulli was awarded the 21st Century Teaching and Learning Award in 2010 for Henrico County Public Schools in recognition of her innovative use of instructional technology.

Jeffrey D. Wilhelm is a professor of English education at Boise State University and the founding director of the Boise State Writing Project. His research agenda centers on engagement in reading and assisting reluctant and struggling readers through various modalities such as drama, visual art, technology, and inquiry contexts. He is the author or coauthor of fourteen books about literacy education, including *"You Gotta BE the Book"* (winner of the NCTE Promising Research Award) and *"Reading Don't Fix No Chevys"* (winner of the David H. Russell Award for Distinguished Research in English Education).

Angela M. Woods graduated from Meredith College in 1999 and earned her National Board Certification in English/Language Arts in 2004. She teaches ninth-grade English and young adult literature at Garner Magnet High School. She is currently working toward her master's degree at North Carolina State University.

Corbin Wright has been teaching in Henrico County, Virginia, for six years and was named one of Henrico's Teachers of the Year in 2009. She is currently English department chair for Glen Allen High School, a pilot school in twenty-first-century learning initiatives. She frequently conducts research within her classroom on topics such as technology in education and alternative writing methods.

Carl A. Young, associate professor of English language arts and middle grades education in the Department of Curriculum and Instruction at North Carolina State University, teaches courses in English methods, teaching composition, content area reading and writing, new literacies, and emerging technologies. He conducts research on new literacies, participatory media, e-portfolios, and other technology applications in English education. Selected publications have appeared in *English Education, English Journal, Journal of Literacy Research,* and *Reading Psychology.* Young serves in leadership roles in CEE and as chair of the English Education SIG of the Society for Information Technology and Teacher Education (SITE). He also serves as lead editor of the English language arts section of *Contemporary Issues in Technology and Teacher Education.*

This book was typeset in Palatino and Helvetica by Barbara Frazier.
Typefaces used on the cover are Torino and News Gothic.
The book was printed on 50-lb. Opaque Offset paper by Versa Press, Inc.